Pursuing Excellence
for the Glory of God

Pursuing Excellence for the Glory of God

Toward a Biblical Philosophy
of Christian School Education

KEITH A. CURRIVEAN

WIPF & STOCK · Eugene, Oregon

PURSUING EXCELLENCE FOR THE GLORY OF GOD
Toward a Biblical Philosophy of Christian School Education

Copyright © 2022 Keith A. Currivean. All rights reserved. Except for brief quotations in critical publications or reviews, no part of this book may be reproduced in any manner without prior written permission from the publisher. Write: Permissions, Wipf and Stock Publishers, 199 W. 8th Ave., Suite 3, Eugene, OR 97401.

Wipf & Stock
An Imprint of Wipf and Stock Publishers
199 W. 8th Ave., Suite 3
Eugene, OR 97401

www.wipfandstock.com

PAPERBACK ISBN: 978-1-6667-2344-1
HARDCOVER ISBN: 978-1-6667-2008-2
EBOOK ISBN: 978-1-6667-2009-9

JANUARY 7, 2022

Contents

List of Abbreviations | viii

INTRODUCTION | 1

CHAPTER 1
 What Is Education? | 14

CHAPTER 2
 Toward a Definition of the Philosophy of Education | 24

CHAPTER 3
 Toward a Biblical Philosophy of Christian School Education | 63

CHAPTER 4
 Toward a Christian Understanding of Idealism | 103

CHAPTER 5
 Toward a Christian Understanding of Realism | 116

CHAPTER 6
 Toward a Christian Understanding of Scholasticism | 131

CHAPTER 7
 Toward a Christian Understanding of Continentalism | 138

CHAPTER 8
 Toward a Christian Understanding of Romanticism | 147

CHAPTER 9
 Toward a Christian Understanding of Existentialism | 155

CHAPTER 10

    Toward a Christian Understanding of Pragmatism | 163

CHAPTER 11

    Toward a Christian Understanding of Social Reconstructionism | 173

CHAPTER 12

    Toward a Christian Understanding of Behaviorism | 182

CHAPTER 13

    Toward a Christian Understanding of Developmentalism | 187

CHAPTER 14

    Toward a Christian Understanding of Essentialism | 207

CHAPTER 15

    Toward a Christian Understanding of Perennialism | 212

CHAPTER 16

    Toward a Biblical Philosophy of Christian School Education | 223

APPENDIX 1

    Ars Gratia Ars—Soli Deo Gloria: A Critical Review of Nicholas Wolterstorff's *Art in Action: Toward a Christian Aesthetic* | 267

APPENDIX 2

    Toward a Summative Capstone Project for Students in a K–12 Christian School | 283

APPENDIX 3

    Sample School Profile Based upon a Biblical Philosophy of a Christian School Education | 285

APPENDIX 4 | 291

    Sample Alphabetized Quotes Pertinent to a Biblical Philosophy of a Christian School Education | 291

APPENDIX 5 | 305

    Sample Taxonomy Table of a Multifaceted, Holistic, Eclectic Pedagogy Based upon a Biblical Philosophy of a Christian School Education | 305

Appendix 6 | 308

    A Covenant for Excellence | 308

BIBLIOGRAPHY | 313

List of Abbreviations

AA: *Art in Action*
NW: Nicholas Wolterstorff
WW: *Works and Worlds of Art*

Introduction

THIS BOOK EXPLORES A biblical philosophy of Christian school education with unprecedented scope and acumen. To accomplish this objective, it considers what *education* is (ch. 1), what *philosophy of education* is (ch. 2), and what the ultimate *goal of education* is (ch. 3). Additionally, this book provides a novel Christian overview of twelve philosophies of education (chs. 4–15). Each of those chapters provides an introduction of a particular philosophy of education and some of that philosophy's exemplars. Each of these chapters then concludes with a constructive, Christian critique. Chapter 16 highlights a biblical philosophy of Christian school education—featuring some *contributors*, some *principles*, and some *priorities* for a biblical philosophy of Christian school education, viz. *pursuing excellence for the glory of God*.

This book occasionally utilizes terms such as *pursuing* and *toward*. Although there are several reasons for that—some of which will be addressed in due course, most of these reasons can be summed up in one of two categories of rationale for utilizing this type of language in this book: (1) modesty and (2) movement. Modesty: this book does not claim to be the final statement, but a contribution to others exploring these educational breadths and these philosophical depths. Movement: in the sense that *education* is about growth, development, and other aspects of moving—from where one presently *is* to where it would be preferred for one *to be*. Whereas the argument could be made that discretion is the greater part of valor, what seems even more potent and pertinent for the present author in the writing of this book, is that humility is the greater part of excellence. To put it another way—and to utilize two classical, educational terms: *humilitates* is a great part of *arête*. Concomitant to that development, movement, and growth both in perspective and in probity is the deepening realization that the One who is Perfect commands that *we* be perfect—an aspirational standard *at* which to take aim and *toward* which to make progress, even if complete attainment in this life might never be fully achieved. What applies in this way to *all* of life seems to apply *particularly* to education and to philosophizing about education. Thus, the title for this book is *Pursuing Excellence for the Glory of God*.

Furthermore, when it comes to philosophizing in general and to philosophizing about education in particular, one philosopher says it well: "The problem likely lies in the enormity of 'the big questions' and the puny-ness of our cognitive equipment. If there is a lesson to be learned from the history of philosophy, it is that intellectual humility is a virtue worthy of cultivation."[1] Not dissimilarly, Howard Gardner, a Harvard-educated American developmental psychologist and the John H. and Elisabeth A. Hobbs Professor of Cognition and Education at the Graduate School of Education at Harvard University, prudently admonishes educators, philosophers, cognitive scientists, and anyone else who would enter the domain of learning about learning and thinking about education—and consequently anyone giving deep consideration to and about the philosophy of education—that "keen vigilance and enduring humility should accompany forays into this brave new world."[2]

In light of these aforementioned prioritized intentions, at least four primary audiences are targeted:

1. *Theoreticians.* Inclusive of the historical overview of chapter 1, the philosophical overview of chapter 2, the doxological overview of chapter 3, and the conceptual overviews of chapters 4 through 16, there apparently has never been a single document that has so comprehensively addressed the breadth of coverage as this book. Scholars will benefit from the efficiency of having this vast array at their fingertips in one document.

2. *Practitioners.* Challenged by the depth of the aforementioned chapters, professional practitioners will be aided in their implementation of education, philosophy of education, and a biblical philosophy of Christian school education by the readiness, tidiness, and helpfulness of the quotations, allusions, illustrations, and appendices, as well. The first appendix, for example, takes a particular domain within a biblical philosophy of Christian school education

---

1. Clark et al., *101 Key Terms*, 69.
2. Gardner, *Disciplined Mind*, 83.

and provides a more analytical and critical look at one philosopher's proposal and recommends a more corresponding and coherent Christian approach to arts and aesthetics—an approach consistent with the thesis of this book, *soli Deo gloria*. The subsequent appendices provide a sampling of this present scholar's research for the ready reference of the Christian school educator—no matter his or her role. The content of these appendices has been researched, implemented, and observed to meet criteria of biblical excellence.

3. *Parents, pastors, and other partners*. Without these constituents as the *primary* stewards of the children with whom God has blessed Christian schools, Christian school education *would* not be and *could* not be what it is—and most certainly without parents, pastors, and other partners, Christian school education could never become what it *ought* to be becoming. Without these foundationally important partners in this ministry whose business is Christian education in all that is discussed in this book for Christian schools to be and to become, Christian schooling would fail to optimize its biblically mandated and divinely ordained symbiosis and synergy with the aforementioned parties. Finally, without these critical constituents being versed in the following content and concepts, *they* would not be (as) prepared to do Christian school education in the partnered, excellent, and God-glorifying way presented in this book.

4. *Students* of *and* at *Christian schools*. There have always been, and this side of glory it appears there will always be, learners being educated in the ways of God, both directly by God and by others. Whenever others are involved, there will be learners, and there will be learners *of* learners. This book has *them* in mind, as well—whether they are an astute seventeen-year-old preparing to embark upon his Christian school senior thesis, or someone with a few more full moons under her belt preparing to embark upon her grad class, master's thesis, doctoral dissertation, or professional research grant. May the following pages inform, engage, and inspire them.

5. Most of all, however, *Coram Deo*: God is the primary target audience of this present piece. May he bless and be blessed by these efforts and the aforementioned subsequent and concomitant engagements, as well. *Soli Deo gloria!*

Finally, by way of introduction, with such a substantive portion of this book highlighting twelve schools of thought *within* (i.e., approaches *to*) the philosophy of education, this final section of the introduction intends to clarify the content and intent of chapters 4–15.[3]

To get a running start, a reader may reasonably wonder about *nomenclature*—that is, the names used to identify the twelve schools of thought highlighted in chapters 4–15. *Nomenclature* derives from two Latin terms: *nomen*, meaning *name*, and *calare*, meaning *caller*. *Nomenclature* is etymologically, therefore, *the name something is called*. The *nomenclator* of ancient Rome was the one who announced the arrival of visitors, prompted the actor his lines, or cued the politician of key points. The *nomenclator* of ancient Rome signaled something significant. Similarly, *nomenclature* within chapters 4–15 of this book signals something significant. It denotes either: (1) the names or terms used of a set or system, (2) a set of names or terms used within a system, (3) the method of choosing names, especially within a science or discipline. To address (1) and (2) would be simply to let the reader know that each of the twelve terms used in this book as its nomenclature for titling chapters 4–15 is used not uncommonly in the literature of the philosophy of education. Having said that, however, the author concedes that there seems not to be a single source prior to this book that uses these twelve, all of these twelve, and only these twelve. Thus, raising the question: (3) *id est* reasonable for the reader to wonder about the *method* of choosing these twelve, all of these twelve, and only these twelve as the *nomenclature* for these chapters within this book. For the answer to *that* question, attention is given next to the underlying question of *taxonomy*, i.e., the science of classification.

Taxonomy is derived from two Greek morphemes: *taxis* that denotes *meaning* or *order*, and *nomos* that denotes *law*, *science*, or *method*. Taxonomy, therefore, is the *method or science of classifying*.

In some disciplines some taxonomies are nearly universal, e.g., the Linnean taxonomy of living things.[4] In other disciplines, such as the phi-

---

3. As per the table of contents, chs. 4–15 will each attempt to provide a brief introduction to, a representative historical sampling of, and a Christian critique regarding each of the twelve schools of thought pertaining to philosophy of education as "taxonomized" for this book.

4. In 1735, Carolus Linnaeus published his revolutionary and iconic *Systema Naturae* (The system of nature), a pamphlet delineating his proposed system of the classification of nature. He would later publish subsequent editions which contained more species. Eventually Linnaeus would name more than four thousand animal species and more than seven thousand plant species utilizing his system of binomial

losophy of education, for example, no such conventional classification has yet been established.[5]

In his helpful monograph within the Sage Publications series on Quantitative Applications in the Social Sciences, UCLA professor emeritus Kenneth Bailey writes about *Typologies and Taxonomies: An Introduction to Classification Techniques*.[6] He whimsically analogizes taxonomies to electricity.[7] Ubiquitous and simple, "we use it every day . . . but most of us know very little about how it really works."[8] He proceeds to suggest that "one basic secret to successful classification is the ability to ascertain the key or fundamental characteristics on which the classification is based."[9] He explains that *that* is done by identifying the dividing characteristics between classes of terms and classifying the terms accordingly. Furthermore, such classification ought to have both reasonable exhaustivity (inclusive of all terms being classified) and reasonable mutual exclusivity.[10]

Bailey goes on to distinguish his classification of the terms *taxonomy* and *typology*. The former he describes as applying generally to classifications that are hierarchical, quantitative, evolutionary, or empirical in nature. *Typologies*, on the other hand, at least per Bailey's classification, tend to be more conceptual and multidimensional.

Following Bailey's cue, therefore, the present author submits that the *taxonomy* most appropriate for the purposes of nomenclature within chapters 4–15 of this book (whose classifying does *not* happen to be

---

nomenclature. The 1758 edition of *Systema Naturae* was entitled *System of nature through the three kingdoms of nature, according to classes, orders, genera and species, with characters, differences, synonyms, places*, whose ranking system still finds its way into many introduction to biology textbooks more than two centuries later.

5. For that matter even within the field of biology there are presently non-Linnaen taxonomies, perhaps most prominently: (1) *phylogenetic* systems utilizing non-ranking cladistic clusters based upon relative recency of common ancestor and (2) *phenetic* systems using statistical analyses of similarity within clusters regardless of common ancestry.

6. Originally trained as a mathematician, Bailey earned his PhD in sociology from the University of Texas and became a professor of sociology and interdisciplinary studies at UCLA. (See note below.)

7. And other classifications, as well.

8. Bailey, *Typologies and Taxonomies*, 1.

9. Bailey, *Typologies and Taxonomies*, 2.

10. Bailey, *Typologies and Taxonomies*, 3.

hierarchical, quantitative, evolutionary, or empirical in nature) is not a *taxonomy* at all, but rather a conceptual, multidimensional *typology*.[11]

Nonetheless, with no definitive *typology* of schools of thought within the philosophy of education, part of the challenge of these twelve chapters is in developing a system that is reasonably exhaustive and reasonably mutually exclusive. The method(s) used to overcome the aforementioned challenge(s) in establishing the classification of conceptual, multidimensional typologies for the purposes of this book included the following:

1. Conducting a vast survey of the literature of the philosophy of education (a twentyseven-page bibliography does not even list all of the sources consulted).

2. Enumerating the various classifications and concomitant nomenclatures that dozens of theorists have used within the contexts of the philosophy of education.

3. Vetting such classifications and concomitant nomenclatures against other expert sources; cross-referencing, comparing, and contrasting various definitions, delineations, and distributions.

4. Analyzing the diverse multidimensional and conceptual aspects of the various aforementioned classifications and their concomitant nomenclatures, alongside the anticipated, cited historical figures of chapters 4–15, and synthesizing the cited historical figures of chapters 4–15 into a single typology.

5. Filtering each of the cited historical figures (and their contributions to the philosophy of education) alluded to in chapters 4–15 through the grids of exhaustivity and mutual exclusivity to achieve reasonableness in that dual-standard *sine qua non* of typologies.

6. Classifying and clustering the types by conceptual emphases common among each of the historical figures within a particular typology.

---

11. The etymology of this word is straightforwardly from two Greek-English cognates *tupos*, type, and *ology*, study of.

7. Utilizing key philosophical and educational emphases as primary determiners of which type best classified that particular historical figure.

8. Prioritizing *conceptual* clustering over any type of ancestral clustering.[12]

9. Including each of the cited historical figures in the one type-class most suited to their emphases.

What follows, then, is a brief, introductory overview of this process and of the particulars delineated chronologically within each of the twelve chapters referenced by their respective typology.

One final word of introduction to the first of two overview charts below: With a tip of the hat to Heddendorf and Vos and their thoughtful work on what they call *Hidden Threads: A Christian Critique of Sociological Theory*, in which the so-called *hidden thread* was an element of Christian truth woven into the warp and woof of societies and into the very fabric of sociologies, as well,[13] the present author borrows the term *thread* in the sense of the thematic elements of emphases present in each of the exemplars classified within each of the typologies. These thematic elements tend to include philosophical aspects (i.e., metaphysical, epistemological, or axiological) and educational elements, as well as those common philosophical emphases within that classification or cluster that manifest themselves in rather[14] typologically consistent ways.

---

12. Socrates is included in Continentalism, for example, not because he would have included himself there, nor even because this author is yielding to the suggestion from some Continentalists that Socrates is their source of inspiration for their ideas, methods, or emphases; rather, Socrates is included within this book's chapter on Continentalism because: (1) Socrates is influential and iconic enough that he ought to be included among the historical exemplars; (2) Socrates's educational emphases seem to reasonably fit the emphases of Continentalism as it is classified in this book; (3) Socrates's educational emphases seem to fit the emphases of Continentalism better than Socrates's educational emphases seem to fit any of the other eleven classifications. To use Bailey's differentiator: The clustering within typologies in chapters 4–15 of this book utilizes conceptual, rather than ancestral criteria.

13. Heddendorf and Vos, *Hidden Threads*.

14. The term *remarkable* might not be overstated or dramatic here. For in one of the chapters in particular, for example, the introductory overview cites some of the otherwise stark contrasts that (outside of the prevailing and unifying typology characterizing the school of thought most consistent with the exemplars within that particular cluster of that chapter in this book) otherwise might distinguish even disparate thinkers (were the classificatory lens to be something other than what it has been for

School of Thought	Philosophical common threads	Educational common threads	Other characteristic common threads
Idealism	*Ideas* are ultimate reality.	Ideas, such as beauty, goodness, truth, and justice, compel education.	Education entails educing ideas to one's consciousness and enhancing one's understanding of, appreciation for, and facility with ultimate ideas.
Realism	Reality *really* exists outside of just the mind and ideas.	Realists believe that reality exists in the "real" world of physical objects, including teachers, students, subject matters, and schools.	Truth can be observed and taught. The scientific method complements mathematics, logic, critical thinking, classics, conduct, and character development—all preparing students to become good citizens and flourishing humans.
Scholasticism	Scholastics prioritized the (re-)discovery of transcendental truths that would lead a person (back) to God through a life of moral and religious volition.	One primary methodology for such discovery was the dialectic.	More Socratic than most of the other philosophies of education, scholasticism utilizes disputation as a journey of shared discovery.

---

this project as described above.)

Continentalism	A diverse movement or set of movements that includes postmodernism, phenomenology, and critical theory.	Both epistemology *and* pedagogy are seen to be constructivistic, experiential, idiosyncratic, and subjective.	A descriptive science concerned with the objects and structures of consciousness; a holistic line of understanding that may be more like getting acquainted with a person than like following a demonstration.
Romanticism	Humans (especially children) were believed to be innately, inherently, and naturally good.	Romanticists argue for the least possible restraint in educational contexts and emphasize creativity, literature, poetry, and the performing arts.	Student-focused, student-centered, or student-guided methodologies manifest in so-called organic, open, or "noble savage" pedagogies—all in the passionate pursuit of a free, uninhibited person untainted by the constraints of a restrictive society.
Existentialism	"Existence precedes essence": Belief in the ultimate freedom of individuals to choose to make themselves—creating their own essence.	Education emphasizes human potential in the sense of personal meaning, clarification, and value.	Each human is free (and responsible) for creating one's own essence.
Pragmatism	Belief that that which can be experienced or observed is that which is actually real. Belief that the world is dynamic, evolving, and ever-changing, and that as a result, *truth* is that which "works."	Educational emphases include adaptation, social contextualization, hands-on learning, problem-solving, experimentation, situational ethics, new experiences connected to prior experiences, and the scientific method to prepare students for citizenship, daily living, and careers.	Teaching and learning are comprised of that which allows the learner to navigate the dynamics of his ever-evolving universe and his ever-evolving context.

Social Reconstructionism	Social reconstructionism emphasizes resolving social injustices in a quest for better societies. Social reconstructionists believe that societal and educational systems need to be revolutionized in order to overcome oppression and to improve human conditions.	Educational social reconstructionists claim that education is the solution to the problem(s) of society. Reconstructionistic educators prioritize social reform as the primary aim of education. Curricula focus on community-based learning, bringing the larger world into the classroom, and taking action on real-world issues, such as war, violence, hunger, human trafficking, terrorism, and (other) injustices.	Emphases include notions such as John Rawls's theory of social justice, Axiochus's *eukosmia*, Robert Owen's communitarianism, Horace Mann's normalization of common schools, Catharine Esther Beecher's program to eradicate American illiteracy, Theodore Weld's passion to abolish American slavery, Angelina and Sarah Grimké's promotion of the education of women, and Mahatma Gandhi's dream for India.
Behaviorism	Behaviorism refers to a school of thought in philosophy, in the behavioral sciences, and in education that emphasizes scientific method, objective observation, and psychological approaches to the study of and to the teaching of animals and humans.	A scientific, psychologized, and mechanistic approach to learning theory.	Behavior is what organisms *do*.
Developmentalism	Developmentalists emphasize the systematic development of the child progressing through a sequence of stages of maturation and growth.	The aim of developmental education is to produce students who think creatively and critically by means of stage-appropriate advancements.	Development is achieved by means of stage-appropriate advancements.

Essentialism	Essentialists strive to educate all students with what essentialists determine to be the most essential (e.g., common core of) knowledge, skills, and character.	Essentialists prioritize teachers having the competence necessary to present the aforementioned information in preparation of model citizens. Emphases are given to math, science, history, language, and literature.	The essentialist classroom is often lecture-based, and students take notes. The focus is on students becoming informed about the essential events, people, and institutions that have shaped society.
Perennialism	Perennialists promote education that engages students with great ideas.	Curricula look similar *to* Realist or Essentialist curricula (e.g., math, science, history, literature, language arts, fine arts, athletics, etc.), but not infrequently departs *from* other curricula in at least four ways (see next column).	The reintegration of literature, language arts, social studies, and other humanities back into their historical context. The chronologizing of the delivery of humanities content. The study of one of more of the classical languages. The structuring of the educational system to mirror the stages of the *trivium* (i.e., grammar, logic, and rhetoric).

In summary, the reader is reminded of Bailey's principle: "One basic secret to successful classification is the ability to ascertain the key or fundamental characteristics on which the classification is based."[15] Bailey explains that *that* is done by identifying the dividing characteristics *between* classes of terms, clarifying the defining characteristic(s) *within* a class of terms, and classifying the terms accordingly.

Distilling the aforementioned chart down to the defining characteristic within each school of thought as classified within chapters 4–15 of this book would be to look at the historical exemplars cited within each school of thought through the lens of the *impetus*[16] of each exemplar's

---

15. Bailey, *Typologies and Taxonomies*, 2.
16. Ones *impetus* of and for education (i.e., whether definition, aim, and/or methodology) is used as the defining and unifying aspect *within* each school of thought as well as the distinguishing characteristic *between* each school of thought in chs. 4–15 of this book as highlighted in the second chart in this introduction.

philosophy of education—with *impetus* in this context being defined as *that which motivates, stimulates, focuses, or sustains the philosophies of education represented by historical exemplars within each of the typologies represented respectively within each of the twelve schools of thought highlighted in chapters 4–15 of this book.* That is the classifying method utilized herein per Bailey's conceptual model.[17]

SCHOOL OF THOUGHT	IMPETUS: That which motivates, stimulates, focuses, or sustains the philosophies of education represented by historical exemplars within each of the typologies respectively.
Idealism	*Ideas* are ultimate reality, therefore, education ought to *educe* ideas to one's mind and enhance one's understanding of, appreciation for, and facility with ultimate ideas.
Realism	The physical world is real reality, therefore, education ought to observe and teach truth via the scientific method, mathematics, logic, critical thinking, classics, conduct, and character development preparing students to become good citizens and flourishing humans in the real, physical world.
Scholasticism	Scholastics emphasize transcendental truths that would lead a person to God, therefore, education ought to foster that discovery via dialectic, discussion, and a rich moral life of devotion and service.
Continental-ism	Within continentalistic approaches to truth and to teaching, both epistemology and pedagogy are seen to be personal, constructivistic, experiential, idiosyncratic, and subjective, therefore, education ought to cultivate such a perspective.
Romanticism	Romanticists believe that the individual child is inherently good and naturally curious, therefore, education ought to free the student to pursue natural, personal fulfillment.
Existentialism	Existentialists believe in the ultimate freedom of humans to choose to make themselves, therefore, education ought to foster individual quest for becoming, meaning, and value.
Pragmatism	Pragmatists believe that that which is *real* is observable and evolving—and that *truth* is that which "works," therefore, education ought to emphasize learning-by-doing, problem-solving, situational ethics, and the scientific method—preparing students for citizenship, daily living, and careers.
Social Reconstructionism	Social reconstructionists assert education as the identification of and solution to the problems and injustices of society.

17. This Bailey-like classification by *impetus* also applies to the present author's approach in his own movement toward a biblical philosophy of Christian school education, viz. its *impetus* being *arête: pursuing excellence for the glory of God.*

Behaviorism	Behaviorism distills teaching and learning to a system of stimuli and responses.
Developmentalism	Developmentalists emphasize the systematic development of the child progressing through a sequence of stages of maturation and growth.
Essentialism	Essentialists aspire to educate all students with what essentialists determine to be the most essential knowledge, skills, and character.
Perennialism	Perennialists promote education that engages students with great ideas as introduced via great books, classical languages, and the trivium.

Chapter 1

What Is Education?

ETYMOLOGICAL CONSIDERATIONS

THE ENGLISH TERM *EDUCATION* comes from the Latin term *educere*. *Educere* consists of the prefix *e* which conveys *out* and the phoneme *ducere* which connotes to *lead*. *Educere*, therefore, denotes *leading forth* or *drawing out*. In English *to educate*, according to the *Oxford English Dictionary* is to bring up persons from childhood, as to form their habits, manners, intellectual, and physical aptitudes. More philosophically stated, *educing* entails the following aspects:

1. The eliciting (extracting, drawing out) of a point or an idea by analysis or inference.

2. The direct inference of a particular from particulars.

3. The argument from particulars.

4. The drawing out (or actualization) of a substantial form.[1]

As one scholar summarizes, "*Educing* is *leading forth*—a *leading forth* of the human spirit into the widest range of its potentialities."[2]

---

1. Angeles and Ehrlich, *HarperCollins Dictionary of Philosophy*, 79.
2. Hodgson, *God's Wisdom*, 6.

Within education and the philosophy of education, several other terms emerge in significance, as well. *Methodology*, for example, comes from *meta* and *odos*, which together connote *a path ahead, a chasing after something, a movement toward*. Thus, the notion of *methodology* within the context of education includes *the body or system of postulates, procedures, and paths pursuant of educational ends, aims, goals, and objectives*.

Ancients and contemporaries alike have utilized methods and have cast terms to attempt to capture the essence of education, its philosophy, and the methods entailed within approaches to education and its philosophy.

Much of what we inherit within the scope of a *biblical* philosophy of Christian school education we glean extensively from two ancient cultures, viz. Israel and Greece. "Two words define the cultures of Israel and Greece—words that are intrinsically pedagogical, words that made these cultures into educational enterprises: *torah* and *paideia*. These words are the antecedents of a Christian theology of education, and they are imbedded in it."[3]

Paideia (Plato applied this term to Socrates) was the nurture, upbringing, and disciplining of the child, *pais*. According to Werner Jaeger, *paideia* was the central idea of Greek culture, designating "the formative process of the human personality. *Paideia* involved not only the systematic and consciously sought development of individuals, but likewise the cultivation of the people as a whole."[4]

Torah included information in the everyday speech of the ancient Israelites. It connoted and conveyed instruction given by parents to their children to teach them matters of learning and living.[5] *Torah* was not primarily an intellectual activity but rather was particularly for the attainment of *zekhut*, a quality of virtue, courtesy, restraint, self-renunciation, humility, and mutuality. Thus, wisdom for the ancient Hebrews was *hokmah*, the skill of living life the way life ought to be lived.[6]

Not dissimilarly for the Greeks, *paideia* entailed *sophia*. *Sophia* was wisdom. Hodgson describes *sophia* not as a possessing, displacing, controlling, or abandoning spirit, but as a persuading, educing, nurturing,

---

3. Hodgson, *God's Wisdom*, 12.
4. Eby and Arrowood, *History and Philosophy of Education*, 234.
5. Prov 1:8; 4:1; 6:20; 31:26.
6. Much more will be said about the Hebrew (and, by extension, the New Testament) contributions to a biblical philosophy of Christian school education in later sections of this book.

communicating, and teaching spirit; acting in profound interaction with the human spirit—indeed with the entire cosmos.[7]

A leading educational philosopher explains how this term *paideia* was used by one of the premier philosophers of education.

> Aristotle's educational theory was a systematization of the idea he had developed as he studied various forms of government. *Paideia*, the Greek term for the taking on of culture, had by Aristotle's time changed from meaning the education of children to meaning the cultivation of human character and behavior. In his desire to restore vitality of the declining *polis*, Aristotle developed his educational philosophy.[8]

No trivial aspect of Aristotle's *paideia* was its intended end of *eudaimonia*—human flourishing. To achieve *eudaimonia*—and thus to flourish as a human—required three prerequisite types of knowledge:

1. *Episteme*: scientific knowledge. In contrast to *doxa* (common belief or personal opinion), *episteme* was Aristotle's term for justified true belief. Its intended end was understanding.

2. *Techne*: technical knowledge, such as skills and crafts. Like *episteme* it had a set of principles, but unlike *episteme* its end was *making* in a craftsman sort of way.

3. *Phronesis*: practical knowledge, political insight, and particularizing wisdom. It was the most practical of the three types of knowledge in the sense of providing the knowledge of what to do in a particular context or situation.[9]

Systematizing the acquisition of these three types of knowledge, *paideia* was assembled into a comprehensive curriculum called *enkuklios paideia*. Enkuklios paideia was literally the Greeks' *circle of learning*—encompassing the vast breadth of coverage necessary for an education toward full-orbed wisdom.[10]

In this tradition a *pedagogue* was one who would lead (*agein*) the child (*pais*) through this *enkuklios paideia*. The *pedagogue* was the tutor

---

7. *Wisdom* in English comes from an Old English term meaning "to see," and thus, "to know."

8. Gutek, *Historical and Philosophical Foundations*, 49–60.

9. Perhaps not unlike the French concept of *savoir-faire*.

10. Not dissimilarly, a term from Latin derivation, *curriculum* means the course that one runs in the teaching-learning enterprise.

or the teacher.[11] In some educational systems, however, the *pedagogue* was not always necessarily a person, *per se*. For example, in the cave allegory, "The historical Socrates is committed to awakening[12] each and every person to self-scrutiny."[13] Similarly also in Plato's *magnum opus*, *The Republic*, the ancient sage portrays a state whose core purpose and highest virtue is education. "Sophia-god engenders *paideia*, and *paideia* yields life-enhancing wisdom, a wisdom that takes the form of critical thinking, heightened imagination, and liberating practice."[14] Thus, to the ancient Greek, or so it seems, the *pedagogue* could be a person, a group of persons, a flickering fire, a shifting shadow, a divinity, a group of divinities, or even just wisdom herself.[15]

Each of these aforementioned notions of *paideia* entailed cognitive considerations, but they also entailed characterological ones, as well. For example, *eukosmia* was part of the *enkuklios paideia*. *Eukosmia* entailed etiquette. More than mere manners,[16] *eukosmia* was obedience to particularly prescribed order and discipline.[17]

The New Testament utilized several key Greek terms in and around the semantic domain of *education*. These terms tended to have similar diachronic and synchronic denotations and connotations to the extrabiblical sources, but their canonized utilizations seem to warrant particular consideration. One Christian scholar summarizes the New Testament terms pertaining to education as follows.

1. *didasko* ("to teach"—Acts 2:42; 2 Tim 3:16).
2. *didaskalos* ("the teaching"—1 Tim 2:7; 2 Cor 12:28; Eph 4:11).
3. *paideuo* ("to provide guidance or training"—Eph 6:4; 2 Tim 3:16).
4. *pkatecheo* ("to be informed"—Acts 18:25; Roman 2:18; 1 Cor 14:19).
5. *noutheteo* ("to shape the mind" 1 Cor 4:14; Eph 6:4; Col 3:16).

11. Eventually the English term *teach* derived from the Germanic root, *teik*, which meant "to show," and thus, "to present, or to offer a view."

12. Not dissimilarly *Dabar* in Hebrew was a term of enlightening. In Greek the *logoi spermatikoi* was the truth that spawned life.

13. Nussbaum, *Cultivating Humanity*, 26.

14. Hodgson, *God's Wisdom*, 8.

15. Proverbs 8 provides a biblical exemplar of the personification of Wisdom and its role in compelling adherents through the curriculum of human flourishing.

16. Not dissimilarly, from Latin, *prudentia* has been described as the right appreciation and application of ethics in practical cases.

17. McInerny, *Common Things*, 159.

6. *matheteuo* ("to disciple" used in the Gospels for followers, learners, or disciples).
7. *oikodomeo* ("to build up" 1 Cor 3:9; 8:1; 1 Thess 5:11; 1 Pet 2:5).
8. *paratithemi* ("to commit" 1 Tim 1:18; 2 Tim 2:2).
9. *ektithemi* ("to expound or explain" Acts 11:4; 18:26; 28:23).
10. *hodegeo* ("to guide" John 16:13; Matt 15:14; 23:16, 24; Rev 7:17).[18]

Another Christian scholar synthesized these terms and their concomitant concepts into the following description: "Education as growth in wisdom is evoked by God's Wisdom (*sophia tou theou*) which challenges the foolishness of worldly wisdom (*sophia tou kosmou*)."[19] Whether foolish or wise, education entails thoughts, and thoughts entail ideas. *Eidos* is *idea*.

Aristotle categorized educational *eidos* into seven divisions of the liberal arts.[20] These seven liberal arts included the three arts of the Trivium, i.e., Grammar, Dialectic (logic), and Rhetoric, plus the four arts of the Quadrivium, i.e., Arithmetic, Geometry, Astronomy, and Music. These liberal arts were considered secular.

On the other hand, Hodgson argues that education itself is *not* secular. He asserts that "education is an essentially religious activity, with a religious object as the ultimate referent of education (truth, goodness, beauty, holiness, eternity, divinity) and a religious power as its ultimate teacher (Platonic ideas, the highest good, the divine Spirit, God, Christ, Wisdom, Torah)."[21] "God as teacher . . . is something primordial, mysterious, and overwhelming. . . . Today that God is our true teacher means that no absolute system of human beliefs is possible—no fideism, for truth always transcends what we can know and express, and therefore, what is demanded of human beings is recognition of our own finitude, and humility before the subject matter."[22]

Hodgson goes on to argue that this religious basis for education can be traced back to before Aristotle—even before Plato—and on through to virtually *all* of the major educational theorists up until at least Alfred

---

18. Anthony, *Evangelical Dictionary of Christian Education*, 84.
19. 1 Cor 1:18—2:13.
20. More on these seven later in the book.
21. Hodgson, *God's Wisdom*, 8.
22. Hodgson, *God's Wisdom*, 11.

North Whitehead. The latter, certainly no friend to the Christianity, famously declared, "The essence of education is that it be religious."[23]

Furthermore, William Perry writes about "faith." *Faith* as mature commitment entails an "investment of personal responsibility and energy, an affirmation of what is one's own, a definition of one's identity, [even] in a relative world."[24] Even Harvard's Gardner speaks of "transpersonal intelligence." Peter Hodgson paraphrases this term of transpersonal intelligence as, "Persons [not being limited to] self-knowledge and fellow-knowledge, but [having] an intrinsic intelligence of the whole—of the world, the ultimate, the values and truth."[25]

Whether secular or religious, the history of education—and the terms entailed in describing it, present the student of the philosophy of education with a challenge of diversity (if not disparity) of definitional contributions. Rich indeed are the tributaries that flow into the stream of language used to describe and delineate aspects of education.

Fast-forwarding two thousand years, the *lebensgeschichte* of education is a storied history indeed. This storied history of education covers a vast domain and creates a circuitous path winding through the world of *ideas*—ideas about ideas, about people, about God, and about how people come to have ideas about ideas, about people, and about God, and about how these ideas cross their paths, come to their minds, and conform their souls and its concomitant choices to some standard or ideal. Education is *more* than just something cognitive, characterological, and teleological, but it is not *less*.

Additionally complicating matters, extensive contemporary progressivism, underlying pragmatism, and ubiquitous consumerism have all contributed to an increase of *edu*-metric[26] and psychometric approaches to schooling in particular and to education in general. Whether *edu*-metric assessment or psychometric diagnostics, whether at the individual, classroom, grade, school, district, regional, national, or

---

23. Whitehead, *Aims of Education*, 14.
24. Hodgson, *God's Wisdom*, 5.
25. Hodgson, *God's Wisdom*, 6.

26. *Edu-metric* is defined (and distinguished from the more traditional *psychometric*) as a utilization of "approaches to assessment which focus on authentic tasks and acknowledge cognitive complexity. Unlike psychometric approaches which emphasize differences between learners on the normal curve, *edumetric* approaches focus on individual learning on within-individual growth," as cited at https://dictionaryofeducation.co.uk/component/glossary/Glossary-1/e/edumetric-300/.

associational levels, whether any of these so-called progressive aspects of education is warranted or beneficial, the current bent has not necessarily seemed to achieve its intended ends. "The lesson of a century of research and reflection is that potential is multifaceted, ubiquitous, and crudely assessed through psychometrics. Sadly, the imprimatur of scientific respectability expropriated by [edu-metrics or by] psychometrics has been lent to programs of testing that have not only distorted the curriculum, but destined generations of students to second-rate schooling."[27]

Not unlike what Poythress has observed, "Technical terms [and tedious tests] may *some*times be defined with the explicit purpose of eliminating fuzziness on the boundaries."[28] Sometimes it seems, however, at least in the history of the philosophy of education, that *that* elimination of fuzziness has not necessarily been achieved in terms of what *education* is and how it ought to be defined and done.

HISTORICAL CONSIDERATIONS

Whether expressed in English ("standing on the shoulders of giants")[29] or stated in Latin ("*nanos gigantum humeris insidentes*"),[30] exploration by starting with and in some way building upon previous explorations and discoveries, predominates the method of chapters 4–16 of this book. Admittedly somewhat voluminous, these chapters represent a sampling of the vast and varied historical contributions to the exploration, delineation, and appreciation of what education is, has been, and ought to be. Ambitious readers will note much has been left on the cutting floor. What remains represents the core, the compendium, the chronology, and the critical considerations of philosophers, philosophers of education, and a few other contributors. Such contributors and contributions continue to provide a corpus to examine, a summit to ascend, and perchance a giant or two—or two hundred—upon whose shoulders the present author and readers can find themselves perspectivally perched. From such a perch one can see more vastly what education is, has been, and ought to be in order to eventually see more perceptively what philosophy of education

---

27. Thomas, *Education*, 82.

28. Poythress, *Symphonic Theology*, 67.

29. As attributed to Isaac Newton in 1676 when he said, "If I have seen further, it is by standing on the shoulders of giants."

30. As attributed to Bernard of Chartres in the twelfth century.

is, has been, and ought to be. With such informed perspective, one ought then to be able to see more clearly what a biblical philosophy of Christian school education is, has been, and ought to be.

As an overview to the next chapters, the following table highlights some features of the models of educational emphases in summary.[31]

Philosophical emphasis	Thinkers that have described education thusly
Character, morality	Plutarch (Spartans), Herbart, Christian educators
Happiness	Aristotle, James, Mill
Truth	Socrates, Christian educators
Citizenship	Aristotle, Luther, Milton
Mastery of nature	Bacon, Huxley, Christian educators
Religion	Comenius and other Christian educators
Mental power, discipline	Scholastics, Locke, Van Dyke
Preparation for the future	Kant, Christian educators
Preparation for eternity	Egyptian, Christian educators
Habits	Aristotle, Rousseau, James, Christian educators
Unfolding	Froebel, Hegel, many Christian educators
Holy life	Froebel and other Christian educators
Interests	Herbart, Rousseau, Organicists
Knowledge	Scholastics, Ward, Christian educators
Complete living	Egyptians, Greeks, Spencer, Christian educators
Culture, liberal education	Dewey, Adler, Christian educators
Skill	Primitive, Butler, Moore, Christian educators
Inheritance of Culture	Butler, Dewey, Christian educators
Socialization	Greeks, Harris, Dewey, Christian educators
Social efficiency, organization of experience	Primitive, Dewey
Growth	Greeks, Romanticists, Dewey, Rogers, Christian

Arguably the perennially probing query of what *is* education persists. Even premier thinkers in the field concede to what they call the "diffuse state of affairs" of defining education.[32] Some philosophers of education question whether education is amenable to precise analysis at all.[33] Some other philosophers even suggest that the definition of education is

---

31. This table is adapted from Byrne, *Christian Approach to Education*, 97.
32. Phillips and Siegel, "Philosophy of Education," para. 2.
33. Peters, *Oxford Readings in Philosophy*, 3.

an "essentially contested concept."³⁴ Nonetheless, as Poythress observed, "Technical terms [such as *education*] may sometimes be defined with the explicit purpose of eliminating fuzziness on the boundaries."³⁵ That is what the present author shall attempt presently to do.

TOWARD A DEFINITION OF EDUCATION

Although the present author acknowledges a vast array of denotations, a broad scope of connotations, and an abundant list of illustrations³⁶ of the term *education*—meanings that may in fact provide viable contributions to understanding *education* in particular contexts—within the context of this book (and if perhaps serving no other purpose than to provide a particular referent by which to contextualize the comments of the remainder of this book, if not a lens through which to see and a grid through which to filter the content and the concepts to be explored and explained herein), the present author cautiously offers the following working definition of *education*.³⁷

*Education is the act, the process, or the product of imparting or acquiring knowledge or understanding, or of developing skills or competencies, or of cultivating the capacities of reasoning, judgment, values, or virtues—thereby preparing oneself or others for mature and flourishing life.*³⁸

Akin to Vygotsky's *zone of proximal development*, a *gängelwagen* not only provides a literal aid to the development of many soon-to-be-walkers, it also offers a metaphor for the educational environment of a child, as well. Such an educational environment and the defining of the

---

34. Winch and Gingell, *Key Concepts*, 73.
35. Poythress, *Symphonic Theology*, 67.
36. Chapters 4–16 of this book highlight many such illustrations.
37. As referred to earlier, a partial method of defining education in this present book is one of abduction, viz. distilling from the more than four thousand years of historical, philosophical definitions of education the salient and substantive common denominators of what thinkers seem to have thought education entails.
38. *Mature, flourishing,* and other terms and concepts like them appear not infrequently throughout the history of the philosophy of education. What is less common is how these terms are defined and what—in the various definitions and delineations of education—these types of terms allude to. The careful reader will note as (s)he proceeds through chs. 4–15 of this book the various elements that each school of thought in general and many of the individual theorists in particular prioritize in their view of what contributes to a mature and flourishing person—and what contributes to a person developing those qualities, as well.

irreducibly important and foundationally critical components of such aspects is what the author portends to do in this proposed working definition of *education*.

Not less than encompassing and addressing medium, method, and message, *education* firstly references *the act, the process, or the product* of teaching or learning. Secondly *education*, even within its vast array of divergent definitions, seems universally to entail something multi-modal. These various modes often receive technical titles such as cognitive, affective, and behavioral—or more colloquially coined concepts such as head, heart, and hands. Thus, thirdly, *education* seems to universally entail some aspect of those three domains represented in the definition as *imparting or acquiring knowledge or understanding, of developing skills or competencies, or of cultivating the capacities of reasoning, judgment, values, and virtues*. The aims of education are as vast as the history of the philosophy of education itself. Nonetheless, it seems abductively reasonable to say that education aims at *preparing oneself or others for mature and flourishing life*.

So, the working definition of *education*—the present author's *gängelwagen*, as it were—and for the purposes of this book will be: *Education is the act, the process, or the product of imparting or acquiring knowledge or understanding, or of developing skills or competencies, or of cultivating the capacities of reasoning, judgment, values, or virtues—thereby preparing oneself or others for mature and flourishing life.*

Chapter 2

Toward a Definition of the Philosophy of Education

SOMEWHAT ALONG THE LINES of John Frame, the present author observes the difficulty to "draw any [comprehensive and definitive] distinction between a Christian theology and a Christian philosophy.... Since philosophy is concerned with reality in a broad, comprehensive sense, it may well take it as its task to 'apply the Word of God to all areas of life.' That definition makes philosophy identical with, not a subdivision of, theology."[1] Although Frame's statement is undoubtedly controversial and although it states the case more emphatically and narrowly than the present author would, nonetheless, the present chapter, which is intended to move the reader from a definition of education toward a philosophy of education, will in fact utilize traditional tools, texts, and taxonomies consistent with philosophy. It will do so, however, also with an eye toward a Christian theological grid of interpretation of these analytical, philosophical *particula*.

CONCEPTUAL CONSIDERATIONS: WHY PHILOSOPHY OF EDUCATION IS IMPORTANT

Doing education and doing philosophy about education is germane to human nature. "Education *is*, because man *is*."[2] "So long as people are

---

1. Frame, *Doctrine of Knowledge of God*, 85.
2. Maritain, *Education at the Crossroads*, 1.

curious and questioning about the fundamentals of their beliefs and can be bothered and brave enough to examine them properly, philosophy will go on."[3] So, in one sense it can be said that every human is a learner, an educator, a philosopher, and even a philosopher of education. In another sense, the aforementioned discipline of the philosophy of education requires certain *loci* and *foci* not necessarily so germane to everyday life. Such *loci* and *foci* within educational contexts include the fundamental questions of philosophy itself. "An education that fails to consider the fundamental questions of human existence—the questions of life and the nature of truth, goodness, beauty, and justice—with which philosophy is concerned—is a very inadequate type of education."[4]

Although generally abstract and analytical in nature, such fundamental questions intentionally asked and skillfully answered profer profound practicality in teaching and in learning. Gadamer, for example, promoted the notion of philosophy of education having *practical* value. He even described such *theory* as the "highest intensification and purification of practical action."[5]

Furthermore, as many have quipped, "The philosophy of the classroom in one generation will be the philosophy of society in the next generation."[6] What educators *do* (not to mention *why* they do what they do) has distinct and durative effects. Thus, as Abraham Lincoln proclaimed, education is "the most important subject which we, as a people, can be engaged in."[7]

The history of educational philosophy, however, demonstrates at least as much fluctuation as the history of philosophy itself or of the history of education itself. Many educators seem all too ready to be swayed by the latest theoretical whim, or perhaps worse, not to give any intentional thought whatsoever to what their educational philosophy is and why. To that point it was John Shand who wryly—if not Seuss-ian-ly—observed, "One can stand here or one can stand there, indeed anywhere, but in no case if one stands at all can one simply stand nowhere, nor is

---

3. Shand, *Philosophy and Philosophers*, 310.
4. Knight, *Philosophy and Education*, v.
5. Lammi, "Conflict of Paideias," 6.
6. Copan et al., *Philosophy*, 7.
7. Peterson, *With All Your Mind*, 6.

talk of standing always somewhere illegitimate because one cannot talk of standing nowhere."[8]

The present author concurs with Shand. "Philosophy is not a luxury; indeed it becomes a necessity just as soon as people are able and willing to think . . . about their beliefs."[9] The same should be said about the philosophy of education.

Strauss observes, "There are as many definitions of philosophy as there are philosophers."[10] He cites the following issues that play a role in the history of the philosophy of education:

1. The problem regarding our awareness of the boundaries of our experience, and the urge to contemplate what lies beyond these limits.

2. The way in which the problem of human knowledge, truth, and insight touches upon the boundary questions of science—education included.

Another Dutch Reformed philosopher defined philosophy as "the structural analysis of all temporal reality (to the extent that is accessible to theoretical inquiry) in the perspective of its totality, that is to say, in accordance with the dynamics of all created reality in its divergence and disclosure from its Origin, its functioning under a correlate law, and its convergence and concentration in its destination."[11]

Approaching the topic of deriving a philosophy of education from the perspective of a worldview similar to the one alluded to above, Cowan suggests that a philosophy of education needs to answer at least three fundamental questions:[12]

1. What is education?

2. What are the aims, goals, or intended ends of education?

3. How does one accomplish those aims, goals, or intended ends of education?

Easy enough? Perhaps not.

---

8. Shand, *Philosophy and Philosophers*, 310.
9. Shand, *Philosophy and Philosophers*, ix.
10. Strauss, *Discipline of the Disciplines*, 1.
11. Troost, *What Is Reformational Philosophy*, 2.
12. In a phone conversation between the present author and Dr. Steven B. Cowan.

CONCEPTUAL CONSIDERATIONS: WHY PHILOSOPHY OF EDUCATION IS CHALLENGING

"The history of education is dotted with such terrible failures, as the chart of a difficult channel is starred with wrecks."[13] Navigating such a treacherous passage has proved challenging throughout the history of the philosophy of education. Navigating such a treacherous passage requires skill, intentionality, and perspective. Navigating such a treacherous passage is what this section attempts to do. The navigating begins with two ancient philosophical polarities utilizing the same term—in very different ways. The term (a term to which the reader has already been introduced) is *paideia*. The philosophers are Plato and Aristotle.

It was Alfred North Whitehead who once suggested that the history of philosophy is nothing but a series of footnotes to Plato.[14] The conceptual navigation of the difficulties endemic to the philosophy of education, therefore, appropriately launches there.

"Plato proposed that all knowledge-claims be examined for objective truth. He taught 'dialectic'—the art of dialoguing and reasoning through the interplay of ideas."[15]

> When pleasure and love—and pain and hatred—spring up rightly in the souls of those who are unable as yet to grasp a rational account of such phenomena, they will consent thereunto through having been rightly trained in fitting practices: this consent, viewed as a whole, is goodness. This student is rightly trained in respect of pleasures and pains, so as to hate what ought to be hated—right from the beginning to the very end, and to love what ought to be loved.[16]

And, as Simmons would comment, "This isn't just reading and writing and counting. This is *paideia*";[17] it was education for *all* of life. Ideas, ideals, and interplay between the ideas, ideals, and the Socratic tutor and students. This was Platonic *paideia*.

Subsequent to Plato, on the other hand, Aristotle utilized the same term (*paideia*) as Plato had, but he did so in a rather contrasting way

---

13. Highet, *Art of Teaching*, 177.
14. Allen and Springsted, *Primary Readings*, 1.
15. Peterson, *Philosophy of Education*, 99.
16. Peterson, *Philosophy of Education*, 99.
17. Simmons, *Climbing Parnassus*, 56.

to Plato's idealism. Aristotle, an educational realist, took this whole-life *paideia* education-model in a rather different direction.

In his commentary bearing Aristotle's name, Barnes says of Aristotle that he "bestrode antiquity like an intellectual colossus. No man before him had contributed so much to learning. No man after him could hope to rival his achievements."[18] Thus, when it comes to navigating the difficulties of the philosophy of education, to overlook this sapient sentinel would be an oversight indeed.

Aristotle philosophically observed about education, "The difference between one and another training in habits in our childhood is not a light matter, but important—rather, all-important."[19] This all-important matter seemed to occupy a lot of Aristotle's thinking and writing.

> Aristotle's educational theory was a systematization of the idea he had developed as he studied various forms of government. *Paideia*, the Greek term for the taking on of culture, had by Aristotle's time changed from meaning the education of children to meaning the cultivation of human character and behavior. In his desire to restore vitality of the declining *polis*, Aristotle developed his educational philosophy.[20]

As was noted earlier, no trivial aspect of Aristotle's *paideia* was its intended end of *eudaimonia*—human flourishing. To achieve *eudaimonia*, and thus to flourish as a human, required three prerequisite types of knowledge: *episteme*, *techne*, and *phronesis*. Systematizing the acquisition of these three types of knowledge, Aristotle's *paideia* was assembled into a comprehensive curriculum called *enkuklios paideia*.

Such were the two titanic tributaries of influence on the flow of the philosophy of education: Plato and Aristotle. From these seminal sources, more than a dozen additional schools of thought emerged.[21] Surveying thousands of years of humans attempting to navigate the treacherous waters of education and philosophizing about that education, the challenge becomes increasingly clear. Of man and the history of man's complexities and challenges, many sociologists use the term *excedentarite incloturable*, i.e., "definitions can neither claim to enclose man nor contain him in precise conceptual boundaries. Rather it is recognized that the human

---

18. Barnes, *Aristotle*, 1.
19. Aristotle, *Nichomachean*, 2.1.
20. Gutek, *Historical and Philosophical Foundations*, 49–60.
21. Such will be explored in chs. 4–16.

being is always more than what we can say, and this seemingly incomprehensible being is what is to be educated."[22]

Navigating the historical tension between the quintessential idealism of Plato's philosophy of education on the one hand and Aristotle's realism on the other presents a challenge.[23] That notwithstanding attempting to fathom the fathomless complexities of what it means to be human as a necessary prerequisite (in some way and to some extent) to knowing what *educating* a human is, presents additional challenges.

Furthermore, additional complicating matters seem to contribute to the challenge, as well. "*Mindlessness* is the most pertinent and accurate criticism of American education. . . . Educators have failed to ask the larger question of purpose."[24] When it comes to doing philosophy of education in the twentieth century, there is the complicating matter of what could be called the challenge of the mind: Do educators even think about the philosophy entailed by and endemic to their teaching and to their students' learning? What is education's origin, purpose, end, or aim anyway?

Compoundingly, Ronald Nash critiques, "America's educational crisis is not exclusively a crisis of the mind . . . it is a crisis of the heart."[25] Akin to C. S. Lewis's famed critique of education in *The Abolition of Man*, that education and its philosophies have become like men without chests, void and vacuous of the heart and soul of what's most important to what education ought to be, Nash identifies an additionally complicating matter: the crisis of the heart. So, whether primarily a crisis of the head, of the heart, or even of the hand, the challenge is challenging.

Intensifying the challenge even further is the complexity of a question that seems to have eluded thinkers throughout the ages. "In every field there are a few very simple questions which are highly embarrassing because the debate which forever arises around them leads only to perpetual failure and seems consistently to make fools of the most expert."[26] There is what has been called "manifold problems involved in determining

22. Ggita, *Jacques Maritain*, 8.

23. The reader will note such differences as (s)he reads the subsequent chapters on the various schools of philosophies of education. Platonic idealism and Aristotelian realism are just two of the fountainheads of the many tributaries eventuating from this diverse source.

24. Knight, *Philosophy and Education*, 3–4.

25. Nash, *American Heart*, 29–30.

26. Erickson, *Childhood and Society*, 23.

what philosophy of education is."[27] In the philosophy of education such a question seems to be what *is* the philosophy of education.[28] "The question of what *is* philosophy of education opens a Pandora's box of other questions."[29] The metaphysics, epistemology, and axiology of reality, of knowledge, of understanding, of learning, of thinking, of beauty, goodness, and truth, and of ultimate ends—just to name a few.

The twentieth century, on the one hand—as R. S. Peters has optimistically proffered—offered significant help in this matter—of overcoming the aforementioned challenges of defining and doing the philosophy of education—by providing unprecedented breadth and precision of *coverage* on the philosophy of education.[30] On the other hand, the twentieth century *also* brought with it a proliferation of perspectives in interpreting matters pertinent to doing the philosophy of education.[31] For example, one of the century's most influential thinkers notably postured: "Philosophy has been disdained by Sigmund Freud and dismissed by him as nothing but one of the most decent forms of the sublimation of repressed sexuality."[32]

Somewhere between Peters's optimism on the one hand and Freud's cynicism on the other, lay a vast semantic domain—a field white unto harvest for thinkers to think about what education is and about what the philosophy of education is. As one such thinker pithily but poignantly observed, "Philosophizing about education is not the same as theorizing about philosophy of education. In a very real sense, this is not a book *in* philosophy of education, it is *about* it."[33] So, what *is* it, and what *ought* it be about?

Lucas contributes the following considerations: "'What is your reason for existing? What good are you to us?' When one considers seriously

---

27. Lucas, *What Is Philosophy of Education*, 199.
28. Peters, *Philosophy of Education*, 3.
29. Lucas, *What Is Philosophy of Education*, iii.
30. Peters, *Philosophy of Education*, 1–7.
31. As noted earlier, the reader will note such differences as (s)he reads the subsequent chapters on the various schools of philosophies of education. The present point is not to elaborate on such proliferations presently, but to juxtapose Peters's point of increased clarity with the counterpoint of proliferation of perspective, e.g., fundamentalism vs. liberalism; mechanistic views of pedagogy vs. romantic ones; Darwinism vs. Intelligent design; etc.
32. Frankl, *Will to Meaning*, 61–62.
33. Lucas, *What Is Philosophy of Education*, iv.

how difficult it is for an educational philosopher to make meaningful, even to his own classes of prospective teachers, the problems in educational theory which he discusses, there is little wonder that he finds difficulty in talking to the less-formally educated populace."[34]

John Palms, a university president and prolific author, beckons educators to recognize their wider obligation to society in this regard. With a tip of his hat to Maritain, Palms urges educators to recognize the intellectual *crossroads* to which the academy has come, and with Christian fervor, he exhorts educators to recognize the centrifugal forces pulling at the fabric of society.[35]

Not dissimilarly Strauss cites Dutch philosopher Henk van Riessen as describing philosophy as "that discipline constantly involved in wrestling with 'boundary questions' (*grensvragen*)."[36]

On the other hand, Gowin seems to erroneously assert,

> Occasionally, a philosopher will claim to have found a logical connection between metaphysics or epistemology and educational practices, but analysis invariably reveals either that his metaphysical or epistemological method is a disguised value judgment, or that the connection is a psychological rather than a logical one.... Although metaphysics and epistemology have been parts of philosophy, the sciences have rendered them irrelevant.... All of this is merely a way of saying that philosophy of education is about:
>
> 1. clarifying the problems of education (analysis)
> 2. presenting possible alternatives (synthesis).[37]

The present author concedes that the philosophy of education is likely not *less* than analysis and synthesis, but argues that it may be *more*. This book will present a model and utilize methods that *do* entail metaphysics and epistemology (along with axiology) as foundations upon which to build philosophy of education; it will also explore connections from which to infer what education and the philosophy of education are.

Christianly navigating the aforementioned difficult passage of the history of the philosophy of education, intensifies in some ways and clarifies in other ways the questions at hand. Pazmiño, for example,

---

34. Lucas, *What Is Philosophy of Education*, 307.
35. McInerny, *Common Things*, 19.
36. Strauss, *Philosophy*, 1–3.
37. Lucas, *What Is Philosophy of Education*, 206–9.

insightfully advocates a "careful blending of the various philosophies and practices" of the foci of education.[38] Benson explains,

> As there is no *one* Protestant philosophy or *one* liberal philosophy, so there is no *one* evangelical philosophy of Christian education. Yet all of these philosophies have certain commonalities which enable the theories within each to be subsumed under a generic rubric. As such there is an evangelical philosophy of Christian education. The commonalities or foundation stones of an evangelical philosophy are theological. The deity of Jesus Christ and the authority of Scripture are the touchstones of evangelical theology. To the evangelical, an authoritative Bible answers with certitude the two questions upon which a philosophy of education should be constructed: What is humankind? What is his or her purpose?
>
> Education within evangelicalism is an interesting blend. Throughout this [twentieth] century evangelicals have been extremely eclectic. They have been reactive and action-oriented, rather than polemical and theoretical. Their concern for numerical growth and the vigor of an individual's Christian experience often have superseded a reflectively developed philosophy of education. This was not a studied intentionality. Rather it progressed quite naturally from the historical context in which evangelicalism found itself.[39]

Finally, although perhaps a bit overstated, Max Scheler insightfully indicts,

> Christianity has never, or only in weak ways, come to a philosophical picture of the world and of life, a picture that sprang originally and spontaneously out of Christian experience. There never was and is not now a "Christian philosophy," unless one understands by this an essentially Greek philosophy with Christian ornamentation. But, there is a system of thought that, springing up from the root and essence of Christian experience, observes and discovers the world.[40]

To attentively experience, to keenly observe, and to systematically discover and document aspects about one's world all contribute to philosophical exploration. It is to such philosophical exploration of that world of educationally pertinent ideas that these next sections move.

38. Pazmiño, *Foundational Issues*, 124–25.
39. Benson, "Evangelical Philosophies," 53.
40. Westphal, *Postmodern Philosophy*, 248–49.

CONCEPTUAL CONSIDERATIONS TOWARD A PHILOSOPHY OF EDUCATION

DeWeese and others have identified the inescapable questions of philosophy of *any* kind, including the philosophy of education: What is philosophy? What is real? How do I know? How should I live? Thus, the implied inescapable questions pertinent to this book on educational philosophy include: What is philosophy of education? What is a biblical metaphysics for Christian school education? What is a biblical epistemology for Christian school education? What is a biblical axiology (including both ethics and aesthetics) for Christian school education? The following figure summarizes the process to follow.[41]

FIGURE 1

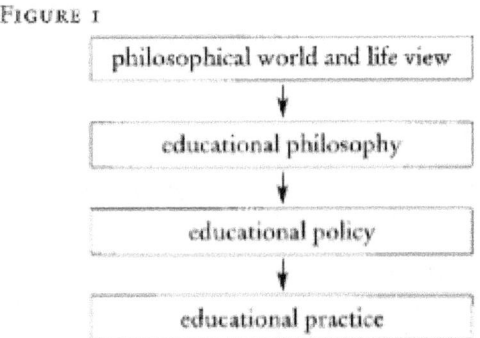

As Peterson urges,

> Philosophy of education is an extremely valuable subject for Christians. . . . We need a whole way of thinking about education—that is, a philosophical outlook that relates religious commitment to educational concerns, so that we can intelligently address whatever educational problems we face. The main point of contact between educational philosophy and Christianity is their mutual attention to the same basic conceptual questions.[42]

Peterson proceeds to urge Christian philosophers of education to abduce from the perennial essentials, "*Quod ubique, quod simper, quod ab omnibus creditum est*,"[43] i.e., that which one Christian philosopher of

---

41. Peterson, *With All Your Mind*, 6.
42. Peterson, *With All Your Mind*, 9.
43. Peterson, *With All Your Mind*, 10. "That which has been everywhere and always

education has referred to as the "historic, ecumenical orthodoxy."[44] Such foundational beliefs are sequentially:

1. Descriptive

2. Analytic

3. Synthetic

4. Normative[45]

This next section attempts to accomplish each—assembling that type of clear, coherent, corresponding, and constructive philosophical framework[46]—a foundational worldview upon which to build a biblical philosophy of Christian school education.

METAPHYSICS

Thinkers who have written about philosophy of education have been quite diverse in their approach to the study of what is real. Many have attempted to avoid—or even escape—the indisputable foundationality of this discipline. That notwithstanding,

> metaphysics has a close relationship to education, for all thinking, all knowing, and all teaching are metaphysical in nature. In order that a metaphysics of education be possible there must be a uniformity and rationality in the world and an individual capable of transmuting this outer intelligence into inner meaning. Such an educational metaphysics traces the intelligence in the school, and the thought in subject matter back to a Supreme Intelligence which is the presupposition and fundamental reality of existence and of education.[47]

> By virtue of the fact that God's specifications provide metaphysics, we can conclude that the "metaphysics" of a bookmark includes the complexities for how human beings may use it with significance. The world is complicated. God made it so. The complexities fit together into a whole because of the wisdom

---

by everyone believed" (Peterson's translation).

44. Peterson, *With All Your Mind*, 10.
45. Peterson, *With All Your Mind*, 15–17.
46. Vokey, *What Do Philosophers Do*, 24.
47. Fleshman, *Metaphysics of Education*, 146–47.

of God's plan, not because one aspect can be "reduced" to another.[48]

"He who is," is what Gilson calls the *ultima thule* of metaphysics, the One in whom Thomism and Augustinianism converge and the One to whom Platonism and Aristotelianism unwittingly ultimately point, i.e., that God is the great I am, the *ipsum esse*—existence itself.[49]

The Apostle Paul extends this realization. In Acts 17, for example, Paul enlightens the pagan Athenians that the "Unknown God," the immovable mover, is also the ground of all being—"the One in whom we live, and move, and have our very being." Not a "*deus ex machina*," but rather a viable, *bona fide*, "innate idea of a supremely perfect Being."[50]

On the other hand, Spinoza seems to take this too far and equivocates (the "nature" of) God and Nature.

> "By *Natura naturata* I understand whatever follows from the necessity of God's nature, or from any of God's attributes, i.e., all the modes of God's attributes insofar as they are considered as things that are in God, and can neither *be* nor be *conceived* without God." Spinoza's metaphysics of God is neatly summed up in a phrase that occurs in the Latin (but not in the original Dutch) edition of the *Ethics: God, or Nature*, (i.e., *Deus, sive Natura*): That eternal and infinite being we call God, or Nature, acts from the same necessity from which he exists.[51]

Not unlikely, God does in fact act from the same necessity and nature from which he exists, but that does not necessarily equate God with nature, as Spinoza seems erroneously to argue. Contradistinctively, Carl Henry observes that the loss of knowing God as *Logos* included the bond of intelligibility between man and nature subordinating a supposedly unintelligible cosmos to man as intellectual voyager.[52]

Revelatio naturalis and *revelatio verbalis* were the Reformers' notion of the *perpiscuitas* of God putting himself on display through creation and through Scripture. Not dissimilarly, Maritain, a Catholic educational philosopher in the Thomist tradition, asserts that metaphysics properly includes an investigation into the cause of being—i.e., God, in whom the

---

48. Poythress, *Redeeming Philosophy*, 284.
49. Gilson, *God and Philosophy*, 63–73.
50. Gilson, *God and Philosophy*, xxi, 81–82.
51. Nadler, "Baruch Spinoza," para. 30, 32.
52. Henry, *God, Revelation, and Authority*, 169.

act of existing is subsistent. Since Maritain holds that *being* is something that is grasped through intuition, one is not surprised to see that he will argue that one can attain knowledge of the existence of God not only through the Thomistic five ways, but also through intuition.

Following Aquinas more closely in other methodological ways, however, Maritain holds that the philosophical discipline of metaphysics deals with being as *being* (*ens inquantum ens*), i.e., it "investigates the first principles of things and their highest causes."[53] Maritain also holds that there are certain fundamental metaphysical questions to which Aquinas's responses are largely correct, though they may not be complete as they stand. Maritain adopts, against John Duns Scotus, Aquinas's general position on analogy, on being, and on the need for analogical terms and concepts. Again, in answer to the problem of unity and plurality—e.g., how can a thing be individual and distinct and yet a member of a class of things of the same kind?—Maritain follows Aquinas: that we have to distinguish what a thing is (its nature or essence, which it shares with things of the same kind), from the fact that it is (i.e., that it has its own 'act of existing'). When it comes to the analysis of the nature and the unity of sensible beings, including human beings, Maritain employs Aquinas's distinction between the form and the matter of a thing; nature or essence reflects the form, whereas the individuality is determined by the matter.[54]

From a similar tradition, Gilson referred to what he called philosophical "halfway houses" filled with those who either on the one hand were "spellbound by science" or on the other hand were "inebriated with God." Eschewing each of these erroneous extremes, Gilson advocated for a comprehensive, coherent, Christian conception of metaphysics: "We should keep the truth and keep it whole. It can be done. But only those can do it, who realize the *He* who is the God of the philosophers is HE WHO I."[55] This assertion brings the present author to his concluding comment in this section on metaphysics. The comment is an allusion from the Protestant polymath Poythress: the metaphysics of the world set the stage for the unveiling of truth, i.e., God's Truth.[56] Thus, this book turns its attention next to epistemology.

---

53. Sweet, "Jacques Maritain," para. 18.
54. Sweet, "Jacques Maritain," para. 18.
55. Gilson, *God and Philosophy*, 114, 102, 144.
56. Poythress, *Redeeming Philosophy*, 268.

EPISTEMOLOGY

Cowan and Spiegel succinctly define epistemology as the, "branch of philosophy concerned with the source, scope, and limits of knowledge."[57] Boudy suggests, "Educational epistemology can be thought of as a logical assessment of the schemata needed by the learner to comprehend and to interpret problems."[58] Such would include "a body of propositions containing what Gilbert Ryle calls 'knowings *that*' and 'knowings *how*.'"[59] As Poythress insightfully comments, "Human knowledge always involves the coherent interlocking of normative, situational, and existential perspectives.[60] Such an interlocking perspective provides the basis for the present author's attempt to articulate a comprehensive, Christian epistemology as the foundation upon which a biblical philosophy of Christian school education is built.[61]

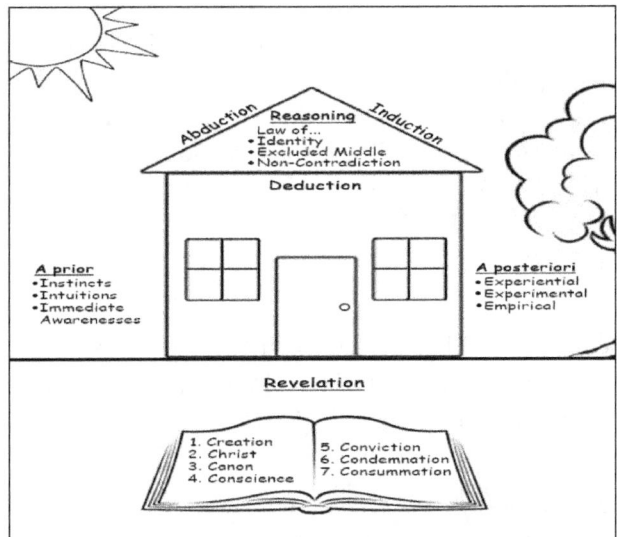

57. Cowan and Spiegel, *Love of Wisdom*, 21.
58. Broudy, *Uses of Schooling*, 54.
59. Broudy, *Uses of Schooling*, 53.
60. Poythress, *Redeeming Philosophy*, 196.
61. This original diagram illustrates such a comprehensive, Christian epistemology. A comment about each segment of the illustration follows the diagram.

Revelation: God's Word

As Alston asserts, "Epistemology cannot be the very first of our intellectual enterprises. We must already have some knowledge before we can reflect on what it is to know something."[62]

The foundation, therefore, of all knowledge and understanding, that upon which a full-orbed epistemology is constructed, is that which God has chosen to reveal.[63] He reveals through his word.[64] God speaks, has spoken, and will eventually speak his word through creation, Christ, canon, conscience, conviction, condemnation, and consummation.

Creation

When God speaks, even the nonexistent universe listens and leaps into action. *Ex nihilo* God spoke everything into existence by his word, thereby revealing aspects of his person, his plan, and the weight of his glory and grace.[65] Dispelling the darkness of the *tohu bahovou*,[66] bringing order to where there had been utter and ultimate chaos, and filling the limitless void with an unlimited unveiling of Beauty, Goodness, and Truth, God said, "Let there be," and there *was*.

Christ

Coequal, coeternal, and coexistent with the Father, the second person of the Trinity is the very Word of God incarnate.[67] Not only the substitutionary atonement for our sin, Christ also simultaneously reveals God

---

62. Crisp et al., *Knowledge and Reality*, 89.

63. "The secret things belong to the Lord our God, but the things that are revealed belong to us and to our children forever, that we may do all the words of this law" (Deut 29:29).

64. Greene, *Reclaiming the Future*, 100, suggests, "The Word of God is *the* unifying element in all reality."

65. Gen 1:1–28; Job 38:1—42:6; and particularly Rom 1:19–20, "For what can be known about God is plain to them, because God has shown it to them. For his invisible attributes, namely, his eternal power and divine nature, have been clearly perceived, ever since the creation of the world, in the things that have been made. So they are without excuse."

66. ESV translates this Hebrew idiom "without form and void" (Gen 1:2).

67. John 1; Col 1:15–20; Heb 1:1–12.

to man and reveals the *proto-man* to man, as well—putting on display to humans how humans ideally ought to live—even while accomplishing the necessary and sufficient work for redeeming man back to God.

Canon

The inspired Scriptures reveal God's written word. From Genesis to Revelation, the sixty-six books of the Bible authoritatively and truthfully instruct us doctrinally, inspire us doxologically, and inform us historically about the way of God with man.[68] Furthermore, "all Scripture is breathed out by God and profitable for teaching, for reproof, for correction, and for training in righteousness, that the man of God may be complete, equipped for every good work."[69] As such, Scripture is the standard against which to measure truth claims. Furthermore, it is not only regulative, it is normative: "The truth of the Bible is the basic axiom of Christian theism. It is there alone that one learns what God is. It is there alone that one learns what man is, what children are, and what education ought to be."[70]

Conscience

Not unlikely part of *imago Dei* or common grace, conscience comes from God as an internal tug toward truth and goodness. As the Apostle Paul

---

68. As summarized in Gundry, Meadows, et al., *Four Views*, 18, how one goes about observing, interpreting, and applying the revealed truth of Scripture comes down to hermeneutics. Evangelicals generally ascribe to one of (or to some combination of) the following models for approaching Scripture: (1) Grammatical-Historical; (2) Principalizing; (3) Redemptive-Historical; (4) Drama-of-Redemption; (5) Redemptive-Movement. Listed here from the most literal to the least literal, the aforementioned taxonomy provides a target of approaches, whose epicenter can be viewed as the ideal intersection, convergence, or union of all five approaches employed context-appropriately and to some appropriate degree in order to see all that God unveiled in the revelation of his written word. As N. T. Wright put it, it is not "the authority of Scripture" but "the authority of God exercised through Scripture." Thus, the Bible canonizes God's ultimate, foundational, revealed, written authority—the basis which goes before, beneath, and beyond contextual beliefs and situational behaviors. Others have also added other approaches to the list above, such as: (1) literary/postmodern, (2) philosophical/theological, and (3) canonical views (Porter and Stovell, *Biblical Hermeneutics*). A more in-depth discussion can be found in Osborne, *Hermeneutical Spiral*.

69. 2 Tim 3:16–17.

70. Clark, *Christian Philosophy of Education*, 43.

writes, "They show that the work of the law is written on their hearts, while their conscience also bears witness, and their conflicting thoughts accuse or even excuse them."[71] Conscience helps humans know right and wrong.

Conviction

God reveals himself and his standards through the convicting work of his Spirit. "And when he comes, he will convict the world concerning sin and righteousness and judgment."[72] The third person of the Trinity does his work (of both comforting and) of convicting efficiently, efficaciously, and eternally significantly.

Condemnation

From the moment Satan sank his venom into Eve, the corrupting and depraving effects of sin and the curse have resulted in deleterious noetic effects on humans. One day God will speak an end to the pervasiveness and even to the presence of sin as it is presently known. "By the same word, the heavens and earth that now exist are stored up for fire, being kept until the Day of Judgment and destruction of the ungodly."[73] Such eventual judgment provides prescient knowledge of who God is and of how he handles sin.

Consummation

Ultimately, God will speak—and this present age will come to an end, and the new heavens and the new earth will come into being. The epistemic prescience of this metaphysical reality is to be an axiological aphorism beckoning humans to right thinking, right being, right living, and right educating.

> But do not overlook this one fact, beloved, that with the Lord one day is as a thousand years, and a thousand years as one day. The Lord is not slow to fulfill his promise as some count

---

71. Rom 2:15.
72. John 16:18.
73. 2 Pet 3:7.

slowness, but is patient toward you, not wishing that any should perish, but that all should reach repentance. But the day of the Lord will come like a thief, and then the heavens will pass away with a roar, and the heavenly bodies will be burned up and dissolved, and the earth and the works that are done on it will be exposed. Since all these things are thus to be dissolved, what sort of people ought you to be in lives of holiness and godliness, waiting for and hastening the coming of the day of God, because of which the heavens will be set on fire and dissolved, and the heavenly bodies will melt as they burn! But according to His promise we are waiting for new heavens and a new earth in which righteousness dwells. Therefore, beloved, since you are waiting for these, be diligent to be found by him without spot or blemish, and at peace.[74]

Thus, the sevenfold word of God reveals God to man through creation, Christ, canon, conscience, conviction, condemnation, and consummation. As one Christian educational philosopher applies this type of epistemological taxonomy, he concludes, "All knowledge is revelation. In the words of Herman Bavinck, 'The purpose of God's revelation according to Scriptures is this very thing: that man shall learn to know God, and hence may have eternal life.'"[75]

In addition to such truth being a conveyor of life, Arthur Holmes summarized six implications of relating such truth to God as its Source:

1. To say that truth is absolute rather than relative means that it is unchanging and universally the same.
2. Truth is absolute not in or of itself but because it derives intimately and ultimately from the one, eternal God. It is grounded in his "metaphysical objectivity," and that of his creation.
3. Absolute propositional truth, therefore, depends on the absolute personal truth (or fidelity) of God, who can be trusted in all he does and says.
4. All knowledge ultimately bears witness to the truth God reveals. Both the intelligibility of nature and the cognitive powers of man attest to God's fidelity.

---

74. 2 Pet 3:8–13.
75. DeJong, *Teaching for a Change*, 140–41.

5. The propositional truth of the Biblical revelation likewise depends on and bears witness to the personal fidelity of God, and the ultimate unity of truth is specially revealed in Jesus Christ.
6. Human knowledge is, therefore, not detached and purely theoretical but intensely personal. Because truth captures the hearts and minds of men, it admits of epistemological subjectivity. Because knowledge depends on God's fidelity, the believer's pursuit of knowledge can express this trust in God.[76]

A Posteriori Knowledge and Empiricism

Complementing the foundational means of knowledge (i.e., revelation) and corresponding to knowledge that is arrived at *a posteriori*, empirical knowledge entails both informal experience and formal experimentation. In the words of one philosopher of education,

> Experience becomes intelligible only in so far as the mind orders the phenomena. The educated mind orders experience with the resources of the arts and the sciences. While the informed sources for interpretation—common sense, common knowledge, common images—that may be acquired without intuition, the interpretive use of schooling according to the concepts and judgment of the learned, is its most distinctive contribution to the individual and the society.[77]

Experience

In utero humans begin experiencing vast experiences—nonstop. Each of these experiences affects synapses, informs thinking, and shapes the experience of subsequent experiences. The five senses provide the primary (if not the exclusive) means by which humans experientially know. Such sensory-perceptive knowledge is generally reliable.[78]

---

76. Holmes, *All Truth Is God's Truth*, 37.
77. Broudy, *Uses of Schooling*, 20.
78. A helpful discussion of this in Alston, *Reliability of Sense Perception*.

Experimentation

Archimedes, Copernicus, Newton, Locke, Hume, Einstein, Crick, and Watson are both sentinels *for* and beacons *of* empiricism, but they are not unique in this mode of knowing. Every human engages and obtains knowledge empirically. Per Common Sense philosophers, "The mind has immediate access to the world. . . . Thus, an individual can have fairly direct epistemic access to the facts of nature. . . . Such is epistemic optimism."[79] But, more than optimism, it is epistemic realism. Humans know through experiences, some of those experiences entail testing hypotheses; thus, experimentation.

Reasoning

The capstone or roof of the house of knowledge and knowing is rationality or reasoning. Reasoning is clear, cogent, coherent thinking. It comes in three basic forms: abduction, induction, and deduction.

Abduction argues to the best explanation. It is the form of inference which proceeds from an observation or a set of observations to a hypothesis which allegedly best (or most simply) explains or accounts for the observation(s). A Supreme Court justice, for example, may abduce her opinion from all the presented evidence.

Induction utilizes premises to give reasonable grounds for a conclusion, such as in arguing from particulars to generals. It infers from premises that not unlikely support a conclusion—even if those premises (unlike deduction) do not necessarily ensure the conclusion. A *Project Lead the Way* high school freshman may conclude inductively in his Biomedical Tech class, for example, that the perpetrator must be a certain individual given the evidentiary correlation.

---

79. Clark et al., *101 Key Terms*, 14.

Deduction utilizes true premises and valid argumentation to conclude with certainty.[80] It argues from premises to reach a logically necessary conclusion.[81] A first-year logic student, for example, may deduce:

1. All bachelors are not married.

2. Professor Jones is a bachelor.

3. Therefore, Professor Jones is not married.

Reasoning appropriately employs *each* of these three forms of argument. It also appropriately employs each of the following three *laws of logic*.

THE LAWS OF LOGIC

"Philosophically, logic is at least closely related to the study of *correct reasoning*. Reasoning is an epistemic, mental activity. So, logic is at least closely allied with epistemology."[82] "Aristotelian logic was essentially classificatory, for it sought to set out valid (and invalid) connections between statements through recasting them into the subject-predicate form, and developed the syllogism as a calculus of class inclusion and exclusion."[83]

> But the particular value of *modern logic* is that in a computer-like way, it enables us to formulate very complex statements and to perform feats of elaborate and sophisticated deduction which we would not be capable of otherwise, just as the casting of scientific results into a mathematical notation may not only give them consistency, making them precise and clear, but, as it were, do some difficult thinking for us by unfolding the implications

---

80. Per Aristotle, "A deduction is speech (*logos*) in which, certain things having been supposed, something different from those supposed results of necessity because of their being so. Each of the 'things supposed' is a premise (*protasis*) of the argument, and what *resulting of necessity* is the conclusion (*sumperasma*). The core of this definition is the notion of *resulting of necessity* (*ex anankês sumbainein*). This corresponds to a modern notion of logical consequence: X X results of necessity from Y Y and Z Z if it would be impossible for X X to be false when Y Y and Z Z are true. We could therefore take this to be a general definition of valid argument" (*Prior Analytics* I.2, 24b18–20).

81. For further discussion, see Smith, "Aristotle's Logic."

82. Shapiro, "Classical Logic," para. 4.

83. Torrance, *Theological Science*, 247.

of our scientific models beyond what we could determine with our empirical statements alone.[84]

Thus, "this is the task of *formal* logic, not to be concerned, however, with the processes of inquiry but to *be* the formal science of coherent statements that sets out their conditions and formulates their principles."[85] "Clearly logic or the *scientia generalis* will be of value for any *scientia specialis*,"[86] including establishing an epistemological framework for a biblical philosophy of Christian school education.

Consistent with the particular biblical philosophy of Christian school education espoused in this book, J. P. Moreland explains:

> These [three following] fundamental laws [of logic delineated below] are true principles governing reality and thought and are assumed by Scripture. Some claim they are arbitrary Western constructions, but this is false. The basic laws of logic govern all reality and thought and are known to be true for at least two reasons: (1) They are intuitively obvious and self-evident. Once one understands a basic law of logic, one can see that it is true. (2) Those who deny them use these principles in their denial, demonstrating that these laws are unavoidable, and that it is self-refuting to deny them.
>
> The basic laws of logic are neither arbitrary inventions of God nor principles that exist completely outside God's being. Obviously, the laws of logic are not like the laws of nature. God may violate the latter (say, suspend gravity), but he cannot violate the former. Those laws are rooted in God's own nature. Indeed, some scholars think the passage, "In the beginning was the Word [logos]" (John 1:1) is accurately translated, "In the beginning was Logic (a divine, rational mind)." For example, even God cannot exist and not exist at the same time, and even God cannot validly believe that red is a color and that red is not a color. When people say that God need not behave "logically," they are using the term in a loose sense to mean "the sensible thing from my point of view." Often God does not act in ways that people understand or judge to be what they would do in the circumstances. But God never behaves illogically in the proper sense. He does not violate in His being or thought the fundamental laws of logic.[87]

---

84. Torrance, *Theological Science*, 250.
85. Torrance, *Theological Science*, 246.
86. Torrance, *Theological Science*, 250.
87. Moreland, "Three Laws of Logic," para. 7.

The three laws of logic are as follows: law of identity, law of excluded middle, and law of "non-contradiction."

Law of Identity

X is X. "The law of identity says that if a statement such as 'It is raining' is true, then the statement is true. More generally, it says that the statement X is the same thing as itself, and it is different from everything else. Applied to all realty, the law of identity says that everything is itself and not something else."[88]

Law of Excluded Middle

Either X, or non-X. "The law of the excluded middle says that a statement such as 'It is raining' is either true or false. There is no other [*tertiem quid*] alternative."[89]

Law of Non-contradiction[90]

Not simultaneously X and non-X in the same way. "The law of non-contradiction says that a statement such as 'It is raining' cannot be both true and false in the same sense. Of course, it could be raining in Missouri and not raining in Arizona, but the principle says that it cannot be raining and not raining at the [precisely] same time in [precisely] the same place."[91]

Immediate Awareness

The term innate can be used for this category, but not necessarily in a strictly narrow, technical sense. This domain of knowledge entails *a*

---

88. Moreland, "Three Laws of Logic," para. 3.

89. Moreland, "Three Laws of Logic," para. 5.

90. Ronald Nash quoted in Sproul, *Not a Chance*, 145. "Strictly speaking, the law of non-contradiction cannot be proved. The reason is simple. Any argument offered as proof for the law of non-contradiction would of necessity have to assume the law as part of the proof. Hence, any direct proof of the law would end up being circular. It would beg the question."

91. Moreland, "Three Laws of Logic."

priori knowing and knowledge, including but not necessarily limited to instincts and intuition.

Instincts

Instincts are inborn, innate, or even involuntary inclinations, impulses, activity, tendency, or action. For example, human hearts "know" how to beat, even without being taught—at least in the conventional sense of the term *taught*. Ethology is a distinct discipline developed largely to study intrinsic, inherited, and instinctual aspects of creatures.[92] The discipline attempts to ferret non-educated and non-environmental elements of the creatures' behavior, broadly speaking. Ethologists define instincts as *any behavior that is present but is unlearned or not resultant from any previous experience*, e.g., a reflex. Generally speaking Darwinists argue that such instinctual behavior is hardwired into species from previous generations' experience, and largely creationists (as well as others committed to Intelligent Design) infer these instinctual behaviors to be part of the design of the Designer preparing the particular species or the particular individual for a readiness to know certain preparatory behaviors prior to having the otherwise necessary experience or education to know that right response at the moment of the triggering event.[93]

---

92. Ethology has unfortunately historically been largely predominated by Darwinists. Intelligent design theorists and creationists alike, however, seem to be increasingly contributing significantly to this growing field.

93. Early in the twentieth century, Behaviorists had all but eliminated *instincts* as part of the informed discussion on behavior in preference for their more programmed understanding of a mechanistic view of behavior. Van Nostrand's 1961 book, *Instincts*, seems to have been particularly influential in instincts' reentry into mainstream epistemic consideration. Interestingly the subtitle chosen for the book was *An Enduring Problem in Psychology*. From the book comes the following delineation of what comprises *instinct* in distinction from the other modes or means of knowing: "To be considered instinctual, a behavior must: (a) be automatic, (b) be irresistible, (c) occur at some point in development, (d) be triggered by some event in the environment, (e) occur in every member of the species, (f) be immodifiable, and (g) govern behavior for which the organism needs no training—although the organism may profit from experience and to that degree the behavior is modifiable."

Intuition

Into which category to place *intuit*-eds and *intuit*-ings, whether intuition is a distinct faculty, to what extent intuitions are mere opinions, or whether they are beliefs or tendencies that make certain beliefs attractive to us all transcend the scope of this book.[94] But, affirming that "we have intuitions about what we can trust to be true,"[95] and acknowledging that such a capacity or insight does constitute a viable aspect of a full-orbed epistemology does not.

For many thinkers (educators and philosophers alike), for example Husserl, this area of knowledge was so definite, distinct, and diverse that they would employ multiple terms to reference types of knowledge in this domain.

1. *Wesensschau*—an immediate intellectual vision or grasping of essences, which is part of the Husserl "pre-philosophical, natural attitude."[96]

2. *Zu den Sachen selbst*—"To the things themselves," or "just as experienced by consciousness" independent of empirical data, rational inquiry, revelation, or other "theoretical or metaphysical presuppositions."[97]

3. *Lebenswelt*—the "lived-world," of which sciences are derivative and parasitic. Shand explains, "Objects already appear to us loaded with a significance that points beyond themselves: their meaning points to their own horizon, which is currently not present in the experience, and defines them as the objects they are and indicates the context in which the objects occur."[98]

4. *Eidetic intuitions*—reduced or residual impression of essences.

5. *Epoche*—suspension of judgment about an object, even about its existence or non-existence.[99]

---

94. Van Inwagen, "Account of Personal Identity," 305–19.
95. Poythress, *Redeeming Philosophy*, 197.
96. Shand, *Philosophy and Philosophers*, 222–24.
97. Shand, *Philosophy and Philosophers*, 310.
98. Shand, *Philosophy and Philosophers*, 229.
99. Shand, *Philosophy and Philosophers*, 229.

AXIOLOGY

As a subsequent complement to metaphysics and epistemology, axiology is the study of value and worth; the collective discipline entailing aesthetics and ethics and their subdisciplines; the foundation for the aforementioned subdisciplines. *Axio* comes from the Greek morpheme *axia*, which meant value or worth. Fundamentally, axiology (the third of the three major disciplines within philosophy) studies that which is beautiful, good, and true.

Aesthetics

Aesthetics is the first subdiscipline within axiology. Whether a critical reflection on art or a more constructive inquiry into matters of taste, appreciation, and quality, aesthetics considers what is beauty, what is beautiful, and what is beautification.[100]

Ethics

Derived from the Greek term *ethikos*, which came from *ethos* which meant *habit*, ethics studies that which is good, right, moral, and just—or not. The ethics presented in this book distill down to three principles:

1. The theological principle.

    1. God is God; we are not.
    2. God himself is the source and standard of what is beautiful, good, and true.[101]

2. The deontological/teleological principle.[102]

---

100. For more on these considerations, the reader is directed to appendix 1.

101. Herman Bavinck, quoted in Van Til, *Defense of the Faith*, 295, "It is God himself who witnesses to all men. And it is man himself, created as he is in God's image who must, in spite of himself, listen to this testimony and consent to it." Nonetheless, unlike Van Til, the present author does not ascribe to theological volunteerism, a perspective from which Van Til seems to have taught that God could have determined whatever he wanted to determine to be beautiful, good, and true. With many others, the present author's position includes God himself (*rex lex*) in his very nature as the source and standard of all ethics and excellencies.

102. The present author asserts that these two approaches to ethics are merely two sides of the same coin: the former emphasizing the duty, obligation, or ought-ness of

1. God says that humans ought to fear him and to keep his commandments.
2. God's greatest commandments are to love him with all one's heart, mind, soul, and strength—and to love others as one would be loved.

3. The doxological principle.

   1. God says humans are to glorify him in all that they do.
   2. God says that we do that most and best by love, joy, peace, patience, kindness, goodness, faithfulness, gentleness, self-control, truth, grace, and whole-hearted excellence—doing everything as a diligent steward doing all one does as from, through, and unto him.

This previous section has highlighted philosophical aspects of a Christian worldview. It has done so as substance to the foundation upon which to construct a biblical philosophy of a Christian school education. To do so it considered metaphysics, epistemology, and axiology. In each of those areas, God is considered to be the one from whom, through whom, and to whom being, knowledge, and beauty, goodness, and truth derive their origin, purpose, and destiny. Therefore, it seems most efficient, most effective, most reasonable, and most eternally significant for a biblical philosophy of a Christian school education to be intentional, comprehensive, intensive, and coherent in its efforts to base everything it is and does on these foundational truths. Furthermore, however, those truths tend to be multi-faceted, if not complex. That is what this next section briefly addresses: complexity theory for a biblical philosophy of a Christian school education.

COMPLEXITY

A careful reader will notice a movement toward a philosophy of education that entails aspects of complexity and consilience. Complexity and consilience are developing disciplines whose quantum ways and means offer much at this point of the present discussion. As one expert in the field of complexity observes, "Once an ordinary noun describing objects

---

what is right and wrong, and the latter emphasizing the ideal and intended ends of what is right. The "material"—as well as the "value"—of the "coin," so to speak is the (moral) perfection of God, *lex rex*.

with many interconnected parts, now [*complexity*] designates a scientific field with many branches."[103]

Complexity,[104] in the context of a quantum discipline being employed interdiciplinarily and as a lens through which to perceive otherwise confounding sets of considerations, has been defined as "the property of a real world system that is manifest in the inability of any one formalism being adequate to capture all its properties. It requires that we find distinctly different ways of interacting with systems. Distinctly different in the sense that when we make successful models, the formal systems needed to describe each distinct aspect is *not* derivable from each other."[105]

Holland suggests that each complex system exhibits *emergence*, "the action of the whole is more than the sum of its parts . . . where the aggregate exhibits properties *not* attained by summation."[106] And, so it is—the present author proposes—with education, with the philosophy of education, and with a biblical philosophy of Christian school education.[107] Every lesson, every plan, every word, and every interaction contribute exponentially to an ever-increasingly laden labyrinth of complexity.[108]

---

103. Holland, *Complexity*, 1.

104. For the remainder of this present discussion the term *complexity* will be utilized to convey the hand-in-hand concepts of complexity and consilience. For further discussion of the idio-nuances of consilience *per se*, the inquisitive and ambitious reader is encouraged to consider Edward O. Wilson's helpful book, *Consilience: The Unity of Knowledge*.

105. As defined Mikulecky, "Complexity Science," 30.

106. Holland, *Complexity*, 1, 4.

107. Terms such as combinatoric play, complicated subsystems, aggregate aspects, bottom-up *and* top-down merely begin to scratch the surface of the tip of this educational iceberg.

108. One critical consideration and not infrequently an invaluable tool within complex systems is Zipf's law. Named after the twentieth-century American linguist who popularized this principle observed hundreds of years earlier, Zipf's law is an empirical principle utilizing probability distribution statistics not infrequently in the social and physical sciences whose data can be approximated with remarkable resemblance to a particular distribution. Recent work has been done applying Zipf's law in as simple a complex system as reproduction. In this context Zipf's law describes a reproducer as an entity that develops and has a material overlap between the "parent" and "progeny" as follows:

x begets y iff $y \neq x$ and x is (part of) the efficient cause of y (where x and y always refer to individuals).

x materially overlaps y iff there is a physical part z, of x at time t which is a physical part of y at time $t \neq t'$.

Although, "we are still a long way from an overarching theory of complexity, there is strong evidence that such a theory is possible."[109] Perhaps such a theory for schools, education, philosophy of education, and a biblical philosophy of Christian school education is even further off. Notwithstanding, it seems to the present author to deserve increased attention for future study to consider the implications of complexity theory in this critical domain.

Accordingly, what our present situation seems to call for is a complex, many-leveled struggle, which Taylor suggests is neither fragmented nor *uni*-disciplinary and which "embraces both [*grandeur* and *misere*] . . . to give us undistorted insight into our era that we need to rise to its greatest challenges."[110]

As one scholar-practitioner has observed, complexity has proved more complex but also more interdisciplinarily helpful than first anticipated.[111]

> This is [one of] the reason[s] why quantum physics seems to offer such a hopeful arena. For the most widely accepted

---

x progenerates y iff *x* begets *y* and *x* materially overlaps *y*.

Reproduction is a process of progeneration the result of which is an increase in numerically distinct objects of a given kind.

x is a *reproducer* iff *x* was the product of progeneration and *x* has the capacity to develop the capacity to progenerate.

Reproduction is a composite process of progeneration and development, the result of which is an increase in numerically distinct objects with the capacity to develop the capacity to progenerate (or progenerate directly).

x is a *reproducer* iff *x* was the product of progeneration and *x* has the capacity to reproduce.

x acquires something, *p* (a part, a property), iff *p* is not a part/property of *x* at time *t*, but *p* is part/property of *x* at some later time *t'*.

x develops iff *x* acquires the capacity to reproduce.

In the context of education, "parent" becomes akin to the developer, e.g., teacher, tutor, text, etc., and "progeny" becomes akin to that which is developed, e.g., lecture, lesson, student, etc. Although its original genesis lay outside of the pedagogical domain, it is inserted here by analogy and its extension to education is done so *a fortiori*. For although *both* teacher and student are *reproducers* at many times and in many ways virtually every school day, there also exist many *other* constituent variables and *reproducers*—exponentially compounding the following flow of complexity. And so it goes; everyday in every way. Every lesson, every plan, every word, every interaction—another reproducer contributing exponentially to an ever-increasingly laden labyrinth of complexity.

109. Holland, *Complexity*, 90.

110. Taylor, *Ethics of Authenticity*, 120–21.

111. Swenson, *Hurtling toward Oblivion*, 61.

interpretation of the equations of quantum probabilities holds that the limitations on our knowledge of quantum states are intrinsic to the world itself. It is not that better theories or measuring apparatus will someday allow us to specify the location and momentum of a subatomic particle [simultaneously] with exact precision.[112]

Such is both the plight and the possibility of the post-Einsteinian world. Less certain in one sense, but more precise in another. And, so it is with the simultaneity of considerations necessary for a full-orbed biblical philosophy of Christian school education: Each of the aforementioned dynamics from the previous sections of this chapter presently positing upon the educator and the student in a precise, yet not fully certain type of way.

In describing the challenge of how to Christianly educate children within the context of quantum complexity, for example, Michal Anthony suggests that "there really aren't any pure theories that can be condensed into a neatly packaged, descriptive paradigm."[113]

Such contemporary realization is not entirely new. In many ways it seems substantively akin to what Scottish Presbyterian philosopher Francis Hutcheson (1694–1746) described about three hundred years ago; he referred to it as "unity in variety."[114]

> Similarly to Hutcheson but notably contrary to Hobbes, Bacon, and Kant—all of whom used a dichotomous scheme to classify the sciences, Dooyeweerd adopts the principle of linear filiation (akin to *complexity*) used by Auguste Comte. Dooyeweerd identifies fifteen irreducible, interrelated sciences; listed below in descending order of complexity from the top to the bottom, are the following aspects of a complex system of a biblical philosophy of Christian school education.
>
> 1. Pistical
> 2. Ethical
> 3. Juridical
> 4. Aesthetic
> 5. Economic
> 6. Social

---

112. Clayton, *God and Contemporary Science*, 193.
113. Anthony, *Your Child's Spiritual Formation*, 1.
114. Scruton, *Beauty*, 162.

7. Linguistic
8. Historical (culture molding)
9. Analytical (logic, thought)
10. Psychical (sensation)
11. Biotic (life)
12. Physical (energy)
13. Movement
14. Spatial
15. Numerical[115]

Even several leading contemporary secular philosophers of education seem to be increasingly tending toward these tensions that Hutcheson and Dooyeweerd addressed and that complexity theorists discuss:

> I adopt this ecumenical [eclectic, or *complexity*] approach for two reasons. First, I want to show that a "multiple intelligences" approach is flexible, it can be employed in studying sharply focused topics, as well as generic ones. Second, not every aspect of multiple intelligences can be used with equal effectiveness for every pedagogical goal. . . . The pedagogical challenge is to figure out which entry points hold promise for particular understandings.[116]

One Christian educational philosopher illustrates these aspects of complexity like this:

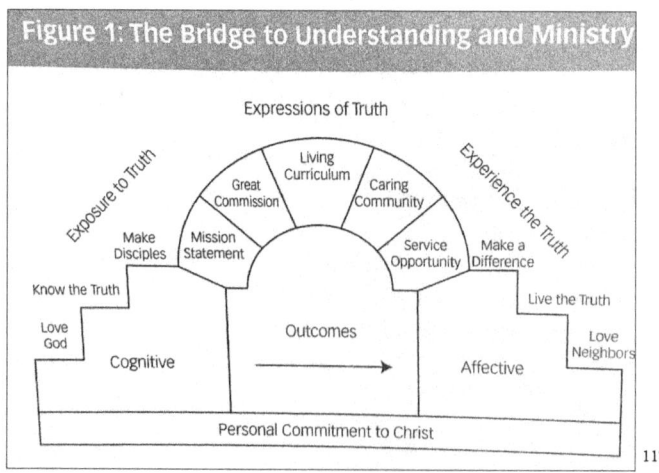

[117]

---

115. Clark, *Introduction to Christian Philosophy*, 94–95.
116. Gardner, *Disciplined Mind*, 188.
117. Braley et al., *Foundations of Christian School Education*, 322.

TOWARD A DEFINITION OF THE PHILOSOPHY OF EDUCATION

So, how one *achieves* consilience within such complexity in the context of a full-orbed philosophy of education becomes the next question. To probe that question, three other aspects of complexity within education and the philosophy of education will briefly be addressed, i.e., *learning, mind,* and *syntality*. The subsequent section will then consider Christian complexity as it applies to education and the philosophy of education. But, first a brief word about *learning, mind,* and *syntality* as aspects of complexity in education.

From a renown developmental psychologist, we read, "*Learning* is now seen as *situated*—as occurring in specific [complex] contexts, with particular identifying features and purposes."[118] Resultantly, many interdisciplinary tools are wielded. For example, learning "is the process by which behavior is changed and, ideally, improved through experience . . . guided by an expert."[119] And, "the aim of educational psychology [one such interdisciplinary tool] is to understand how learning processes may be most effectively guided."[120]

> To *learn* is to engage in an experience that affects the psychological functioning of the individual in ways that will result in changes in his behavior. The word "learning" is used to refer to both the process and the result. As a process, learning refers to the experiences the learner goes through, his internal and external activity, and his reactions to the situation in which he defends himself. As a product, learning refers to the changes that occur—the ways in which the learner is different or the actual changes in his behavior. These changes may be temporary or relatively permanent.[121]

In addition to *learning*, such interdisciplinary complexity also necessitates considerations regarding what the *mind* is. Part of the tension or even apparent disparity in defining *mind* is what Wallach and Wallach address in their complexity approach to what they call seven views *of* the mind.

> Implicitly or explicitly, the views have left their imprint not only upon philosophers and students of philosophy but also upon professional and students in various fields, especially

---

118. Gardner, *Disciplined Mind*, 97.
119. Bernard, *Psychology of Teaching and Learning*, 481.
120. Bernard, *Psychology of Teaching and Learning*, 6.
121. Clayton, *Teaching and Learning*, 35.

in psychology. . . . It matters for everybody how the mind is *viewed*,[122] not only for intellectual reasons but also because different views promote different ways of thinking of ourselves and different ways of being. . . . While each of them [i.e., the seven views of the mind] have certain virtues, none of them seemed entirely satisfactory.

Our "circumnavigation" is replicated here. Think of each as a port of call on our voyage, with a chapter devoted to each. . . . The reader is invited to join us on our tour and to consider whether, despite the problems we find with each view,[123] a solution to our problem may be at hand if we undertake an integration of their respective virtues.[124]

1. Mind as Distinct from the Physical World.
2. Mind as a Manner of Speaking.
3. Mind as Behavior.
4. Mind as Software in the Head.
5. Mind as Brain.
6. Mind as Scientific Construct.
7. Mind as Social Construct.[125]

Like the very theory they espouse[126] regarding the multi-affectedness and complexity of a seven-view view of the mind, they observe, "Mental concepts are classificatory that enable us to assign categories. . . .

---

122. What Wallach and Wallach seem to be arguing for is something more methodological than ontological. They do not seem to be arguing that the *mind* actually *is* these seven different things in the same way at the same time, which would not be ontologically viable. Rather they seem to be attempting to provide their readers with a set of seven different lenses through which to consider such a complexity as *mind*. Each of the seven lenses, so to speak, lends itself to inspection of the mind in a contextually appropriate way. For example, the neuroscientist is not encouraged to "see" mind as brain and only as brain, but to primarily look through the lens of *mind as brain* when studying the brain to learn about the mind, but also to have in mind while conducting neuroscience that any and all contributions that neuroscientific perspective can provide in terms of insights regarding what the mind is and how it functions do not entail the entirety of even how to *look* at what the mind is let alone what it *actually* (i.e., ontologically) is.

123. One significant deficit of their immensely helpful contribution to this vital discussion is the conspicuous absence of something like a possible eighth view they could call "Mind as *Imago Dei*."

124. Wallach and Wallach, *Seven Views of Mind*, x–xi.

125. Wallach and Wallach, *Seven Views of Mind*, v.

126. Again, what Wallach and Wallach seem to be arguing for is something more methodological than ontological, *per se*.

Each of the seven views in this book makes an essential point that seems correct. . . . These [seven] points provided the building blocks that we drew upon in developing our answer to the [mind] problem. It is an answer, we believe, that is able to acknowledge, appreciate, and account for mental concepts."[127] "Without the presence in psychology or philosophy or neuroscience of *each* of the seven views, we could not have come to the conclusion offered here."[128]

In addition to *mind* and to *learning*, another application of complexity in education and the philosophy of education is *syntality*. "Although *syntality* is a term used in more than one context within education and with different connotations in each context, one such usage is as an approach to accelerated learning accomplished by bringing together numerous learning techniques in a holistic approach to learning."[129] *Syntality* in those contexts refers to diverse dynamics of interplay between personalities of learners, or even to the process by which to bring multiple diverse dynamics from various disciplines or methodologies to the learning context.[130]

---

127. Wallach and Wallach, *Seven Views of Mind*, 99.

128. Wallach and Wallach, *Seven Views of Mind*, 99.

129. Anthony, *Evangelical Dictionary*, 677.

130. Other examples of complexity in education and the philosophy of education exist, as well. The present author is not alone in looking through the lens of complexity to inspect aspects pertinent to this book such as syntality, mind, learning, education, and the philosophy of education. Recently Wiley-Blackwell published a multiauthored work in which more than ten philosophers of education contributed to a book entitled *Complexity Theory and the Philosophy of Education*. Most notably the editor—also a contributor, Mark Mason, professor of philosophy and educational studies—summarizes a few of the "simultaneities" that he and his colleagues observe in a complexity approach to the philosophy of education:

1. *knower and knowledge*, where complexity theory, by considering both simultaneously, aims to move beyond the common distinction between teachers' representing the established and objective knowledge of the curriculum while pedagogically fostering subjective knowing in learners;
2. *transphenomenality*, where complexity theory offers insights that can be had only by the simultaneous consideration of factors normally associated with apparently quite different phenomenal levels of explanation;
3. *transdisciplinarity*, where complexity theory offers insights that can be had only by the simultaneous consideration of factors normally associated with apparently quite different disciplinary perspectives;

CHRISTIAN COMPLEXITY

Similarly (at least in some ways) in 1987 Poythress penned his probing *Symphonic Theology*, which he subtitled *The Validity of Multiple Perspectives in Theology*. The present author summarizes here a few salient and pertinent insights from that important and paradigmatic work.[131]

1. Models, diagrams, and analogies can play a key role in discovery.[132]

2. Even when the exact same data are considered different conclusions can reasonably be concluded.[133]

---

4. *descriptive and pragmatic* insights, where an emphasis in complexity research has recently moved beyond careful descriptive accounts of complex phenomena toward deliberate attempts to prompt the emergence and affect the character of such phenomena—an emphasis well-suited to the pragmatic concerns of many educationists;

5. *representation and presentation*, where representations contribute to the shape of possibility, being partial rather than comprehensive, active rather than inert implicated rather than benign;

6. *affect and effect*, in the terms of which Davis argues that educators and educational researchers are uniquely positioned to contribute to complexity thinking, most obviously because of the transphenomenal nature of the educational project, the transdisciplinary character of educational research, and the interdiscursive nature of educational thought;

7. *education and research*, where Davis suggests that educational research and educational practice might be considered aspects of the same project, e.g., expanding the space of human possibility by exploring the space of the existing possible (Mason, *Complexity Theory*, 5–6).

131. Although a detailed explanation of Poythress's work in this regard transcends the scope of this book, in summary its inclusion within this section serves primarily two purposes: (1) to validate from the perspective of a highly regarded Christian polymath (which Poythress is—having earned doctorates in both science *and* theology) that a Christian worldview is not incompatible with complexity, nor vice versa; (2) to suggest some of the ways and means that their compatibility can be observed, appreciated, and implemented when (like the sons of Issachar) a God-fearer endeavors to understand his context and to engage (within) that context with the transcendent and transformative truths of God.

132. Poythress, *Symphonic Theology*, 12.

133. Poythress, *Symphonic Theology*, 10.

3. The use (i.e., *mis*-use or *over*-use) of perspective is fraught with danger.[134]

4. It is misleading to say that all perspectives are valid.[135]

5. The use of multiplicity of perspective does not constitute a denial of the absoluteness of truth.[136]

6. The use of multiplicity of perspective constitutes the richness of truth and builds upon the fact that human beings are limited.[137]

7. Each perspective has (at most) partial knowledge—not complete or perfect grasp of all truth.[138]

8. Each perspective needs to strive to stand outside of itself and its [epistemic] limitations.[139]

9. Each perspective . . . [140]

    1. Has a separate focus.
    2. Is dependent on others and is intelligible only in the context of the others.
    3. If expanded far enough will involve another.
    4. Can contribute to a symphonic perspective.
    5. Is like a facet on a jewel.

10. The content of Truth is both one and many.[141]

11. As Wittgenstein dubbed, there are often "family resemblances."[142]

---

134. Poythress, *Symphonic Theology*, 12.
135. Poythress, *Symphonic Theology*, 44.
136. Poythress, *Symphonic Theology*, 45.
137. Poythress, *Symphonic Theology*, 45.
138. Poythress, *Symphonic Theology*, 45.
139. Poythress, *Symphonic Theology*, 52.
140. Poythress, *Symphonic Theology*, 36–37.
141. Poythress, *Symphonic Theology*, 51.
142. Poythress, *Symphonic Theology*, 66.

12. Symphonic theology [or by analogy a symphonic approach to a biblical philosophy of Christian school education] shows its greatest distinctiveness in its method for synthesis:[143]

    1. Use of a variety of perspectives to examine a topic.
    2. Use of the preemption method of argument (i.e., incorporating the other perspective's strong point).
    3. Dissolve poorly posed questions and debates based merely upon semantics.
    4. Enrich reconciliation of apparently opposing emphases.[144]

It was the sons of Issachar that were commended because of their intentionality to have ideas that were well thought out within their historical, cultural milieu—allowing them to "understand the times," no matter how complex. To have ideas that are well thought out today—to be understanding of the times—includes the recognition of the Copernican shifts of complexity and consilience.

Ultimately, "the truth of God's mind is rich."[145] "Only God's knowledge of Himself is nonmysterious,"[146] which provides no guarantee of complete transparency, complete mastery, or complete eradication of any and all mystery for humans. Therefore, Christian philosophers and educators alike seek, as Poythress urges, "loyalty to [God's] truth."[147]

Connecting the dots of truth, complexity, and education, Allen suggests that "of all the beautiful truths pertaining to the soul which have been restored and brought to light in this age [of complexity], none is more gladdening or fruitful of divine promise and confidence than this—that man is the master of thought, the molder of character, and the maker and shaper of condition, environment, and destiny."[148] Allen goes on to argue, "Mind is the Master power that moulds and makes, and Man is Mind, and evermore he takes the tool of Thought, and, shaping what he

---

143. Poythress, *Symphonic Theology*, 96.

144. One endeavoring to do a biblical philosophy of Christian school education—especially one endeavoring to do so with and within complexity is encouraged to do two things: (1) consider and incorporate some of the elements alluded to here from Poythress's book; (2) use Poythress's book as a resource to elucidate some of his suggestions more definitively.

145. Poythress, *Redeeming Philosophy*, 186.

146. Poythress, *Redeeming Philosophy*, 104.

147. Poythress, *Redeeming Philosophy*, 186.

148. Allen, *As a Man Thinketh*, 14.

wills, brings forth a thousand ills: he thinks in secret and it comes to pass: Environment is but his looking glass."[149] Paraphrasing Jesus he continues, "A man is literally what he thinks, his character being the complete sum of all his thoughts. . . . Act is the blossom of thought, and joy and suffering its fruits."[150] "The vision that you glorify in your mind, the Ideal that you enthrone in your heart—this you will build your life by, this you will become."[151]

To that end and with the complexity of God's aseity, singularity, and absoluteness of truth in mind, "The primary end of education [is] not the acquisition of useful information or skills needed for a particular occupation in life, but the cultivation of the mind."[152] "The true object of education is to help the growing man by means of discipline and knowledge, to realize and determine himself"[153] by and before God.

TOWARD A DEFINITION OF (A BIBLICAL) PHILOSOPHY OF EDUCATION

Having already arrived at a definition of *education*, the present author prepares for the next step down the path, i.e., defining the *philosophy of* education. The term *philosophy*, according to the *Oxford Dictionary*, denotes aspects such as:

1. An academic discipline.

2. The study of fundamental nature.

3. The study of the theoretical bases for a particular discipline, e.g., education.

4. The theory, attitude, or orientation that acts as a guiding principle for one's approach to a particular discipline, e.g., education.

Thus, a working definition for the purposes of this book would be that the *philosophy of education is both the academic discipline which studies the fundamental nature of education, its foundational constituents, and*

---

149. Allen, *As a Man Thinketh*, 5.
150. Allen, *As a Man Thinketh*, 9.
151. Allen, *As a Man Thinketh*, 47.
152. Ggita, *Jacques Maritain*, 73.
153. Ggita, *Jacques Maritain*, 22.

its theoretical bases, as well as the theory, attitude, and orientation that acts as a guiding principle for one's approach to education—which is the act, the process, or the product of imparting or acquiring knowledge or understanding, or of developing skills or competencies, or of cultivating the capacities of reasoning, judgment, values, or virtues—thereby preparing oneself or others for mature and flourishing life.

Chapter 3

Toward a Biblical Philosophy of Christian School Education

"We cannot educate man unless we know what he really is."[1] *That* is where a *biblical* philosophy of *Christian* school education comes in. Nonetheless, as James Pluddemann (not unlikely quoting Frank Gaebelein) wryly assessed, "[Sometimes] Christian education is neither."[2] Pluddemann, Gaebelein, et al. tragically observed much in Christian school education that failed to be and do what it ought to be and do, largely because it had failed to have a thoroughgoing biblical philosophy of and for itself. This third of three introductory chapters portends to contribute to mitigating such a lack by surveying several aspects of a biblical philosophy of Christian school education with movement toward one.

PROLEGOMENA: SCRIPTURAL AND PRESUPPOSITIONAL CONSIDERATIONS

The following is a sampling of Scriptures salient to a biblical philosophy of Christian school education. Granted *all* Scripture is God-breathed and arguably profitable for this exercise. These passages, however, seem particularly germane to some aspect or another of a biblical philosophy

---

1. Ggita, *Jacques Maritain*, 91.
2. Lebar, *Education That Is Christian*, 9.

of Christian school education. To that end, after each quotation a brief contextualizing comment is provided.

Genesis 1:1

"In the beginning, God created the heavens and the earth."

Paradigmatically this passage establishes first things first: God is *the* Uncaused Cause, Originator of *all* there is. Genesis 1 establishes God as the One from whom, through whom, and to whom are all things.[3] God, therefore, has the right to define the terms of what it means to *be* human—and, what it means to *educate* humans.

Genesis 1:26–28

"Then God said, 'Let us make man in our image, after our likeness. And let them have dominion over the fish of the sea and over the birds of the heavens and over the livestock and over all the earth and over every creeping thing that creeps on the earth.' So God created man in his own image, in the image of God he created him; male and female he created them. And God blessed them. And God said to them, 'Be fruitful and multiply and fill the earth and subdue it, and have dominion over the fish of the sea and over the birds of the heavens and over every living thing that moves on the earth.'"

Humans are *imago Dei*: God's image bearers created to put him on display to one another, to the onlooking universe, and ultimately back to God, himself. What all *imago Dei* entails transcends the scope of this book, but it seems reasonable that *imago Dei* at least includes humans being what one can see God being in Genesis 1, i.e., creator and communicator. God created humans (at least in part) to join him in *creatio continuo* and *communicatio continuo*.[4]

Exodus 20:20

"Moses said to the people, 'Do not fear, for God has come to test you, that the fear of him may be before you, that you may not sin.'"

3. Rom 11:33–36.

4. (No small) part of what it means to be human is working with God on behalf of God communicating and creating in ways that will put him on display.

A fortiori if this passage applies to the divinely delivered Decalogue, how much more ought it apply to the Christian school handbook. Compliance or conformity to some man-made code is not the end game. Rightly regarding God (and others) and rightly relating to him (and others) *is*. Reverential awe and responsive obedience deserve cultivation in one's policies and procedures, as well as in one's prescriptive and proscriptive behaviors. Any code and concomitant consequences or commendations ought to point students *toward* God—not *away* from him. For many this may mean a rereading and even a rewriting of the parent-student handbook to distill the salient, scriptural precepts and principles out from any anthropocentric fear of man and any material that may incline humans away from a proper relationship with God—and concomitantly with others and with the rest of the created order. God wants trust, reverence, and obedience. He knows what is right, and he urges Christian schools to that end.

Deuteronomy 6:4

"Hear, O Israel: The Lord our God, the Lord is one."

There is one God, and this God is one. The ontic and epistemic contributions of *adonai eloheynu; adonai echad* are profound. No one other than Yahweh is Lord. He is the Source of all there is and of all that is revealed.

But, there also seems to be an ethical aspect to this divine disclosure, as well—especially juxtaposed to four hundred years in Egypt,[5] where polytheism ruled the day: Many gods, therefore, many ways of doing things. If someone in ancient Egypt, for example, wanted the blessing of the sun, (s)he would try to appease the sun god; if the Nile, then the river god. Each domain of life would have had its alleged sovereign. But, if (i.e., *since*) there is *one* God and that God is *one*, there is, therefore, only *one* way of doing things, i.e., *his* way. His way, the passage goes on to explain, is that humans love him with their entire being and to convey that his way is the right way to the next generation from the moment they arise in the morning until the moment they go down at night—and every moment in between.

---

5. Not to mention the polytheistic tendencies of many ancient Palestinians that God's people would soon be encountering.

Deuteronomy 29:29

"The secret things belong to the Lord our God, but the things that are revealed belong to us and to our children forever, that we may do all the words of this law."

God chooses to reveal himself and to reveal beauty, goodness, and truth, but he chooses not to reveal everything. Whether he reveals or conceals, he does so to prompt trust and obedience in the context of relationship with him and others.

1 Samuel 2:26

"Now the boy Samuel continued to grow both in stature and in favor with the Lord and also with man."

Samuel was a godly child. He provides an exemplar of what theocentric child development looks like: growing, maturing, and relating well with God and others.[6]

Job 28:28

"And he said to man, 'Behold, the fear of the Lord, that is wisdom, and to turn away from evil is understanding.'"

God is the infinite and perfect Source of knowledge, wisdom, and understanding. He reveals that the axiological aspects of the universe are based upon the epistemological and metaphysical aspects of the universe in general—and upon him as *lex rex* in particular.[7]

---

6. Very similarly it was said of Jesus at age twelve that "the child grew and became strong, filled with wisdom. And the favor of God was upon him. . . . And Jesus increased in wisdom and in stature and in favor with God and man" (Luke 2:40, 52).

7. The book of Job has much to say that is pertinent to a biblical philosophy of Christian school education. Perhaps most profound is the LORD's answer to Job and Job's response to God found in chs. 38–42. Additional illustrations of important and impactful truths include, "Hear my words, you wise men, and give ear to me, you who know; for the ear tests words as the palate tastes food. . . . Let us choose what is right; let us know among ourselves what is good" (Job 28:28; 34:2–4).

Psalm 1, 19, 139, and 150

These psalms in their entireties seem to encapsulate essential aspects of a biblical philosophy of Christian school education. Psalm 1 portrays the *telos* of a godly person living wisely and flourishing; that is the aim of a Christian school education. Psalm 19 portrays God as the purveyor of both general and special revelation, and it portrays the one who hears and heeds God as both redeemed and rewarded; the former is the epistemological bases of a Christian school education, and the latter is the impetus. Psalm 139 poetically portrays the anthropology of a Christian school education. Psalm 150 portrays the doxological climax of the Psalms, the doxological *summum bonum* of life, and the doxological goal of a Christian school education.

Proverbs 1:7

"The fear of the LORD is the beginning of knowledge; fools despise wisdom and instruction."

Many of the proverbs illustrate the distinction between the wise person who seeks, savors, and submits to God's providential will and ways, versus the fool who ignores, disregards, or even shuns God's wisdom and his wooing. This verse from Solomon's opening chapter has become for many a quintessential referent of the aforementioned contrast. The juxtaposition is not just ironic, it is telling; it is not just telling, it ought to be paradigmatic. A biblical philosophy of Christian school education ought to render reverential awe to the Creator God; that in and of itself ought to be that to which and by which Christian school and its adherents recalibrate as the starting point of every day, every lesson, every conference, etc.; *that* ought to be *the* beginning point of everything that a Christian school is and does.

Proverbs 8:1–36

"Does not wisdom call? Does not understanding raise her voice?"

An entire chapter is given to revealing Wisdom personified. She beautifully beckons passersby. Those who heed her call receive a blessed life; those who do not, end in death. A biblical philosophy of Christian school education ought to cultivate a lifelong love of wisdom.[8]

Ecclesiastes 7:18

"It is good that you should take hold of this, and from that withhold not your hand, for the one who fears God shall come out from both of them."

Although there are some radical and even extreme aspects to biblical Christianity and therefore to any philosophy of education espousing the aforementioned worldview, there is also a profound and extensive sense in which something akin to a golden mean is not infrequently that which is biblical and best. Examples could include pursuing academic excellence but not the extreme of having an anxious student body; enforcing the truth of the handbook standards, but doing so with grace;[9] cultivating creativity, but encouraging so within God-honoring parameters and guidelines, etc. Balance, moderation, and shalom are part of the flourishing of a biblical philosophy of Christian school education that rightly reveres God and concomitantly discerns direction, which is not infrequently neither to the right nor to the left—or sometimes, some of both.

Ecclesiastes 12

"Remember also your Creator in the days of your youth, before the evil days come and the years draw near. . . . This is the end of the matter; all has been heard. Fear God and keep his commandments, for this is the whole duty of man. For God will bring every deed into judgment . . . whether good or evil."

Having pondered the vicissitudes of life, Qoheleth concludes:

1. Theologically: God is God; we are not.

---

8. Even etymologically this makes sense: *sophia* is wisdom and *phileo* is love. So, rightfully one who does *any* philosophy ought to do so as a love of wisdom, let alone one who does a *biblical* philosophy of Christian school education.

9. The discussion of biblical balance in the context of Christian school discipline deserves its own book. Some salient Scriptures include: Gen 1:27; Deut 6:4–9; 29:29; Prov 3:11–12; 13:24; Eccl 12; Mic 6:8; John 1:17, 29; 3:16–21; 1 Cor 11:1; 2 Cor 2:5–11; 5:14–18; Gal 6:1–15; Eph 4:15; Phil 2:12–16; 3:12–16; Col 3:1–17; Jas 5:16; 1 John 1:9; Jude 20–25. See also comment above on Exod 20:20.

2. Deontologically: We ought to do what God says to do.

3. Doxologically: What God wants from us is *us*: our obeisance and our obedience.

John 8:31, 32, 47

"If you abide in my word, you are truly my disciples, and you will know the truth, and the truth will set you free. . . . Whoever is of God hears the words of God. The reason why you do not hear them is that you are not of God."

John Feinberg, Nancy Pearcey, and D. A. Carson have a lot to say about this matter of truth.[10] Perhaps (at least in some ways) more than ever, truth is under attack—if not under siege. Postmodernity may have eroded some aspects of authority speaking into the lives of the next generation, but discipling, mentoring, and pointing the next generation to the absolute, liberating, life-giving, and transformative truth of Jesus and his word need (at least as much as ever) to be pertinent to one's biblical philosophy of Christian school education.

Romans 1:19-20

"For what can be known about God is plain to them, because God has shown it to them. . . . For his invisible attributes, namely, his eternal power and divine nature, have been clearly perceived, ever since the creation of the world, in the things that have been made. So they are without excuse. . . . For although they knew God, they did not honor him as God or give thanks to him, but they became futile in their thinking, and their foolish hearts were darkened."

> Ironically, this whole model of *knowing* in Romans 1:18–32 seems to leave open a surprisingly positive role for human reason [even] in religious knowing. Many exegetes have observed that, for all its limitations, human reason is presented in these verses as a faculty which is, in principle, capable of attaining truth about God. It is simply crippled by the idolatrous

---

10. Citations of their books, respectively (in this book's bibliography), *No One Like Him*, *Total Truth*, and *The Gagging of God*, provide the inquiring reader an opportunity to explore these matters further.

tendencies of the human moral will. By implication, this would suggest that if one's moral faculties were repaired, one's reason might be free[er] to operate [more like] as it was [originally] intended.[11]

Romans 11:33–36

"Oh, the depth of the riches and wisdom and knowledge of God! How unsearchable are his judgments and how inscrutable his ways! For who has known the mind of the Lord, or who has been his counselor? Or who has given a gift to him that he might be repaid? For from him and through him and to him are all things. To him be glory forever. Amen."

Revelation, mystery, and providence are all intended to a singular, doxological end, i.e., God's glory. Therefore, *soli Deo gloria* ought to be the bottom line of a biblical philosophy of Christian school education, because it ought to be the bottom line of life.

2 Corinthians 10:4–5

"For the weapons of our warfare are not of the flesh but have divine power to destroy strongholds. We destroy arguments and every lofty opinion raised against the knowledge of God, and take every thought captive to obey Christ."

Every thought that every student in Christian education has is ideally to be taken captive to Christ. So also, every thought of every biblical Christian endeavoring to do philosophy of education ought to be taken captive to Christ, as well.

Ephesians 2:10

"For we are his workmanship [*poiema*], created in Christ Jesus for good works, which God prepared beforehand, that we should walk in them."

This is the identity that each entity has (if they are) in Christ. What profound implications for a biblical philosophy of Christian school education that not only is each individual an *imago Dei*,[12] if they are

---

11. Scott, *Paul's Way of Knowing*, 22.
12. Gen 1:27.

already regenerated,[13] they are also God's *poiema*—his handiwork, his masterpiece, his poetry in motion with a divine design to do good works that God prepared in advance for that individual uniquely to do.

Hebrews 5:8, 14

"Although he was a son, he learned obedience through what he suffered . . . solid food is for the mature, for those who have their powers of discernment trained by constant practice to distinguish good from evil."

If the perfect Son of God *"learned* obedience," *a fortiori* how much more do mere mortals—faculty, families, students, and staff alike—need to *learn* obedience. If he learned through suffering, and he is the prototype, then it goes to reason that (at least) *some* of the challenging aspects of Christian school education can be lessons in obedience.[14] May Christian schools be committed to sinking their teeth into the mature and maturing meats of perspective, perseverance, practice, and discernment.

James 1:19–20; 3:13–18

"Everyone should be quick to listen, slow to speak and slow to become angry for man's anger does not bring about the righteous life that God desires. . . . Who is wise and understanding among you? By his good conduct let him show his works in the meekness of wisdom."

Undeniably education entails intellectual development. More than achieving merely intellectual development, however, godly character, godly wisdom, and godly lives ought to be vital parts of Christian school education.[15]

---

13. Eph 2:8–9.

14. Jesus said it quite plainly to his followers: "In this world you will have trouble; but, be of good cheer, I have overcome the world" (John 16:33).

15. Scripture is replete with such revelation. Pertinent passages include Mic 6:8; Matt 5–7; Rom 12–14; Jas 1:26–27; 3:13; 2 Pet 1:3–9; 3:18; Jude 24–25; and Gal 5:22–23, which cites love, joy, peace, patience, kindness, goodness, faithfulness, gentleness, self-control as indicative of a maturing life flourishing with the fruit of the Spirit.

Colossians 1:28–29

Finally,[16] Paul's paradigmatic passage of Col 1:28–29, in which the apostle inspired by the Spirit expands this vision of Christian education. "We proclaim him, teaching everyone and admonishing everyone with all his wisdom, so that we might present everyone complete in Christ. To this end I labor, struggling with all his energy so powerfully working in me."

Replete with educational implications this passage portrays the *who*, *what*, *why*, and *how* of Christian education. The *who* in this passage entails the one(s) teaching, the one(s) being taught, and the One whose proclamation provides the substance of the educational exchange.

First Paul pictures a pedagogical partnership as he utilizes first-person plural for the ones proclaiming. In contradistinction to the Gnostics of the day, no secret society precludes partnering in reaching and teaching this next generation with the transformative truth of a theocentric educational experience. The Christian school movement has not infrequently referenced such partnership as a three-legged stool of parent, Christian school, and local church;[17] these three biblically viable institutions together proclaiming the centrality of Christ.

Whether counting or calculus, alphabet or algebra, Bible or band, science or science fiction, classroom or boardroom, the centrality of Christ occupies the centrality of the argument of Colossians and the impetus for the Christian school. Even as the vain, Christ-less philosophies of the first century preyed upon the minds of ancient Asia Minor, so also the tepid and vacuous worldviews of the twenty-first century command our attention and demand a Christ-full response. "We proclaim *him* . . ." Proclaiming Christ as central not only to *Christ*ian truth, but to *all* truth differentiates substantively *Christ*ian education from secular curriculum.

Such Christian curricular cogency and cohesion contrasts with any exclusive mystery religions of that day or this—such as within the gnostic framework, only special prerequisite qualifiers allowed for further elucidation. Contrastingly, in Christian education, the apostle unveils the audience as *everyone*. Some Christian schools, therefore, practice so-called open admission, others require a profession of faith at least from one parent to satisfy the terms of the prior partnership implied in the aforementioned subject of the predicate of proclamation. In either case,

---

16. There are many other passages that could be mentioned, and some of those will be later in this book, including but not limited to 2 Tim 2:15.

17. Or, the three-strand cord of Eccl 4:12, which "is not easily broken."

it warrants noting that Paul uses a particularly emphatic construction. In Col 1:28 alone the word *everyone* gets used three times. By virtue of the hermeneutical principle of repetition, a careful reader can deduce a particular Pauline emphasis. Perhaps controverting human tendencies toward preferences, comfort zones, or even teacher's pets, this inspired text preempts such particularity, requiring rather a relational regard for each and every student as being a viable recipient of Christian education.

The *what* of Col 1:28–29 entails teaching, admonishing, and wisdom. *Teaching (didasko)* covers a broad semantic domain and a concomitantly broad pedagogical domain, as well. This broad pedagogical domain likely includes but is not limited to didactic, demonstration, and other deliveries, as well. Some have referred to this as pertaining to the cognitive domain of the *head*. Admonishing (*noutheteuo*), on the other hand, connotes that aspect of education alluded to in the antiquated axiomatic adage, "Students don't care how much you know, until they know how much you care." This so-called cognitive and affective domain pertains to the *head* and to the *heart*. Finally, wisdom (*sophia*) not unlikely hearkens back to Paul's native Hebrew term *hokmah*. *Hokmah*, generally translated *wisdom*, refers to the skill of living. Used of carpenters exacting a precise cut, mariners navigating a stormy sea, teachers preparing and presenting well-crafted lessons, or students developing the craft of living life the way life was designed to be lived, the *hands* that execute such a life have been well-educated in the behavioral domain of *wisdom*.

The *why* of Col 1:28–29 of presenting everyone *complete* in Christ conveys a teleological aspect of education. Maturity, well-roundedness, preparedness, flourishing; such pursuits constitute the bull's-eye at which Christian education takes aim everyday in every way. Additionally and noteworthily, Paul utilizes a singular *end* in 1:29, "to this end." Just having noted multiple means of proclaiming, teaching, and admonishing, Paul demonstrates that each of those aspects of Christian education come together toward a *single* end.

The *how* of Col 1:28–29 involves three components: *each* of us; *effort*; *energy*. Contrasting with the *we* of the *who* at the opening of the passage in v. 28, Paul utilizes first-person *singular* when it comes to *how* Christian education gets done in v. 29. It seems that the implication includes individual responsibility in the actual *doing* of Christian education. Whether teacher, student, parent, or administrator, each member of the Christian school educational endeavor as an individual maintains individual dignity and responsibility for an aspect of the education. Paul, the exemplar, asserts that collectively (*we*) proclaim, but individually (*I*), i.e., *each* of us, ought to exert the effort necessary and sufficient for true, transformative Christian education to transpire.

He describes such *effort* with ascending intensity. "To this end I labor, struggling . . ." not passively, but actively; not perfunctorily, but intentionally; not meagerly, but energetically for each educator (again, whether teacher, student, parent, or administrator), the standard is *laboring* and *struggling*—in other words, working hard at doing it well.

Finally, Paul identifies the Source by which all of the aforementioned gets accomplished. None other than the *energy* of Christ which so powerfully works within each believer engaged in the Christian educational enterprise. Anything less than that eternal, infinite, immutable, reliable, durative Source would prove insufficient for such an infinitely important engagement, but *his* energy in and through each individual laboring and struggling proves both necessary and sufficient for the ends of a biblical philosophy of Christian school education as delineated in Col 1:28–29.

WELTANSCHAUUNG: WORLDVIEW—
A THOUGHT EXPERIMENT

He was about three years old at the time. Keith Arthur Currivean Jr. had just arrived to his grandparents' house for a Christmas celebration. Enamored by a big red balloon, the youngster walked around for hours with the newly discovered object in front of his face. Concomitant to this peculiar pastime was, of course, the fact that everything that Keith looked at he saw as red, and conversely everything that looked at him saw him as red, too.

That is a picture of *Weltanschauung*. Popularly referred to as worldview, *Weltanschauung* is the interpretive gird through which all of life is filtered; it is the lens through which all of life is seen—and thru which all of life sees the observer, and it is the set of fundamental core beliefs to which an adherent holds, as well as the resultant behaviors (most broadly defined) of those fundamental core beliefs.

Philosophers occasionally simplify the categories of consideration within a worldview as origin, purpose, and destiny: (1) Origin: that *from* which something came; (2) Purpose: that *for* which that something exists; (3) Destiny: that end *toward* which that something is (i.e., *ought* to be) headed. Romans 11:36 distills a comprehensive, Christian worldview down to a singular, salient statement.[18] "For from him and through him and to him are all things, to him be glory forever."

Admitting the analogical limitations of any metaphor as a just descriptor for such a vast complex of metaphysics, epistemology, and axiology, the present author nonetheless suggests the big red balloon illustration as a helpful lens—quite accurate and descriptive to the various aspects of the *phenomena* and *noumena* associated with *Weltanschauung* and its concomitant philosophical considerations.

Another apt analogy is a foundation. In his sermon recorded in Matthew's gospel, Jesus describes lives built upon rock versus lives built upon sand. One foundation withstood the rigors of life, the other did not. And, so it is with a worldview. Foundational to all of how one lives life, his worldview must be solid in each of the following regards:

1. Consistent with (and not inconsistent with) the laws of identity, excluded middle, and non-contradiction.

2. Coherent within itself—and not internally inconsistent or self-stultifying.

3. Correspondent to reality with categorically appropriate controls for different types of knowledge (e.g., empirical, rational, revelational, intuitive, etc.).

4. Comprehensive and capable to address all of life whether metaphysical, epistemological, axiological, aesthetic, ethical, etc.

The *Weltanschauung* to which the present author subscribes is the Christian worldview of biblical theism. Although woefully disparate, dissonant, or even disobedient as the author can be at times to that worldview, the author would nonetheless assert the all-inclusive, all-intensive, and all-extensive ways, means, and ends that *that* biblical Christian worldview would and should have in life. One such area is that of faith-learning integration within ones biblical philosophy of Christian school education.

---

18. See above for further comments on Rom 11:33–36.

FAITH-LEARNING INTEGRATION

By definition of each of its three terms alone (i.e., *faith*, *learning*, and *integration*) this concept begs a worldview, but not just *any* worldview. It demands a (to be read "*the*") worldview that is sturdy enough to build everything upon it, since *everything* would be entailed by faith, learning, and integration. biblical Christianity is such a worldview.

As per the Pauline passage above,[19] biblical Christianity solidly addresses origin, purpose, and destiny in a consistent, coherent, correspondent, and comprehensive manner. (In making such an assertion the present author is not making any claims to have cornered, articulated, or mastered such a worldview in its finest and fullest.)

Thus, it can be said that the lens is ready—the balloon is inflated and in place. Now the Christian-scholar-practitioner just needs to "look for and see" the integrative opportunity of *creatio concursivo*! The foundation has been laid, all that has to be done is to build an infrastructure of a biblical philosophy of Christian school education from within which an interdisciplinary impact can be constructed to glorify God via educational excellence, i.e., *arête*.

HISTORICAL CONSIDERATIONS

"It is true that our chief duty consists, according to the profound saying of the Greek poet, Pindar, in becoming who we are, nothing is more important for each of us, or more difficult, than to become a man. Thus, the chief task of education is above all to shape man or to guide the evolving dynamism through which man forms himself as a man."[20] In other words, in contrast to twentieth-century Darwinian, Skinnerian, and Dewey-ian philosophies of education, "education is not animal training. The education of man is a human awakening."[21]

Human awakening within the context of school does not happen within a vacuum. It takes shape within a certain milieu. "The *school milieu* or environment—the atmosphere in which teaching and learning

---

19. Rom 11:33–36.
20. Maritain, *Crossroads*, 17.
21. Ggita, *Jacques Maritain*, 7.

take place—helps to shape the students' social and intellectual attitudes and values . . . norms and dispositions."[22]

Paideia was such a milieu for many of the ancient Greeks. "What in Greek *paideia* had been the formation or *morphosis* of the human personality, [in Christianity] becomes for the Christian the *meta*-morphosis of which Paul had spoken of in Romans 12:1–2:[23] 'Do not be conformed to this world, but be transformed by the renewing of your minds.'"[24]

In that sense the priority of human awakening and milieu-shaping are the most important and impactful issues that schools can address. "The greatest need of Christian schools is that they be *Christian* in the fullest sense of the word. . . . They must seek to develop a positive educational philosophy built upon a distinctly Christian worldview."[25]

At the end of *Republic*, readers find Socrates chiding himself for not having intellectually dined well. "The Socratic admission is meant to teach us that the 'appetite' for inquiry must find gratification in a disciplined way, if truth (the mind's natural 'nutrition') is to be obtained."[26]

Many thinkers have seen school education as an integral component of developing that appetite and a necessary part of a healthy, flourishing individual prepared to live and contribute to others living life.[27] The process was to be constructive.

Not dissimilarly Tertullian famously asserted, "Christian are made, not born."[28] No small part of *being made* is the choices one makes. There is an existential quality to life—that it is not the dreams we dream, but the choices we make.[29] "It should be noted, however, that what Paul Tillich

22. Gutek, *New Perspectives*, 185.

23. Which obviously, but neither incidentally nor trivially, follows immediately after Rom 11:32–36 as quoted above.

24. Jaeger, *Early Christianity and Greek Paideia*, 87.

25. Knight, *Philosophy and Education*, xiii.

26. McInerny, *Common Things*, 144.

27. Thomas, *Education*, 115.

28. Seymour and Miller, *Theological Approaches*, 133.

29. This quote is attributable to Dr. Joseph Stowell, former president of Cornerstone University. Prior to his ministry at Cornerstone, he was president of Moody Bible Institute. Prior to that, he was pastor of Highland Park Baptist Church, where he worked alongside the superintendent of Southfield Christian School, a ministry of HPBC. There he would speak to chapel, not infrequently emphasizing this existential quality of living a Christian life well.

correctly called the 'existential elements' in early Christian theology and a full-blown existential philosophy are two separate entities."[30]

Nonetheless, Christian school students cannot and ought not just *know* the truth. As Søren Kierkegaard suggested, "The highest of all is not to understand the highest, but to act upon it."[31] Christian school students ought to grow in their *knowing* the truth *and* in their *doing* of it, as well.

Conceiving of participating in truth and acting upon it predates Tillich and Kierkegaard. In his Christian classic on education of a previous century, Henry Ephraim Robins writes, "The true idea of relationship (between God and man) involves the presence of God in every highest activity of man; to separate them is not simply to deny man a power he needs, it is to break a unity and to set a part of the power to do what the whole power ought to do as one." He goes on to explain that "the glory of Christianity is that it reveals the provision and supplies the means whereby man may be renewed in the spiritual life of God, so that whatever he does in any sphere of action may be energized and consecrated by one living motive." Finally, he insists upon biblical, Christian *truth* as the instrument of regeneration, the means of development, and the comprehensivizing of all of life in every realm.[32]

Even secular, contemporary neuroscientists acknowledge this mystery and complexity of our nature. A nature behind which is not only a drive to survive, but the even more fundamental force of faith, which is the hope and motivation that ideally result in the skills and disciplines to successfully motivate life to the best means and ends.[33] Dr. Newberg, one such secular, contemporary neuroscientist, for example, demonstrates that such faith manifest through reflecting on transcendent truths, for example, actually favorably alters brain chemistry and circuitry.[34]

In more overtly Christian terms, Richard H. Niebuhr refers to this as the *fiduciary* aspect of faith. He describes it in relationship to a "radically monotheistic center of value and power."[35]

Gregory Kerr, a contemporary Thomist, a philosophy professor, and a teacher in the tradition of Maritain, observes, "Educators [ought to]

30. Knight, *Philosophy and Education*, 85.
31. Taylor, *Myth of Certainty*, 95.
32. Robins, *Christian Idea*, 23–25.
33. Newberg, *Principles of Neurotheology*, 20–21.
34. Newberg, *Principles of Neurotheology*, 23.
35. Seymour, *Theological Approaches*, 148.

want to provoke growth in human beings, to make them better. . . . We want to teach them how to 'know' truth, goodness, and beauty simply[36]—and then to feed for eternity"[37] This is what Kerr calls the *sine qua non* of Christian education. What this all looks like within the context of a biblical philosophy of education and within the framework of Christian school is what will be considered next.

CONSIDERATIONS PERTAINING TO APPLYING A BIBLICAL WORLDVIEW TO A SCHOOL FRAMEWORK

One prominent non-theist educational expert asserts, "Effective education can take many different forms, but certain features must be present. Those who run a school—or a network of schools—must have a clear vision of what they want to achieve."[38] It is such a clear vision that this section endeavors to hone.

    36. Hearkening back to a day in which such a simple *Coram Deo* mindset ruled the day, Charles Taylor and James K. A. Smith reflect on *How (Not) to Be Secular* in "this present age" (with a tip of their hats to Kierkegaard). The two probingly ponder, "What's the shape of the existential terrain in which we find ourselves in late modernity? Where are the valleys of despair . . . the pitfalls and dead ends?" They cite several obstacles in the present generation, which create impediments to implementing the aforementioned biblical philosophy of Christian school education: (1) Yawning existential abyss; (2) Indifference to Higher things; (3) Agnostically cross-pressured spaces; (4) Breezy illogic; (5) Flourishing individualism; (6) Secularism or secularity; (7) The aridity of neo-Nietzchean wastelands; (8) A theological shift to anthropocentrism and its concomitant eclipse of grace—and the fading of mystery. Not merely the privation of unbelief, but the "production of a new option—the possibility of exclusive humanism as a viable *social imaginary*—a way of constructing meaning and significance without any reference to the divine or transcendence" (Smith, *How [Not] to Be Secular*, 26). The antidote to such impediments, according to Taylor, is a return to the Reformed "radical simplification" (Taylor, *Secular Age*, 77). He distills such as follows:
    1. Sanctification of ordinary life:
       a. A refusal of sacred/profane distinctions.
       b. A recognition of domestic life as a sphere of grace.
    2. Alter orientation:
       a. Everyone to be expected to live all their lives *coram Deo*.
       b. Everyone to be expected to live all their lives *soli Deo gloria* (Smith, *How [Not] to Be Secular*, 35–39).
    37. McInerny, *Common Things*, 101.
    38. Gardner, *Disciplined Mind*, 112.

Gordon Clark observes that not infrequently Christian education lacks philosophical vision. As he says, "Most educators, unfortunately, have little philosophy and oscillate among aggregates of discordant opinions.... This rejection of the very basis of Christianity pervades all their teaching.... That these two alternatives [Christian theism and any non-Christian view] ... must differ *toto coelo* from that of Christian theism ought to be immediately evident."[39] He goes on to assert that "there is only one philosophy that can really unify education and life. That philosophy is the philosophy of Christian theism."[40]

One philosopher of education summarizes well the examination, analysis, and synthesis (both positive and negative) that Christian educators and Christian philosophers of education need to do when it comes to surveying the historical contributions of educators and philosophers of education. "In conclusion, it can be said that Christians will probably find something in each of these philosophies that they see as helpful, true, or good. They also probably will find some things that do not fit the biblical picture."[41] Knight continues, "The individual Christian should rather seek to utilize the insights offered by the modern [and ancient] philosophies to develop a personal philosophy of education that roots itself in the biblical worldview but has been enriched by noting the insights of other viewpoints."[42] Such appropriate assimilation and intentional integration should be judicious and discerning. "The teaching of any topic in a Christian school is not a modification of the approach used in non-Christian schools. It is rather a radical reorientation of that topic within the philosophical framework of Christianity."[43] The framework is constructed from the model that God has revealed.

This model began at least as early as creation. Out of everything that God spoke *ex nihilo* into being, only one part of creation was created in the very image of its Creator. Fathomless mystery entailed in that single attribute alone, philosophers, theologians, and countless other thinkers have spent innumerable hours and spilled measureless ink in attempts to fathom the fathomless: What *does* it mean to be human: *imago Dei*, *homo sapiens*, man, woman, boy, and girl?

---

39. Clark, *Christian Philosophy of Education*, 11–12.
40. Clark, *Christian Philosophy of Education*, 21.
41. Knight, *Philosophy and Education*, 62.
42. Knight, *Philosophy and Education*, 87.
43. Knight, *Philosophy and Education*, 236–37.

ANTHROPOLOGY TOWARD A BIBLICAL PHILOSOPHY OF CHRISTIAN SCHOOL EDUCATION

If one is going to educate humans and to philosophize about educating humans, one needs to define what it means to *be* human. "We cannot educate man unless we know what he really is."[44] As Maritain assessed, "If we wish to perceive what a Christian philosophy of education consists of, it is clear that the first thing to do is to try to bring out what the Christian idea of man is."[45] Wolterstorff explains that "every philosophy of education grows out of an image of man in the world, so we must begin by looking at some main features."[46] What does it mean to be human?[47]

Yale professor Robert Calhoun classifies a meta-analysis of categorical answers to the question about who man is. He summarizes his findings as follows:

1. Just a person (common sense).

2. A complicated animal (science).

3. A sample of the universe (philosophy).

4. A servant of Superior values and powers (religion).[48]

The anthropology of this section of this book pursues a particular version of the last of those four options.

---

44. Ggita, *Jacques Maritain*, 91.
45. Edmund *Christian Idea of Education*, 173.
46. Wolterstorff, *Educating for Responsible Action*, 7.
47. Whatever it means to be human, and however one answers the fundamental anthropological questions—whether, in what way, and to what extent humans choose good or not-good needs to be considered at least in some way and to some extent. Per Victor Frankl, for example, "Man is never driven to moral behavior; in each instance he decides to behave morally." For those plumbing the depths of man's body, brain, mind, and spirit (e.g., educators and those philosophizing about education), Frankl cautions this work between (what he calls) the "two realms" of "science and religion." It is, therefore, a border area, and as such a no-man's-land. And, yet—what a land of promise! (Frankl, *Man's Search for Meaning*, 158, as well as Frankl, *Doctor & the Soul*, 284). Nonetheless, a thorough rendering of this question deserves its own book and transcends the scope and intent of this present book.
48. Calhoun, *What Is Man*, iii.

From a Christian perspective, "the critical anthropological conception for education is the Imago Dei."[49] First, God created man in his image. Secondly, that Christ became man (and even became sin), so that he might redeem man back to God. "The belief that God, *theos*, became human, *anthropos*, in the person of Jesus Christ is fundamental to Christian anthropology. According to this belief, Christians seek to be formed and transformed according to the norms of selfhood in the life and teachings of Jesus Christ."[50]

"The image of God is not something man *has*, somewhere inside of him, or somewhere on the surface, as if God had first created man and then stamped him with a signet ring. No, the image of God is not something man *has*, man *is* the image. First Corinthians 11:7 pointedly says, 'He [man] is the image and glory of God.'"[51] It is what D. F. M. Strauss refers to as the uniqueness and mystery of being human.[52] "Man is created in God's image. He is therefore like God in everything in which a creature can be like God."[53] As Pascal observed:

> For, in fact, what is man in nature? A *nothing* in comparison with the infinite, an *all* in comparison with the nothing, a *mean* between nothing and everything. He is infinitely removed from two extremes, and his being is no less distant from the nothing from which he is drawn than from the infinite where he is engulfed.... Man is but a reed, the most feeble thing in nature, but he is a thinking reed. It is not necessary that the universe arm itself to crush him. A vapor, a drop of water suffices to kill him. But if the universe were to crush him, man would still be more noble than that which killed him, because he knows that he dies and the advantage that the universe has over him, the universe knows nothing of this. Thus, all our dignity consists in thought.[54]

49. Seymour, *Theological Approaches*, 246.
50. Seymour, *Theological Approaches*, 146.
51. Clark, *Biblical Doctrine of Man*, 9.
52. Strauss, *Discipline of the Disciplines*, 104–42.
53. Van Til, *Defense of the Faith*, 13.
54. Clark, *Christian Philosophy of Education*, 139. "Car enfin qu'est-ce que l'homme dans la nature? Un néant à l'égard de l'infini, un tout à l'égard du néant, un milieu entre rien et tout. Il est infiniment éloigné des extremes, et son être n'est pas moins distant du néant d'où il est tire que de l'infini où il est englouti.... L'homme n'est qu'un Roseau, le plus faible de la nature, mais c'est un roseau pensant. Il ne faut pas que l'univers entire s'arme pour l'écraser. Une vapeur, une goutte d'eau suffit pour le tuer. Mais quand l'univers l'écraserait, l'homme serait encore plus noble que ce qui le tue, parce qu'il sait

TOWARD A BIBLICAL PHILOSOPHY OF CHRISTIAN SCHOOL EDUCATION 83

Taking that one step further, Susanne Johnson, associate dean at SMU's Perkins School of Theology, summarizes four biblical contributions to the anthropological aspect of a Christian philosophy of education:

1. We are created beings: *nephesh*, persons into whom God breathed his breath of life.

2. We are rooted in bodily, historical existence: human soul abides in the human body.

3. We are given a share in who God is and what God does: both individually and corporately we participate in God's creative and redemptive work.

4. We exist in relationship to that God who creates and loves: both individually and corporately, we share in a community of relatedness with God and others.[55]

She contrasts that with two of the prevailing secular schools of thought:

1. *Self-actualization* supplants *imago Dei* and love for God and others, and it overlooks or underplays the reality of human sin and self-deception as profound hindrances to Christian growth and change.

2. *Eudaimonism* tends to reduce commitments to God and others to mere utilitarian or individualistic pursuit.[56]

Donovan Graham offers an anthropological antidote to such secularism in schools, i.e., the reestablishing of biblical norms regarding the learner, the learning process, and the teacher.[57] "This approach involves looking for principles and concepts derived from the Word, both directly and through inference, that will form a *framework* for redemptive teaching."[58] This is what he calls a "genuinely Christian" education.[59]

Perry Downs and Ted Ward, prominent scholars of Christian education, use a drawing of a human hand to illustrate what they call the "interwoven" or "holistic" aspects of human nature:

---

qu'il meurt et l'avantage que l'univers a sur lui; l'univers n'en sait rien. Anisi toute notre dignité cinsiste dans la pensée."

55. Seymour, *Theological Approaches*, 129–30.
56. Seymour, *Theological Approaches*, 127–28.
57. Graham, *Teaching Redemptively*, 209–11.
58. Graham, *Teaching Redemptively*, 13.
59. Graham, *Teaching Redemptively*, xv.

Common to much Christian education literature are discussions of the spiritual aspect of people. But it is more appropriate to see the "spiritual" as the essence of what humans are, rather than as an aspect. Scripture describes us as spiritual in the core of our beings. In this illustration, the spiritual essence of the person resides in the palm of the hand, indicating that each aspect of the person interacts with and is influenced by the spiritual. Each finger represents an aspect of the human personality:

1. Physical
2. Cognitive
3. Affective
4. Social
5. Moral[60]

Consequently, "the greatest need you and I have—the greatest need of collective humanity—is renovation of our heart. That spiritual place within us from which outlook, choices, and actions come has been formed by a world away from god. Now it needs to be transformed."[61]

Similarly, Dallas Willard and J. P. Moreland diagnose "empty selves" whose "meaningless morass" mandates a manifest of maturation as follows:

1. The recovery of the importance of the Christian mind.

2. The renovation of the heart and spiritual formation.

3. The restoration of the power of the Holy Spirit at the center of the Christian life.

Moreland calls this approach to Christian anthropology, "a revolution on behalf of the cause of Christ."[62] To this end, D. Bruce Lockerbie argues that Christian education in general and Christian schooling in particular can be both "essential and beneficial."[63]

Dr. Jeff Myers emphasizes the estimated ten thousand decisions that students in school make daily. Desiring to cultivate a growing number of those decisions being God-honoring ones, Dr. Myers's operative question as he directs Summit Ministries is, "How do we cultivate a hunger and

---

60. Downs, *Teaching for Spiritual Growth*, 75.
61. DeWeese, *Doing Philosophy*, 49.
62. Moreland, *Kingdom Triangle*, back flap.
63. Wiens and Wiens, *Building a Better School*, 21–47.

thirst for righteousness?" His partial answer includes educators facilitating students' growth in:

1. Understanding the Faith.

2. Understanding the Times.

3. Understanding the Culture.

He describes Christian teaching as "putting another rung in the double helix of Truth and Relationship in the mind of students."[64] Such teaching would be contributing to a student's maturation and flourishing, indeed.

A Biblical Illustration

Biblical anthropology has a rich and varied history, and no small part of that history has to do with children flourishing. One Old Testament minor prophet portrayed it well.

"A good place to grow up in." That is how Zechariah describes it. Foretelling the time of Christ's coming kingdom, and forth-telling the beauty, goodness, and truth of being God's people, doing God's work, in God's way, the Old Testament prophet pictures the idyllic ideal—painting a prophetic portrait of kingdom come. At that time, swords will be turned into plowshares, lions will lay down with lambs, and children will be playing, laughing, and filing the place with delight (cf. Zech 8:5).

What a picture: The God of the universe describing the way things ought to be (and will be!) and using within that description children making noise, having fun, and being filled with delight. The passage goes on to describe the source of such a blessing, as well as the outcome. The source: God, and his dealing with his people in righteousness and faithfulness. The outcome: "A good place to grow up in."

As Christian schools assemble, may *that* be their anthropology, and may *that* be their vision, mission, and passion: That the God of righteousness and faithfulness would rule the school every day in every way, that children would attend with joy and resolve, and that the Christian school would in fact be, "a good place to grow up in."

---

64. From an unpublished speech of Dr. Myers in St. Louis, Spring 2017, that the present author attended.

STEWARDSHIP

To that end and by those means, "the school is based upon a biblical philosophy of life. Its objectives are biblical, not humanistic. The (Christian) school exists because of this philosophy and its objectives."[65] No small part of that philosophy and its concomitant objectives includes the opportunity and responsibility of human individuals and institutions to be stewards of everything that is God's, i.e., everything.

Psalm 24:1 plainly declares, "The earth is the Lord's and *everything* that is in it." Therefore, each of us is a steward of that which is rightfully God's, which is everything.

1. Everything belongs to God (Ps 24:1).

2. Each person is a steward of God's stuff (Gen 1:27–30).

3. A steward has responsibility (1 Cor 4:2).

4. Part of a steward's responsibility is to provide for one's family (1 Tim 5:8).

5. Part of a steward's responsibility is to give back to God in proportion to what has been entrusted to that person (Luke 12:47–48).

6. Part of a steward's duty is to faithfully optimize himself in the following domains:
    a. Spiritual.
        i. Relationship with God.
        ii. Pursuit of goodness and truth.
    b. Occupational.
        i. Engagement.
        ii. Employment.
        iii. Vocare.
    c. Social.
        i. Intrapersonal.
        ii. Interpersonal.
    d. Physical.
        i. Salubriousness: habituated wellness of sleep, nutrition, and exercise.
        ii. Temple maintenance.

65. Lowrie, *Christian School Board Members*, 129.

iii. Intellectual.
    1. Critical analyses.
       a. Read.
       b. Write.
       c. Reason: math and logic.
       d. Rhetoric.
i. Comport oneself.
ii. Relate to others.
iii. Speak:
1. Logos.
2. Pathos.
3. Ethos.
    2. Cultural awareness.
    3. Creative arts.
iv. Emotional.
    1. Accurately knowing one's feelings.
    2. Appropriately showing one's feelings.

Such a holism as integral to the flourishing of educated humans is part of what the ancients had in mind when they wrote about *paideia* and *arête*. Thus, the following sections address lexical aspects of those key terms.

Arête: Lexical Considerations

Bruce Lockerbie describes three ultimate traits of students immersed in comprehensive education, i.e., *paideia*.[66] He cites the following:

1. *Dike*—a sense of justice and rightness.

2. *Time*—a sense of honor.

3. *Arête*—virtue or excellence.

Frankena suggests that even though *arête* is often translated as "virtue," it is better translated by "excellence."[67] As another scholar puts it, "No [single] English word or phrase captures the exact meaning of *arête*. The nearest equivalents are 'excellence' and 'virtue'. But there is something

---

66. The three are the classical Greek terms for justice, honor, and excellence.
67. Frankena, *Three Historical Philosophies*, 15.

more to *arête* which cannot be expressed in words. There is something of the Divine in it."⁶⁸ Aristotle described *arête* as:

> Concerned with emotions and actions in which one can have excess of deficiency or a due mean. For example, one can be frightened or bold, feel desire or anger or pity, and experience pleasure and pain in general, either too much or too little, and in both cases wrongly: whereas to feel these feelings at the right time, on the right occasion, towards the right people, for the right purpose and in the right manner, is to feel the best among them, which is the mean amount—and best amount is of course the mark of virtue.⁶⁹
>
> Some thinkers hold that *arête* is a gift of nature, others think we become good by habit, others that we can be taught to be good. Natural endowment is obviously not under our control, it is bestowed on those who are fortunate, in the true sense, by some divine dispensation. Again, theory and teaching are not equally efficacious in all cases, the soil must have been previously tilled if it is to foster the seed, [and] the mind of the pupil must have been prepared by the cultivation of habits.⁷⁰

Famously summarizing the *ethike* aspect of arête, Aristotle quips, "Excellence is an art won by training and habituation. We do not act rightly because we have virtue or excellence, but we rather have those because we have acted rightly. We are what we repeatedly do. Excellence, then, is not an act, but a habit."

David Hicks, a moral classicist, observes, "*Arête* expresses the life that knows and reveres, speculates and acts upon the Good, that loves and re-produces the Beautiful, and that pursues excellence and moderation in all things."⁷¹

Jon Mills, an educational philosopher, added:

> Human excellence [*arête*] is not a specific experience, feeling, activity, or action, but rather it is what Aristotle calls a *hexis* and what Dewey refers to as a *habit*. A *hexis* is not just a skill, capability, or an answer that may be retrieved from a fund of knowledge at any given moment, instead it is a disposition, which may

---

68. Uebersax, "Areté."

69. Simmons, *Climbing Parnassus*, 57. In the present author's view, "*the* mark of virtue" should read "*a* mark of virtue."

70. Simmons, *Climbing Parnassus*, 57.

71. Hicks, *Norms and Nobility*, 21.

be said to be always present.⁷² As Kant put it, "Education must be the moralization of man. He is to acquire not merely the skills needed for all sorts of ends, but also the disposition to choose only good ends."⁷³

Princeton-educated Berkeley professor of classical archaeology Stephen G. Miller illustrates the enduring excellence denoted by *arête* with a quotation from Homer's *Iliad*. "These prizes are placed in competition awaiting the horsemen. If we Achaians were not competing for the sake of some other hero, I myself would take the first prizes away to my tent. You know by how much my horses surpass all others in their *arête*, for they are immortal"⁷⁴ Overlooking the hubris latent in that citation, a careful reader will note the *quantity* of the *quality* of *arête*—a surpassing excellence.

Aristotle used it of men of virtue, valor, and habituation; Homer used it of high-brow horses; Christian educators use it of themselves, their students, their subjects, and their pursuit of the very Christian excellence to which God has called them.

Scripture is replete from cover to cover with illustrations and mandates for God's people to do God's work in God's way. Such is *arête*; such is Christian excellence.

Harold Best, former dean of the Wheaton Conservatory of Music, summarized it as follows: "Excellence is both absolute and relative—absolute because it is the norm of stewardship and cannot be avoided or compromised, and relative because it is set in the context of striving, wrestling, hungering, thirsting, pressing on from point to point and achievement to achievement."⁷⁵ Within the context of a biblical philosophy of Christian school education, *arête* entails *pursuing excellence for the glory of God*.

Soli Deo Gloria: (For the) Glory of God (Alone)

School, schooling, and all that school and schooling can entail can all be done for any number of reasons or because of any number of motivations. A biblical philosophy of Christian school education singularizes

---

72. Mills, *Pedagogy of Becoming*, 6.
73. Mills, *Pedagogy of Becoming*, 7.
74. Miller, *Arete*, 2.
75. Lockerbie, *Christian Paideia*, 91.

the end and the impetus of all of a school's pursuits: *soli Deo gloria*, i.e., only for God's glory. In the words of more than one Christian school motto: *pursuing excellence for the glory of God*. That is the *raison d'etre*.

In his essay "Truth and the Supremacy of Christ in a Postmodern World," Voddie Baucham Jr. argues that the ultimate questions of life are answered in Col 1:12–21. "Ultimately, this is what Christian theism tells us:

1. Who am I? I am the crown and glory of the creation of God.

2. Why am I here? I am here to bring glory and honor to the Lord Jesus Christ."[76]

Thus, the ultimate philosophical questions of origin, purpose, and destiny are answered substantively in that one reality: *soli Deo gloria*.

Furthermore, Piper extends that logic universally to all of life. Somewhere between paradise and paradise may not exactly be paradise, but it ought to have the same *locus* and focus as eternity past and eternity future, i.e., glorifying God. "The whole creation awaits the kingdom yet to come, while it praises the Maker. Within this context the Christian thinks and lives. There can be no legitimate division of life into the secular and sacred, no separation of fact from value, no divorcing of human purposes from God. Anthropocentrism [ideally] gives way to a thoroughly theocentric approach to everything."[77]

Theocentrism does not just make for good theology theoretically speaking, it also makes for good school life very practically speaking. "The solution to the secular educational dilemma is simple, for there is no dilemma for the discerning Christian. There is no choice to be made, for God is central; both students and subjects are essential, but neither one is central."[78] God alone ought to be the central priority of any biblical philosophy of Christian school education.

This paradigm is not new. Biblical Christianity has realized theocentrism as being the ideal foundation for ones worldview and philosophy for generations. "We have learned long ago, in the language of the Westminster Shorter Catechism, that the 'chief end of man is to glorify God and to enjoy Him forever.' God gives us knowledge not so that we may puff out our chests and brag about our intelligence or scholarships but

---

76. Piper and Taylor, *Supremacy of Christ*, 67.
77. Piper, *Supremacy of Christ*, 67.
78. DeJong, *Teaching for a Change*, 13.

that we may be His servants, to know Him, to glorify Him, and to enjoy Him forever. The world exists for God's glory, not ours."[79] "To know and to love God is man's highest good."[80] "Christ will not be glorified," argues Köstenberger, "... if evangelicals fail to hold fast to a robust understanding of [this] biblical truth."[81]

Although these truths may not be new, they deserve a renewed focus and fervor. "A Christian worldview beckons us to the pursuit of excellence in all things. Our divinely created nature tends toward fulfillment and longs for a measure of perfection in earthly life . . . our general Christian calling is satisfied by giving our best efforts as service to God"[82]—our utmost for his highest in all of life, including within a biblical philosophy of Christian school education.

Pursuing Excellence for the Glory of God

At least since the time of the ancient Greeks, education has promoted *eudaimonia*, or something like it; *eudaimonia* is the flourishing good life. Such quality of life, however, seems to be more about movement toward an ideal than a point of arrival. As Carl Rogers suggests, "The good life is a process, not a state of being. It is a direction not a destination."[83]

At least since Aristotle, there has been an aspect of philosophy that has emphasized *ta pros ta telos*, which connotes *not the end, but that which is toward the end*. As in philosophy in general, so that much more in a biblical philosophy of Christian school education, it is about moving *toward* the end of perfectly glorifying God in all one is and does.

"[Educational] philosophy is a *progress* which causes us to become more fully and makes us better."[84] But, especially in a biblical philosophy of Christian school education, there ought to be a teleological movement toward the ultimate end.

As theologian Cornelius Plantinga observes, "The person who pursues [education] in hope shapes his or her life accordingly for service in the kingdom. The motto of Wheaton College, for example, one of

---

79. DeJong, *Teaching for a Change*, 140.
80. Holmes, *Christian Perspective*, 22.
81. Köstenberger, *Excellence*, 14.
82. Peterson, *With All Your Mind*, 131.
83. Rogers et al., *Person to Person*, 187.
84. Mills, *Pedagogy of Becoming*, 27.

the leaders in the Christian college movement, has it exactly right: 'For Christ and His Kingdom.'"[85]

The Apostle Paul epitomizes this mode of living. "Not that I have already obtained this or am already perfect, but I press on to make it my own, because Christ Jesus has made me his own. Brothers, I do not consider that I have made it my own. But one thing I do: forgetting what lies behind and straining forward to what lies ahead, I press on toward the goal for the prize of the upward call of God in Christ Jesus."[86]

That is what *pursuing* in the context of a biblical philosophy of Christian school education ought to look like. Not that what Christian school education ought ultimately to be about is actually even fully attainable this side of glory, but that *that (ta pros ta) telos* nonetheless compels the educator and the learner alike to the heavenward call of doing whatever we do in word or deed—*all* to the glory of God.

As Carolyn Caines contrasted conventional standards of what being educated might mean and concluded, "If one day I see the world as God sees it, and come to know Him, whom to know is life eternal, and glorify God by fulfilling His purpose for me, then, I have become educated!"[87]

PROLEGOMENA TOWARD A BIBLICAL PHILOSOPHY OF CHRISTIAN SCHOOL EDUCATION

A biblical philosophy of Christian school education informs a well-rounded school program of academic, artistic, athletic, relational, moral, and spiritual excellence from a biblical, Christian worldview by God's grace and for God's glory. Each of these ingredients is irreplaceably important. The means is God's grace; the end is God's glory; the constituent programmatic components include academic, artistic, athletic, relational, moral, and spiritual aspects; the standard is excellence; the integrative core is a biblical, Christian worldview.

Everything affects and is affected by one's worldview. It is the lens not only through which one sees the world, but also the lens through which one is seen, i.e., through which lives manifest one's most basic beliefs. A biblical, Christian worldview informs all of life, impacts every entailment

---

85. Plantinga, *Engaging God's World*, xiii.
86. Phil 3:12–14.
87. Schultz, *Kingdom Education*, 154.

of educational excellence, and encompasses the loci of historic, biblical Christian theology. Such a worldview necessarily and sufficiently informs a biblical philosophy of a Christian school education.

PHILOSOPHICAL-THEOLOGICAL PRECEPTS TOWARD A BIBLICAL PHILOSOPHY OF CHRISTIAN SCHOOL EDUCATION

Such an educational framework entails the following philosophical-theological precepts. This section provides an extended syllogism[88] deducing what a Christian school ought to be and do.

1. God is the self-existent, eternal, triune, perfect Creator, Sustainer, Ruler, and Judge.

2. He is the One from whom, through whom, for whom, and to whom everything exists.

3. Everything exists by his grace and for his glory.

4. I exist.

5. Therefore, I exist by his grace and for his glory.

6. To glorify God is to put his communicable attributes on display for his glory and for others' good.

7. God is True, Beautiful, and Good.

8. He created everything that exists *in substantiva*, and everything that exists *in substantiva* is true, beautiful, and good.

9. Everything else exists *in privation*; everything else is sin; everything else falls short of the glory of God.

10. All sin is culpability before God and results in death, decay, and dying. Such is the result of sin and its concomitant, comprehensive, and curdling curse.

11. Prior to sin and its curse, the universe was good—*very* good.

---

88. Succinctly connecting the dots of the previous sections into a single constellation.

12. Prior to the universe, the triune God of Father, Son, and Holy Spirit coequal, coeternal, community coexisted eternally in perfection and glory.

13. In the beginning God created the heavens and the earth, i.e., *everything*, i.e., all *else* that is *not* himself (e.g., time, space, matter, etc.).

14. Although he is the source *of* all creation, he is distinct *from* creation.

15. He spoke creation into existence *ex nihilo*.

16. All creation was good; humankind was *very* good.

17. Part of the very goodness of humankind is having been made *imago Dei*.

18. Part of the very goodness of humankind of having been made in *imago Dei* entails what is seen of God via the Genesis 1 creation account up to that inception of humankind, i.e., that of God being both communicative and creative.

19. Part of the very goodness of humankind of having been made in *imago Dei* entails being relational with God, with others, and with the rest of creation.

20. Part of the very goodness of humankind of having been made in *imago Dei* and being relational with God, with others, and with the rest of creation is having been made to be in perfect, harmonious, sinless relationship with God.

21. Another part of the very goodness of humankind, on the other hand, was also freedom.

22. Freedom of *that* kind is volition to choose to do—or to choose to refrain from doing.

23. Humankind not only can—it cannot *not*—choose, i.e., humans are volitional and act volitionally: *doing becoming being*.

24. Among other things, humankind volitionally opposed the good, acceptable, and perfect will of God by doing a thing that God as the perfect Creator, Sustainer, Ruler, and Judge had prohibited. In so

doing humankind became a being separated from perfect fellowship with God.

25. Thus, and thereby sin and its concomitant curse of death, decay, and dying came upon all creation.

26. Since that moment and until the eventual moment of Christ's consummation of the ages, all creation has groaned, now groans, and will continue to groan for redemption.

27. In Christ, there can be redemption.

28. In Christ, God is both just and justifier.

29. Christ came fulfilling prophecy, being born of the Virgin Mary, living perfectly and exemplarily, dying sacrificially and substitutionarily, rising victoriously and redemptively, and ascending intercedingly.

30. When Christ ascended, God sent his Holy Spirit.

31. The Holy Spirit convicts of sin, righteousness, and judgment.

32. The Holy Spirit regenerates, converts, and indwells all believers sealing them for the day of the Lord and equipping them for service and sanctification until that day.

33. That day will come.

34. In the meantime, all creation groans for redemption.

35. Our part in that creative-redemptive enterprise is relationship with God, relationship with others, and relationship with the rest of creation via purposeful and stewardly work.

36. Both relationships and purposeful and stewardly work predate sin and its curse.

37. Nonetheless, relationships and purposeful and stewardly work have been deleteriously affected, challenged, and intensified by sin and its curse.

38. Schools are to help prepare people for those relationships and for that work.

39. Christian schools are to prepare students for those relationships and for that work *soli Dei gratia* and *soli Deo gloria*!

40. The preparation for that work and for those relationships is best done in the context of a comprehensive, cohesive, canonical, theocentric metaphysic, epistemology, and axiology, i.e., that God and his Truth, Goodness, and Beauty are before, beneath, and beyond all we are and can ever fully know, and that all we are and can ever know is rightly targeted only, fully, and eternally at the bull's-eye of a doxological teleology, i.e., that life is about relationship, stewardship, and worship—and all of that is to be prioritized, pursued, and practiced by God's grace and for God's glory.

41. This can be done efficiently, effectively, and eternally significantly when it is done in the context of a well-rounded school program of academic, artistic, athletic, relational, moral, and spiritual excellence from a biblical, Christian worldview by God's grace and for God's glory.

42. This can be done efficiently, effectively, and eternally significantly when it is done in a strategic partnership between the school, the family, and the local church. The school is the professional—trained to teach; the church is the local assembly—commissioned by God for spiritual authority and community; and the family is the institution primarily accountable to God for the children with whom he has entrusted them.

BIBLICAL PRINCIPLES TOWARD A BIBLICAL PHILOSOPHY OF CHRISTIAN EDUCATION

This next section highlights observations from Scripture. These scriptural highlights delineate a biblical philosophy of Christian school education.

1. Children are created in the image of God and thereby are imbued and endowed with dignity, value, significance, and worth (Gen 1:27).

2. Children are a gift from God (Num 5:28; Deut 7:13; 28:4–11; Ps 127:3; Lam 4:2).

3. Children are desirable (Gen 9:7; Deut 6:3; Luke 1:24–25).

4. Children are to be taught that all creation puts God on display (Gen 1; Ps 1, 19, 139, 150; Rom 1; 11:33–36; Col 1; Heb 1).

5. Children are to be taught and trained in how to relate to God, to others, and to creation (Gen 1:28; 2:15; Exod 12:26–37; 23:19; Deut 4:9–10; 6:1–7; 31:12–13; Ps 78:4–6; Prov 22:6; 1 Tim 4:4–5).

6. Children are to be taught to love, fear, and obey God (Prov 8:32; Eccl 12; Jer 2:30; 3:22; Eph 6:1; Col 3:20; 2 Pet 3:18).

7. Children are to enter God's presence and enjoy his companionship (Ps 8:2; 34:11; 103:13; Mal 2:15; Matt 21:15; Mark 10:13–16).

8. Children are to be led to Christ and not away from him (Matt 18:1–6).

9. Children that are regenerate are God's handiwork created in Christ Jesus to do the good works which he prepared in advance for them to do (Eph 2:10).

10. Children are to grow up in their Head who is Christ by being taught to speak the truth in love (Eph 4:12–16).

11. Children are to be gently shepherded (Ps 23; Ezek 34:1–31; John 10:14–18).

12. Children are to be protected and provided for (1 Sam 20:42; Ezra 8:21; Matt 6:25–34; 7:7–11).

13. Children are to be taught and trained by parents and others partnered with the parents, the children, and God (Deut 1:31; Deut 6:4–9; 1 Sam 1:27–28; 3:1–10; Prov 1:1–9; Isa 7:15; Luke 2:39; 8:39; Acts 26:4; Rom 14:19; Eph 4:11–13; 6:4).

14. Children are to be developed holistically (1 Sam 2:26; Luke 2:40, 52).

15. Children ought to praise God through the use of their bodies, through the use of music, and through the use of the arts and sciences (Gen 1–2; Pss 19, 150; Luke 2:52; Rom 11:33—12:2; 1 Cor 3:16; 6:12–20; 9:24–27; Eph 5:15–21; 1 Tim 4:6–10).

16. Children are to be trained in how to use Scripture well (Matt 4:1–11; 2 Tim 2:14–26).

17. Children are to be taught, reproved, corrected, and trained in righteousness by means of a right use of Scripture (2 Tim 3:16).

18. Children are to be discipled and disciplined (Prov 3:11–12; 13:24; 19:18; 23:13; 29:15–17; Eph 6:4; Titus 2:1—3:9).

19. Children are to be encouraged and equipped (Exod 31:1–5; Eph 6:1–4; 1 Tim 5:8; 2 Pet 3:18; 3 John 4).

20. Children are to be taught that everything they do is to be done wholeheartedly, excellently, to the best of their ability, and for the glory of God (Ps 33:1–22; Rom 11:36; 1 Cor 10:31; Col 3:17, 23–24).

21. Children are to be taught that everything they do is to be done with a God-honoring orderliness (Ps 50:23; 90:9–12; 1 Cor 14:40).

22. Children are to be taught that everything is to be done in light of the brevity and importance of time—and in light of the certainty and infiniteness of eternity (Exod 20:20; Job 28:28; Ps 39:4–5; 90:9–12; Matt 25; Jas 4:11—5:12).

23. Children are to be taught that everything they do is to be done peaceably—and with forgiveness (Judg 11:13; Matt 18:15–35; Mark 4:39; 9:50; Rom 12:9–21; Eph 4:29; 6:21–24; Phil 4:4–9; Col 3:12–17).

24. Children are to be helped in cultivating a Christian worldview (Exod 20:20; Job 28:28; Ps 32:8; Eccl 12:1–13).

25. Children are to be guided in the identification and cultivation of life's organizing principles (Job 34:1–4; Ps 19; Prov 1–31; John 8:38).

26. Children are to be taught to listen for and to listen to God and others well (Prov 1:5; 18:2, 13, 15; Jas 1:19–20).

27. Children are to be assisted in knowing and showing God's Spirit dwelling in them and producing fruit through them (Gal 5:22–23; 2 Tim 2:20–26; 2 Pet 1:3–9).

28. Children are to be taught that everything they do will have a natural proneness to human flesh, which by nature is contrary to God's

Spirit (Gen 3:1–24; Deut 29:16–28; Judg 21:25; Job 38:1—42:6; Gal 5:16–21; Eph 6:10–20; Heb 5:14; Jas 4:1–10).

29. Children are to be taught that everything they do is to be done as a process of learning obedience; a process of learning to choose obedience; and a process of choosing obedience (Deut 6:1–25; 21:21; 30:11–20; 32:46–47; Josh 23:11—24:24; Prov 1:1–9; 8:1–36; Heb 5:8, 14; Jas 3:13–18).

30. Children are to be taught that we are saved by God's grace through our faith and that *that* grace and faith are the basis for receiving everything we need for life, for godliness, and for overcoming the fallenness of sin, of self, and of secular world (Eph 2:8–9; Titus 2:11–13; 2 Pet 1:3–9; 1 John 5:4).

31. Children are to be pointed in the direction of *arête* as the doxological and deontological teleology of all of life (Deut 29:29; Matt 25:14–30; Rom 11:33–36; 1 Cor 10:31; 15:58; Col 1:28–29).

PEDAGOGICAL PRAXES TOWARD A BIBLICAL PHILOSOPHY OF CHRISTIAN EDUCATION

This section operationalizes a biblical philosophy of Christian school education with goals pertinent to its worldview. These goals entail pertinent pedagogical praxes.

1. Prioritize practices of holistic development entailing academic, artistic, athletic, relational, moral, and spiritual excellence.

2. Maintain the centrality of God—and of what he has revealed and of how he relates—in all of the curriculum, co-curriculum, and extra-curriculum.

3. Prioritize (as primary) loving God with all one's mind, heart, soul, and strength. Prioritize loving others (as secondary).

4. Prioritize excellence.

5. Create an optimal environment in which the teacher teaches and the students learn.

6. Establish rules that are clear, concrete, consistent, coherent, and Christ-honoring.

7. Enforce rules kindly, calmly, confidently, consistently, congruously, caringly, correctingly, and Christ-honoringly.

8. Develop character; do not just modify behavior.

9. Derive all pedagogical praxes directly from Scripture or by deduction from Scripture.

10. Cultivate the disciplines of truth, beauty, goodness.

11. Train the students in the liberal arts and sciences.

12. Teach not only *what* to learn, but *how* to learn.

13. Read well. Read good. Read a lot.

14. Introduce the students to great ideas through great books.

15. Teach Christian truth, beauty, and goodness.

TOWARD A BIBLICAL PHILOSOPHY OF CHRISTIAN SCHOOL EDUCATION

Based upon the working definitions within and the prescribed the purposes of this book: *philosophy of education is both the academic discipline which studies the fundamental nature of education, its foundational constituents, and its theoretical bases, as well as the theory, attitude, and orientation that acts as a guiding principle for one's approach to education, i.e., the act, the process, or the product of imparting or acquiring knowledge or understanding, or of developing skills or competencies, or of cultivating the capacities of reasoning, judgment, values, or virtues—thereby preparing oneself or others for mature and flourishing life.*

That end is accomplished by being God's person doing God's work in God's way. This next section of this book summarizes that *summum bonum* within the context of a biblical philosophy of Christian school education.

Although the present author acknowledges a vast array of denotations, a broad scope of connotations, and an abundant aforementioned list of illustrations of the term *biblical philosophy of Christian school education*—meanings that may in fact provide viable contributions to understanding *biblical philosophy of Christian school education* in particular contexts, within the context of this book—the present author offers the following working definition of a *biblical philosophy of Christian school education* for the purposes of this book.

Noetic

1. Regain that which was lost in the fall.

2. Renew minds and concomitantly transform learners by means of the liberating mechanisms of Beauty, Goodness, and Truth.

3. Teach students to think God's thoughts after him.

4. Demonstrate the theocentric foundations of each and of all of the academic disciplines and cocurricular domains for development.

5. Promote a sense of divine *Weltanschauung, apologia,* and *vocare* within each student as a steward of God's stuff—truth, time, talent, treasure, and *creation continuo*.

Relational

1. Reach and teach this next generation by God's grace and for God's glory.

2. Cultivate great commandment and great commission living.

3. Speak the truth in love.

4. Engage in the "one another's" of the New Testament for God's people doing God's work in God's way.[89]

---

89. "One another" comes from the Greek term *allelon*, which occurs 100 times in 94 verses containing 47 admonitions to Christians on how to comport themselves and how to interact with others. These become the standard for relationships among all the constituents of a Christian school.

5. Cultivate an individual spirit of and a collective culture of love, joy, peace, patience, kindness, goodness, faithfulness, gentleness, and self-control.

Doxological

1. Do all of this in such a way (the *quality* of arête) and to such an extent (the *quantity* of arête)—excellently and wholeheartedly as unto the Lord (the motive, the impetus, and the goal of *soli Deo gloria*).

2. Reorient and recalibrate teachers' and learners' modes, means, and motives to being from God, through God, and to God (Rom 11:36).

Thus, summatively, a biblical philosophy of a Christian school education is that which entails and incorporates the aforementioned noetic, relational, and doxological aspects. What seems to do so succinctly, saliently, substantively, and scripturally is *arête: pursuing excellence for the glory of God!*

Chapter 4

TOWARD A CHRISTIAN UNDERSTANDING OF IDEALISM

CHAPTERS 4–15 CATALOG TWELVE (other) schools of thought. Each chapter will briefly introduce the school of thought, representatively overview historical persons of import within that school of thought, and Christianly critique each school of thought. The first is *Idealism*.

Idealism,[1] when it comes to theories of education, could be referred to as *idea*-ism.[2] Idealism purports the notion that *ideas* are the actual and ultimate reality.[3] Thus, ideas, such as beauty, goodness, truth, and justice, compel education. The fleeting impressions of the sensory world are to be overcome with the light of reason, by means of eternal truth, and through developing ones rational thinking. Education entails educing latent ideas (back) to consciousness and expanding one's understanding of, appreciation for, and facility with ultimate ideas.

Heraclitus (535–475 BC) described "mind as fire," which he defined as an infinite mass of substance—uncreated, eternal, and identical with the universe. He considered *logos* (reason) to be the process which governed the universe. "The *logos* is hidden within humanity. We become

---

1. Or, what might be more precisely termed *idealistic philosophies of education*.

2. Not unique to the present author, the term is of indefinite origin as it applies to this school of thought.

3. As has been observed, not all educational idealists "reject matter (the material world); rather, they hold that the material world is characterized by change, instability, and uncertainty, whereas some ideas are enduring; thus, *idea-ism* might be a more correct descriptive term for this philosophy." (See Ozmon, "Idealism and Education," 7.)

intelligent by drawing in the divine *logos* we breathe." Finally, the *telos* or aim of education—and of life—was simply and comprehensively captured in his saying that it is the *character* of man that is his destiny.[4]

Anaxagoras (ca. 500–428 BC) wrote, "Mind (*nous*) orders all things."[5] From one of his significant fragments we read these thoughts that he posited about the mind (*nous*):

> The rest have a portion of everything, but *Mind* is unlimited and self-ruled and is mixed with no thing, but is alone and by itself. For if it were not by itself but were mixed with something else, it would have a share of all things—if it were mixed with anything. For in everything there is a portion of everything, as I have said before. And the things mixed together with it would hinder it so that it would rule nothing in the same way as it does being alone and by itself. For it is the finest of all things and the purest, and it has all judgment about everything and the greatest power.[6]

Plato (427–347 BC) has been called "the first educational philosopher."[7] Many educational philosophers consider him to be the fountainhead of idealism, as well. In chapter 4 of the *Republic* he asks, "How shall we educate them, then? Or is it hard to improve on the educational system which has evolved over a long period of time? This, as you know consists of exercise for the body and cultural studies for the mind."[8]

In his "Allegory of the Cave," Plato answers his aforementioned question.

> Here's a situation which you can use as an analogy for the human condition—for our education, or lack of it. Imagine people living in a cavernous cell down under the ground, at the far end of the cave, a long way off, there's an entrance open to the outside world. They've been there since childhood, with their legs and necks tied up in way which keeps them in one place and allows them to look only straight ahead, but not to turn their heads. There's firelight burning a log way further up the cave behind them, up the slope between the fire and the prisoners,

---

4. Pojman and Vaughn, *Classics of Philosophy*, 10, 15.
5. Pojman, *Classics*, 11.
6. Anaxagoras, quoted in Patzia, "Anaxagoras," para. 27.
7. Eby, *Ancient and Medieval*, 345.
8. Pojman, *Classics*, 144.

there's a road . . . a place between themselves and their audience and above which they show their tricks.⁹

Continuing his dialog with Glaucon and extending his cavernous educational metaphor, Plato rhetorically asks,

"What do you think would happen if they were set free? Well, my dear Glaucon . . . only God knows," the ancient concedes. On the other hand, "if this is true, we must bear in mind that education is not capable of doing what some people promise. They claim to introduce knowledge into a mind which doesn't have it, as if they were introducing sight into the eyes which are blind. So, what education should be is *the art of orientation*."¹⁰

Plato proceeds to describe three divisions of the human mind in need of an education of orientation:

1. Philosophical.

2. Competitive.

3. Avaricious.

And, "due to its experience, intelligence, and rationality . . . then it is the philosophical type with his appreciation for rationality, whose tastes are closest to the truth."¹¹

Nonetheless, Plato seems to express curiosity if not concern about the possible deleterious effects of writing philosophically about the mind of learners.

> This discovery of yours [King Thamus had been questioning Thoth about what he had observed in his travels to Egypt, i.e., this discovery of writing and the claim that that would make them wiser and more able to remember] will create forgetfulness in the learners' souls because they will not use their memories, they will trust to the external written characters and not remember of themselves. The specific which you have discovered is an aid not to memory, but to reminiscence, and you will give your disciples not truth, but only the semblance of truth; they will be hearers of many things and will have learned nothing.¹²

---

9. Pojman, *Classics*, 173.
10. Pojman, *Classics*, 175–76.
11. Pojman, *Classics*, 184.
12. Plato, *Phaedrus*, §275.

Interestingly, Plato seemed to prioritize music over many other aspects of teaching and learning. "Musical training is a more potent instrument than any other, because rhythm and harmony find their way into the inward places of the soul, on which they mightily fasten, imparting grace, and making the soul of him who is rightly educated graceful."[13]

Consistent with that priority of grace and gracefulness, "Convention tells us, as you know, that it's best to remain as unruffled as possible when disaster strikes and not to get upset," and "the ability to think about the incident . . . under the guidance of reason to make the best possible use of one's situation."[14]

Plato established a structure for this system of schools as follows:[15]

Age	School	Development or studies
Birth to 3 years	Infancy	Bodily growth, sensory life, no fear, child reacts to pleasure or pain.
4 to 6 years	Nursery	Play, fairy tales, nursery rhymes, myths, ridding one of self-will.
6 to 13 years	Elementary	Play, poetry, reading, writing, singing, dancing, religion, manners, numbers, geometry.
13 to 16 years	Instrumental	Play the cithara, religious hymns, memorize poetry, arithmetic.
16 to 20 years	Gymnastic and military	No more formal intellectual training, in light of formal gymnastics and military training.

Philo (ca. 20–ca. 50), a neo-Platonist of the Alexandrian school, utilized imagination, interpretation, and allegory as some of his primary philosophical, hermeneutical, and educational tools. Wielding a distinctively neo-Platonic approach to the Christian Scriptures, to doctrine, and to history, Philo advocated moral education. "The greatest of all propositions is virtue, for it is conversant about the most important of all materials, namely, about the universal life of man."[16]

---

13. Plato, *Phaedrus*, §401.
14. Pojman, *Classics*, 199.
15. Adapted from Eby, *Ancient*, 389.
16. Gamble, *Great Tradition*, 154.

Augustine (354–430) wrote profoundly, introspectively, and theologically about education. "You have made us for yourself, and restless is our heart until it comes to rest in you."[17] "Augustine observed children with care, attention, and empathy. He lamented their extreme vulnerability. . . . The questions Augustine leaves us with are these: How can we attend to children in a world that is driven by adult concerns? How shall we understand and nurture the moral lives of children? How can we educate for virtue?"[18] His response to these and other educational questions seem to reveal his true colors as both undeniably classical—in the traditions Plato and of Cicero—and yet profoundly Christian. For example, his list of virtues combines faith, hope, and love with the cardinal excellencies of prudence, justice, fortitude, and temperance. To develop these, however, is not just a matter of Aristotelian habituation, Platonic recollection, or Socratic illumination; Augustine refers to Romans 7 and finds good company in the Apostle Paul illustrating that a person can *know* what is good and even *want* to do good, and yet not do it. Augustine calls these sins of omission and commission, and no Kohlbergian or Piagetian development can solve that conundrum—only what Augustine calls the inner teacher of Christ.

Summatively, "learning, according to Augustine, is an inner illumination. It is of Divine origin, and it is not reducible to simply following rules. One may come to know eternal truths, not by recollecting our vision of Platonic forms from a previous life, but because God has made our intellect in such a way that it is naturally suited to see truths in the Divine light."[19]

Sir Thomas More (1478–1553) composed an early utopian essay. His utopian system was extensively Platonic. In it the home was abandoned in favor of training for service to the state, and the people had one book in which was written all of the sciences.[20]

Immanuel Kant's (1724–1804) famous observation that "the human being is the only creature that needs to be educated,"[21] seems to beg the question of the definition of education. Does not the baby bird observe flight? Might not the fledging horse model some of its first steps from the

---

17. Augustine, *Confessions*, 1.
18. Bunge, *Child in Christian Thought*, 78–102.
19. Curren, *Companion*, 59.
20. Eby and Arrowood, *Development of Modern Education*, 244.
21. Cahn, *Classic and Contemporary Readings*, 152.

grown equesters in its purview? Does not the primate show its offspring which fruit to pick? Let alone countless other counterexamples that could be provided.

Nonetheless, there seems to be *something* provocative and perhaps profound in Kant's quote. What other creature takes notes on *The Old Man and the Sea*, or attempts to master differential equations under the guidance of an instructor? Kant goes on to suggest that to have trained a child is "not enough; rather, what really matters is that they have learned to think."[22] Summarily Kant suggests, "Education must be the moralization of man. He is to acquire not merely the skills needed for all sorts of ends, but also the disposition to choose only good ends."[23] "He is merely what education makes him."[24]

Kant categorized good educational ends as follows:

1. Duties to oneself:
   a. Obligatory duties.
      i. To preserve oneself.
      ii. To be truthful.
      iii. To respect oneself.
      iv. Not to be . . .
         1. Miserly.
         2. Servile.
   b. Meritorious duties.
      i. To seek one's own natural perfection.
      ii. To seek one's own moral perfection.
2. Duties to others:
   a. Obligatory duties.
      i. To keep promises.
      ii. To be truthful.
      iii. To respect others.
      iv. To maintain law and order.
   b. Meritorious duties.
      i. To promote others' happiness.
      ii. To be grateful.
      iii. To be sympathetic.

22. Cahn, *Classic*, 157.
23. Mills, *Becoming*, 7.
24. Frankena, *Three Historical Philosophies*, 83.

iv. To be friendly and sociable.

To such educational ends "children ought to be educated, not for the present, but for a possibly improved condition of man in the future."[25] Part of that future is the impact that the educated individual can have on society. Kant says, "Education makes a man a citizen (*Burger*) and equips him for civil society (*bergerliche Gesellschaft*); he seems to mean by this that education makes him (or at least *should* make him) a good citizen of the state in which he lives."[26] In conclusion, Kant concedes that "a child must play, but he must also learn to work, and where can the inclination to work be cultivated so well as at school? School is a place of compulsory culture."[27]

Johann Gottfried Herder (1744–1803) used the term *Bildung*[28] rather than the more conventional term *Erziehung*.[29] Furthermore,

> Whereas the psychologists of the time were carefully distinguishing various human faculties (e.g., conation, feeling, knowledge), Herder stressed the unity and indivisible wholeness of human nature. Consciousness and *Besonnenheit* ("reflective discernment") are not simply "higher" faculties added to an animal foundation, instead, they designate the structure of the individual as a whole with qualitatively unique human desires and human sensitivities. Since human instincts and sensitivities are subject to reflection, or "broken off" (*gebrochen*), however, the human individual is "the first liberated member of creation."[30]

Georg Wilhelm Friedrich Hegel (1770–1831) suggested that "God evokes, drives, fulfills, and in some sense *is* the pedagogical process, the education-event. God is now conceived as spirit (*Geist*) rather than merely idea of good: God is subject or mind, as well as substance."[31] Hegel utilized very particular and rather technical terms to specify aspects of his philosophy of education. *Pädogogik* is the art of making

---

25. Frankena, *Three Historical Philosophies*, 97.
26. Frankena, *Three Historical Philosophies*, 103.
27. Frankena, *Three Historical Philosophies*, 119.
28. *Bildung* connotes *education* in the sense of formation. It conveys the German notion of self-cultivation. It presupposes a philosophy of education linking idealistic philosophy with personal development and cultural assimilation.
29. *Erziehung* connotes education in the sense of acquisition of skills, knowledge, and judgment.
30. Irmscher, "Johan Gottfried von Herder," para. 8.
31. Hodgson, *God's Wisdom*, 42.

human beings ethical. *Volkserzieher* is the enlightened religious educator. Education involves a transition from a naturalistic, self-seeking, egoistic will (*Willkür*) to a universal, inter-subjective, free will (*freie Wille*).

William T. Harris (1835–1909), superintendent of the St. Louis schools during the 1870s, founded the *Journal of Speculative Philosophy* and would eventually become the United States Commissioner of Education. He is considered to be among the most influential philosophical idealists on American education.[32] His Christian ideals and his commitment to reform education in schools fueled his efforts to launch kindergartens, to install libraries in all schools, to require strict morality, and to include grade school and high schools in the public school system.

Charlotte Mason (1842–1923) suggested that "knowledge is passed like the light of a torch, from mind to mind, and the flame can be kindled at original minds only." Mason was the founder of PNEU (Parents' National Education Union), which holds—along with Ms. Mason's eventual twentieth-century protégé, Karen Glass—the following presuppositions about education:

1. Children are born as persons.

2. Children are responsible persons.

3. Children (not the teachers) are responsible for learning via the work of self-effort.

4. Children ought to be educated on real ideas, within their natural environment by means of development of good habits and by means of exposure to living ideas and concepts from birth.

5. Teachers provide sympathy and occasional elucidation.

6. Teachers must provide ample nourishment for the mind.

7. Teachers should rely upon a child's natural desire for knowledge.

8. Teachers should create a healthy learning environment.

9. Teachers should view education as consisting of three instruments:
    a. Atmosphere.
    b. Discipline.

---

32. Knight, *Philosophy and Education*, 45.

c. Life.
10. Teachers should view the leaner as needing to develop two internal loci:
   a. The student's will.
   b. The student's reason.
11. Teachers should regard the following curricular considerations:
   a. Testing should not determine curriculum.
   b. Curriculum should be designed to meet universal human needs.
   c. Curriculum should satisfy the demands of the human desire to know vastly.
   d. Curriculum should address all three sorts of knowledge proper to a child:
      i. God.
      ii. Self.
      iii. Universe.
   e. Curriculum should reflect that the knowledge of God:
      i. Is most indispensable.
      ii. Is most "happy-making."
      iii. Ranks first in importance.
   f. Curriculum should include reading the Bible.
   g. Curriculum should manifest the following values:
      i. History should give us greatness of mind.
      ii. Literature should warm the imagination.
      iii. Citizenship should offer us examples to emulate.
      iv. Composition should be learned naturally around other subjects.
      v. Foreign language should make use of narration.
      vi. The arts should be appreciated before they are imitated.
      vii. Science and geography should:
         1. Avoid utilitarian minimizing.
         2. Involve "common knowledge" and introduce the student to the delight and variety of association, apprehension, and appropriation.
      viii. Mathematics should engage the science of proportion and ingenuity.
12. Their motto for students is, I am. I can. I ought. I will.[33]

33. Mason and Glass, *Mind to Mind*. See also https://charlottemasoninstitute.org/.

Alfred North Whitehead (1861–1947) coauthored *Principia Mathematica* with Bertrand Russell and became known for a metaphysical system whose tenets contributed substantively to the foundation for process theology. His book *The Aims of Education* argues that "culture is activity of thought, and receptiveness to beauty and humane feeling. Scraps of information have nothing to do with it. A merely well-informed man is the most useless bore on God's earth. What we should aim at producing is men who possess both culture and expert knowledge in some special direction."[34] He insisted on the "interest in the *sine qua non* for attention and apprehension."[35]

Paul Elmer More (1864–1937), an essayist and editor, was trained at Washington University and Harvard University. A Christian Platonist, More exhorted educational leaders that "other men are creatures of the visible moment; the aristocrat of the mind is a citizen of the past and of the future. And such a charter of citizenship it is the first duty of the college to provide."[36]

> There is no need to dwell on this aspect of the classics. He who cares to follow their full working in this direction, as did our English humanist, may find it exhibited in Plato's political and ethical scheme Aristotle—as spokesmen for their people, it would be *eleutheria*, liberty. The freedom to cultivate the higher part of a man's nature—his intellectual prerogative, his desire for truth, his refinements of taste—and to hold the baser part of himself in subjection, the freedom also, for its own perfection, and indeed for its very existence, to impose an outer conformity to, or at least respect for, the laws of this inner government on others who are of themselves ungoverned. Such liberty is the ground of true distinction.[37]

Irving Babbitt (1865–1933),[38] founder of the New American Humanism movement, was trained in classics at Harvard, where he returned

---

34. Cahn, *Classic*, 211. In the present author's view, the suggestion that "scraps of information have nothing to do with it" is overstated.

35. Cahn, *Classic*, 216.

36. Gamble, *Great Tradition*, 560.

37. Gamble, *Great Tradition*, 569.

38. Babbitt manifested significant Aristotelian influence, but he is included in this chapter on Idealism because of the prevailing Platonism that seems to permeate his writing. Plato's *Republic* seemed particularly influential in terms of Babbitt's philosophy of education as argued in this 1935 thesis: https://doi.org/10.1093/mind/XLVI.184.468.

to teach from 1894 until his death. His students included T. S. Eliot. He advocated "a Socratic concern for carefully defined terms, clear principles of discernment of that which is worthy of our love, and a belief that the individual will and appetite must always be restrained. His *New Humanism* (as distinguished from John Dewey's secular humanism) rejected both Baconian power over nature and Romantic sentimental humanitarianism as proper goals for education."[39]

> A sober reflection on the history of the ancient republics might put us on our guard against many of the dangers to which we ourselves are exposed. It might cure us in part of our cheap optimism. It might, in any case, make us conscious of that tendency of which Machiavelli had so clear a vision—the tendency of a state to slip down an easy slope of prosperity into vice.... This high message contained in classical literature calls for the active exercise of our own best faculties, of our intellect and imagination, in order to be understood.[40]

Twentieth-century constructivist theologian and philosopher of religion Bernard Meland (1899–1993) proposes a post-pragmatism argument against the primacy of information, practices, morals, or even technological advances as essential to education. He argues for a "higher goodness."[41] Spiritual in nature, this *higher goodness* simultaneously incorporates and transcends the aforementioned aspects of education. It includes devotion, discernment, reflection, imagination, and something spiritual. He posits a type of a Whiteheadian transformative pedagogy.

1. Education and life formation.

2. The rhythm of education.

3. Constructive and interactive knowledge.

4. Education as the practice of freedom.

5. Connected teaching and cooperative learning.

Sam Rocha,[42] professor of philosophy of education at the University of British Columbia, observes,

---

39. Gamble, *Great Tradition*, 538.
40. Gamble, *Great Tradition*, 555–57.
41. Hodgson, *God's Wisdom*, 4.
42. See also http://www.samrocha.com/ for more information on this philosopher's

> Everyone comes into direct contact with education. Read for the truth. Write and speak to show what seems true. Ask questions to get what might be true. Attend classes to seek the truth. Do not settle for shallow, impoverished answers. With courage, with the tough, loving attitude that genuine seriousness brings, philosophy and education yield knowledge. Knowledge is not enough. We must understand that . . . Love alone is necessary and sufficient for all things. Everything else is secondary.[43]

For idealists *ideas* are ultimate reality, therefore, education ought to *educe* ideas (back) to one's mind and enhance one's understanding of, appreciation for, and facility with ultimate ideas. Idealists have a lot to offer the philosophy of education. Among other things they tend to emphasize good thinking (e.g., reading, reasoning, and reflection) about good ideas (e.g., beauty, goodness, truth, and justice). Many idealists also strive for a healthy balance of historical awareness, cultural sensitivity, and preparedness for what might lie ahead. Furthermore, they tend to have a sense of transcendence—that there is something or Someone that is bigger, better, and beyond the immediate sensory realities. Additionally, they generally aspire to the development of noble character and character traits such as wisdom, virtue, and love. Finally, they are strong in positing that education entails educing ideas to consciousness and expanding one's understanding of, appreciation for, and facility with ultimate ideas.

Nonetheless, they are not generally as strong in recognizing that much of education is not just educing *back* to consciousness former ideas, but that it also involves educing *toward* ideas yet to be learned. Additionally, educational idealists tend to be Platonic dualists[44] in the sense of prioritizing the real reality of the realm of ideas over the realness of the corporal world, which they claim is a mere shadow of the real world of ideas. A biblical philosophy of Christian school education does not posit Platonic dualism in that way or to that degree.

The book of Colossians is particularly pertinent in this regard. Part of Paul's priority in penning that epistle was as a polemic against Gnosticism. Gnostics (the Idealists of *that* day and region) were dualists, as well. Notions such as demi-gods (such as Christ) providing intermediary

---

model of education.

43. Rocha, *Philosophy and Education*, 9–51.

44. In philosophy there are a variety of non-dualist idealists, as well. Berkeley, for example, considered by many to be the father of modern idealism, is not a dualist. Guyer and Horstmann, "Idealism," 199–225.

servicing between the high gods and humans, esoteric mystery knowledge for only a select few humans, and the inherent evil of the physical world are all addressed correctively in Colossians. Christ is the Godhead bodily, that the physical world is fallen, but it was originally created good, that Christ in us is the assurance of our access to and eventual place in glory, and that education is to be about proclaiming him as present, prominent, and preeminent in all things—whether counting, calculus, or character development.

Idealists need to learn to set their minds and hearts even *higher* than their esoteric ideas—on to Christ himself, who sits at the right hand of God. Education is not (just) about *educing* us back to Edenic ideations, but rather *educing* us *even* higher to the heavenward call in Christ Jesus.

Chapter 5

Toward a Christian Understanding of Realism

REALISM TEACHES THAT REALITY exists outside of just the mind and esoteric ideas. Realists believe that reality exists in the "real" world of physical objects including teachers, students, and subject matter(s). Truth can be observed and taught. The scientific method complements mathematics, logic, critical thinking, classics, and character development in a curriculum of preparing students to become good citizens and flourishing humans.

Encompassing a vast array of thinkers, realism ranges from relativists (e.g., Protagoras) to non-relativists (e.g., Bloom), from theists (e.g., Descartes, Carson) to atheists (e.g., Nagel, Paine) and to polytheists (e.g., Egyptians), from substance dualists (e.g., Locke, Descartes) to materialists (e.g., Nagel). Nonetheless a common thread running through their philosophies of education is the priority that "thinking proceeds from things as they actually *are* to their critical analysis."[1]

For the educational realist, the physical world is really real. Therefore, education ought to observe and to teach real-world truth, so that students can become good citizens and flourishing humans in the real, physical world.

First, primitive education was among the earliest of systematized approaches to education, per se. It tended toward realism. As such, it tended to address four categories of emphasis:

---

1. Noddings, *Philosophy of Education*, 10.

1. To help persons make the most of their environment—to feed, clothe, shelter, and protect themselves.

2. To help persons to get along with their closest relations—family and otherwise.

3. To help persons feel at home and at peace—such as religious attitudes, practices, and beliefs.

4. To help afford opportunity for meaningful expression—including language, music, dance, painting, and drama.[2]

Egyptian education advanced beyond some of those earlier and more primitive and rudimentary aims. Scholars highlight the following curricular objectives in the ancient Egyptian system of education:

1. Domestication of animals.

2. Tribal unification and government.

3. Architecture and construction.

4. Irrigation.

5. Embalming.

6. *Esprit de corps*.

7. Familial life and domestic functions.

8. Arts, e.g., sculpture, painting, textiles, pottery, furniture, and metallurgy.

9. Arithmetic.

10. Geometry.

11. Astronomy.

12. Mechanics.

13. Geography.

14. Medicine.

---

2. Eby, *Ancient and Medieval*, 5.

15. Alphabet and writing.

16. Didactic and rhetoric.

17. Military and professional training.[3]

Conspicuously absent, however, from Egyptian pedagogy were two disciplines that were emphasized in many other ancient curricula and co-curricula. "It is not customary at all among them to have received any instruction in wrestling or music . . . they considered music not only useless, but even harmful, since it makes the spirit of listeners effeminate."[4] And, they seem to have found little to no pedagogical value in the almost universal sport of wrestling.

Protagoras (ca. 490–ca. 420 BC) claimed that his students would develop the irreplaceably important skills of "prudence in affairs private as well as public; he will learn to order his own house in the best manner, and he will be able to speak and act for the best in the affairs of the city."[5] A student of Democritus, a sophist, a relativist, and a pre-Socratic agnostic, Protagoras popularly posited that "man is the measure of all things." He was among the first to emphasize grammar—as the scientific knowledge of the use of language. He prioritized beginning education at a young age, cultivating disposition, and utilizing exercise.[6]

Herodotus (ca. 484–425 BC) observed the importance and impact of tradition and regiment in the training of young men. "Convention is the king of all men."[7] His contributions to education and its philosophies included his historical accounts of educators and their approaches to learning and learners.

Aristotle (384–322 BC) famously observed that "all men by nature desire to know." In 335, Aristotle returned to Athens and founded his Lyceum or *Peripatus* to introduce students to a breadth of studies in pursuit of the *summum bonum*, i.e., *eudaimonia*. His educational aim was to produce a young man who would be charming in person and graceful in manners, a beautiful soul in a beautiful body, habituated to well-ordered

---

3. Eby, *Ancient and Medieval*, 36–107.
4. Eby, *Ancient and Medieval*, 81.
5. Eby, *Ancient and Medieval*, 314.
6. Eby, *Ancient and Medieval*, 318.
7. Eby, *Ancient and Medieval*, 302.

behavior.⁸ Furthermore, his comments about education and the philosophy thereof seem even more descriptive today than ever.

> At present, opinion is divided about the subjects of education. People do not take the same view about what should be learned by the young, either with a view to human excellence or a view to the best possible life, nor is it clear whether education should be directed mainly to the intellect or to moral character, whether the proper studies to be pursued are those that are useful in life, or those which make for excellence, or those that advance the bounds of knowledge. . . . Men do not all honor the same distinctive human excellence and so naturally they differ about the proper training for it.⁹

Isocrates (436–338 BC) is sometimes referred to as "the most successful professional teacher of antiquity," and "one of the few who had a definite theory of education."¹⁰ For him both oratory and *arête* represented more than mere ornamental polish on the young man, but actually the foundational core of his exacting and training. "Geometry, astrology, eristic dialogues are good for the young, if only as employing them, but they do not make practical men. By an educated man I understand one who can deal with all that comes upon him day by day, who is honest and mannerly in society, who rules his desires, who is not spoiled by good fortune."¹¹

Whereas Axiochus advocated a boy starting school at age seven and the Athenians advocated entry at age six, Xenophon (ca. 428–ca. 354 BC) disagreed with setting any particular beginning age altogether. "In every part of Hellas except Sparta, those who claim to give their sons the best education, as soon as ever the child understands what is said to him, at once make one of the servants his *paidagogos*, and at once send him off to school to learn letters and music and the exercises of the Palaestra."¹² Fastidious about deportment and attire, Xenophon emphasized justice, temperance, and courage. Although a journalist, himself, he ideally sought to prepare soldiers; consequently, he ironically *de*-emphasized any literary training for advanced students.¹³

8. Boyd, *History of Western Education*, 88.
9. Knight, *Philosophy and Education*, v.
10. Eby, *Ancient and Medieval*, 339.
11. Eby, *Ancient and Medieval*, 341.
12. Eby, *Ancient and Medieval*, 238–39.
13. Eby, *Ancient and Medieval*, 338–39.

Christine de Pizan (ca. 1363–ca. 1430), born in Italy but reared by her father, a court physician to King Charles of France, married young and after the death of both her husband and her father, she supported herself and her children through her writing. *The Book of Body Politic* delineates many of her views on education.

> Virtue must regulate human life in all its works.... Human happiness comes from being virtuous.... Because we are expressly commanded to love God, the first thing is to introduce the child of the Prince to this love very early and to teach him simple little prayers appropriate to the understanding of the child.... And when the child comes to learn his grammar then the tutor should begin to use a bit more subtle words and teaching, according to how he sees what the child is able to understand, and thus, little by little, teach more and more, just as a nurse increases the food of the child according to his growth.... I dare say there is no treasure the like of understanding. Who would not undertake any labor, you champions of wisdom, to acquire it?[14]

Pier Paolo Vergerio (1370–1444) authored *Character and Studies Befitting a Free-Born Youth*, which became a widely utilized textbook for a hundred years. In it he urged students to strive for wisdom and virtue, and not for material profit or idle pleasure. "The one is fit for free men, the other fit for slaves."[15] He continues, "What way of life can be more delightful, or indeed more beneficial, than to read and write all the time: for moderns to understand things ancient, for present generations to converse with their posterity, and thus to make every time our own, both past and future?"[16]

Aeneas Silvius (1405–1464), a classicist, a cardinal, a bishop, and eventually the pope (Pius II), emphasized liberal arts, religious studies, and character development. As for style, he promoted brevity, fullness, simplicity, and elegance. *The Education of Boys* was one of his most influential works.

> And is it not fitting that the king should have a liberal education, that he may garner truth for himself in the books of philosophers? ... Nothing is more excellent than intellect and reason. ... The disciplines are interconnected and a person cannot

---

14. Gamble, *Great Tradition*, 322–31.
15. Gamble, *Great Tradition*, 313.
16. Gamble, *Great Tradition*, 312.

gain one unless he acquires the light of another.... Therefore, greatest attention and zeal must be given to letters.... Receive this further instruction and learn what authors you should read while you are a boy. They are poets, historians, philosophers, and orators. For we shall reserve the theologians for another time, although some of those included under the name of philosophers might be given to a boy without danger, as we shall afterwards indicate.... We shall have to speak more in detail in other books as the periods of your life will require if God, the Creator of the world, and the Author of our soul will prolong our life.... But do you meanwhile so endeavor to practice and learn what you have been taught is proper for a boy that you may be most eager for the other parts of this work.[17]

Desiderius Roterodamus Erasmus (1466–1536) was a cosmopolitan renaissance humanist. In 1516 he authored *The Education of the Christian Prince*. He "believed that the revival of interest in the classics and classical style would contribute to a reexamination of the Bible as the pure source of God's revelation, free from the accretions of Medieval scholasticism."[18] Erasmus asserted that "to be a schoolmaster is next to being a king. Do you count it a mean employment to imbue minds of your fellow-citizen in their earliest years with the best literature and with the love of Christ, and to return them to their country honest and virtuous men? In the opinion of fools, it is a humble task, but in fact it is the noblest of occupations."[19] "Erasmus' students read Aristotle in the original Greek and found that he actually contradicted what they had found in their round-about translations from the Muslims."[20] As one scholar observed, "His strong affirmation [is] of the Christ-centered purpose of education. ('All studies are for this one object . . .')." Finally, from his *On Education for Children*:

> Nature, the mother of all things, has equipped brute animals with more means to fulfill the functions of their species, but to man alone, she has given the faculty of reason, and so she has thrown the burden of human growth upon education. Therefore, it is right to say that the beginning and the end, indeed, the total sum of man's happiness, are founded upon a good upbringing and education.[21]

17. Gamble, *Great Tradition*, 342–52.
18. Gutek, *Foundations of Education*, 95.
19. Gaebelein, *Christian Education in Democracy*, 172.
20. Kienel, *History of Christian School Education*, 1:251.
21. Gamble, *Great Tradition*, 360–61.

Sir Thomas Elyot (ca. 1490–1546), an English diplomat and scholar, advocated humanists' ideas, including the education of women. Advocating for the educating of women, Elyot published the *Defense of Good Women*. In this essay, Elyot supported Thomas More and other humanists' ideal of educated wives who would be prepared to provide intellectual companionship for their husbands and educated training for their children.

Published posthumously, Roger Ascham's (ca. 1515–1568) *The Schoolmaster* delineates three "earnest respects" for education to prioritize and practice.

1. Truth of religion.

2. Honesty in living.

3. Right order in learning.

As a humanist and a utilitarian, Peter Ramus (1515–1572) exercised sustained effort to affect educational reform in the following regards:

1. The principles of observation and of nature should govern all studies—particularly in higher education.

2. The principle of system provided the logic behind his schema:

    1. Law of truth.
    2. Law of justice.
    3. Law of wisdom.

3. The principle of practice refers to his penchant for having students read widely and then utilize the content from their reading in a variety of critical and creative ways.[22]

Wolfgang Ratke[23] (1571–1635) proposed the following educational endeavor:

1. How the Hebrew, Greek, Latin, and other tongues may be learned both by young and old, more easily and in very much shorter time.

2. How, not only in High German, but, also, in all other tongues a school may be established, in which all arts and sciences may be thoroughly learned and propagated.

---

22. Eby, *Development of Modern Education*, 213–16.
23. Often now known as *Ratich*, a name he likely would never have known.

3. How, in the whole Empire one and the same speech, one and the same government, and finally one and the same religion, may be pleasantly introduced and peacefully maintained.[24]

Rene Descartes (1596–1650), the father of modern philosophy, departed from the Scholasticism of his day. Popularly and profoundly, he observed *Cogito ergo sum*: "I think, therefore, I am." Although not a philosopher of education *per se*, some scholars suggest that "there is no thinker who has exercised a more decided influence on the destinies of education."[25] In summary, Descartes's educational influence included posits such as, "Never accept anything for true which I did not clearly know to be such . . . what was presented to my mind so clearly and distinctly as to exclude all ground of doubt."[26] Furthermore, he believed that all primary ideas are innate, and that the growth of knowledge came "merely in drawing out the implications of these principles. . . . The fundamental process of learning is rational, constructive thinking."[27]

John Locke (1632–1704), a classicist as well as a physician, waxes classically when he describes that man has little more to wish for if he but has a sound mind in a sound body. "As the strength of the body lies chiefly in being able to endure hardships, so also does that of the mind. And the great principle and foundation of all virtue and worth is placed in this, that a man is able to deny himself his own desires, cross his own inclinations, and purely follow what reason directs as best, though the appetite lean the other way."[28] To that end, a teacher "should remember that his business is not so much to teach him all that is knowable, as to raise in him a love and esteem of knowledge, and to put him in the right way of knowing and improving himself, when he has a mind to it." He seemed to "show a sympathetic understanding of children. Remembering how he hated the rote learning of his own education, Locke proposed a curriculum tailored to the needs and aptitudes of the individual child. . . . Good health and good character were to be valued over intellectual learning."[29]

"Eventually Anthony Benezet (1713–1784) wrote primers, spelling books, and a grammar handbook for mothers living far from any school

---

24. Eby, *Development of Modern Education*, 248.
25. Eby, *Development of Modern Education*, 233.
26. Eby, *Development of Modern Education*, 234.
27. Eby, *Development of Modern Education*, 234.
28. Cahn, *Classic and Contemporary Readings*, 106.
29. Anthony, "John Locke," 436–37.

to use in teaching their children at home . . . [but] he never lost sight of the need for even a classically-educated student to receive a 'useful or practical education, including knowing the essentials of business and account keeping.'"[30]

Thomas Jefferson (1743–1826), an advocate of republican education, had been influenced by the likes of Thomas Paine's *Common Sense* theories and Crevecoeur's correspondence theories. Jefferson envisioned education as a necessary foundation for a free people who governed themselves democratically through representative institutions. Resting on his political philosophy and rooted in the Enlightenment, Jefferson conceived of three broad goals for civic education in this new republic:

1. State-supported and locally controlled schooling should provide the people with a basic literary, mathematical, and historical foundation.

2. Schools should be agencies of identifying, selecting, and preparing the most talented persons for leadership via higher education.

3. Popular education should advance human liberty and freedom by safeguarding the individual's natural rights.[31]

About Americans of his time and their education then and into the future, French philosopher and cultural historian Alex de Tocqueville (1805–1859) wrote:

> Everything about him [i.e., early Americans] is primitive and unformed, but he is himself the result of the labor and the experience of eighteen centuries. He wears the dress, and he speaks the language of cities; he is acquainted with the past, curious of the future, and ready for argument upon the present; he is, in short, a highly civilized being, who consents, for a time, to inhabit the backwoods, and who penetrates into the wilds of the New World with the Bible, an axe, and a pile of newspapers.
>
> It cannot be doubted that, in the United States, the instruction of the people powerfully contributes to the support of a democratic republic, and such must always be the case, I believe, where instruction which awakens the understanding is not separated from moral education which amends the heart. But I by no means exaggerate this benefit, and I am still further from thinking, as so many people do think in Europe, that men can be instantaneously made citizens by teaching them to read and

---

30. Lockerbie, *Passion for Learning*, 241.
31. Gutek, *Historical and Philosophical Foundations*, 187.

write. True information is mainly derived from experience, and if the Americans had not been gradually accustomed to govern themselves, their book-learning would not assist them much at the present day.[32]

Mary Wollstonecraft (1759-1797), proponent of women's education, argued that since "every person [is] endowed with the power of reason, [every person has] the right to an education." By education she explains that "the sense of the word is not precisely defined, such an attention to a child as will slowly sharpen the senses, form the temper, regulate the passions as they begin to ferment, and set the understanding to work before the body arrives at maturity; so that the man may only have to proceed, not begin, the important task of learning to think and reason."[33] She concludes that virtue is founded on knowledge; that we need mankind (both male and female) to be more virtuous, which "is scarcely possible unless they be educated."[34]

Edward Copleston (1776-1849), bishop of Llandaff, moral philosopher, and provost of Oriel College in Oxford, argued,

> There must be surely a cultivation of the mind, which is itself good: a good of the highest order, without any immediate reference to bodily appetites, or wants of any kind. If this liberal instruction be first provided, and if the intellect be duly prepared by correct Logic, and pure Mathematical science, there is no analysis, which of the business of life may afterwards call upon him to investigate, beyond reach of a moderate understanding.[35]

Trained as an Episcopalian priest, Albert Jay Nock (1870-1945) became an author and a publisher and was a "Jeffersonian individualist who defended political, economic, and intellectual freedom while at the same time mercilessly exposing and condemning vulgar materialism and the false promises of mass democracy."[36]

> An educational system was set up in our country, and lavishly endowed in response to the noble sentiment of parents for the advancement of their children. It was to be equalitarian, as the average man understood equality, that is to say, everybody

32. Phaman, "Alexis de Tocqueville," para. 3, 5.
33. Cahn, *Classic and Contemporary Readings*, 175-76.
34. Cahn, *Classic and Contemporary Readings*, 184.
35. Gamble, *Great Tradition*, 498-513.
36. Gamble, *Great Tradition*, 579.

should be regarded as able to take in its benefits. It should be democratic, as the average man understood democracy, that is to say, no one had any natural right to anything that everybody could not get.

"Bring on your children, and we will put them through this process under the sanction of an equalitarian and democratic theory."

It did not work.[37]

Eric Voegelin (1901–1985), Vienna born, bred, and educated, was a political philosopher who preferred an Aristotelian, classical approach to education. "The climate of our universities is certainly hostile to the life of reason but not every man is agreeable to having his nature deformed by the 'climate' or, as it is sometimes called, the 'age.' There are always young men with enough spiritual instinct to resist the efforts of 'educators' who pressure for 'adjustment.' . . . Through the life of reason, man realizes his freedom."[38]

For R. S. Peters (1919–2011), "education involves the nurture of a 'rational passion' associated with commitment to the worthwhile. The implication for education has to do with cognition—with logical thinking and the resolution of moral dilemmas."[39] Peters wrote: "Respect for truth is intimately connected with fairness, and respect for persons, which together with freedom, are fundamental principles which underlie our mortal life and which are personalized in the form of the rational passions."[40]

David Malet Armstrong (1926–2014), an Australian philosopher, was renowned for his factualist ontology, his functionalist theory of the mind, and his externalist epistemology. Each of those views has contributed significantly to the contour of the Australian teacher education programs.

Allan Bloom (1930–1992) bemoaned the fact that "these great universities—which can split the atom, find cures for the most terrible diseases, conduct surveys of whole populations and produce massive dictionaries of lost languages—cannot generate a modest program of general education for undergraduate students. This is a parable for our

---

37. Gamble, *Great Tradition*, 579–82.
38. Gamble, *Great Tradition*, 651–58.
39. Johnson and Reed, *Philosophical Documents in Education*, 162.
40. Johnson and Reed, *Philosophical Documents in Education*, 162–63.

times."[41] He addressed social woes and identified what has been called the "intellectual confusion and moral quandary of the American academy." He suggested a return to the learning communities of liberal arts and of deep-thinking skills.[42]

Princeton- and Oxford-educated Rhodes Scholar, head of school, and philosopher of education David V. Hicks suggests that "modern criticism of general education focuses mostly on the symptoms of the school's declining academic standards. . . . But the reality behind the image has changed, and administrative cosmetics are no more salubrious than Band Aids on bullet holes."[43]

He advocates for systemic change. He argues that educators need to recall "the purpose of education is not the assimilation of facts or the retention of information, but the habituation of the mind and body to will and act in accordance with what one knows."[44] He advocates for a moral classicism as a model of educational theory and methodology.

William Glasser (1925–2013), a psychiatrist who posited Reality Therapy, proposed a humanistic approach to education in his *Schools without Walls*. In addition to promoting student responsibility, he fundamentally argued that schools failed to educate, because they failed to establish warm relationships, to cultivate students' self-worth, and to love. "The role of the school should be to provide a warm and nonthreatening environment in which those needs can be met. This atmosphere will provide an effective context for learning."[45] (Whereas on the surface this may seem to belong more in the chapter on Existentialism or Romanticism, ultimately Glasser advocated three aspects of Realism as foundational to his entire educational theory, i.e., realism, responsibility, and right-and-wrong.)

Thomas Nagel (b. 1937), philosopher of the mind and ethics, authored *Mind and Cosmos* (2012), in which he argues against a reductionist view of the origin and emergence of consciousness in general and against Darwinist view in particular. Furthermore, he wrote an article entitled "Public Education and Intelligent Design," which ignited debate as to whether, in what way, and to what extent Intelligent Design should

41. Anthony, *Evangelical Dictionary*, 92.
42. Anthony, *Evangelical Dictionary*, 92.
43. Hicks, *Norms and Nobility*, 107.
44. Hicks, *Norms and Nobility*, 20.
45. Knight, *Philosophy and Education*, 113.

be taught in public schools. More central to Nagel's realism in terms of a philosophy of education, however, is his writing on Aristotle's *eudaimonia* as the *ergon* for humans.[46]

> We must identify with the highest part of ourselves rather than with the whole. The other functions, including the practical employment of reason itself, provide support for the highest form of activity but do not enter into our proper excellence as primary component factors. This is because men are not simply the most complex species of animal but possess as their essential nature a capacity to transcend themselves and become like gods. It is in virtue of this capacity that they are capable of *eudaimonia*.[47]

Ben Carson (b. 1951) cites Jesus[48] and Aristotle,[49] respectively, as paradigmatic thinkers about education and excellence. Carson's model of realism in education in the pursuit of excellence entails:

1. T—Time and Talents are to be recognized as gifts from God.
2. H—Hope for good things and be Honest.
3. I—Insight should be gleaned from great books and good people.
4. N—Be Nice to all people.
5. K—Knowledge should be recognized as a key to living rightly.
6. B—Books should be read actively, widely, and well.
7. I—In-depth learning skills should be developed.
8. G—God: Never get too big for him.[50]

A graduate of the King's College and a PhD in philosophy from University of Southern California, Harry Brighouse is a professor of philosophy at University of Wisconsin, is director of its Center for Ethics and

---

46. *Ergon* refers to the doings of something, that for which a thing is "designed." A hammer's *ergon*, for example, is pounding. Aristotle argued for *eudaimonia*, i.e., human flourishing as the *ergon* of a human. Nagel seems to concur, but he beckons beyond Aristotelian *eudaimonia* to a more particularized flourishing, i.e., reason as the differentiator of humans from other creatures.
47. Taggart, "Nagel on Aristotle," para. 6.
48. "As a man thinks in his heart, so is he."
49. "We are what we repeatedly do. Excellence then is not an act but a habit."
50. Carson, *Think Big*.

Education, codirector of the Spencer Foundation's Initiative on Philosophy in Educational Policy and Practice, and has written extensively on education, including a book entitled *On Education* (2006), in which he summarizes his views as follows:

> The guiding normative idea of this book has been that education should promote human flourishing, when human flourishing is understood in a pluralistic fashion. Schooling should:
>
> 1. Facilitate the powerful self-interest children have in becoming autonomous, self-governing adults.
> 2. Enable children to become economically self-reliant, insofar as that is possible.
> 3. Enhance children's prospective wellbeing.
> 4. Produce responsible, deliberative citizens who are capable of accepting the demands of justice and abiding by the norm of reciprocity.[51]

Realists believe that the physical world is real reality, therefore, education ought to observe and teach truth via the scientific method, mathematics, logic, critical thinking, classics, conduct, and character development whereby preparing students to become good citizens and flourishing humans in the real, physical world. Realism rightly teaches that reality exists outside of just the realm of the mind and esoteric ideas. Realists believe that reality exists in the "real" world of physical objects, including schools, teachers, students, and subject matter, as well. They rightly regard truth, but many of them overly emphasize its observableness.

The scientific method rightly complements mathematics, logic, critical thinking, classics, cocurricular arts and athletics, and the development of conduct, character, and citizenship—all within a well-rounded curriculum of preparing students to become good citizens and flourishing humans. Many realists, however, might overemphasize rationality, science, or *eudaimonia*. God is the real *source* of all truth, and some of that truth eludes validation in a beaker or a syllogism, and he is the *end* of all education—it should be for his glory.

Realism, nonetheless, contributes significantly to education and to the philosophy of education, but a Christian critique of realism's impetus is critical. Per the Apostle Paul in Rom 11:33–36, and fundamentally distinguishing from other realists' view of the ultimate reality of the

---

51. Brighouse, *On Education Thinking*, 131.

physical world, the ultimate truth of reason, and the ultimate value of *eudaimonia*: (1) *God* is the one *from* whom everything exists. (2) *God* is the one *through* whom everything is sustained. (3) *God* is the one *to* whom everything ought to be aimed; to *God* be glory forever and ever.

Chapter 6

Toward a Christian Understanding of Scholasticism

SCHOLASTICS EMPHASIZED TRANSCENDENTAL TRUTHS that would lead a person to God. The goal of medieval education in general and of scholasticism in particular, therefore, tended to be overtly religious, prioritizing the rediscovery of these transcendental truths and a concomitant devotion to transcendental truths that would guide a person through a life of moral volition and religious service.

One methodology for such discovery was the dialectic. To the medieval mind discussion and debate were an art, a science, and even entertainment. More Socratic than most of the other schools of thought,[1] scholasticism utilized disputation as a journey of shared discovery.

An early and important work of Anselm of Canterbury (ca. 1033–1109)—albeit less widely known than some of his other *magnum opuses*—included an introduction to scholasticism's pedagogical methodology, viz. *De Grammatico*. Among other contributions, Anselm is famously known for his view of integration and the primacy of faith. "'I believe that I may know,' says Anselm. The meaning was not that he would take leave of common sense, but that religious authority must reveal the meaning of brute facts and the value of effort, of feeling, and of emotion."[2]

---

1. With the not unlikely exception of Continentalism. (See note on Socrates in that chapter.)

2. Eby, *Ancient and Medieval*, 741.

Sometimes referred to as the Socrates of the Middle Ages, Peter Abelard (1079–1142) was called the most popular teacher of his time. He sought "consensus truth-making," and suggested, "By doubting we are led to inquiry, and by inquiry we attain the truth."[3]

Monastic educated and head of school for the Victorines, Hugh of St. Victor (1096–1141) suggested three qualities contributed to a student's preparedness for study: endowment, practice, and discipline. The opening of his *De Sacramentis* delineates his view of education:

> All the arts of the natural world subserve our knowledge of God, and the lower wisdom—rightly ordered—leads to the higher. The trivium serves the literal meaning, the quadrivium the figurative meaning. Above and before all these is that divine Being to whom Scripture leads by faith and works; in the knowledge of whose truth and the love of whose excellence man is restored to his true nature.[4]

John of Salisbury (ca. 1120–1180) confessed, "Thus I learned by experience an evident lesson, that, just as dialectic facilitates other disciplines, so, if studied alone, it remains lifeless and sterile, nor does it stimulate the soul to bear fruits of Philosophy, unless it conceives elsewhere."[5]

> I myself am of the opinion of those who believe that a man cannot be literate without knowledge of the authors. Copious reading, however, by no means makes the philosopher, since it is grace alone that leads to wisdom. . . . The first task for man aspiring to wisdom is the consideration of what he himself is: what is within him, what without, what below, what above, what opposite, what before, and what after: *Noti Seliton* (know thyself). . . . Such contemplation bears fourfold fruit: benefit to self, affection for neighbor, scorn for the world, and love.

John Milton (1608–1674), a poet, a polyglot, and a professed follower of Jesus, famously penned these words in his *Of Education*: "The end then of learning is to repair the ruins of our first parents by regaining to know God aright, and out of that knowledge to love Him, to imitate Him, to be like Him, as we may the nearest by possessing souls of true

---

3. Kienel, *History of Christian Education*, 1:98.
4. Gamble, *Great Tradition*, 255.
5. Lockerbie, *Passion for Learning*, 99.

virtue, which being united to the heavenly grace of faith, makes up the highest perfection."[6]

Educated by the then relatively recently founded Franciscans, Bonaventure (1221–1274) went on to the University of Paris, where he was granted his doctorate degree the same day as Thomas Aquinas. His *Journey of the Mind to God*, written in 1259 while Bonaventure was leading the Franciscans, provided spiritual guidance and care for university students. Wisdom, peace, love, grace, and the need for the centrality of Christ and for prayer permeated this student handbook.

> His symbolic interpretation of Scripture and his mysticism may sound foreign to modern ears, but his advice regarding the preconditions of learning is timeless. Certainly, Bonaventure's ideal standard is a reminder that the "integration of faith and learning" has behind it a long history of careful reflection. Bonaventure could not have imagined a university ever wanting to separate faith and learning.[7]

Aquinas (1225–1274) integrated Aristotle's philosophy of natural realism with the doctrines of the church. As Catholic scholar Isaac Doughton has quipped, "What a strange prank of history that the pagan Aristotle, who died more than 300 years before Christ was born, should have become the dominant master of mind in the Christian Church!"[8] Thomism, as an educational philosophy, found a home in many (especially) Catholic institutions of higher learning.[9] Aquinas advocated teachers being involved in the life of their students, as well as in the own scholarly pursuits.

A. G. Sertillanges (1863–1948) was a Dominican, a French theologian, and a neo-Thomistic philosopher. His call for students was to embrace the intellectual life requiring obedience, persistence, effort, self-discipline, long self-examination, and a devotion to truth.[10]

> All of this is not intended to narrow down the field of intellectual research and to confine it to exclusively religious study. That will be evident. I have already said that every truth is practical, that every truth has a saving power. But I am indicating a spirit,

---

6. Gamble, *Great Tradition*, 467.
7. Gamble, *Great Tradition*, 299–300.
8. Kienel, *History of Christian Education*, 1:95.
9. Gutek, *Historical and Philosophical Foundations*, 90.
10. Gamble, *Great Tradition*, 572–73.

and this spirit, both in general and because of what is opportune at the present time, excludes mere dilettantism.

It also excludes a certain archaeological tendency, a love of the past which turns away from present suffering, an esteem for the past which seems not to recognize the universal presence of God. Every age is not as good as every other, but all ages are Christian ages, and there is one which for us, in practice, surpasses them all, our own. In view of it are our inborn resources, our graces of today and tomorrow, and consequently the efforts that we must make in order to correspond with them.

Let us not be like those people who always seem to be pallbearers at the funeral of the past. Let us utilize, by living, the qualities of the dead. Truth is ever new. Like the grass of morning, moist with glistening dew, all the old virtues are waiting to spring up a fresh. God does not grow old. We must help our God to renew, not the buried past and the chronicles of a vanished world, but the eternal face of the earth.[11]

French philosopher Jacques Maritain (1882–1973) employs metaphysical considerations in analyzing what education is. "In order to discuss the dynamic factors in education, we must naturally reckon first with the Platonic conception: that all learning is in the learner, not in the teacher."[12] Alluding to *Phaedo*, Maritain concedes some "great truth" within Platonism, but he suggests that it may be exaggerated in its assertion of the preexistence of knowledge from the start of human souls. "The teacher does possess knowledge that the student does not have. He actually communicates knowledge to the student whose soul has *not* previously contemplated the divine Ideas before . . . [more of a] *tabula rasa*, as Aristotle put it."[13] The student is neither an angel nor a lump of clay. Between those two extremes the learner is a "living being that possesses an inner vitality. . . . Ready-made knowledge does not, as Plato believed, exist in human souls. But the vital and active principle of knowledge does exist in each of us."[14] The teacher becomes a "dynamic factor," a ministerial agent, an *ars cooperative naturae*—an artist subservient to nature. On the other hand, "The plastic and suggestible freedom of the child is harmed and led astray if it is not helped and guided."[15]

11. Gamble, *Great Tradition*, 573–78.
12. Cahn, *Classic and Contemporary Readings*, 371.
13. Cahn, *Classic and Contemporary Readings*, 371.
14. Cahn, *Classic and Contemporary Readings*, 372.
15. Cahn, *Classic and Contemporary Readings*, 373.

Jacques Maritain represents his view:

> Creativity, or the power of engendering, does not belong only to material organisms, it is a mark and privilege of life in spiritual things also. . . . The intellect in us strives to engender. It is anxious to produce, not only the inner word, the concept which remains inside of us, but a work at once material and spiritual like ourselves, and into which something of our soul overflows. Through a natural super-abundance the intellect tends to express and utter outward, it tends to sing, to manifest itself in a work. The key concept on aesthetic judgments is that of excellence.[16]
>
> I advance of the opinion, incidentally, that, and the general educational scheme, it would be advantageous to hurry the four years of college, so that the period of undergraduate studies would extend from 16 to 19. Thus, after the years of secondary education, dealing primarily with national and foreign languages, comparative grammar, history, natural history, and the arts of expression, we would have the following for four years of undergraduate school during which the student enters and encompasses the university of liberal arts: comprising: first, mathematics, and literature and poetry, second, logic, third, foreign languages, and the history of civilization. The year of natural sciences and fine arts, comprising: first, physics and natural science, second, fine arts, mathematics, literature and poetry, third, history of the sciences. The year is philosophy comprising: first philosophy, that is to say, metaphysics and philosophy of nature, theory of knowledge, psychology, second, physics and natural science, third, mathematics, literature and poetry, fine arts. The year of ethical and political philosophy comprising: first, ethics, overcome and social philosophy, second, physics and natural science, third, mathematics, literature and poetry, fine arts, history of civilization and history of sciences.[17]

Étienne Gilson (1884–1978) was an educational Thomist. He suggested that "the active power, therefore, generally needs time to master completely the matter to which it is applied; as with fire which does not instantaneously consume all its inflammable material nor succeeds in setting it alight at once, but gradually deprives it of its opposing dispositions until it finally masters and assimilates it completely."

---

16. Peterson and Evans, *Philosophy of Education*, 44–45.
17. Maritain, *Crossroads*, 66–68.

Of the scholastic educational philosophers—whether of that medieval time, e.g., Aquinas, or whether nearly a millennium later, e.g., Gilson—it can be said what was said of Aquinas himself:[18]

> He held that the learner has the active potency to arrive at knowledge of the unknown through discovery. All teaching must be guided by this principle. The signs and symbols that the teacher presents to the student must enable the latter to relate them to the first principles which support what he already knows. The teacher, then, must possess explicit knowledge to those first principles. As for curriculum, since the learner's intellectual knowledge is rooted in sense knowledge, he must acquire a knowledge of the material world before advancing to the world of metaphysics, which considers beings that exist apart from matter—that is, pure forms. Truth is rooted in the existence of things, and therefore the path to truth is the order of existence as it is apprehended by man.[19]

The goal of medieval education in general and of scholasticism (which prevailed in many Western universities circa AD 1000–1500 and still does in certain circles today) in particular was generally overtly religious, prioritizing the rediscovery of transcendental truths that would lead a person to God. With a name derived from the Latin *scholasticus*, which refers to things pertaining to school, it is appropriate that this system of thinking put such emphasis on academics. Methodologies for such discovery included doubt, philological analysis, and *a priori* knowledge (or even speculation),[20] but the aforementioned may have been overly prioritized with too little regard given to empirical and other *a posteriori* sources of truth, e.g., experimentation, linguistics, document-evidence, history, and other firsthand observations. Finally, many early scholastics tended to be Ptolemaic,[21] not just in their cosmogony, but also in their other sciences,[22] as well. Rightly, they highly regarded both revelation and

---

18. Quoted in Gangel and Benson, *Christian Education*, 114.

19. Quoted in Gangel and Benson, *Christian Education*, 114.

20. A helpful discussion of these methodologies and their historical development and significance can be found in Eby and Arrowood, *History and Philosophy*, 740–55.

21. The Ptolemaic system of cosmogony, among other things, posited that the earth was the fixed center of the universe.

22. There was a synchronic tendency of many medieval thinkers to be Ptolemaic in their view not only of cosmogony, but analogously to see man in general and individual man in particular to be centrist in one's capacity to seek, to discover, and to know truth, as well. Virtually all of the Ptolemaic tendencies of the earth being the center

reason—the Bible *and* human intellect; wrongly some may have *over*-emphasized neo-Platonic methods of discovery and not unlikely *under*-emphasized the noetic effects of the fall and its concomitant curse.[23]

---

of it all were abandoned at the time of the Copernican revolution bringing with it a prevalent heliocentrism. What is not as clear is if some neo-scholastics such as Gilson and Maritain have altogether abandoned a kind of epistemological anthropocentrism whose regard for man's individual epistemic capacity might be too elevated and whose view of the noetic effects of the fall might be too understated.

23. J. P Moreland and William Lane Craig provide a helpful discussion of this notion of the noetic effects of the fall in their *Philosophical Foundations for a Christian Worldview*, 18, 27, 164.

Chapter 7

TOWARD A CHRISTIAN UNDERSTANDING OF CONTINENTALISM

AS NEL NODDINGS, PROFESSOR emerita of philosophy of education at Stanford University, observed, "American philosophers of education have been [significantly] influenced by movements in Continentalism."[1] She goes on to describe this diverse movement (or a set of movements) referred to as Continentalism as including critical theory, phenomenology, hermeneutics, and postmodernism. She characterizes critical theory as the opposite of analytic philosophy, which "prizes detachment and the search for a neutral form of truth embedded permanently in language or the real world; critical theory insists that such detachment is both intellectually and morally irresponsible."[2] Noddings describes phenomenology as "a descriptive science concerned primarily with the objects and structures of consciousness."[3] Per Richard Rorty, hermeneutics in this Continental sense[4] is the "holistic line of argument that says we shall never be able to avoid the 'hermeneutical circle'—the fact that we cannot understand the parts of a strange culture, practice, theory,

---

1. Noddings, *Philosophy of Education*, 61.
2. Noddings, *Philosophy of Education*, 72.
3. Noddings, *Philosophy of Education*, 70.
4. The use of this term in this context is not the generic, conventional, "art and science of interpretation," but rather a particular school of thought, viz. a particular approach *to* hermeneutics.

language, or whatever. . . . This notion of understanding is more like getting acquainted with a person than like following a demonstration."[5] Finally, Noddings suggests that "when we look more deeply into [postmodern] epistemology, we will see that [many] contemporary educators are caught up in something called 'constructivism,'[6] which is thought by some to be an epistemological position and by others to be a *post-epistemological position*."[7]

Within each of the aforementioned continentalistic approaches to truth and to teaching, both epistemology and pedagogy are seen to be personal, constructivistic, experiential, and subjective. Therefore, Continentalists emphasize that education ought to cultivate such a personal, constructivistic, experiential, and subjective perspective in both the educator and in the student, as well.

Socrates (ca. 469–399 BC),[8] considered by many to be the father of Western philosophy, advised that "the unexamined life is not worth living." During his time, "the Athenian Areopagus was the official body which exercised a perfunctory supervision over all civic affairs and, likewise, over the education of the young. But it exercised little influence so

---

5. Noddings, *Philosophy of Education*, 76–77.

6. Based in no small part on the work of Jerome Bruner, *constructivism* asserts that people create (i.e., *construct*) their own understanding of reality by means of their idiosyncratic experiences and their personal reflections on those experiences. Constructivism posits learning as an active process—in the sense that learners *actively* create their own subjective representations of objective reality. New information gets connected with and assimilated by means of prior knowledge. Learners select experiential information, establish working hypotheses, and make subjective decisions regarding their constructed understanding of reality.

7. Noddings, *Philosophy of Education*, 78.

8. Many have suggested that this aforementioned perspective, as well as the roots of the aforementioned movements, grow out of the soils of Socrates. Socrates is included in this chapter *not* because he *was* a constructivist, a phenomenalist, a postmodernist, etc. He was not. He is included in this chapter for at least four reasons: (1) his influential if not iconic contributions to the history of the philosophy of education warrant inclusion in this book; (2) many thinkers in this chapter would point back to Socrates as being seminal or at least inspirational to their theory; (3) Socrates's educational emphases seem to reasonably fit the emphases of Continentalism as it is classified in this book; and (4) Socrates's educational emphases seem to fit the emphases of Continentalism better than Socrates's educational emphases seem to fit any of the other present eleven classifications. (In other words, to use Bailey's differentiator: The clustering within typologies in chs. 4–15 of this book utilizes *conceptual*, rather than *ancestral* criteria; his educational emphasis like the others represented in this chapter was largely about perspective and process.)

far as the actual educational practices were concerned," with the exception of mandating certain studies: "Were not the laws, which have charge of education, right in commanding your father to train you in music and gymnastic?"[9]

Socrates questioned such status quo. He believed that wisdom begins with admitting one's own ignorance; that self-knowledge is the ultimate wisdom; and that people could arrive at truth through a process of questioning. Although, as a teacher himself, he would speak with people of all classes, he preferred students who demonstrated "a readiness to learn, a power of retaining, self-control, and an ambition to excel in practical affairs."[10] His peripatetic style, his maieutic methodology, and his dialectical intent distinguished his approach from many who had preceded him. Although a bit of an iconoclast, Socrates did agree with the Areopagus on at least one aspect of education, i.e., that boys should commence their official schooling at age six.

Nicholas of Cusa (1401–1464) utilized paradox and irony to expose the presumption of scholastic theology that claimed to have successfully fathomed the unknowable depths of the knowledge of God. "Since ultimate truth is too simple to be known by human reason, it must be perceived by its opposite, which is *docta ignorantia* (i.e., *Learned Ignorance*, the title of his *magnum opus*.)."[11]

Friedrich Schleiermacher (1768–1834) was among many who categorized disciplines such as Christian education as "applied theology," with the task of formulating "rules of art" to guide the Christian educator.[12] Practically speaking, "Christian educators are challenged to devise curriculum that are consistent with the intellectual capacities of persons and, at the same time, evoke the imaginative character of the gospel."[13]

Friedrich Froebel (1782–1852), founder of kindergarten, was influenced heavily both by the idealism of Fichte and Hegel, as well as by the increasingly prevailing trends in science of his day.[14] Most fully in his book entitled *The Education of Man* (1826),[15] Froebel posited learning

9. Eby, *Ancient and Medieval*, 226–27.
10. Eby, *Ancient and Medieval*, 323.
11. Lockerbie, *Passion for Learning*, 126.
12. Seymour, *Theological Approaches*, 219.
13. Seymour, *Theological Approaches*, 253.
14. Gutek, *Historical and Philosophical Foundations*, 259.
15. Gutek, *Historical and Philosophical Foundations*, 265.

as *induction*. Written in obscure prose, he attempted to weave often disparate strands of philosophical idealism, Christian mysticism, romanticism, and science into a coherent educational philosophy. He emphasized art, architecture, and music in his curricula—including his 1843 classic, *Mutter und Kose Lieder* (Mothers Songs, Games, and Stories).

Regarded by many as one of the most influential Protestant thinkers of the twentieth century, Karl Barth (1886–1968) did not write much about education, per se, but from a section in *Church Dogmatics*, the following insights and perspectives are summarized.[16]

1. Children are needy beginners.

    1. Inept, inexperienced, unskilled, and immature.
    2. Sheer readiness to learn.

2. A child is characteristically to be at play.

    1. Untoiling involvement.
    2. Self-forgetfulness.
    3. Joyous objectivity.
    4. Clear-sighted cheerfulness.

3. Readiness to step into freedom.

    1. Relatively unencumbered.
    2. Readily apprehends God's call.

Author of *Truth and Method on Hermeneutics* (1960), Hans-Georg Gadamer (1900–2002) did not write extensively on education either, yet he "is credited with developing a hermeneutics not as an attempt to prescribe a method or set of methods for understanding, but to discover what is common to all modes of understanding and to show that understanding is never a subjective relation to a given 'object' but to the history of its effect."[17] The same author illustrates the application of this in the classroom. "It is critical for teachers to establish rapport with students to help them proceed from the already acquired experiences to the new ones, to apply the new language items to the personal life experiences, and to practice vigorously."[18]

---

16. Bunge, *Child in Christian Thought*, 393.
17. Cubukcu, "Gadamer's Philosophical Hermeneutics," 110.
18. Cubukcu, "Gadamer's Philosophical Hermeneutics," 115.

Cambridge philosopher Michael Oakeshott (1901–1990) commented that "to see oneself reflected in the mirror of the present modish world is to see a sadly distorted image of a human being, for there is nothing to encourage us to believe that what has captured the current fancy is the most valuable part of our inheritance, or that the better survives more readily than the worse. And nothing survives in this world which is not cared for by human beings."[19] Influenced heavily by Kant, Dilthey, and Hegel, Oakeshott described education and the other "human sciences"[20] as being not just interpretive, but *doubly* interpretive—since such disciplines study human behavior, which Oakeshott described as being interpretive itself.[21]

Revered by many as one of the most influential Catholic thinkers of the twentieth century, Karl Rahner (1904–1984) wrote,

> It is only in the child that the child in the simple and absolute sense of the term really begins. And that is the dignity of the child, his task and his claim upon us all that we can and must help him in this task. In serving the child in this way, therefore, there can be no question of any petty sentimentality. Rather it is the eternal value and dignity—that we are concerned with. . . . Who only becomes a share-er in God's interior life, that he becomes that child which he only begins to be in his own childhood.[22]

What Peter Berger refers to as "signals of transcendence, Rahner extends to actually defining child as infinite openness to the Infinite."[23]

Marianna Papastephanou (born c. 1970), a prominent and influential contemporary European philosopher of education, observes that the philosophy *in* and *of* education is often expected to consist of the

---

19. Gamble, *Great Tradition*, 636.

20. Oakeshott used the term *Geisteswissenschaften*, i.e., the sciences of mind, ideas, or culture.

21. Oakeshott seems to be using *interpretive* similarly to *subjective*. One interprets one's experiences subjectively and per that interpretation not only creates understanding for oneself via any science; but his larger point in this context seems to be that *that is doubly* the case in all of the human sciences (including education), because of the need for an *inter*-personal as well as an *intra*-personal feedback loop. In other words that first interpretive cycle not only creates a meaning for that particular interpreted experience, but it also then becomes a filter through which subsequent experiences get ("doubly") interpreted.

22. Bunge, *Child in Christian Thought*, 45.

23. Bunge, *Child in Christian Thought*, 443.

application of more general philosophy to the particularities of this field of education.[24] Elsewhere she suggests, "Philosophy *of* education is one of those fields that is marked by the ambivalence of the genitive 'of.' Due to the ambiguity of the genitive, whether education is the object of philosophy, or the subject thereof becomes unclear."[25] Papastephanou argues for a "kinetic interconnection" of *both* (what some might refer to as the "plenary" use of the genitive).[26]

> The issue of the presencing of unique subjectives in their intimate relation with the presencing of others is seminal for education.[27] It has profound significance for understanding the quality of space and of intellectual, volitional, and emotional bodies that occur within schools as educational institutions—that is to say their qualities as places of education.[28] But the realization of the

---

24. Ruitenberg, *What Do Philosophers Do*, 103.

25. Ruitenberg, *What Do Philosophers Do*, 130.

26. Christians do not lack illustrations of this *genitive*-ambiguity. Famously the Apostle Paul states that it is the love *of* Christ that compels us (cf. 2 Cor 5:14). Non-plenary grammarians would not unlikely suggest that *of* in this context would be *either* objective or subjective. If objective, then Christ being the object of our love would be that which compels us; i.e., "the love that we have for Christ compels us." If, on the other hand, the genitive *of* were to be read as a subjective genitive, then Christ would be the subject—the one doing the loving; i.e., "the love with which Christ loves us is that which compels us." If someone were to invoke a *plenary* (i.e., *both* objective *and* subjective at the same time, but in a converse or complementary way), then it would suggest that in some way and to some extent that it is *both* "the love that we have for Christ that compels us" and "the love with which Christ loves us that compels us." Papastephanou is not a non-plenary grammarian when it comes to the "grammar" of the "*of*" between the subject and the object of learning. Papastephanou invokes a plenary interpretation of the "*of*" between the subject and the object of learning. She sometimes calls this symbiotic relationship between the learner and that which is learned a "kinetic interconnection." *Kinetic* denotes movement; *interconnection* denotes a *mutual* or *dynamic* relationship in which a person, thing, or idea is linked or associated with some other person, thing, or idea. Papastephanou suggests that there is actually dynamic interplay (in almost a complexity or even a quantum type of way) between learner and that which is learned. In Papastephanou's philosophy of education, as soon as the student steps into the stream of learning, the posit that neither the student nor the stream is the same ever again, is a critical realization for educators of this ilk to facilitate students stepping into streams of kinetic interconnection.

27. In other words, she believes that it is very important to consider the context *and* the content of one's intended learning as a symbiotic element of the one learning and his/her learning process.

28. In other words, she believes that it is vitally important that schools regard the aforementioned *kinetic interconnection* between the learner and that which is being learned (as well as other learners) as holistically impactful on the learning endeavor.

rich potential of the expiration of schools conceived in this way requires the inclusion rather than the occlusion of the interiority of the individual.[29] Proper account needs to be taken of what one might term the "phenomenological self," with its own felt intentionality and intelligence that is both[30] always potentially transformatively engaged and subtly existentially enduring.[31]

Claudia Ruitenberg, assistant professor of the philosophy of education at the University of British Columbia, explores these notions, as well.

> To be a true description of consolidated meetings, action, praxis, and the event (and the enlarged thought they require) presupposes the exigency to learn, to desire knowing, and to respond

---

29. In other words, she believes that schools generally do not "breathe" this way anymore—as they once did, but that to reintroduce *kinetic interconnection* of the individual learner and its contextual particularities would allow the flow of school and learning to become (again) what it ought to be.

30. In other words, she believes in yet another plenary interpretation, viz. that the student *and* the stream *both*—that both change (in some way and to some extent) *and* stay the same (in some way and to some extent).

31. Ruitenberg, *What Do Philosophers Do*, 53. Subsequently Papastephanou, an eminently influential—albeit esoteric, if not even obfuscatious for some readers—European philosopher of education, asserts that the method that seems most suitable to the task is comprised of the following steps:

1. Critically locate one of the reasons for the philosophical objectification (especially in its institutional form) in the fashionable dualism between everydayness and epiphany, on which educators have so far remained silent.
2. To employ Sartre's idea of the practical-inert as an illustration and, in so doing, to go against the tendency in philosophy of education to neglect Sartre because he is no longer fashionable in general philosophy.
3. To take assessment as an example of an educational practice that is often regarded unfavorably, as stale, and uninspiring and unavoidably emerging from a supposed immersion of practico-inert everydayness, and to undo this by educationally rehabilitating centrality any redemptive politics and transcendent praxes.
4. To make the connections between the practico-inert and both Arendt's and Badiou's negative treatment of issues that are central to educational research, such as knowledge, human sciences, and statistics.
5. And, finally, to make the suggested subjective genitive mode more explicit by making educational philosophy "answer them back" precisely by showing how, if approached in the appropriate manner, some inexorable statistics may reveal philosophical-political inadvertence or complicity.

to everydayness thoughtfully. Instead of setting "epiphanic" notions as primary aims or ideals of philosophy, thus reducing education to the practico-inert, we must acknowledge instances where learning should be an end-in-itself and can affect the disruption of inert realities, philosophies, and sciences. If one does not learn to wander, reality remains unnoticed and non-thematicised. One asks to view questions, the search for truth is not set on course. In this way, method is the response to *aporia*; *aporia* is the rebirth of method, and education and philosophy are allies. Challenge to respond to the singularity that comes from the real life, to find a path, is, amongst other things, an invitation to (re)education and demand for a message somewhat unique.[32]

Continentalists come in a variety of shapes and stripes. Within all of the aforementioned continentalistic approaches to truth and to teaching, however, both epistemology and pedagogy are seen to be personal, constructivistic, experiential, and subjective. Education, therefore, is seen as largely the cultivation of such a perspective. These theories may sound appealing to some readers—and confounding to others. What is indisputable, however, is the significant impact that continentalists have had on the philosophy of education in Europe and America over the past century or so. That impact continues today.

Some of that impact may come as a result of some of the positive attributes and contributions of many of these theories. Favorable characteristics such as the following characterize no small part of these writings: authenticity, self-awareness, self-knowledge, interpersonal sensitivity, childlike faith, tolerance of doubt, looking beyond oneself and one's own limited epistemic background, and a desire to loosen up intellectual boundaries and uncover transformative truths.

Nonetheless, continental philosophies of education tend to be imprecise, evocative, and obfuscatory. They also seem to understate or even eschew absolute truth, authorial intent, and the perspicuity of the written text. Furthermore, most of the aforementioned thinkers overemphasize the contextualization or cultural-conditioned aspects of knowledge and of knowing. On the other hand, *analytical* approaches to philosophy (in

---

32. Ruitenberg, *What Do Philosophers of Education Do*, 146–47. Herein Ruitenberg merely paraphrases Papastephanou. In other words, she, too, believes in the integral importance of the symbiotic relationship between learner and that which is learned, and that the optimal path forward in learning entails the intentionally aware (and yet ambling) consolidation of meetings, action, praxis, and the event into a simultaneously subjective and objective learning singularity.

general and Christian analytical approaches to philosophy in particular) address these inadequacies and provide correction to these *errata* by emphasizing clear definitions and rigorous argumentation. A biblical philosophy of Christian school education must be built upon the scriptural foundations discussed in chapter 3 of this book, including the absoluteness, immutability, and eternality of truth as revealed by God through his word.

Chapter 8

TOWARD A CHRISTIAN UNDERSTANDING OF ROMANTICISM

ROMANTICISM IS CONSIDERED BY many to represent (or at least *seems* to be or *strives* to be) a philosophy of freedom—extolling the natural, primitive, uninhibited, and unbridled knowledge of and expression of oneself. Largely a reaction to scientific rationalization, Rousseau and many of the other Romanticists represented in this chapter believed that all humans—in particular children—were inherently good and naturally curious. Therefore, these Romanticists argued for the least possible restraint in educational contexts to allow the individual student to flourish most naturally. In terms of curricular emphases, creativity, literature, poetry, and the performing arts take front stage. Student-focused, student-centered, and student-guided methodologies manifest themselves in so-called organic, open, or "noble savage" pedagogies—all in the passionate pursuit of the student developing as a free, uninhibited, loving person untainted by the artificial constraints of an otherwise oppressive educational system and an otherwise restrictive society.

A bit of an iconoclast, Jean-Jacques Rousseau (1712–1778), prophet of Naturalism and advocate of child-centered educational practices,[1] abandoned the arguments of the deists and many of the philosophers of his day. In lieu of such conventional Enlightenment thinking, Rousseau advocated *amour de soi* ("love of self," often translated "self-esteem")[2]

---

1. Gutek, *Historical and Philosophical Foundations*, 135.
2. Rousseau held *amour de soi* in contradistinction to *amour proper*, which he

as the conduit through which the child's identity could be healthfully formed around natural instincts. Rousseau routinely asserted counter-classical content: "The only habit the child should be allowed to acquire is to contract none."[3] "Habit, routine, and custom mean nothing to [a child]. What he did yesterday has no effect on what he does today."[4]

At times Rousseau seems to take some epistemic leaps without substantiating his claims either with scientific evidence or with logical arguments, such as when he asserts unequivocally and without description or defense, "Children's first sensations are wholly in the realm of feeling."[5] On the other hand, some of his intuitions seem founded and evocative. "Nature wants children to be children before they are men. If we deliberately depart from this order, we shall get premature fruits which are neither ripe nor well-flavored, and which soon decay."[6] From the closing words of Emile himself, this insight from a young man regarding the role of teacher: "Lead me to imitate you, and enjoy your well-deserved rest."[7] Rousseau emphasized *amour de soi* as fundamental to healthy child development.

Johann Heinrich Pestalozzi (1747–1827), a proponent of educating the heart and the senses, authored *How Gertrude Teaches Her Children* (1801), in which Pestalozzi largely aligned his theories of education with Rousseauean rhetoric and ideology. He taught his son according to these ideologies, as well.[8] Pestalozzianism impacted schools in the United States largely in three phases:

1. Pestalozzi's methods were introduced in America by William Maclure and Joseph Neef.

2. Pestalozzi's theories were promoted by concerted efforts of Henry Bernard, common school pioneer.

---

disdained as mere selfishness.
3. Cahn, *Classic and Contemporary Readings*, 125.
4. Cahn, *Classic and Contemporary Readings*, 133.
5. Cahn, *Classic and Contemporary Readings*, 125.
6. Cahn, *Classic and Contemporary Readings*, 127.
7. Cahn, *Classic and Contemporary Readings*, 152.
8. Gutek, *Historical and Philosophical Foundations*, 150.

3. Pestalozzi's educational model was distributed by Edward A. Sheldon's development of a full-scale teacher education program at the Normal School at Oswego, New York.[9]

After Prussia was defeated by Napoleon, the German philosopher Johann Gottlieb Fichte (1762–1814) convincingly argued that the only hope his nation had would be in the adoption of the Pestalozzian system of education. His nation then became a land of "schoolmasters and pupils."[10] Elementary schools became public and free. "Illiteracy disappeared. School attendance was required of all children from six to fourteen years of age. The teachers, who were almost all men, were selected and trained with great care."[11]

Not infrequently called the "Father of Modern Liberal Theology," Friedrich Daniel Ernst Schleiermacher (1768–1834) was a German biblical scholar, theologian, and philosopher known for his attempts to reconcile the criticisms of the Enlightenment with Protestantism. In 1818 he famously preached a series of sermons on the Christian home, in which he conveyed many of his thoughts on childhood and education. "Like Rousseau, he saw play as a significant part of the learning process. He advocated cultivating the virtue of obedience daily from the very beginning. Parents, however, should not undertake the religious formation of children alone; pastors and schools should also participate."[12]

"Each age must write its own books,"[13] wrote Ralph Waldo Emerson (1803–1882), pioneer of New England Transcendentalism, which has been described as "an American literary, political, and philosophical movement of the early nineteenth century."[14] In his famous speech entitled *Transcendentalism*, Emerson famously posited the following regarding the process of knowledge acquisition:

> It is well known to most of my audience, that the Idealism of the present day acquired the name of Transcendental, from the use of that term by Immanuel Kant, of Konigsberg [sic], who replied to the skeptical philosophy of Locke, which insisted that there was nothing in the intellect which was not previously in the

9. Gutek, *Historical and Philosophical Foundations*, 169.
10. Eby, *Development of Modern Education*, 680.
11. Eby, *Development of Modern Education*, 680.
12. Bunge, *Child in Christian Thought*, 279.
13. Conway, *American Literacy*, 75.
14. Goodman, "Transcendentalism," para. 1.

experience of the senses, by showing that there was a very important class of ideas, or imperative forms, which did not come by experience, but through which experience was acquired, that these were intuitions of the mind itself, and he denominated them Transcendental forms.[15]

The philosophical explorations of Henry David Thoreau (1817–1862) into self and the world "led him to develop an epistemology of embodied perception and a non-dualistic account of mental and material life. . . . Thoreau's work anticipates certain later developments in pragmatism, phenomenology, and environmental philosophy, and poses a perennially valuable challenge to our conception of the methods and intentions of philosophy itself"[16]—not to mention the philosophy of education.

Marietta Pierce Johnson (1864–1938) was an educational reformer and a Georgist.[17] In 1907 she founded a progressive school called The School of Organic Education.[18] Mrs. Johnson thought that children should live natural lives and not be forced to read at a young age. She required crafts and dancing to complement academic curriculum. Mrs. Johnson advocated schools with no homework, no exams, no grades, and no failures. Her school peaked in the 1920s, not unlikely in no small part due to John Dewey's favorable review of Mrs. Johnson and of her school.[19]

Herbert Kohl (b. 1937) is considered to be the father of the *open school movement* and the originator of the term *open classroom*.

> The role of the teacher is not to control his pupils but rather to enable them to make choices and to pursue what interests them. In an open classroom, a pupil functions according to his sense of himself rather than what he is expected to be, It is not that the teacher should expect the same of all his pupils. On the contrary, the teacher must learn to perceive differences, but these should

---

15. Goodman, "Transcendentalism," para. 1.

16. Furtak, "Henry David Thoreau," para. 1.

17. Georgism was a largely nineteenth-century, American economic philosophy named after economist Henry George who advocated a single-tax system.

18. Now, this school is known as the Marietta Johnson School of Organic Education in Fairhope, Alabama.

19. The Organic School, "About Us," http://www.fairhopeorganicschool.com/about-us/.

emerge from what actually happens in the classroom during the school year, and not from preconceptions.[20]

Patricia Heidenry,[21] a contemporary St. Louisan, shocked many readers with her *New York Times Magazine* article in 1975. "My husband and I are keeping our children out of school."[22] She describes homeschooling as idyllic. "By chance I read *How Children Learn* by John Holt shortly after I read *Summerhill*. Everything Holt said about how children learn reflected what I was observing in my own children."[23]

One of Mrs. Heidenry's children, Margaret, later described the family's curriculum and daily schedule as follows:

- 9:30: Reading.
- 10:00: Mathematics.
- 10:30: Science.
- 11:00: Yoga and tea break (with parents).
- 11:30: Drawing and painting.
- 12:30: Lunch.
- 1:30: Writing:
    - Monday and Tuesday: Play of the week.
    - Wednesday: Correspondence.
    - Thursday and Friday: Writing and illustrating stories.
- 2:30: History and geography.
- 3:00: Yoga and break.
- 6:30: Spanish.

Years later, the mother sent all of her four children back to school, but she claims that all four of her children—largely due to years of being schooled at home—had become among "the warmest, sweetest people you will ever meet."

Margaret concludes her article with these allusions to her mother: "In her article, my mother laid out the basic tenets of her approach to educating us. 'They work at their own pace,' she wrote. 'They have no

---

20. Kohl, *Open Classroom*, 20.

21. In the homeschool movement, there can be found curricula and philosophies of education representing each of the thirteen schools of thought covered in this book. This particular homeschool family, the only one explicitly referenced as such in this book, seems to represent Rousseau's romanticism. So, it is listed in this particular chapter. An entire book could be done on, for example, thirteen divergent schools of thought within the homeschool community in late twentieth-century America.

22. Cahn, *Classic and Contemporary Readings*, 302.

23. Cahn, *Classic and Contemporary Readings*, 303.

assignments to complete. . . . I am not teaching the children. I am permitting them to learn."

> My mother concluded her *Times* article by emphasizing that educating her children at home was a reflection of her most cherished beliefs. "Children's lives are more than products that must be molded until they adapt well to society, or to another school, or to the work force. As it is now, a child's life is very much bound up with schools and schooling, and that animating force that gives life to each child is ignored." Today she still holds that her work was not in vain. "You're all well-adjusted and happy. And, all of you are close to one another. What else could I possibly want?"[24]

Kieran Egan writes about *Open Education*, which extends Rousseaueanism to the removal of "any and all" obstacles. "Open Education is optimistic in its assessment of human nature, believing that children's curiosity will lead them naturally towards things of educational value, so that if each child's interests are allowed to determine his or her activities in school, they—better than any externally imposed scheme—will lead to the best education for that child."[25]

Open education is motivated by a belief that learners desire to exercise agency in their studies. Specifically, people engaged in the learning process want to conduct inquiries about potential topics of study, to have a hands-on educational experience instead of a strictly textbook-focused education, to take responsibility for their educational decisions, to experience the emotional and physical side of education, to understand how education and community are related, and to have personal choice in the focus of their classroom studies. These learners do a great deal for one another in promoting learning.

Egan posits that learning in a group environment or contributing to a group is beneficial to the learner. Collaborative group work has substantial benefits, such as increased participation by all of the group members, better understanding and retention of material, mastery of skills essential to success, and increased enthusiasm that can spur the participant on to independent learning.

The philosophy of an open education centers on student learning and sees the teacher become the learning assistant. Teachers are

---

24. Heidenry, "Home-Schooling Anarchists."
25. Cahn, *Classic and Contemporary Readings*, 308.

to observe, guide, and provide materials for the learners. The teachers should facilitate not dominate the learning process. Open education is optimistic in the belief that the freedom of choice and student direction will promote a better quality of learning.

One organization committed to such Open Education is www.openlearning.com. This group writes:

> We understand that for students to learn deeply, they need to be active, engaged, inspired, and involved. They need to interact with their peers, connect dots between new and current knowledge, and they need to have fun in the process! We promote dynamic communication through fun and interactive learning communities, where students can discuss and reflect on their experiences, share relevant and meaningful media, and connect with their peers in a safe and positive learning space.[26]

Open education, organic education, Rousseauism, and other forms of Romanticism portray a beautiful picture of a free child and a flourishing adult. One of their greatest assets is *a* high view of humanity; one of their greatest liabilities is *their* high view of humanity. In other words, no one should have a higher view of humanity than Christians.

Christians believe that every person is created in the *imago Dei*, and is imbued with individuality, beauty, dignity, and infinite worth.[27] Furthermore, Christians believe that everyone who has been saved by grace through faith has been so saved unto the good works that God has laid out in advance for that individual to do—as the *poiema* of God that redeemed person is.[28]

However, Christians also believe that in Adam and Eve all humans fell, and that the spiritual, noetic, and relational effects of the fall and its concomitant curse affect each human with a finite, fallible, and fallen nature. So, for Christian educators to see their students rightly, they need to see people like Jesus saw people, i.e., as sin-bent sheep needing a shepherd.[29]

Romanticism is considered by many within education to represent a philosophy of freedom—extolling the natural, primitive, uninhibited, and

---

26. As cited at www.openlearning.com.
27. Gen 1:26–28; Ps 139.
28. Eph 2:8–10.
29. Matt 9:36, which says, "When [Jesus] saw the crowds, he had compassion for them, because they were harassed and helpless, like sheep without a shepherd."

unbridled knowledge of and expression of oneself. Romanticists believe that all humans—in particular, children—are inherently good and independently curious. Therefore, these theorists argue for the least possible restraint in educational contexts in order to free the student to pursue natural, personal fulfillment. However, in light of the depravity of every student and the inherent bent away from what is beautiful, good, and true, Romanticists' student-focused, student-centered, or student-guided methodologies and curricula should give way to more sage-on-the-stage, truth-based, biblio-centric, God-focused approaches to education in order to provide curricular content and clarity and to construct fence-posts of God's revealed beauty, goodness, and truth within which the student can more freely and more rightly graze.

Chapter 9

Toward a Christian Understanding of Existentialism

THEMES OF EXISTENTIALISM ARE both ancient and contemporary, individual and systems, intentionality and being, absurdity and meaning, religious and nonreligious, dialogue and choice. To put all of the following thinkers under one umbrella is a bit of a stretch even for an umbrella as expansive as *existentialism*. Nonetheless, for each of the following thinkers, and for any other educational existentialist, a key component is the freedom of humans to choose to make themselves.

"In this sense, 'existence precedes essence. We make ourselves; we create our essence.'"[1] Educational existentialists believe in the ultimate freedom of humans to choose to make themselves, therefore, educational existentialists emphasize that education ought to foster a student's individual quest for becoming, for achieving meaning, and for clarifying value.

Existentialistic education emphasizes individual existence, freedom, and choice. It posits that each student defines his own meaning. Existentialist educators endeavor to provide pathways for students to explore their own values, meanings, and choices—via discussions, creative projects, and choice of topics to study. The student is to determine their own identity and essence by means of a dialogue between self and

1. MacIntyre, "Existentialism," 147.

society: considering both oneself within a particular cultural context and considering cultural values in relation to oneself.

Joseph Jacotot (1770–1840) posited emancipatory equality or the *panecastic* method.[2] It was based upon four principles:

1. All men have equal intelligence.

2. Every man has received from God the faculty of being able to instruct himself.

3. Humans can teach even what they do not know.

4. Everything is in everything and can be taught and learned by anyone.

Maria Montessori (1870–1952) was a proponent of early childhood education. Her son, Mario, would later establish the AMI (Association Montessori Internationale) in 1929, which embodied his mother's "scientific pedagogy" that "all children at birth possess a psychic power, an inner self-teacher that stimulates their own self-directed learning."[3]

1. The principle of freedom to explore the environment in order to gain greater independence.

2. The development of the will—the moral sense—by choosing the material with which to work, one will engage and one will respect the rights of others to choose their own material.

3. The power of attention, in which the child concentrates on accomplishing a task.

4. The principle of work, by which a child stays at a task, often performing repetitive actions, until it is mastered.

Martin Buber (1878–1965), a famous Austrian Jewish existential philosopher, once concluded his 1926 educators' conference comments by advocating an "inner religious impulse" to serve the One who is "able to do what humans beings cannot do on their own—not only to form, but to *transform* and even to create."

---

2. Derived from the French *panécastique*, "everything in each," which he had transliterated from the Greek *pan* (all) and *ekaston* (each).

3. Gutek, *Historical and Philosophical Foundations*, 368.

"When all [cultural] figures are shattered, when no figure is able to any more dominate and shape the present human material, what is there left to form? Only the image of God. That is the indefinable, only factual, direction of the responsible modern educator."[4]

Buber defines education as the *imitatio Dei absconditi sed non ignoti*.[5] Buber later suggests that education is not insignificantly about an individual rediscovering their internal unity—a unity, which he argues, is analogous and even "related mysteriously to the dynamic unity of the whole, the eternal."[6] Thus, the educator who helps bring human beings back to their own unity will help to put them again "face to face with God."[7]

> Trust, trust in the world, because the human being exists—that is the most inward achievement of the relation in education. Because this human being exists, meaninglessness, however hard-pressed you are by it, cannot be the real truth. Because this human being exists, in the darkness the light lies hidden, in fear of salvation, and in the callousness of one's fellow-men the great Love.[8]

Editor, novelist, conservationist, and existential philosopher of education Harold Titus (1888–1967) hailed the fundamental significance of the philosophy of education. "An education that fails to consider the fundamental questions of human existence—the questions of life and the nature of truth, goodness, beauty, and justice, with which philosophy is concerned—is a very inadequate type of education."[9] He de-emphasized studying the history of thought or the methodology of education in deference to what he considered basic human questions.

Carl Rogers (1902–1987) began his formal training for ministry at a seminary and then crossed the street, matriculated to Columbia University, and abandoned Christianity in favor of secular humanism. Ascribing to many of Maslow's manifests, Rogers extended the reach of secular humanism in education in general and of developmentalism in particular. "The organism has one basic tendency and striving—to actualize,

---

4. Hodgson, *God's Wisdom*, 4.
5. I.e., the imitation of God who is hidden, but not unknown.
6. Hodgson, *God's Wisdom*, 4.
7. Hodgson, *God's Wisdom*, 4.
8. Buber, *Between Man and Man*, ix.
9. Knight, *Philosophy and Education*, v.

maintain, and enhance the experiencing organism."[10] To achieve ones *summum bonum* of self-actualization, Rogers posited three necessary and sufficient relational and pedagogical conditions:

1. Empathy.

2. Congruence.

3. Unconditional positive regard.[11]

He writes about the following five aims of education:

1. Open to experience: both positive and negative emotions are to be accepted. Negative feelings are not denied, but worked through (rather than resorting to ego defense mechanisms).
2. Existential living: being in touch with different experiences as they occur in life, avoiding prejudging and preconceptions. Being able to live and fully appreciate the present, not always looking back to the past or forward to the future, but rather living in the moment and for the moment.
3. Trust feelings: feeling, instincts and gut-reactions are paid attention to and trusted. People's own decisions are the right ones, and they should trust themselves to make the right choices.
4. Creativity: creative thinking and risk taking are features of a person's life. Creativity involves the abilities to adjust, to change, and to seek new experiences.
5. Fulfilled life: the person is happy and satisfied with life, and always looking for new challenges and experiences.[12]

Benjamin Spock (1903–1998) did not "adhere to the old-fashioned regimented methods of child-rearing. His advice went against the grain of what most child-development experts of the times advocated, among them noted children's expert Dr. John Watson, who insisted that 'kissing and coddling infants is taboo.'"[13] Advocating a more intuitive approach to working with children, Spock encouraged adults, "You know more than you think you do."[14] "A child is born with a greater capacity to love than

---

10. Rogers, *Client-Centered Therapy*, 487.
11. Rogers, *Client-Centered Therapy*, 487.
12. McLeod, *Carl Rogers*, para. 14–18.
13. Conway, *American Literacy*, 237.
14. Conway, *American Literacy*, 235.

to hate, to build than to destroy, and to profit from every chance to learn and to mature."[15]

Victor Frankl (1905–1997), an Austrian neurologist and psychiatrist, became a Holocaust survivor and founder of Logotherapy. Logotherapy offers significant educational implications and existential insights. In contrast to many other existentialists, humanists, and developmentalists of his day, however, Frankl insisted:

> Freedom, however, is not the *last* word. Freedom is only part of the story and half of the truth. Freedom is but the negative aspect of the whole phenomenon whose positive aspect is responsibleness. In fact, freedom is in danger of degenerating into mere arbitrariness unless it is lived in terms of responsibleness. That is why I recommend that the Statue of Liberty on the East Coast be supplemented by a Statue of Responsibility on the West Coast.[16]

Frankl's emphases on individual responsibility, on focused purposefulness, and on the potency of sustaining and being sustained by one's substantive *raison d'être* continue to provide guidance to educators, inspiration to students, and correctives to existential angst, existential nihilism, and existential despair found in so many of his contemporary existentialists.

Van Cleve Morris (1921–2013) authored multiple influential books on an existential philosophy of education, including *Existentialism in Education*; *Philosophy and the American School*; and *Principals in Action*. His points of emphasis have been summarized as each student and every teacher realizing that (s)he is a:

1. *Choosing* agent: unable to avoid choosing their way through life.

2. *Free* agent: absolutely free to set the goals of life.

3. *Responsible* agent: personally accountable for free choices as they are revealed in how life is lived.[17]

Parker Palmer (b. 1929), a Quaker and a Berkeley grad, is the founder and senior partner of the Center for Courage and Renewal, which

---

15. Conway, *American Literacy*, 238.
16. Frankl, *Man's Search for Meaning*, 209–10.
17. Knight, *Philosophy and Education*, 81.

oversees the "Courage to Teach" program for K–12 educators across the country. He suggests that

> the culture of disconnection that undermines teaching and learning is driven partly by fear. But it is also driven by our Western commitment to thinking in polarities, a thought form that elevates disconnection into an intellectual virtue. The way of thinking is so embedded in our culture that we rarely escape it, even when we try.
>
> But my deeper hope comes with Rilke's words, "and the point is to live everything." Of course, that is the point! If I do not fully live the tensions that come my way, those tensions do not disappear, they go underground and multiply. I may not know how to solve them, but wrapping my life around them and trying to live out their resolution, I open myself to new possibilities and keep tension from tearing me apart.[18]

Written for school teachers and teachers-in-training, Jacques Rancière's (b. 1940) *The Ignorant Schoolmaster: Five Lessons in Intellectual Emancipation*[19] challenges educators to consider equality as a starting point—not a destination. In other words, Rancière suggests that an uneducated or unintelligent person could teach another ignorant person, and conversely that "there is stultification whenever one intelligence is subordinated to another; whoever teaches without emancipating stultifies. . . . I must teach you that I have nothing to teach you."[20]

Tim Herrmann references a meta-analysis of best practices and principles of what he calls "effective education":[21]

1. Relational: Encourage contact between students and teacher.

2. Responsive: Develop reciprocity and cooperation among students.

3. Active: Use engaging learning modalities.

4. Purposeful: Provide prompt and particular feedback.

5. Dynamic: Emphasize time on task.

---

18. Johnson and Reed, *Philosophical Documents in Education*, 258–76.

19. Originally titled *Le Maître ignorant: Cinq leçons sur l'émancipation intellectuelle*, published in 1987.

20. Rancière, *Ignorant Schoolmaster*, 18, 15.

21. Beers, *Soul of Christian University*, 81.

6. Challenging: Communicate high expectations.

7. Diverse: Respect the varied talents and styles of learning with the classroom.

Calvin Miller (1936–2012), evangelical pastor, seminary professor, and author of more than seventy books, penned these practically poignant, very Christian, and yet extremely existential words:

> The edge is a good address. It is a good place to remember our temporariness. It teaches us to spend our time wisely. So, our last days can become our best days.
> Life is good. So is God.
> And, life with God is full of glorious daybreaks. After all, it was God who gave me the courage to walk the edges of a life that was never mine!
> May we all not take for granted each and every daybreak and remember we are living a life that is ultimately not ours.[22]

Themes of existentialism are both ancient and contemporary, individual and systems, intentionality and being, absurdity and meaning, religious and nonreligious, dialogue and choice, existence and essence. To put all of the aforementioned thinkers under one umbrella is a bit of a stretch—even for an umbrella as expansive as *existentialism*. Nonetheless, for each of the aforementioned thinkers, and for any other educational existentialist, a key component is the freedom of humans to choose to make themselves.

"In this sense, 'existence precedes essence. We make ourselves; we create our essence.'"[23] Educational existentialists believe in the ultimate freedom of humans to choose to make themselves, therefore, educational existentialists emphasize that education ought to foster a student's individual quest for becoming, for achieving meaning, and for clarifying value.

To summarize a single, comprehensive, and coherent response to existential philosophies of education would likely primarily entail acknowledging their emphases on human freedom and its concomitant responsibility. Whether for an atheist like Sartre, a Jew like Buber or Frankl, a liberal like Herrmann or More, or an Evangelical like Calvin Miller, freedom and responsibility rule the day. But, the perceived source,

---

22. Miller quoted in, Stezter, "Calvin Miller Has Died" para. 7–10.
23. MacIntyre, "Existentialism," 147.

purpose, and destiny of that freedom and responsibility differ diametrically depending on the particular thinker's worldview. Although existentialism is not likely a sustainable, comprehensive philosophy in the sense that analytical philosophy is; and although existentialism is not a sustainable, comprehensive worldview like biblical Christianity is; nonetheless, some elements of existentialism bear regarding and implementing judiciously, prudently, and Christianly.[24] Freedom[25] and responsibility are such a conjoined element.

On the other hand, such judicious, prudent, and Christian regard for educational existentialism cannot be without significant caution. Such caution appropriately and primarily focuses on most of educational existentialists' errant metaphysics, epistemology, and axiology. An individual student may be free and concomitantly responsible, but not so free as to create his or her own reality, truth, or value.

God is sovereign. God spoke everything into existence—imbuing its essence, value, and meaning. God reveals truth, and he sets (i.e., he *is*) the standard of right and wrong. He sends his Son that we might be free from sin, death, and hell; whom he sets free is free indeed; and it is in fact for freedom's sake that Christ has set us free, but biblical, Christian freedom is freedom *from* the slavery of law, sin, and death, and freedom *to* live in the Spirit—free to live an abundant life with fruit of, in, and by the Spirit. An individual student can and ought to be shepherded in *this* kind of *ultimate* freedom—any other freedom is not real freedom at all.[26]

---

24. One such element is freedom and concomitant responsibility that seems so prevalent in Paul's portrait of Christian living captured in Gal 5:1—6:10. One Bible scholar and educational leader comments that "it's not the dreams you dream, but the choices you make." This rather existential sentiment (and its Christian college presidential source) will be included in ch. 16.

25. Critically important is the distinction between existentialists' notion of individual freedom entailing one's ability to create one's own essence. A biblical philosophy of Christian school education would need to consider the ultimate corrective to that, viz. the sovereignty of God. This truth has extensive and intensive implications for one's philosophy of what it means to be human and what it means to be educated. As cited on multiple occasions earlier in this book and in the closing chapter, as well, the essence of being human is not something that the individual human creates, but that the Creator spoke that individual into existence, knit that person together in his mother's womb, and is (in the case of the redeemed) re-creating that individual as his *poiema*—cast in the character of Christ to do the good works that God laid out in advance for him/her to do.

26. Gen 1; John 8, 10; John 15; Gal 5:1—6:10.

Chapter 10

Toward a Christian Understanding of Pragmatism

Although pragmatism as a philosophy is largely a late nineteenth-century and early twentieth-century American phenomenon, (1) elements[1] of it extend back at least as far as Democritus, and (2) its impact on educational philosophy can still be extensively observed today. Sometimes referred to as "experientialism,"[2] this school of thought emphasizes that which can be experienced or observed as that which is actually real. Pragmatists believe that the world is dynamic, evolving, and ever-changing, and that as a result, *truth* is that which "works"—i.e., that which allows the learner to navigate the dynamics of his ever-evolving universe and his ever-evolving context. Educational emphases include social contextualization, adaptation, hands-on problem-solving, cross-curricular integration, experimentation, situational ethics, new experiences connected to prior experiences, educative-growth, associated living of democracy, the scientific method, and preparing students for citizenship, daily living, and careers.

According to Democritus (ca. 460–ca. 370 BC), known as the "laughing philosopher" (due to his emphasis on cheerfulness), the knowledge of truth is difficult, since perception coming through the senses is subjective, and truth is not. Democritus argues that from the senses humans

---

1. No pun intended.
2. Or, *instrumentalism*.

derive differing impressions. As a result, our judgment of what is actually and objectively true is blurred.

According to Democritus there are two kinds of knowing. He calls the one "legitimate" (*gnēsiē*, "genuine") and the other "bastard" (*skotiē*, "secret"). The "bastard" knowledge is concerned with the perception through the senses, therefore, it is insufficient and subjective. The "legitimate" knowledge can be achieved only through inductive use of the intellect synthesizing sensory data. All sense data from the "bastard" knowledge must be filtered through reasoning. Only through this mechanism can one attempt to escape the false perception of the "bastard" knowledge and begin to grasp the truth through the inductive reasoning—a primitive precursor to inferential aspects of inductive sciences of much later periods of history.[3] He applied his own methods to his advances in atomism, geometry, and astronomy.

Vitruvius (ca. 70–ca. 25 BC) wrote about architecture and its concomitant sciences of aesthetics, acoustics, optics, geography, and engineering. This Roman designer wrote extensively about educating engineers. He posited that the engineering student should become "a man of letters, a skillful draftsman, a mathematician, familiar with scientific enquiries, a diligent student of philosophy, acquainted with music, not ignorant of medicine, learned in the responses of the jurisconsults, and familiar with astronomical observations."[4] Such a polymath approach to education was to prepare the engineer for his work, for his career, for his hands-on betterment of society.

Christian Thomasius (1655–1728) and Christian Wolff were among the scholars of their day that asserted that all that Aristotle had said was false. Their distrust of antiquities extended beyond one Athenian to a general rejection of and radical disregard for the classics as viable bases for education. They contended that "the lack of progress in science and philosophy was due to the pedantic adherence to Latin as the medium of expression."[5] The teacher's "task is to seek the truth through his own investigation, and to lead his students to do the same. Independent thought is the right and duty of everyone."[6]

---

3. Sylvia, "Democritus."
4. Eby, *Ancient and Medieval*, 550.
5. Eby, *Development of Modern Education*, 344.
6. Eby, *Development of Modern Education*, 345.

In his *On the Study Methods of Our Time*, Italian philosopher, historian, and humanist Giambattista Vico (1668–1744) declared, "Let our efforts not be directed towards achieving superiority over the Ancients merely in the field of science, while they surpass us in wisdom; let us not be merely more exact and more true than the Ancients, while allowing them to be more eloquent than we are; let us equal the Ancients in the fields of wisdom and eloquence as we excel them in the domain of science."[7]

Johann Friedrich Herbart (1776–1841) has been called the "father of the modern science of education"[8] and the "father of modern psychology."[9] An influential German philosopher, psychologist, and educator, Herbart had a major impact on American education up to and eventually through John Dewey. Freeman Butts and Lawrence Cremin summarize the essence of Herbart's ideas:

> Herbart argued that the mind itself was nothing but a set of perceptions and ideas that had been linked together as the individual received impressions from the external world. Simple perceptions and simple ideas became associated and were built up into more complex combinations known as the "apperceptive mass" which was the mind. When two or more ideas have been closely related by frequent, or recent, or vivid association, they will be more likely to continue to be related in future similar experiences. Teaching must take account for the association of ideas by making sure that new subject matter is related in the student's mind to his former ideas.[10]

Mary Lyon (1797–1849) founded the Mount Holyoke Female Seminary. She later authored its *Principles and Design*:

> It is principally devoted to the preparing of female teachers. At the same time, it will qualify ladies for other spheres of usefulness. The design is to give a solid, extensive, and well-balanced English education, connected with that of general improvement, that moral culture, and those enlarged views of duty, which will prepare ladies to be educators of their children and youth, rather than to fit them to be mere teachers, as the term has been technically applied. Such an education is needed by

---

7. Gamble, *Great Tradition*, 488.
8. Eby, *Development of Modern Education*, 758.
9. Kienel, *History of Christian School Education*, 1:259.
10. Kienel, *History of Christian School Education*, 1:259.

every female who takes charge of a school, and sustains the responsibility of guiding the whole course and of forming the entire character of those committed to her care. And when she has done with the business of teaching in a regular school, she will not give up her profession; she will still need the same well-balanced education at the head of her own family and in guiding her own household.[11]

John Stuart Mill (1806–1873), philosopher of utilitarianism and proponent of liberalism, provided perhaps the most complete rendition of his philosophy in his *Introduction to the Principles of Morals and Legislation* (1789). His analysis of educational theory is akin to his Utilitarian tutors Jeremy Bentham and James Mill. He posits that it is possible and desirable to frame social, political, and educational policies that advance the interest of both the individual and the society. The kind of society that Mill advocated would recognize the values of individual freedom of thought and expression and encourage disinterested and objective examination and action on social issues. Mills's preferred a kind of individualism that looked beyond special interests to true social progress[12] and to something better than "mere unguided instinct."[13]

Herbert Spencer (1820–1903) advocated individualism, science, social Darwinism, and its concomitant curricular emphases. He emphasized:

1. Self-preservation and physical health of the body.

2. The self-preservation of human life by providing the necessities of life such as earning a living.

3. Rearing and educating children.

4. Maintaining proper social and political relationships such as civic education.

5. Making time for miscellaneous leisure activities that provide enjoyment and satisfaction such as art, literature, drama, poetry, and music.[14]

---

11. Lockerbie, *Passion for Learning*, 264.
12. Gutek, *Historical and Philosophical Foundations*, 290.
13. Cahn, *Classic and Contemporary Readings*, 209.
14. Gutek, *Historical and Philosophical Foundations*, 304.

Methodologically,

1. Begin with children's immediate and direct experience.

2. Use concrete situations before moving on to abstract problems.

3. Let children learn from the natural consequences of their actions rather than from artificial rewards and punishments.

4. Avoid rote memorization of highly verbal lessons.

5. Impress on children the practical application of what they are learning.[15]

William James (1842–1910), a philosopher and medical doctor, is considered by many to be the "Father of American Psychology." Among other impacts in the field of education, he is recognized as having been the first professor to offer a psychology course. Along with Charles Sanders Peirce and John Dewey, James was one of the early and influential pragmatists in America. He defined truth as that which could prove useful to the user; he argued that the vast array of an individual's experiences could only be made meaningful through a kind of radical empiricism, and he held to a syncretistic epistemology prioritizing the simultaneity of correspondence and coherence.

John Dewey (1859–1952) was a pragmatist philosopher and progressive educator.[16] His version of pragmatism could be called experimentalism and can be summarized with the following process-oriented methodology.[17] "The child's life is an integral, total one. He passes quickly and readily from one topic to another, as from one spot to another, but is not conscious of transition or break."[18]

Dewey describes the aims of education as "enabling individuals to continue their capacity for growth."[19] He argues that minds and mental states are not in and of themselves, but are "purposeful engagement in a course of action,"[20] and even that "no thought, no idea, can possibly be

---

15. Gutek, *Historical and Philosophical Foundations*, 304.

16. "John Dewey did more to shape educational methodology than anyone else in the twentieth century," according to Pearcey, *Total Truth*, 238.

17. Pearcey, *Total Truth*, 344–45.

18. Cahn, *Classic and Contemporary Readings*, 221.

19. Cahn, *Classic and Contemporary Readings*, 242.

20. Cahn, *Classic and Contemporary Readings*, 253.

conveyed as an idea from one person to another."[21] Thus, "processes of instruction are unified in the degree to which they center in the production of good habits of thinking."[22]

Dewey insightfully lamented extremes in educational foci: "On the one hand, there will be reactionaries that claim that the main, if not the sole, business of education is transmission of the cultural heritage. On the other hand, there will be those who hold that we should ignore the past and deal only with the present and the future."[23]

John Dewey's experimental or process-oriented method consisted of five phases:

1. The person encounters something different, a new experience or deviant particular that stops the flow of ongoing activity. It is in the context of this new element that the person finds herself or himself in a problematic situation. Note that the problematic situation can be used educationally when a student or group of students encounters a problem needing to be solved.
2. For the person to solve the problem, the element that is blocking activity must be located and defined. The question needs to be asked, "What is causing the problem?" Once a definition is posed, the person can begin to locate and solve the problem. In the educational situation, the ability to define the problem correctly is an important skill. The definitional phase of problem solving, if correctly done, will point the learner to the resources needed to solve the problem.
3. After the problem has been located and defined, it is then possible to gather information, do research, and consult the previous experience that will shed light on the problem and point to its resolution. In the educational situation, this phase may involve researching in the library, conducting interviews, and collecting information. In this stage, the teacher functions as a resource person who facilitates students' research activities.
4. Next comes the conjectural stage, in which tentative hypotheses of possible action are structured. The person or group reflects on the possible actions and mentally explores the consequences of each. Now the question becomes, "If I do this, what is the likely result?" In the educational situation, the goal is to develop reflective

---

21. Cahn, *Classic and Contemporary Readings*, 257.
22. Cahn, *Classic and Contemporary Readings*, 259.
23. Dewey, *Experience and Education*, 78.

attitudes that contribute to planning skills. Such plans, called "ends in view," give direction to experience.

5. The last stage involves acting on the tentative hypothesis that is likely to resolve the problem by affecting the projected and desired consequences. If the problem is solved, the procedures of the complete act of thought have been followed correctly. If it is not resolved, the process needs to be reexamined to identify mistakes that have interfered with its solution. If the problem is solved, the person resumes activity and adds the particular problem-solving episode to her or his network of experience. In the educational situation, the final step of the problem-solving sequence is of crucial importance. Unlike many conventional school situations where problem-solving stays strictly academic, it requires action, an empirical test. It is this stage that avoids the dualism of theory and practice and integrates them into complete thinking.[24]

George Albert Coe (1862–1951) was a philosophical Darwinian and a theological liberal. He describes his approach to a theory of education as "presentism."

> Of course, we cannot reconstruct anything unless we are acquainted with it; we cannot take a creative part in the moral order without intelligence as to its present and its past. But the focal point of true education is not acquaintance with the past, it is the building forth of a future different from the present and from the past. Moreover, creative education implies that the nature and the degree of this difference are to be determined within and by means of the educative process; they cannot be dictated or imposed; they cannot be discovered by exegesis of any historical document.[25]

Ferdinand C. S. Schiller (1864–1937), Oxford-educated German philosopher and pragmatic humanist, argued against the Idealism that was rather prevalent in both British and American philosophy during his time. Of Schiller and his pragmatic approach to education and learning, it was said:

> He was a man whose training in the hard-headedness of science never completely subdued his soft-hearted belief that men are not merely automata, strictly determined in a mechanical

---

24. Gutek, *Historical and Philosophical Foundations*, 344–45.
25. Gangel, *Christian Education*, 306.

world, but are, to some degree, the makers and shapers of their world. He was a man who was eternally ready to lend a sympathetic ear to the wildest of theories, because he could not be convinced that all wisdom was of the academy or that there was only one clearly marked road to truth.[26]

Historian, Christian humanist, and non-secular pragmatist Christopher Dawson (1889–1970) produced about twenty books, including *The Crisis of Western Education* (1961). In that essay, his *magnum opus*, he wrote:

> So long as the Christian tradition of higher education still exists, the victory of secularism even in a modern technological society is not complete. There is still a voice to bear witness to the existence of the forgotten world of spiritual reality in which man has his true being. . . . The ultimate end of the whole process is a state of spiritual communion in which every individual shares in the experience of the whole and contributes according to his powers to the formation of "the final pooled intelligence," to use Dewey's expression, which is in the democratic mind.[27]

Israel Scheffler (1923–2014), Harvard University professor of philosophy of science and education, describes what he calls the "democratic ideal" in education. He posits the fundamental consideration of education and the philosophy of education being those ideals of democracy. He asks rhetorically, "What should be the purpose and content of an educational system in a democratic society?"[28]

Although pragmatism as a philosophy is largely a late nineteenth-century and early twentieth-century American phenomenon, its impact on educational philosophy can still be extensively observed today. Educational pragmatism emphasizes experiential, observable reality. It espouses that the world is dynamic, evolving, and ever-changing, and that as a result, *truth* is that which "works," and that which "works" is truth. Pragmatists further delineate a truth that works as that which allows the learner to navigate the dynamics of his ever-evolving universe and his ever-evolving context. Educational emphases rightly include socialization, adaptation, hands-on problem-solving, critical thinking, cross-curricular integration, scientific method, experimentation, new

---

26. Porrovecchio, "F. C. S. Schiller," 515–16.
27. Gamble, *Great Tradition*, 226–28.
28. Cahn, *Classic and Contemporary Readings*, 346.

experiences being connected to prior experiences, and educative growth. Furthermore, Dewey, one of its most notable proponents, documented a desire that education would rightly avoid the extremes of eschewing the transmission of cultural heritage as a viable component of education *whatsoever* (on the one extreme), and seeing the transmission of cultural heritage as the *sole* purpose of education (on the other extreme).

Nonetheless, despite distinct contributions, pragmatism generally overemphasizes one of the four aspects of a full-orbed Christian epistemology: *experiential* knowledge.[29] In so doing pragmatists seem to fallaciously overemphasize experiential knowledge as the *sole* source of knowledge and truth to the virtual exclusion of the other three sources of knowledge and truth, i.e., revelation, rationality, and intuition having their proper place at the epistemic table. Furthermore, to a large degree, pragmatists have been philosophical materialists and either agnostics or atheists. Additionally, even a casual reading of almost any of the pragmatists' premier documents lends itself to seeing the underlying Darwinism in much of what is said. Finally, fatally flawed is pragmatism's definition of truth; fundamentally pragmatism is based upon the logical fallacy of affirming the consequence, and it logically leads to relativism.[30] Therefore,

29. Including empiricism.

30. For a helpful discussion of this important matter, the inquiring reader would do well to read Nancy Peracey's *Total Truth*, 229–47. Highlights of her salient presentation include: "Pragmatism is a Darwinian view of knowledge. . . . [It] rejected the older view that the human mind is *transcendent to* matter, in favor of the Darwinian view that mind is *produced by* nature. . . . For the pragmatists, this naturalizing of the mind was the most revolutionary impact of Darwinian theory. It seemed to imply that mental functions are merely adaptations for solving problems in the environment. . . . So, the question each individual must ask is: 'Which things are worth the most?' Whatever you decide, *that* is your truth. . . . Each individual has to become an autonomous decision maker, determining his values strictly on his own. . . . Teachers are not instructors but 'facilitators,' guiding students as they try out various pragmatic strategies as they discover what works for them. . . . Thus, pragmatism inevitably leads to pluralism of beliefs, all of them transient and none of them eternally or universally true." In summary, two lines of analyses seem to suffice: (1) If biblical, Christian truth is not relativistic, then a system of truth-claims that posits some form of relativized truth is not biblical or Christian. Pragmatism is system of truth-claims that posits some form of relativized truth by arguing that truth is that which works for an individual in a particular context which relativizes the truth to a particular individual within a particular context. Therefore, pragmatism is not a biblical, Christian system of truth. (2) Affirming the consequent is a logical fallacy which fallaciously argues that "if P, then Q. Q, therefore P." Clearly erroneous, affirming the consequent can slide insidiously into ideas, such as in the case of Pragmatism: "If something is true, it should work. If it works, then it is true." Pragmatism inherently employs a logical

its educational foundations and concomitantly its educational aims are inexorably skewed.

---

fallacy at the foundation of its epistemology; therefore, it does not work as a rival to the truth of biblical, Christian truth upon which one can construct a biblical philosophy of a Christian school education.

Chapter 11

Toward a Christian Understanding of Social Reconstructionism

Like some of the other schools of thought, so also with Social Reconstructionism, it is less like a monolithic, systematized philosophy per se than it is a cluster of related emphases—a typology of similar impetuses. Emphases within this cluster of Social Reconstructionism typologies include notions such as John Rawls's theory of social justice, Axiochus's ancient etiquette and ethic (*eukosmia*), Robert Owen's communitarianism, Horace Mann's normalization of common schools, Catharine Esther Beecher's program to eradicate American illiteracy, Theodore Weld's passion to abolish American slavery, Angelina and Sarah Grimké's promotion of the education of women, Mahatma Gandhi's dream for India, and many other valuable and viable causes. Social Reconstructionist theories place tremendous value and responsibility on education to liberate individuals oppressed by some societal injustice; they claim that education is the solution to the problem(s) of society. In summary, Social Reconstructionism asserts education as the identification *of* and solution *to* the problem(s) of society.

Axiochus (ca. 455–ca. 405 BC) emphasized *eukosmia*. More than mere manners, *eukosmia* transcended even etiquette. Axiochus considered *eukosmia* to be comportment with a prescribed order and discipline, as captured in the following excerpt: "And, all the time of his youth is spent under overseers which are set over him by the Areopagus, from which labors young men, being once freed, are yet overlaid with greater cares and more weighty thoughts, touching the ordering of his state and the trade of life."[1]

Catharine Macaulay (1731–1791) wrote *Letters on Education*, in which she affirmed her Anglican theism as a basis for sound thinking, teaching, and learning: "The thoughts of a fatherless universe, and a set of beings let loose by chance or fate on one another, without other law than power dictates and opportunity gives a right to exact, chills the sensibility of the feeling mind into indifference and despair."[2] Notably, she argued for the education of women and the for equality of the sexes: "When the [female] sex has been taught wisdom by education, they will be glad to give up indirect influence for rational privileges."[3]

Hannah More (1745–1835) was a contemporary with, a cobelligerent alongside of, and a supporter of William Wilberforce. In addition to her political ties and her evangelical bent, she authored multiple influential educational texts, including *Strictures on Female Education* (1799) and *Hints towards Forming the Character of a Young Princess* (1805).

Robert Owen (1771–1858) was an idealist, utopian, communitarian, educator, social planner, reformer, and innovator. His utopian communitarianism rivaled Marx's scientific socialism. "Perhaps the most useful legacy that Robert Owen left to education was that of the utopian thinker who used social imagination to project a vision of a better world."[4]

Horace Mann (1796–1859) was a leader of the Common School Movement. Challenges of increased urbanization, industrialization, cultural diversification, and ecumenicalization seemed to spur Mann on to active Whig party political engagement. He also tended toward educational emphases such as professionalization of the teaching vocation, communalization of values among schools, and the normalization of so-called common schools or public schools.

Catharine Esther Beecher (1800–1878) envisaged a plan to eradicate American illiteracy and the concomitant "evils" she associated with the lack of education among the children of the United States at that time.

> The educating of children, that is the true and noble profession of a woman—that is what is worthy the noblest powers

---

1. Eby, *Ancient and Medieval*, 272.
2. Johnson, *Philosophical Documents in Education*, 62.
3. Johnson, *Philosophical Documents in Education*, 67.
4. Gutek, *Historical and Philosophical Foundations*, 252.

> and affections of the noblest minds. . . . Every one of the evils portrayed here, it is in the power of American women fully to remedy and remove. Nothing is wanting but a knowledge of the evils, and a well-devised plan for uniting the energies of our countrywomen in the effort, and the thing will be speedily and gloriously achieved. It is the immediate object of this enterprise now presented, to engage American women to exert the great power and influence put into their hands, to remedy the evils which now oppress their countrywomen, and thus at the same time, and by the same method, to secure a proper education to the vast multitude of neglected American children all over the land. The plan is, to begin on a small scale, and to take women already qualified intellectually to teach, and possessed of missionary zeal and benevolence, and, after some further training, to send them to the most ignorant portions of our land, to raise up schools, to instruct in morals and piety, and to teach the domestic arts and virtues.[5]

Theodore Weld (1803-1895), an influential abolitionist, helped establish schools in Perth, New Jersey, and Lexington, Massachusetts. The schools admitted both males and females, as well as students of all races. Weld taught Conversation, Composition, and English Literature. In 1838, Weld married Angelina Grimké, an abolitionist and women's rights advocate, and relocated to Belleville, New Jersey, where in 1839 he and the Grimké sisters authored *American Slavery as It Is: Testimony of a Thousand Witnesses.*[6]

Angelina Grimké (1805-1879) and her older sister Sarah (1792-1873) published *The Education of Women* (1850), in which they presented what they asserted as a biblical argument for the equality of education for men and women.

> It is a remarkable fact that Christ made no distinction between the responsibilities of men and women. He addressed them the same precepts, required from them the same evidence of discipleship, and called upon them in the same language to fulfill their glorious destiny. . . . Think not because I thus speak, that I would withdraw women from the duties of domestic life, far from it; let her fulfill in the circle of home all the obligations that

---

5. Lockerbie, *Passion for Learning*, 241.
6. Lockerbie, *Passion for Learning*, 253-57.

rest upon her, but let he not waste her powers on inferior objects when higher and holier responsibilities demand her attention.[7]

Booker T. Washington (1856–1915) asserted that "no race can be lifted until its mind is awakened and strengthened.... The doubt cannot be much affected by abstract arguments, no matter how delicately or convincingly woven together.... Our pathway must be up through the soil, up through swamps, up through forests, up through streams, the rocks, up through commerce, education, and religion."[8]

Jane Addams (1860–1935) was committed to educating the underprivileged. She advocated a kind of socialized education, not unlikely as concomitant to her work with urban, industrialized, and uneducated immigrants, as well as to her experience at Hull House, which some would call an urban *paideia* of life skills and knowledge.

W. E. B. Du Bois (1868–1963), sociologist, historian, and activist for the rights of African Americans, asserted that "the Negro race, like all races, is going to be saved by its exceptional men. The problem of education, then, among Negroes must first of all deal with the Talented Tenth. ... Human education is not simply a matter of schools, it is much more a matter of family and group life.... Education must not simply teach work—it must teach *life*."[9]

To that end, he continues with his emphasis on practical training:

> Children must be trained in knowledge of what the world is and what it knows and how it does its daily work. These things cannot be separated: we cannot teach pure knowledge apart from actual facts, or separate truth from the human mind. Above all we must not forget that the object of all education is the child itself—and not what it does or makes.[10]

Mahatma Gandhi (1869–1948), father of Indian independence, suggested *love* as the core of the educational enterprise:

> Scientists tell us that without the cohesive force amongst the atoms that comprise this globe of ours, it would crumble into pieces, and we would cease to exist. As even there is a cohesive force among animate beings, which is *love*. We notice it between father and son, between brother and sister, friend and friend.

---

7. Lockerbie, *Passion for Learning*, 260–61.
8. Johnson, *Philosophical Documents in Education*, 138–39.
9. Johnson, *Philosophical Documents in Education*, 140–43.
10. Johnson, *Philosophical Documents in Education*, 416.

> But we have to learn to use that force among all that lives, and in the use of it consists our knowledge of God. Where there is *love*, there is life; hatred leads to destruction.[11]

Additionally, in *India of My Dreams*, Gandhi cast his vision that

> true education of the intellect can only come through a proper exercise and training of the bodily organs, e.g., hands, feet, eyes, ears, nose, etc. In other words, an intelligent use of the bodily organs in a child provides the best and quickest way of developing his intellect. But unless the development of the mind and body goes hand in hand with a corresponding awakening of the soul, the former alone would prove to be a poor lop-sided affair. By spiritual training I mean education of the heart. A proper and all-around development of the mind, therefore, can take place only when it proceeds . . . with the education of the physical and spiritual faculties of the child. They constitute an indivisible whole.[12]

Margaret Sanger (1883–1966) carried the torch of social education, which was fueled by her conviction about birth control. She claimed to "instruct women in the things they need to know."[13]

In 1921, A. S. Neill (1883–1973) founded what he called a modern school, Summerhill, in Leiston, England, about one hundred miles from London. The school was known for optional lessons, no timetables, and an emphasis on play. "I am not decrying learning. But learning should follow play. And learning should be deliberately seasoned with play to make it palatable." Neill prioritized what he called love, freedom, self-determination, and self-expression—all within a context of what Neill referred to as "*final faith* . . . a complete belief in the child as a good, not an evil, being."[14] "I hold that the aim of life is to find happiness. . . . Education should be a preparation for life. Our culture has not been very successful. Our education, politics, and economics lead to war. Our medicines have not done away with disease. Our religion has not abolished usury and robbery. Our boasted humanitarianism still allows public opinion to

---

11. Johnson, *Philosophical Documents in Education*, 388.
12. Gutek, *Historical and Philosophical Foundations*, 390.
13. Conway, *American Literacy*, 223.
14. Cahn, *Classic and Contemporary Readings*, 296.

approve the barbaric sport of hunting."[15] Neill's desire for education was to make a "difference in confronting the evils of society."[16]

Nelson Goodman (1906–1998) taught epistemology at Harvard, but avocationally he founded and directed Project Zero. Project Zero continues its mission of exploring and enriching the understanding of the arts—and the skills and knowledge endemic to the arts. Goodman once quipped, regarding the prevailing developmentalism of his day, "Kids get smarter as they get older." Perhaps motivated by his own work on projectability as an epistemological concept, he seemed to desire something more strategic in education than the aforementioned banal reductionism of his assessment of some developmentalists.

Maxine Greene (1917–2014), an American educational philosopher, author, activist, and educator, sustained "her unyielding faith in humankind's willingness and ability to build on and transcend their lived worlds."[17] She saw education in general and the arts in particular as *meaning-making* (especially for the oppressed). Akin to a constructivist psychology, *meaning-making* provides a process by which a person can construe, understand, and make sense out of the brokenness of oneself, others, and the world at large. "With situations opening, students may become empowered to engage in some sort of *praxis*, engaged enough to name the obstacles in the way of their shared becoming."[18]

Paulo Freire (1921–1997) posits a liberation pedagogy in which a key concept is *consientizacao*, a Portuguese term that denotes raising a person's consciousness and critical awareness of social, political, and economic conditions and contradictions of persons' lives necessary to identify and mitigate repression and oppression. One scholar summarized, "Schooling was taken out of its four walls and transformed into an education that opened the door to the actual world outside."[19] Freire bemoans what he refers to as a "banking concept" of education, one in which the educator merely "deposits" knowledge into the learner. "Education thus becomes an act of depositing, in which the students are the depositories and the teacher is the depositor."[20]

---

15. Cahn, *Classic and Contemporary Readings*, 299.
16. Cahn, *Classic and Contemporary Readings*, 301.
17. Johnson, *Philosophical Documents in Education*, 159.
18. Johnson, *Philosophical Documents in Education*, 174.
19. Gutek, *Historical and Philosophical Foundations*, 436.
20. Johnson, *Philosophical Documents in Education*, 196.

> In perception properly so-called, as an explicit awareness [Gewahren], I am turned toward the object, to the paper, for instance. I apprehend it as being this here and now. The apprehension is a singling out, every object having a background and experience. Around and about the people of my books, pencils, ankles, and so forth, in these in a certain sense for also "perceived," perceptually there, in the "field of intuition," but whilst I was turn towards the paper there was no turning in their direction, nor any apprehending of them, not even in a secondary sense. They appeared and yet were not singled out, were not posited on their own account. Every perception of a thing has such a zone of background intuitions or background awareness, if "intuiting" already includes the state of being turned towards, and is also a "conscious experience," or more briefly a "consciousness of" all indeed that in point of fact lies in the co-perceived objective background.[21]

Despite all of his innovative thinking and extensive writing, Freire is not unlikely more renowned for a quote he borrowed from Sartre than anything else Freire himself otherwise said. In the second chapter of his book *Situation* (1947), Jean Paul Sartre asserted, as famously quoted by Freire: "Consciousness and the world are given in one blow: essentially external to consciousness the world is essentially relative to it."[22]

James Coleman (1926–1995) was originally trained as a chemist and went on to get his PhD in sociology from Columbia. He was president of the American Sociological Association and professor of sociology at the University of Chicago. He presented his 737-page *Equality of Educational Opportunity* report to President Nixon and congress. By 1971 his recommendations became national policy. "Coleman hailed Nixon's actions as 'the first time there has been positive commitment, supported by resources [$1.5 billion] to create strong and stable integration.'"[23]

Published in 1971 by Austrian philosopher, Catholic priest, and social critic Ivan Illich (1926–2002), *Deschooling Society* chronicles what Illich critiques as the ineffectiveness of institutionalized education.

> Universal education through schooling is not feasible. It would be no more feasible if it were attempted by means of alternative

---

21. Cahn, *Classic and Contemporary Readings*, 384.

22. "La conscience et le monde sont donnés d'un meme coup: exterieur par essence a la conscience, le monde est, par essence relatif a elle." Christiaens, "Basic Ontology," 14.

23. Conway, *American Literacy*, 274.

> institutions built on the style of present schools. Neither new attitudes of teachers toward their pupils nor the proliferation of educational hardware or software (in classroom or bedroom), nor finally the attempt to expand the pedagogue's responsibility until it engulfs his pupils' lifetimes will deliver universal education. The current search for new educational funnels must be reversed into the search for their institutional inverse: educational webs which heighten the opportunity for each one to transform each moment of his living into one of learning, sharing, and caring. We hope to contribute concepts needed by those who conduct such counterfoil research on education—and also to those who seek alternatives to other established service industries.[24]

Knowledge, skills, and learning in general were not the problem from Illich's perspective. For him, *school* itself was the problem. "School, he asserted, because of its characteristics as an institution, failed to make learning meaningful."[25]

Postmodern African American literary scholar and social activist Gloria Jean Watkins (b. 1952), oft know by her pen name, bell hooks (*sic*), writes about education as *spiritual growth*:

> To educate as the *practice of freedom* is a way of teaching that anyone can learn.
> That learning process comes easiest to those of us who teach who also believe
> that there is an aspect of our vocation that is sacred; who believe that our work
> is not merely to share information but to share in the intellectual and spiritual
> growth of our students. To teach in a manner that respects and cares for the
> souls of our students is essential if we are to provide the necessary conditions
> where learning can most deeply and intimately begin.[26]

Social Reconstructionism as a whole emphasizes resolving social injustices in a quest for a better society. Reconstructionist educators prioritize social reform as a primary aim of education. Many reconstructionist educators believe that societal and educational systems need to be revolutionized to overcome oppression and to improve human conditions.

---

24. Illich, *Deschooling Society*, 1.
25. Thomas, *Education*, 115.
26. Hooks, *Teaching to Transgress*, 13.

Curricula generally focus on community-based learning, bringing the larger world into the classroom, and taking action on real-world issues such as poverty, oppression, war, violence, hunger, human trafficking, terrorism, racism, and other injustices.

Of his own particular cause—and of this entire school of thought—A. S. Neill said it well. Neill's desire for education was to make a "difference in confronting the evils of society." *That* is what *all* of the Social Reconstructivists want.

Their desire is well-intentioned. At least in some cases, however, the priority and/or the concomitant program is somewhat, significantly, or even tragically misguided.

According to the Christian worldview, the evils of society do not boil down primarily to a lack of education in general or to the lack of a particular reconstructionist educational reform in particular. Fundamentally, according to a Christian worldview, the evils of society boil down to *evil*—i.e., sin. The solution to sin, however, is not a school program or an anti-school program. It is in the accomplished work of Christ.

The argument can most certainly be made that the desire to right societal wrongs is noble and worthwhile. A corollary argument can also be made that *Christians* should be the ones leading the charge on these types of issues of resolving injustice and righting societal wrongs. The questions become, however, how does a Christian individually, how do Christians collectively, or how does Christian school education specifically address these social ills?[27]

---

27. Over the millennia, Christians have answered these questions in a variety of ways. Discussing how to answer these questions and how to most Christianly resolve such societal injustices goes beyond the scope of this present book. The motivated reader, however, is prompted to explore Richard H. Niebuhr's *Christ and Culture* as a primer for cataloging five postures of Christian engagement within society and culture.

Chapter 12

Toward a Christian Understanding of Behaviorism

BEHAVIORISM[1] REFERS TO A school of thought in the behavioral sciences, philosophy, and education. This movement emphasized scientific method, objective observation, and psychological approaches to the study of and to the teaching of animals and humans. Some say that behaviorism began in 1913 when John Watson authored "Psychology as the Behaviorist Views It," but elements of behaviorism predated that publication, as well. Nonetheless, Watson, a primary proponent of behaviorism, did a lot to formulate and articulate the assumptions and analyses of this very scientific and highly psychologized approach to learning theory. Succinctly stated, Behaviorism attempted to reduce teaching and learning to a system of stimuli and responses.

Joseph Lancaster (1778–1838) led a movement to establish schools that used what he called the "Monitorial System," sometimes called the "Lancasterian" or "Lancastrian" System. In Lancaster's Monitorial System advanced students taught less advanced ones, enabling a small number of adult masters to educate large numbers of students at low cost. From about 1798 to 1830 it was highly influential as an inexpensive method of educating expansive populations of poor children in England. Lancaster utilized this method in schools up to a thousand students. In these schools he devised a token-economy of rewarding appropriate deportment and academic achievement and of punishing misbehavior and lack

---

1. Sometimes referred to as *Behavioralism* or *Learning Theory*.

of satisfactory progress. Lancaster's model is being rediscovered today. Problems with contemporary methods are encouraging concerned persons to reexamine some earlier approaches to learning, such as Lancaster's, and adapt them to current educational environments.[2]

Ivan Pavlov (1849–1936) posited an association theory of thought and a system of conditioned reflexes in his rather materialistic and highly behavioristic theory of learning. His findings and resultant methods provided the bases for much of the behavioristic approaches to classroom management, discipline, and behavior modification so prevalent in so many schools for so much of the twentieth century in America—and beyond.

Edward Thorndike (1874–1949) was a professor of psychology at the Teachers College of Columbia University. He laid the groundwork for reinforcement theory within behaviorism by his work with the law of cause and effect in human behavior. His groundbreaking methodology of using animal subjects to infer human implications was illustrated in his dissertation, entitled "Animal Intelligence: An Experimental Study of the Associative Processes in Animals." This technique eventually led Behaviorists to accomplish advancements such as teaching pigeons to play ping-pong through rewarding the subjects in a prescribed series of successful approximations. These developments eventually led to important and impactful ramifications on the views of human learning, as well.

John B. Watson (1878–1958) presented an address to Columbia University in 1913, entitled "Psychology as the Behaviorist Views It." This officially launched the movement known as Behaviorism. Like many Behaviorists, Watson's dissertation had focused on the behavior of animals, "Animal Education: An Experimental Study on the Psychical Development of the White Rat, Correlated with the Growth of Its Nervous System." In this dissertation, Watson detailed the correlation between myelination in rats' brains and their relative learning abilities.

Watson demurred that all actual mental activity (even in humans) as merely observable physiological function. He claimed that language was merely manipulated habit. He asserted the trainable-ness of any person via his program.

Famously from his book on *Behaviorism*, he boasted,

> Give me a dozen healthy infants, well-formed, and my own specified world to bring them up in, and I'll guarantee to take

---

2. Kienel, *History of Christian School Education*, 1:285.

any one at random and train him to become any type of specialist I might select—doctor, lawyer, artist, merchant-chief and, yes, even beggar-man and thief, regardless of his talents, penchants, tendencies, abilities, vocations, and race of his ancestors.[3]

Georg Lukacs (1885–1971),[4] philosopher and literary and social critic, influenced education in at least two ways:

1. He posited an extension of Pavlovian systems of signals with implication to associative theories of learning.

2. He formulated a three-tiered metaphysic that applied Hegelianism to contexts such as schools, i.e., organic, inorganic, and social structure. Each of the three was distinct from the others by a division between the genuine essence of entities and their appearance.

Lev Vygotsky (1896–1934), a Soviet psychologist, posited a theory of human cultural and biosocial development called cultural-historical psychology. Working in a place and at a time of significant cultural and political upheaval, Vygotsky's behavioral theory of development seems less cognitive and more contextual. "Every function in the child's cultural development appears twice: First, it manifests between people (inter-psychological), and then inside the child (intra-psychological). This applies equally to voluntary attention, to logical memory, and to the formation of ideas."[5]

Behavioristically, Vygotsky wrote about what he termed ZPD, a child's *zone of proximal development*. ZPD refers to the idea that there is an area of activity which is just a bit beyond what a child can already do on his or her own; it is what they can do with some kind of help. It is *this* zone, according to Vygotsky, on which teaching should concentrate.[6]

B. F. Skinner (1904–1990) was a professor of psychology at Harvard University. He coined the term *operant conditioning*, which refers to utilizing reinforcement to strengthen certain desired outcome behaviors. His theory of conditioning can be summarized as follows:

---

3. Watson, *Behaviorism*, 82.

4. With a metaphysic reminiscent of continental dialectic, Lukacs could have been included in that chapter. He is included here, because of his Pavolovian methodology, which seems very behavioristic.

5. Vygotsky, *Mind in Society*, 57.

6. Thomas, *Education*, 75.

1. *Continuous reinforcement* (CR). Each time a specific action is performed, the subject receives a reinforcement. This method is effective when teaching a new behavior, because it quickly establishes a positive association between the target behavior and the reinforcement.

2. *Fixed-interval* schedule (FI). A procedure in which reinforcements are presented at fixed time periods, provided that the appropriate response is made. This schedule yields a response rate that is low immediately after reinforcement but eventually becomes rapid immediately prior to the next scheduled reinforcement.

3. *Variable-interval* schedule (VI). A procedure in which behavior is reinforced after random time durations following the last reinforcement. This schedule yields steady responding, at a rate that varies with the average frequency of reinforcement.

4. *Fixed-ratio* schedule (FR). A procedure in which reinforcement is delivered after a specific number of responses have been made. Fixed-ratio schedules tend to produce very rapid responding, often with breaks of no responding just after reinforcement if a large number of responses is required for reinforcement.

5. *Variable-ratio* schedule (VR). A procedure in which reinforcement comes after a number of responses that is randomized from one reinforcement to the next (e.g., the way most slot machines are programmed to payout). The lower the number of responses required, the higher the response rate tends to be. Variable-ratio schedules tend to produce very rapid responding, often with breaks of no responding just after reinforcement if a large number of responses is required for reinforcement.[7]

Implications for defining and doing education included the following steps that Skinner argued could be used to teach any age-appropriate information or skill to any capable student:

1. Clearly specify the action that the student is to take.

2. Meaningfully break the task down into small achievable, progressive steps—proceeding from the simple to the complex.

---

7. Myers, *Psychology*.

3. Have the student do each actionable-step and appropriately reinforce successful successive approximations.

4. Adjust the reinforcements accordingly so that the student becomes increasingly adapt at achieving the actionable-goal.

5. Change to an intermittent reinforcement to sustain successful achievement of the targeted behavior so taught.

Succinctly stated, Behaviorism attempted to reduce teaching and learning to a system of stimuli and responses. Some of this twentieth-century science actually corroborated some ancient biblical wisdom, including but not limited to notions about reward, punishment, reinforcement, and successive approximations. Behaviorism has contributed to understanding many of the mechanisms within teaching and learning. For example, educators, Christian as well as not, have benefited from classroom management techniques developed by Behaviorism. Some literature[8] suggests that certain student populations (e.g., substance abusers, hearing impaired, mentally handicapped, and behaviorally challenged) seem to respond particularly well to some behavioristic techniques. Even among more mainstreamed student populations, certain behavioristic methodologies get utilized quite routinely (e.g., for classroom management, with academic progress, and in scripture memory). Undoubtedly, much can (still) be learned from Behaviorism's highly scientific approaches to observing how learning transpires.

Nonetheless, Behaviorism as a whole is a worldview that is tepid and vacuous. It is materialistic and mechanistic. It (generally) reduces humans to mere animals, and it (generally) reduces cognition, conation, emotion, and even spirituality down to mere physiological functions preprogrammed by a complex matrix of variables.[9] Conspicuously and tragically absent are the *imago Dei*, the fall, the curse, the redemption, the *poiema*, and the notion that humans are eternal beings with God-breathed souls that need to be shepherded and deserve to be educated—not just programmed.

---

8. One example of ready reference to the following statements. Tayo, "B. F. Skinner's Theory," para. 1.

9. It bears noting that philosophers of the mind have almost universally rejected the Behaviorists' view that mental events are merely observable, mechanistic behaviors.

Chapter 13

TOWARD A CHRISTIAN UNDERSTANDING OF DEVELOPMENTALISM

"OF THE MAKING OF many theories of human development," to paraphrase Qoheleth in Ecclesiastes 12, "there is no end!" Ever since there were humans, there was human development, and ever since there was human development (at least the argument could be made that) there have been theories on and about human development. Nonetheless, at least since the time of the following developmentalists, such theories of human development have been stratified and codified. Each of these theories attempts to see human development *en toto* and to classify insights regarding that development, which can be helpful in any human endeavor, particularly in education.[1] Educational developmentalists emphasize the systematic development of the child progressing through stages of maturation and growth.

Sigmund Freud (1856–1939), an Austrian neurologist and founder of psychoanalysis, continues to extensively influence medicine, psychology, the humanities, and education. He posited development to be predominantly psychosexual in nature. Among other famous sound bites,

---

1. Breaking from the rhythm of the other chapters 4–15 that closed with critical Christian comments, this chapter punctuates each of the first few historical allusions of developmentalism with a brief critique. The reason being, these developmentalists have *that* in common (viz. *some* form of developmentalism), but not much else. A few chapter closing comments will be provided, as well.

the following quote captures some of his apparent cynicism, but also some of his undeniable developmentalism. "But surely infantilism is destined to be surmounted. Men cannot remain children forever, they must in the end go out into 'hostile life.' We may call this *'education to reality.'*"[2]

Sadly, this great intellect was not a follower of Jesus. Actually, he was an atheist. Nonetheless, his theories still resonate with many philosophers of education, and his views on psychosexual development have reverberated through many academic halls of learning across multiple disciplines. Freud's views tend to be cynical, mechanistic, Darwinian, and anti-Victorian. His insights about the vastness of the subconscious and the potency of *intra*personal dynamics elucidate much of an educator's struggle to uncover what lay inside herself and her students. Christian educators should be aware of Freud's views, but they should be wary of them, as well.

Jean Piaget (1896–1980), a renowned and oft-quoted Swiss clinical psychologist, the director of the International Bureau of Education, and a pioneer researcher in child development theory, posited a *cognitive* approach to stage development. Within this model Piaget argued for a cognitive mechanism by which the mind processes information. His claim was that a learner could assimilate and accommodate new learning based upon his current stage of development and based upon prior learning. An adherent to a constructivist theory of knowing, Piaget advocated constructionist-based learning strategies.

Piaget delineated the following model of development:

1. Schemas are the building blocks of knowledge.

2. Adaptation processes are schemas that enable the transition from one stage to another. There are three different types of adaptation processes.

    1. Equilibrium, the force that drives development and the tendency to move toward cognitive balance.
    2. Assimilation, the use of existing schema to handle new learning.
    3. Accommodation, the use of a necessarily new schema to handle new learning.

Per the aforementioned schemas and adaptation processes, Piaget highlighted four stages of cognitive development:

---

2. Freud, *Future of Illusion*, 81.

1. *Sensorimotor*—from birth until about two years old: During the sensorimotor stage, the child learns about himself and his environment by means of engaging in the world physically.

2. *Preoperational*—from when the child starts talking until about seven years old: Incorporating language the child begins to use symbols to represent objects. He seems to assimilate information and appropriates it into his preoperational ideas.

3. *Concrete operational*—from about seven years old to early adolescence: During the concrete operational stage, accommodation begins to increase. The child begins to think more abstractly and to make rational judgments.

4. *Formal operational*—from adolescence through adulthood: Formal operational thinking suggests that a thinker no longer requires concrete objects to make rational judgments. He is capable of abstract, analogical, hypothetical, and logical analyses.

From Piaget the Christian educator can glean much helpful guidance:

1. Approach those whom (s)he leads in age-appropriate and stage-appropriate ways.

2. Exercise phase-shifting whenever addressing students of varying levels.

3. Attempt to remember what it was like at each of the various stages.

4. Engage formal operational abstractions strategically.

Erik Erikson (1902–1994), a psychologist renowned for his *psychosocial* stages of development, foundationally shaped multiple generations of educators and students. His eight stages of psychosocial development are as follows:

1. *Hope: basic trust vs. basic mistrust.* This first stage covers the period from birth until one year old, which according to Erikson was the foundational stage of life. During the first or second year of life, the major emphasis is on the mother and father's nurturing the child, especially in terms of visual contact and touch. The child will develop optimism, trust, confidence, and security if properly cared for and handled. If a child does not experience trust, he or

she may develop insecurity, worthlessness, and general mistrust of the world.

2. *Will: autonomy vs. shame.* This stage covers early childhood around eighteen months until three years old. The child begins to discover independence. At this point, the child has an opportunity to build self-esteem and autonomy as he or she learns new skills and develops a sense of right from wrong. The well-cared-for child is sure of himself, carrying himself with pride rather than shame. During this time defiance, temper tantrums, and stubbornness may also appear. Children tend to be vulnerable during this stage, sometimes feeling shame and low self-esteem during an inability to learn certain skills.

3. *Purpose: initiative vs. guilt.* This stage covers around three to six years old. During this period children experience a desire to copy the adults around them and take initiative in creating play situations. They make up stories with toys, playing out roles in a trial universe, experimenting with the blueprint for what they believe it means to be an adult. While Erikson was influenced by Freud, he downplays biological sexuality in favor of the psychosocial features of conflict between child and parents. Nevertheless, Erikson suggested that at this stage children usually become involved in the classic "Oedipal struggle" and resolve this struggle through "social role identification." If frustrated over natural desires and goals, children may easily experience guilt. The most significant relationship is with the basic family.

4. *Competence: industry vs. inferiority.* This stage covers around six to eleven years old. During this stage, often called latency, children are capable of learning, creating, and accomplishing numerous new skills and knowledge, thus developing a sense of industry. This is also a very social stage of development, and if children experience unresolved feelings of inadequacy and inferiority among peers, they can develop problems in terms of competence and self-esteem. As their world expands, the most significant relationship is with the school and neighborhood. Parents are no longer the complete authorities they once were—although they are still important.

5. *Fidelity: identity vs. role confusion.* This stage covers around twelve until eighteen years old. Up until this fifth stage, development depends largely on what is done *to* a person. At this point, development now depends primarily upon what that person does. An adolescent

must struggle to discover and find his or her own identity, while negotiating and struggling with social interactions, fitting in, and developing a sense of morality and right from wrong. Some children attempt to delay entrance to adulthood and withdraw from responsibilities (moratorium). Those unsuccessful with this stage, tend to experience role confusion and upheaval. Adolescents who are successful with this stage, on the other hand, begin to develop a strong affiliation and devotion to ideals, causes, and friends. The primary tasks become self-discovery, individuation from family of origin, and establishing a philosophy of life.

6. *Love: intimacy vs. isolation.* This first stage of adulthood covers around eighteen to thirty-five years old. Dating, marriage, family, and friendships are important during this stage in life. People tend to seek companionship and love. Many young adults begin to settle down and start families. Young adults seek intimacy and satisfying relationships, but if unsuccessful, isolation may occur. Significant relationships at this stage are with marital partners and close friends.

7. *Care: generativity vs. stagnation.* This second stage of adulthood happens between the ages of thirty-five to sixty-four years old. Career and family are the most important priorities at this stage. Middle adulthood is also the time when people can take on greater responsibilities and control. During this stage working to establish stability and *generativity* (attempting to produce something that makes a difference to society) are critical. Inactivity and meaninglessness are common fears during this stage. Significant relationships are those within the family, workplace, local church, and other community groups.

8. *Wisdom/Ego: integrity vs. despair.* This stage affects the age group of sixty-five years and older. Erikson believed that much of life is forward-looking, preparing for the middle adulthood stage; and then that this last stage involves much reflection, backward-looking. Many older adults look back with a feeling of *integrity*—i.e., contentment and fulfillment, having led a meaningful life and having made valuable contributions to society. Others may have a sense of despair during this stage, reflecting upon their experiences

and failures. They may fear death as they struggle to find a purpose to their lives, wondering "What was the point of life? Was it worth it?"[3]

A Christian educator can glean much helpful guidance from Erikson:

1. The stage(s) at which the educator currently finds both himself *and* his students warrants attention in proactively Eriksonian ways.

2. The stage(s) at which the educator or his students struggled earlier in life warrants consideration—possibly through genogram or other introspective or reflective work and prayer.

3. Finally, the educator and the students alike would do well to learn to "fail" upward. Even the secular Erikson saw failure as cumulative and potentially progressive. Certainly, within the redemptive schemas of Christian grace, no educator—nor any student—needs to fall victim to previous non-successes on his own part or on the part of significant others.

Additional developmental clarity and precision can come through considering theorized stages of *moral* development. Lawrence Kohlberg (1927–1987), University of Chicago educated and professor of psychology at Yale and Harvard, developed what he called Stages of Moral Development.

Level 1 (Pre-Conventional)

1. Obedience and punishment orientation. (How can I avoid punishment?)

2. Self-interest orientation. (What's in it for me?)

Level 2 (Conventional)

3. Interpersonal accord and conformity. (What is the socially acceptable norm of being good?)

4. Authority and social-order maintaining orientation. (What is the prevailing code for law-and-order morality and society at large?)

Level 3 (Post-Conventional)

---

3. Adapted from Erikson, "Erikson's Stages of Development."

5. Social contract orientation. (Laws are social contracts, not rigid edicts.)

6. Universal ethical principles. (Decision are made via abstract principles, categorical imperatives, and a principled conscience informed by universal moral principles and transcultural ethical abstractions such as justice.)

Whereas these stages sound "moral," as well as important and impressive, whereas they have provided much established, respected, and conventional wisdom on the matter, and whereas the stages parallel Scripture in many ways, these stages are not exegeted from the Bible and ought to be filtered through the truth of Scripture and applied accordingly.

Benjamin Bloom (1913–1999), an educational psychologist, categorized the developmental learning processes of education in his famous *taxonomy* of learning:[4]

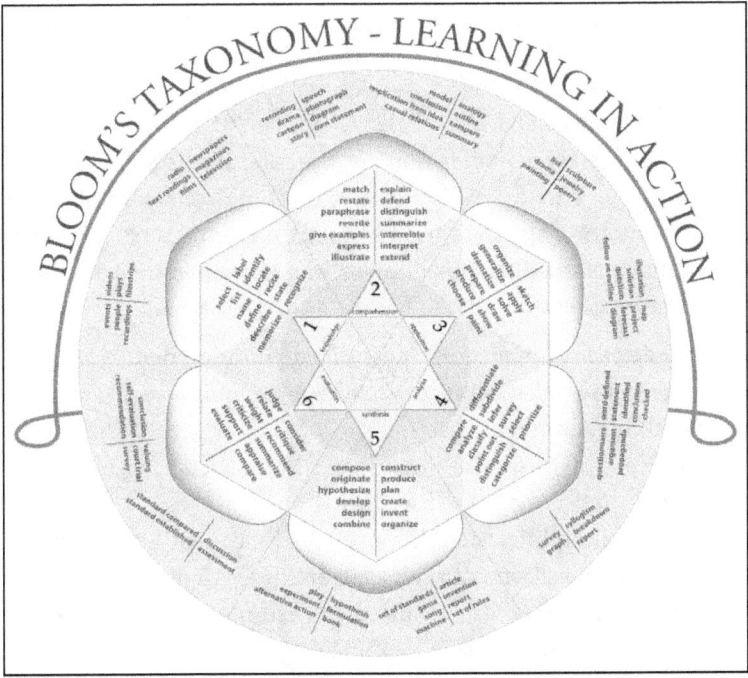

He cast a hierarchy of the mastery of learning in each of the following domains:

4. Tanabe, "Benjamin Bloom."

1. Receiving: The lowest level of learning in which the student passively pays attention; without this level no more advanced learning would occur.

2. Responding: The student actively participates in the learning process; the student not only attends to a stimulus, (s)he also reacts or responds in some way.

3. Valuing: The student attaches a value to an object, phenomenon, or piece of information.

4. Organizing: The student can synthesize various values, information, and ideas; (s)he begins to accommodate them within his/her own schema, comparing, relating, and elaborating on what has been learned.

5. Characterizing: The student has held a particular value or belief that now exerts influence on his/her behavior so that it becomes a characteristic.

Bloom also did extensive work on domains of learning.

1. Skills in the *psychomotor* domain describe the ability to physically manipulate a tool, an instrument, or some other physical object. Psychomotor objectives usually focus on change or development in behavior or skills. This domain was subsequently subdivided by Bloom's successors.
   a. Reflex movements: reactions that are not learned.
   b. Fundamental movements: basic movements such as crawling, walking, or grasping.
   c. Perception: response to sensory stimuli such as visual, auditory, kinesthetic, or tactile discrimination.
   d. Physical abilities: stamina or skills that must be developed for further development such as strength and agility.
   e. Skilled movements: advanced learned movements as one would find in athletics, acting, or dance.
   f. Nondiscursive communication: effective body language, such as gestures and facial expressions.

2. *Cognitive* domain refers to intellectual capacities illustrated ascensively as follows:

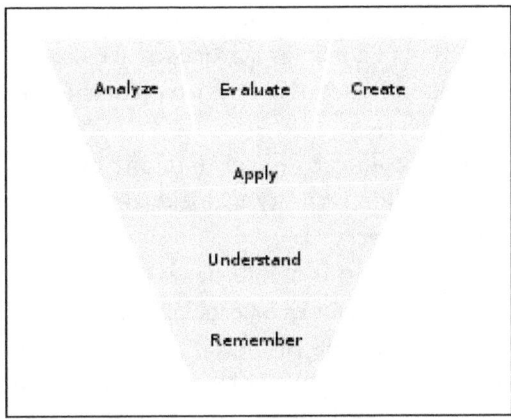

a. Knowledge: exhibit memory of previously learned materials by recalling facts, terms, basic concepts, and other answers.
   i. Knowledge of specifics—terminology, specific facts.
   ii. Knowledge of ways and means of dealing with specifics—conventions, trends and sequences, classifications and categories, criteria, methodology.
   iii. Knowledge of the universals and abstractions in a field—principles and generalizations, as well as theories and structures.
b. Comprehension: demonstrative understanding of facts and ideas by organizing, comparing, translating, interpreting, giving descriptions, and stating main ideas. Illustrations include:
   i. Translation.
   ii. Interpretation.
   iii. Extrapolation.
c. Application: using new knowledge, or solving problems to new situations by applying acquired knowledge, facts, techniques, and rules in some new way.
d. Analysis: examine and break information into parts by identifying motives or causes. Make inferences and find evidence to support generalizations.
   i. Analysis of elements.
   ii. Analysis of relationships.
   iii. Analysis of organizational principles.
e. Synthesis: compile information together in a different way by combining elements in a new pattern or proposing alternative solutions.

      i. Production of unique communication.
      ii. Production of a plan or a proposed set of operations.
      iii. Derivation of a set of abstract relationships among analyzed objects or terms.
   f. Evaluation: present or defend opinions by making judgments about information, validity of ideas, or quality of work based upon a set of criteria.
      i. Judgments in terms of internal evidence.
      ii. Judgments in terms of external criteria.

Harvard-educated Jerome Bruner (1915–2016) contributed to the reversal of what had been the predominance of Skinnerian behaviorism. He postulated that rats had little to do with children, so he advocated observing *children* in the *classroom* to understand how children learned best. Therein, he rediscovered *discovery learning* and the power of simple presentations utilizing formulas, models, and diagrams.[5]

Madeline Cheek Hunter (1916–1994), an American educator, developed a model for teaching, for learning, and for lesson plans which found wide acceptance especially by American schools during the last quarter of the twentieth century. Having developed the model in a laboratory school setting, she wrote extensively about that approach in twelve books, in more than 300 articles, and in seventeen videos. She believed that the most important function of a teacher was decision-making: content decisions, teaching decisions, and learning decisions. She delineated seven components of teaching:

1. Knowledge of human growth and development.
2. Content.
3. Classroom management.
4. Materials.
5. Planning.
6. Human relations.
7. Instructional skills.

She delineated seven components of effective instruction:

---

5. Anthony, *Evangelical Dictionary*, 97–98.

1. Objectives.
2. Standards.
3. Anticipatory set.
4. Teaching (input, modeling, checking for understanding).
5. Guided practice and monitoring.
6. Closure.
7. Independent practice.

David P. Ausubel (1918–2008), a Columbia-trained psychiatrist, established the PhD program in educational psychology at the City University of New York. Largely a Piagetian developmentalist, he advocated varied methodology due to the diverse and complex nature and content of learning and learners. To no small extent, it is from Ausubel that current teachers get much of their contemporary best practices, including but not limited to:

1. Check for understanding.
2. Restatement.
3. Application.

Neil Postman (1931–2003) asserted meaning-making as the most apt metaphor for the teaching-learning enterprise. Along with his coauthor, Charles Weingartner, both of whom were educational critics and promoters of inquiry education, published a chapter called "Meaning Making" in their 1969 book, entitled *Teaching as a Subversive Activity*. The chapter on "Meaning Making" proposed a constructivist philosophy of education (but without using the term "constructivist"),[6] and described

---

6. Constructivism could warrant its own chapter. This particular inclusion in this chapter on Developmentalism (in addition to having included it in the chapter on Continentalism) acknowledges many of Constructivism's roots stemming from the soils of Piagetian theories on individual development in general and on knowledge acquisition in particular. "Constructivism is a learning theory found in psychology which explains how people might acquire knowledge and learn. It, therefore, has direct application to education. The theory suggests that humans construct knowledge and meaning from their experiences." Constructivism is not a specific pedagogy. Piaget's theory of Constructivist learning has had wide ranging impact on learning theories and teaching methods in education and is an underlying theme of many education

why they preferred the term "meaning making" to any other metaphor for teaching and learning.

> In the light of all this, perhaps you will understand why we prefer the metaphor "meaning making" to most of the metaphors of the mind that are operative in the schools. It is, to begin with, much less static than the others. It stresses a process view of minding, including the fact that "minding" is undergoing constant change. "Meaning making" also forces us to focus on the individuality and the uniqueness of the meaning maker (the minder). In most of the other metaphors there is an assumption of "sameness" in all learners. The "garden" to be cultivated, the darkness to be lighted, the foundation to be built upon, the clay to be molded—there is always the implication that all learning will occur in the same way. The flowers will be the same color, the light will reveal the same room, the clay will take the same shape, and so on. Moreover, such metaphors imply boundaries, a limit to learning. How many flowers can a garden hold? How much water can a bucket take? What happens to the learner after his mind has been molded? How large can a building be, even if constructed on a solid foundation? The "meaning maker" has no such limitation. There is no end to his educative process. He continues to create new meanings.[7]

UCLA-trained Piagetian psychologist David Elkind (b. 1931) bemoans Americans' educational proclivity to cultivate a *Hurried Child* of "surrogate self." Contradistinctively, he argues that "all children have, vis-à-vis adults, special needs—intellectual, social, and emotional. Children do not learn, think, or feel in the same was as adults. To ignore these differences, to treat children as adults, is really not democratic or egalitarian."[8]

> Growth in personhood in our contemporary society takes time and cannot be hurried. As we know it, growth occurs in a series of [Piagetian] stages that are related to age. Each stage brings dramatic changes in intellectual capacity, in emotional attachments, and in social relations. The elaboration of these new

---

reform movements. Research support for constructivist teaching techniques has been mixed, with some research supporting these techniques and other research contradicting those results. See more at: http://sydney.edu.au/education_social_work/learning_teaching/ict/theory/constructivism.shtml#sthash.Ml5MIzlv.dpuf.

7. Thomas, *Education*, 94.

8. Elkind, *Hurried Child*, 22.

capacities in all of their complexity and intricacy is a slow and deliberate process. When children are pressured to grow up too fast, important achievements are skipped or bypassed, which can give rise to serious problems later.[9]

Howard Gardner (b. 1943) is a Harvard developmental psychologist. Gardner writes,

> It is up to the educational system as a whole—the educational system in the broadest sense—to ensure that the ensemble of minds is cultivated. In one sense, this is a job of synthesis—making sure that all five kinds of minds are developed. But, equally, it is an ethical obligation: in the years ahead, societies will not survive—let alone thrive—unless we as citizens respect and cultivate the quintet of minds valorized here:
>
> 1. The *disciplined mind* has mastered at least one way of thinking—a distinctive mode of cognition that characterizes a specific scholarly discipline, craft, or profession. Much research confirms that it takes up to ten years to master a discipline. The disciplined mind also knows how to work steadily over time to improve skill and understanding.
> 2. The *synthesizing mind* takes information from disparate sources, understands and evaluates that information objectively, and puts it together in ways that make sense to the synthesizer and also to other persons. Valuable in the past, the capacity to synthesize becomes ever more crucial as information continues to mount at dizzying rates.
> 3. Building on discipline and synthesis, the *creating mind* breaks new ground. It puts forth new ideas, poses unfamiliar questions, conjures up fresh ways of thinking, and arrives at unexpected answers. The creating mind seeks to remain at least one step ahead of even the most sophisticated computers and robots.
> 4. The *respectful mind* notes and welcomes differences between human individuals and between human groups, tries to understand these "others," and seeks to work effectively with them.
> 5. Preceding on a level even more abstract than even the *respectful mind*, the *ethical mind* ponders the nature of one's work and the needs and desires of society in which one lives. This mind conceptualizes how workers can serve purposes beyond self-interest and

---

9. Elkind, *Hurried Child*, 118.

how citizens can work unselfishly [and effectively] to improve the lot of all.[10]

Dr. Daniel Gregory Amen (b. 1954),[11] a *New York Times* bestselling author, psychiatrist, brain disorder specialist, and founder and CEO of his world renown Amen Clinics, puts it plainly: "Change your brain, change your life." Contemporary advances in our empirical understanding of neuroplasticity seem to corroborate ancient wisdom along those lines: "Be transformed by the renewing of your mind."[12] *That* is education.

Psychologists (and educators alike) have carried the torch of Developmentalism for more than a century. Ever since 1879, when Wilhelm Wundt opened his groundbreaking psychology lab in Leipzig, this relatively young discipline has committed to probing the depths of humanness.

In 1950 with the publication of Erikson's *Childhood and Society*, one could argue that a new field of psychology was born: *Developmental* Psychology. Developmental psychology (or the psychology of human development) purports to be the science by which to study processes of the life span. Although far from monolithic, the field tends toward a chronologizing of human development, often into what has come to be known as *stages*.

Whether psychosexual (Freud), psychodynamic (Horney), psychosocial (Erikson), cognitive (Piaget), cultural/historical-proximal (Vygotsky), moral (Kohlberg), etc., Developmentalists or stage theorists suggest a basic, observable, classifiable uniformity and a general universality of certain characteristics and maturation at certain generalized periods of time.

The present author concurs to a significant degree. Many patterns of development can be generalized to offer some helpful contribution to the overall understanding of how humans develop. However, there seems to be limits to those contributions, as well.

What follows, therefore, is a summary of potential limiting factors of what developmental psychology in general and stage theory in particular can, have, and should contribute to a deep understanding of what it means to be human in general, to be mature or maturing in particular, or to eventually be and become educated.

---

10. Gardner, *Five Minds for Future*, 165, 3.
11. Amen's is an individual-centered, neuro-based developmentalism.
12. As cited on www.amenclinics.com.

1. Developmental psychology has likely been most helpful in helping identify and clarify certain age-typical traits of maturation and growth (analogous to biomedical growth charts).

2. Analogous to the growth charts, however, as long as a child is not "off-the-charts," stunted, or inconsistent in his/her progress up the various charts, the helpfulness of such generalized benchmarks seems limited.[13]

3. Broad-based disciplines such as psychology sometimes seem to forget who they are. Psychology is and ought to be the study of the *psyche*, which is individual. Not that studies of many individuals or even groups of individuals ought to be off limits to (or for) psychological inquiry, but rather that the bias of psychology ought to be individually geared. Developmental psychologists (and to some degree many social psychologists and educators) seem to misappropriate that emphasis at times.

4. Concomitantly, whether working with individuals in the classroom or in coaching, counseling, mentoring, advising, etc., it seems more prudent to remember that the individual with whom one is working is just that, an *individual*—not a stage, nor a statistic.

5. Similarly, by extension, although a classroom teacher, for example (or others working with groups of individual persons somewhat simultaneously), can be aided by "reading the growth charts" so to speak, before planning what might be considered age-appropriate lessons, etc., that same teacher (and most certainly that same group of students) is most likely to be most helped by an intuitive and even

---

13. In other words, developmental stages are *descriptive* by nature but are sometimes invoked as *normative*. Care ought to be given not to overly infer from the *is* (even if the *is* is based upon thousands of *is*-es) to the *ought*. Each individual develops individually. Thus, it is also important not to commit the fallacy of composition (concluding it is *so* for the group, because it is *so* for the individual) or the fallacy of division (concluding that it is *so* for the individual, because it is *so* for the group). Finally, it is vitally important to remember that certain aspects of a particular generalized benchmark may pertain to an individual within a particular stage in a way that other certain aspects of a particular generalized benchmark may not. Violation of such would be the fallacy of overgeneralization; each benchmark is a generalization that generally applies to a group of individuals in some way, but each individual within that group develops idiosyncratically specific to each trait.

intentional focus on the individuals (and the group as consisting of individuals). A person they are; a statistic they are not.

6. Presently there seems to already have been much work done. Presently there is yet much work to be done. Not dissimilar to the physicists' quest for a unifying theory, psychologists—arguably much younger in their scientific approach to studying the brain, the mind, and the soul than physicists are to studying the cosmos—continue to forge ahead in systematizing their understanding of the various constituents and contributors to human development (e.g., nature vs. nurture; static vs. dynamic; cognitive vs. affective vs. behavioral; subjective vs. objective; subject vs. object; construct vs. deconstruct; humanism vs. dehumanizing; intrapersonal vs. interpersonal; intra-psychic vs. inter-psychic; conscious vs. subconscious vs. unconscious; genetically predisposed vs. socialized; biology vs. spirituality; inherited vs. learned; collective vs. individual; motivated vs. rewarded; deontological vs. teleological; past vs. present vs. future; conditioned vs. free; determined vs. responsible; healed vs. helped vs. held; self-examined vs. self-explored vs. self-directed; self-aware vs. self-discover vs. self-realized; self-image vs. self-actualized; and universalized vs. unique).

The quest for a full-orbed, biblically-based developmentalism continues. Developmentalists (including stage *and* trait theorists) have contributed significantly to that understanding, and will undoubtedly be looked to in the future to help ferret humanness and the development thereof.

Gabriel Moran, however, challenges these secular notions of developmentalism. "If *human development* is a legitimate term at all, it does not belong exclusively to psychologists. Instead of the psychologist peering into the individual psyche to uncover the laws of development, we have today a complex interdisciplinary task of tracking a movement whose laws depend in part on what is *outside* of the organism."[14]

In the context of a biblical philosophy of Christian school education that would foundationally entail God's word, one such Christian stage theorist, "Donald Oppewal has set forth a teaching methodology explicitly based upon the dynamic epistemology of Scripture."[15] He suggests a

---

14. Seymour, *Theological Approaches*, 147.
15. Knight, *Philosophy and Education*, 81.

three-stage methodology whose aim is dynamic learning for the student by means of transformational teaching from the Bible.

1. In the *consider* phase, the learner is presented with the new material.

2. In the *choose* phase, the options for response are clarified and the implications are explored.

3. During the *commit* phase, students move beyond intellectual understanding, beyond exposure of the moral and other considerations, and toward commitment to act on both the *is* and the *ought*.[16]

In his *Stages of Faith: The Psychology of Human Development and the Quest for Meaning*, James Fowler outlined six stages of maturation into adulthood with theological foundations for psychological and moral development. These stages provide the Christian educator with one scholar's attempt at a faith-learning integration, a biblical contextualization, and a hidden threads analysis of human awakening from a Christian's perspective for Christians in general and for Christian educators in particular.

In his stages of the soul, Moody similarly strives to explore and explain the complexity of spirituality and its development in interdisciplinary terms. He invokes phenomenology, epistemology, and developmentalistic stage theories. Moody presents what appears to be a systematically and systemically biblical summary of the awakening stages of spirituality within the life of Christian educator:

1. The Call.

2. The Search.

3. The Struggle.

4. The Breakthrough.

5. The Return.

The argument could be made that Christian developmentalism has been around for two thousand years or more. As early Christianity became established, as the early church began to grow, as the creeds were formulated, and as individual Christians began to reflect upon what it meant to live and to educate Christianly, various traditions of spiritual

---

16. Knight, *Philosophy and Education*, 248.

development—each with idiosyncratic contributions and deficiencies—developed. Their legacy and influence is still evident today.

1. *Desert Fathers (and Mothers)*. Per the *Oasis of Wisdom* and *The Apophthegmata*, these third- and fourth-century monks and nuns often lived in Egypt and advocated monasticism, asceticism, simplicity, solitude, silence, separation from society, attentiveness to the omnipresence of God, consideration of the struggles of others, and the primacy of gentle love and liberty in the Spirit apart from the world: "Flee, be silent, and pray!"

2. *Benedictine*. Governed by the seventy-three chapters of the Rules of St. Benedict, a fifth-century monk, the dicta of Benedict could be summed up as: *Ora et labora*, i.e., "Pray and work."

3. *Contemplative: The Prayer-Filled Life*. This stream of spirituality steadies one's gaze on the beautiful soul of God through meditation and prayer. Among others, Moravians and Pietists were known for such disciplines.

4. *Holiness: The Virtuous Life*. This tradition stresses inward reformation of the heart and the manifest outward expression of a wholly, holy habituated life. Catholics, Keswicks, and Anabaptists represented this tradition.

5. *Charismatic: The Spirit-Filled Life*. Yearning for the immediacy of God's presence and power, signs, wonders, gifts, and fruit became the litmus that groups such as the Gregorian, the Pentecostals, the Charismatic, and the Liturgical renewal movements emphasized.

6. *Social Justice: The Compassionate Life*. Justice, shalom, and freedom for all became hallmarks of movements such as the Vincentians, the Salvation Army, the Sunday school movement, and the American Civil Rights movement.

7. *Incarnational: The Sacramental Life*. To make manifest in day-to-day life the invisible qualities of God and his goodness are noteworthy of movements such as Eastern Orthodoxy, Renaissance, Romanticism, and Professional Christian Societies.

8. *Evangelical: The Word-Filled Life*. Proclamation of the Bible and the power of God through the gospel are emphasized by this tradition,

e.g., the Dominicans, Reformation, Great Awakenings, Protestant Missionary Movement, and the Student Volunteer Movements.

Taken as a whole and considering these many movements and the major motifs of Christian developmentalism in them and others, it seems prudent to consider the following:

1. Christian developmentalism needs to be examined under diversely interdisciplinary lenses.

2. Christian developmentalism can be examined, but in some ways eludes or transcends certain aspects of objective examination or at least articulation and precision.

3. Christian developmentalism not unlikely requires that a hermeneutic of appropriation trump a hermeneutic of suspicion.

4. Christian developmentalism is first and foremost "a way of life," and not an academic exercise or pursuit.

5. Christian developmentalism is a discipline (or a conglomeration of disciplines) that is necessarily both individual and communal.

6. Christian developmentalism is ultimately not about what we can do for God, but about what he has already done and is continuing to do until he returns.

7. Christian developmentalism is about life united with God and with his children.

8. Christian developmentalism involves involvement in the world socially and soteriologically, albeit somewhat separatistically.

9. Christian developmentalism is a mystery already—but not yet fully—revealed of a divine-human concursive both forming and transforming students and educators alike.

10. Christian developmentalism is about staying in step with the Spirit, conforming to the character of Christ, and abiding and abounding in the love of the Father.

Although multitudinous other contributions could be cited, the aforementioned modeling of interdisciplinarity and integration is exemplary for the Christian educator, whose life and work is and ought to be an integral, integrated, and interdisciplinary whole. That holistic approach then becomes the framework for the model of schooling to be pursued.

Developmentalism can contribute significantly to such a holistically Christian philosophizing about education. Although many of the most prominent trait and stage theorists are not necessarily Christian, their insights and paradigms have much to offer Christian educators willing to expend the energy and effort to sift, to sort, and to submit to the Spirit, of whom it could rightly be said: "All truth is *his* truth." May Christian educators so educate—and be so educated.

Chapter 14

Toward a Christian Understanding of Essentialism

Essentialism strives to educate students with what essentialists determine to be the most essential, foundational, central, basic, or common core of knowledge, skills, and character. Essentialists prioritize teachers having the competence necessary to present the aforementioned essentials in preparation of model citizens. Emphases are given to math, science, history, language, and literature. Essentialists generally eschew vocational courses and promote the identification and assimilation of an agreed-upon body of intellectual information and academic skills. The essentialist classroom is not infrequently lecture based, and students take notes. The focus is on students being informed about the so-called essential events, people, and institutions that have shaped society.

Born Mestrius Plutarchus, he is often known throughout history as Plutarch (ca. 46–ca. 120). Apparently appreciated by later intellectual giants such as Bruni, Erasmus, Elyot, and even Shakespeare, Plutarch's works have been admired and adapted to this current day. Plutarch composed multiple essays on education. For example, his "How the Young Man Should Study Poetry" presents poetry as pertinent preparation to the study of philosophy. In his "On Bringing Up a Boy," he explains, "Perfect men I take to be those who can blend practical ability with philosophy and who can achieve both best and greatest ends—the life of public utility as men of affairs, and the calm and tranquil life as students of philosophy. For there are three kinds of life: the life of action, the life of thought, and the life of enjoyment."[1] Complementarily, "we must not omit to exercise the body also. Our boys must be sent to the teacher of gymnastics and receive a sufficient amount of physical training, both to secure a good carriage and also to develop strength."[2] Finally, "above all things, one should train a child's memory. Memory serves as the storehouse of culture, and hence the fable that Recollection is the mother of the Muses—an indirect way of saying that memory is the best thing in the world to beget and foster wisdom."[3]

Benjamin Franklin (1706–1790) was "long regarded at home and abroad as the quintessential American.... Both famous and revealing is Franklin's account of how he attempted to lead a virtuous life by making a 'little book' in which he allotted a page to each of the virtues and marked his progress as in a ledger."[4] A proponent of self-education, he proposed foreign languages, mathematics, English composition, literature, public speaking, politics, natural sciences, religion, morals, and the practical arts as the bases of an informed electorate and a stable society.

John Henry Newman (1801–1890) was Oxford educated and came to be known as liberal learning's preeminent defender. He delineates "two methods of education, the one aspires to be philosophical, the other to be mechanical; the one rises toward ideas, the other is exhausted upon what is particular and external."[5] He advocated a blending of both.

> The grace stored in Jerusalem, and the gifts which radiate from Athens, are made over and concentrated in Rome. This is true as a matter of history. Rome has inherited both sacred and profane learning; she has perpetuated and dispensed the traditions of Moses and David in supernatural order, and of Homer and Aristotle in the natural. To separate those distinct teachings, human and divine, which meet in Rome, is to retrograde; it is to rebuild the Jewish Temple and to plant anew the four groves of Academus.[6]

William C. Bagley (1874–1946), founder of the Essentialistic Education Society and author of *Education and Emergent Man* (1934), makes

---

1. Gamble, *Great Tradition*, 138.
2. Gamble, *Great Tradition*, 138.
3. Gamble, *Great Tradition*, 139.
4. Bellah et al., *Habits of the Heart*, 32.
5. Gamble, *Great Tradition*, 520.
6. Gamble, *Great Tradition*, 537.

what has been called "The Case for Essentialism in Education." Bagley's book was largely a polemic against the progressivism within American education of his day. He contested that Dewey's pragmatism in particular intellectually hamstrung and morally bankrupt its students. He insisted that a predetermined core of common knowledge should be conveyed to and instilled within all students systematically and disciplinarily. Admittedly akin to perennialism in some ways, Bagley's essentialism emphasized the so-called essential knowledge and competencies necessary to produce prepared citizens—rather than a set of perennial ideas and truths to be addressed and assimilated.

Eric Donald Hirsch Jr. (b. 1928) is professor emeritus of education and humanities at the University of Virginia and perhaps best known for his book *Cultural Literacy: What Every American Needs to Know*. He founded, and he still chairs, the Core Knowledge Foundation.

Per their website,

> The mission of the Core Knowledge Foundation is to advance excellence and equity in education for all children.
>
> To achieve this mission, we offer detailed curricular guidance and materials to schools, teachers, parents, and policy makers—to anyone who believes, as we do, that every child in a diverse democracy deserves access to enabling knowledge.
>
> By providing open access to an exemplary curriculum for preschool through eighth grade, we endeavor to:
> - create literate citizens able to contribute to a democratic society;
> - empower each child to achieve his or her greatest academic potential;
> - shrink the excellence gap between the academic achievement of American students and that of their international peers from high-performing countries;
> - shrink the fairness gap between the academic achievement of American students living in poverty and that of their economically advantaged peers.

And, per Hirsch himself,

> If all of our children are to be fully educated and participate equally in civic life, then we must provide each of them with the shared body of knowledge that makes literacy and communication possible. This concept, central to the Core Knowledge Foundation's goal of excellence and equity in education, takes shape in the Sequence—a pioneering attempt to outline the

specific core of shared knowledge that all children should learn in American schools.[7]

From one of the bastions of essentialism in twenty-first-century America, this summary statement of their adherent essentialism philosophy and practice:[8]

> The Core Knowledge Foundation is dedicated to the mission expressed in our motto—*educational excellence and equity for all children*. To make that mission a reality we offer detailed help and materials to schools, teachers and parents, and effective advocacy grounded in scientific research to citizens and policy makers. We believe that every person in a diverse democratic society deserves equal access to the common knowledge base that draws together its people, while recognizing our differing traditions and contributions. We believe that offering universal access to this shared knowledge is a primary duty of schooling, critical to literacy, and to the closing of the achievement gap between ethnic and racial groups. Most important of all, we believe that shared knowledge, a shared narrative, and shared ideals of liberty and tolerance are indispensable ingredients for effective citizenship and for the perpetuation of our democratic institutions.

Essentialism nobly emphasizes excellence and equity in education and a corpus of so-called essential or core knowledge, skills, and character that ought to be transmitted to students. Their basis for that is largely about promoting democratic values and of preparing solid citizens. They strategically standardized achievement to buoy lower performing schools and students.

Unfortunately, some essentialists prioritize tolerance over truth; many essentialists prioritize a prepared democratic citizenry over an educated *imago Dei*; most essentialists prioritize acquisition of prescribed skills and knowledge over creativity, inquiry, logic, rhetoric, wisdom, or salvation and sanctification. Finally, a (not unlikely unintended) ramification of some essentialist school programs has included not only the buoying up of low-performing institutions and individuals, but also in some cases the so-called dumbing down of other more aspiring

---

7. Hirsch, *Cultural Literacy*.

8. Core Knowledge, "Our Approach," https://www.coreknowledge.org/our-approach/.

individuals or more high-performing institutions to the new norm of whatever is considered *essential*.⁹

---

9. Ted Slater of Regent University provides a helpful critique of Essentialism at http://www.tedslater.com/archives/personal/papers/slater_educational_philosophies.pdf. In addition to documenting some of the aforementioned critiques, Slater also suggests the following critiques: "Teachers are expected to direct the educational process to such an extent that while their students might find the material difficult and, at the time, useless, teachers are assumed to know best what and how their students should be learning at a particular time. The immediate perceived needs of the students are not as important as the more distant goals that educators have set for them. With the instructor's assistance, students can be helped to get down to the hard work of performing a difficult assignment. Nonessential classes such as tap dancing and basket weaving have no place in the essentialists' curriculum. Methods include memorization and drills. Although students might not find these methods interesting, they are expected to discipline themselves to focus their attention to learn the material presented to them in the way it is presented."

Chapter 15

Toward a Christian Understanding of Perennialism

Perennialists promote education that engages students with great ideas. Curricula look similar *to* traditional or Essentialist curricula (e.g., math, science, history, literature, language arts, fine arts, athletics, etc.), but not infrequently depart *from* other curricula in at least four ways:

1. The reintegration of ideas from literature, language arts, social studies, and other humanities back into their historical contexts.[1]

2. The chronologizing of the delivery of humanities content.[2]

3. The study of one or more of the classical languages, most notably Latin, Greek, or Logic.

4. The structuring of the educational system to mirror the stages of the *trivium*:

    1. Elementary school is called (and taught as) Grammar school.

---

1. Unlike traditional curricula, perennialists often do not teach English and History as separate classes, but block them together as omnibus or—more commonly—humanities. Great ideas are then taught in the chronological context of when that idea generally emerged onto the literary-historical scene.

2. Not infrequently, for example, a freshman in high school will start his humanities class(es)—and even his biology class—with, "In the beginning God created . . ." Sophomores might pick-up humanities around the time of Christ; juniors start with the Renaissance; seniors cover modernity and postmodernity.

2. Middle school is called (and taught as) Logic school.
3. High school is called (and taught as) Rhetoric school.

Additionally, the *foci* of education include reading books that are great, teaching ideas that are profound, seeking truths that are enduring, pursuing wisdom that is timeless, and cultivating virtues that are excellent. Cultivation of the intellect is a priority, but so is cultivation of the soul.

Aristophanes (446–386 BC) bemoaned progressive trends in education and advocated conservatism, propriety, and the perennial principles of *paideia*. He described his preferred approach to education—which he claimed had prepared great men to be great as follows:

> *To hear then prepare of the Disciplines rare*
> *Which flourished in Athens of yore*
> *When Honor and Truth were in fashion with youth*
> *And Sobriety bloomed on our shore . . .*
> *Yet these are the precepts which taught*
> *The heroes of old to be hardy and bold*
> *And the Men who at Marathon fought.*[3]

Aristarchus of Samothrace (ca. 220–143 BC) established a school of philology. He emphasized history, language, linguistics, grammar, and transcription. He prioritized fluency with primary source materials. He and his students wrote nearly 1000 commentaries.

Of Cicero (106–43 BC), it is said, "Few men have exercised an influence over the development of literature and of education in western Europe comparable to that of Marcus Tullius Cicero."[4] One of the prominent writers of the golden age of Roman literature, his work is esteemed by Quintilian as the finest Latin oration, and his grammar provided a paradigm for much of the Renaissance model of writing. A proponent of a versed and varied education of the humanities and of the letters, he championed the cause of the liberal arts in his philosophy of education. "Although others may be called men [*homines*], those alone are such who are perfected in the sciences proper to humanity."[5]

Seneca (ca. 4 BC–AD 65) criticized schools of his day for having abandoned the excellence of Platonic instruction and Aristotelian habituation.

---

3. Eby, *Ancient and Medieval*, 272–73.
4. Eby, *Ancient and Medieval*, 543.
5. Eby, *Ancient and Medieval*, 546.

> We dull our fine edge by superfluous pursuits; these things make men clever, but not good. Wisdom is a plainer thing than that, nay it is clearly better to use literature for the improvement of the mind, instead of wasting philosophy itself as we waste other efforts on superfluous things. Just as we suffer from excess in all things, so we suffer from excess in literature. Thus, we learn our lessons, not for life, but for the lecture-room.[6] . . . Betake yourself, therefore, to philosophy if you would be safe, untroubled, happy, and if you wish to be—and, that is most important—free.[7]

Quintilian (35–95), having been a *tricinium fori* (i.e., an apprentice for the year that a young man spent working with a distinguished man as—in this case—his legal and rhetorical assistant and student) of Domitius, he advocated such internships whose goal was to expose the young man to the knowledge, skills, and virtues that had contributed to the patron's success.[8] Quintilian also advocated elementary education as "play school."[9] His many, varied educational innovations included:

1. Study should be balanced with play.

2. Children ought to be "won for learning."

3. Educational toys such as large ivory letters and wax tablets should be used.

4. Reading and writing should be introduced to three-year-olds via games and songs.

5. Rewards ought to be given for good behavior, rather than corporal punishment for bad behavior.

Quintilian recommended a "Great Books" curriculum and character development. "I hold that no one can be a true orator, unless he is also a good man, and even if he could be, I would not have it so."[10] He proceeded to explain that his educational "aim, then, is the education of the perfect orator."[11] Other aspects of his educational emphases included:

---

6. *Non vitae sed scholae discimus.*
7. Eby, *Ancient and Medieval*, 511.
8. Gutek, *Historical and Philosophical Foundations*, 67.
9. Kienel, *History of Christian School Education*, 1:23.
10. Gamble, *Great Tradition*, 106.
11. Gamble, *Great Tradition*, 107.

1. Begin with Greek.

2. Have a thorough education.

3. Search for wisdom. ("All previous ages have toiled that we might reap the fruit of wisdom.")[12]

Where to conduct such an education (whether at a school or in one's home) had become quite debated in his day.

> But the time has come for the boy to grow little by little, to leave the nursery and to tackle his studies in good earnest. This, therefore, is the place to discuss the question as to whether it is better to have him educated privately at home or hand him over to some large school and those whom I may call public instructors. The latter course has, I know won the approval of most eminent authorities and of those who have formed the national character of the most famous states.
>
> Let me now explain my own views. It is above all things necessary that our future orator, who will have to live in the utmost publicity in the broad daylight of public life, should become accustomed from his childhood to move in society without fear and habituated to a life far removed from that of the pale student, the solitary, the recluse. His mind requires constant stimulus and excitement.[13]

As an orator and a historian, Tacitus (ca. 55–ca. 117) emphasized a liberal arts education. "Breadth of culture is an ornament that tells of itself even when one is not making a point of it: it comes prominently into view where you least expect it. . . . I have been extolling a knowledge of law and of philosophy as indispensable to the orator."[14]

Albert (d. 779), the Archbishop Egbert of York's minister school, was the son of prominent parents. He was consecrated to the archiepiscopate on April 24, 767. The reputation of his school, which spread over Europe, was due much to the zeal and learning of Albert himself. The great library there was chiefly collected by him during his many wanderings on the Continent, with Alcuin as his companion. Scholars described this early, energetic educator as follows:

---

12. Gamble, *Great Tradition*, 106.
13. Gamble, *Great Tradition*, 106–27.
14. Gamble, *Great Tradition*, 128–32.

There he (Albert) moistened thirsty hearts with diverse streams of teaching and varied dews of study; busily giving to some the arts of science of grammar (*grammaticae rationis artes*), pouring into others the streams of the tongues of orators; these he polished on the whet-stone of law, those he taught to sing in Aeonian chant, making others play the flute of Castaly, and run with the lyre over the hills of Parnassus. But others, the said master made to know the harmony of heaven and the sun, the labors of the moon, the five belts of the sky, the seven planets, the laws of the fixed stars, their rising and setting, the movements of the air and the sun, the earth's quake, the nature of men, cattle, birds, and beasts, the different kinds of number and various (geometrical) figures; and he gave sure return to the festival of Easter, above all, revealing the mysteries of holy writ, for he opened the abysses of the old and rude law.

The one master taught all the subjects of learning, not only the trivium, grammar, rhetoric, and logic, and the quadrivium, arithmetic, geometry, music, and astronomy, but the subjects of the higher faculties, law, and "above all" divinity. He therefore performed the functions afterwards separated by the division of labor between the Grammar Schoolmaster [and] the Song Schoolmaster.[15]

Among Rabanus Maurus's (ca. 776–856) principal writing was *On the Education of the Clergy*, in which he delineated the curriculum:

1. Grammar
2. Rhetoric
3. Dialectic
4. Arithmetic
5. Geometry
6. Music
7. Astronomy

The seven liberal arts of the philosophers, which Christians should learn for their utility and advantage, we have, I think, sufficiently discussed. We have this yet to add. When those, who are called philosophers, have in their expositions or in their writings, uttered perchance some truth, which agrees with our faith, we should not handle it timidly, but rather take it as from its unlawful possessors and apply it to our own use.[16]

---

15. Kienel, *History of Christian School Education*, 1:67.
16. Gamble, *Great Tradition*, 254.

In correspondence to his friend regarding education, Alfred the Great (849–899) wrote to Bishop Waeferth,

> Therefore it seems better to me, if you agree, for us also to translate some of the books into the language which we all can understand, and for you to see to it, as can easily be done if we have tranquility enough, that all the freeborn youth now in England, who are rich enough to be able to devote themselves to it, be set to learn as long as they are not fit for any other occupation, until that they are well able to read English writing, and let those afterwards be taught more in the Latin language who are to continue learning, and be promoted to a higher rank.[17]

As an excellent epistolary, Petrach (1304–1374) penned pithy prose, not a few of which elucidated his educational views. "Believe me, many things are attributed to gravity and wisdom which are really due to incapacity and sloth."[18] Petrach is credited with rejuvenating the ancient model of liberal education, the *studia humanitatis* of Renaissance humanism. His insistence on the centrality of self-knowledge in education connects him with a long tradition."[19]

Geert Groote (1340–1384), founder of the Brethren of the Common Life, utilized the *trivium* and *quadrivium*, but emphasized the vernacular as well as the classical languages. He was rather ahead of the times by utilizing grade plans, small groups, and even differentiated and leveled instruction per the pace(s) of the students.

Leonardo Bruni D'Arezzo (1369–1444) declared his interest in the education of girls, as well as boys. A Ciceronian by style and Petrarchian by philosophical content, classicism and humanism pulsate from his voluminous compositions and translations—especially Greek works into Latin and Italian. His essay on education appears to be among the first humanistic tracts published on the subject.[20]

Under the patronage of the Medici family, Leonardo Bruni (ca. 1370–1444), a lawyer by trade, gave himself and his students to the study and translation of classic Greek and Latin works. He emphasized both style *and* content as, what he called, "the two sides of learning." In his *On the Study of Literature*, Bruni demonstrated his penchant for the breadth

---

17. Lockerbie, *Passion for Learning*, 89.
18. Gamble, *Great Tradition*, 303.
19. Gamble, *Great Tradition*, 304.
20. Eby, *Ancient and Medieval*, 884.

of a liberal (i.e., liberal arts) education: "We must not forget that true distinction is to be gained by a wide and varied range of such studies as conduce to the profitable enjoyment of life."[21]

Vittorino de Feltre (1378–1446), although diminutive in stature, is recognized to have been mighty in his Christian convictions and enormous in his impact on the Italian renaissance. Generally considered the father of boarding schools, Feltre founded a school to house and to educate Christian boys in classicism, moral philosophy, and literature. He advocated "Christianity and humanism [as] the two coordinate factors necessary to the development of complete manhood."[22]

Dorothy Sayers (1893–1957), an English novelist, playwright, translator, and daughter of a school headmaster, concluded that "the sole true end of education is simply this: to teach men how to learn for themselves, and whatever instruction fails to do this is effort spent in vain."[23] She first delivered her brief "The Lost Tools of Learning" as a lecture at Oxford in 1947. The impact of these educationally famed insights have been so influential and international that its opening paragraph is cited substantively here.[24]

> My views about child psychology are, I admit, neither orthodox nor enlightened. Looking back upon myself (since I am the child I know best and the only child I can pretend to know from inside), I recognize three states of development. These, in a rough-and-ready fashion, I will call the Poll-Parrot, the Pert, and the Poetic, the latter coinciding, approximately, with the onset of puberty. The Poll-Parrot stage is the one in which learning by heart is easy and, on the whole, pleasurable; whereas reasoning is difficult and, on the whole, little relished. At this age, one readily memorizes the shapes and appearances of things, one likes to recite the number-plates of cars, one rejoices in the chanting of rhymes and the rumble and thunder of unintelligible polysyllables, one enjoys the mere accumulation of things. The Pert age, which follows upon this (and, naturally, overlaps it to some extent), is characterized by contradicting, answering back,

---

21. Gamble, *Great Tradition*, 332.
22. Lockerbie, *Passion for Learning*, 121.
23. Sayers, *Lost Tools of Learning*, available online at https://classicalchristian.org/the-lost-tools-of-learning-dorothy-sayers/.
24. Classical education has been the fastest growing approach to education in America since the late twentieth century, and Sayers's speech has prompted no small part of that growth.

liking to "catch people out" (especially one's elders), and by the propounding of conundrums. Its nuisance-value is extremely high. It usually sets in about the Fourth Form. The Poetic age is popularly known as the "difficult" age. It is self-centered; it yearns to express itself; it rather specializes in being misunderstood; it is restless and tries to achieve independence; and, with good luck and good guidance, it should show the beginnings of creativeness; a reaching out towards a synthesis of what it already knows, and a deliberate eagerness to know and do some one thing in preference to all others. Now it seems to me that the layout of the Trivium adapts itself with a singular appropriateness to these three ages: Grammar to the Poll-Parrot, Dialectic to the Pert, and Rhetoric to the Poetic age.[25]

C. S. Lewis (1898–1963) advocated reading "old books." "It is a good rule, after reading a new book, never to allow yourself another new book till you have read an old one in between. If that is too much for you, you should at least read one old one to every three new ones."[26] Lewis explains that

> there is a strange idea abroad that in every subject the ancient books should be read only by the professionals, and that the amateur should content himself with the modern books. . . . Now this seems to me topsy-turvy. . . . Every age has its own outlook. It is especially good at seeing certain truths and especially liable to make certain mistakes. . . . We all, therefore, need to read books that will correct the characteristic mistakes of our own period. And that means old books.[27]

Mortimer Adler (1902–2001) observed, "The human mind naturally tends to learn, to acquire knowledge—just as the earth naturally tends to support vegetation."[28] He identifies three adjustments to modes of teaching and learning to strengthen the basic ways in which the mind can be improved—i.e., what is education and how can it be accomplished and enhanced:

1. Acquisition of organized knowledge.

---

25. Sayers, *Lost Tools of Learning*, available online at https://classicalchristian.org/the-lost-tools-of-learning-dorothy-sayers/.
26. Gamble, *Great Tradition*, 595.
27. Gamble, *Great Tradition*, 595–600.
28. Peterson, *With All Your Mind*, 41.

2. Development of intellectual skills.

3. Enlargement of understanding, insight, and appreciation.[29]

No small manifestation of Adler's educational philosophy was summarized in his 1982 book, *The Paideia Proposal*. In summary, Adler concludes that Great Books and their Great Ideas are the antidotes for contemporary educational malaise: "To make a fresh start, it is only necessary to open the great philosophical books of the past (especially those written by Aristotle and in his tradition) and to read them with the effort of understanding that they deserve. The recovery of basic truths, long hidden from view, would eradicate errors that have had such disastrous consequences in modern times."[30]

Thirty years earlier, Adler had published what to many has become the gold standard of classical education and the great books tradition: *A Synopticon: An Index to the Great Ideas* (1952) is a two-volume index of the great books and the 102 great ideas that Adler and University of Chicago colleague Robert Hutchins identified. The *Synopticon* was originally published as volumes 2 and 3 of *Encyclopedia Britannica*'s series entitled *Great Books of the Western World*.

A Christian humanist, an educational historian, and a classicist, Henri-Irénée Marrou (1904–1977) advocated for a perennialist approach to education. "A classical culture can be defined as a unified collection of great masterpieces existing as the recognized basis of its scale of values."[31]

Tracy Lee Simmons, Hillsdale College professor, writes,

> Classical education was thought to *improve* the learner, not simply to make him more knowledgeable or tolerant or mentally skillful, but better and stronger, just as there survives today a residual belief that one who has read and digested Shakespeare is better, more insightful, than one who has not. Educated men were known for their ability not only to do the right things, but also to say the right things in the right way: *Ars recte loquendi*—the art of correct speaking and writing, and was therefore *initium et fundamentum omnium disciplinarum*—the beginning and basis of all knowledge. No doubt this aptitude and habit, this thirst and hunger for the *mot juste*, paid off. Reading was

---

29. Adler, *Paideia Proposal*, 22.
30. Adler, *Ten Philosophical*, 200.
31. Hicks, *Norms and Nobility*, 107.

not to be broad or "inclusive," but good: it should consist of the best.

Language took front seat—in Latin and Greek. The Humanist ideal laws uttered for new listeners. More to the point, this period, through classical learning, bestowed upon latter generations a recognized corpus, a body of expanded literary, philosophical, and artistic knowledge that . . . fashioned and maintained models of imitation designed for the pursuit of excellence. The educated man and woman were not merely educated. They were *cultured*. And their culture, such as it was, could be proved by the languages they knew and the books they read. . . . No hidebound blindness or hoodwinked drones here. These men were out to achieve results, not merely to enforce mindless routine.[32]

Douglas Wilson (b. 1953), a conservative, Reformed pastor, author, educator, and founder and head of a Christian school and a Christian college in Moscow, Idaho, promotes classical, Christian education. He posits that public schools have failed and that the antidote to failed education is a renaissance of the trivium, the quadrivium, the classical languages, good books, and great ideas—as well as a return to biblical, Christian ideas and ideals.

Contemporary classicists Kevin Clark and Ravi Scott Jain's book on *A Philosophy of Christian Classical Education* is presented here in a nutshell.[33]

---

32. Simmons, *Climbing Parnassus*, 106–19.
33. Clark et al., *Liberal Arts Tradition*, 149.

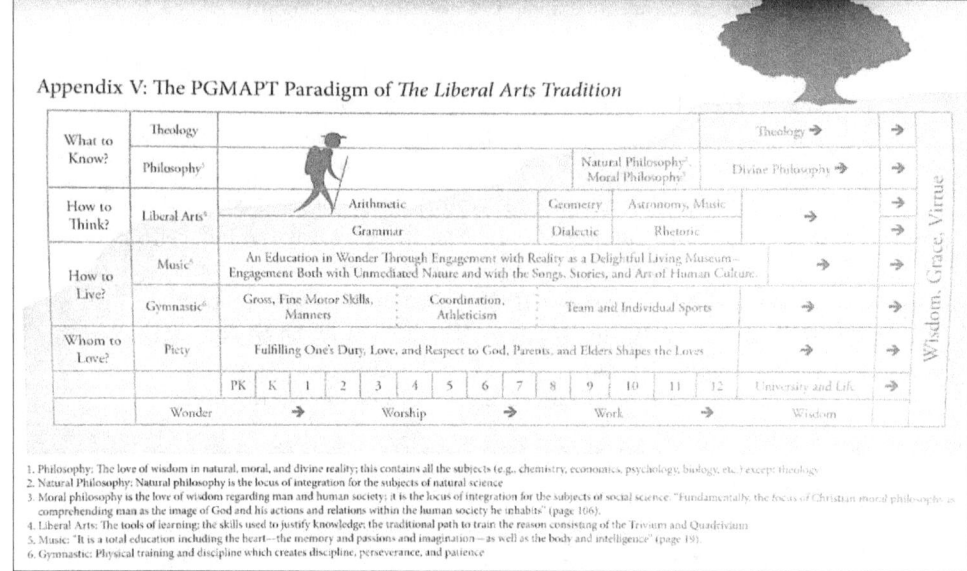

Appendix V: The PGMAPT Paradigm of *The Liberal Arts Tradition*

What to Know?	Theology				Theology →	→	
	Philosophy[1]			Natural Philosophy[2] Moral Philosophy[3]	Divine Philosophy →	→	
How to Think?	Liberal Arts[4]	Arithmetic	Geometry	Astronomy, Music	→	→	Wisdom, Grace, Virtue
		Grammar	Dialectic	Rhetoric		→	
How to Live?	Music[5]	An Education in Wonder Through Engagement with Reality as a Delightful Living Museum—Engagement Both with Unmediated Nature and with the Songs, Stories, and Art of Human Culture.			→	→	
	Gymnastic[6]	Gross, Fine Motor Skills, Manners	Coordination, Athleticism	Team and Individual Sports	→	→	
Whom to Love?	Piety	Fulfilling One's Duty, Love, and Respect to God, Parents, and Elders Shapes the Loves			→	→	
		PK K 1 2 3 4 5 6 7 8 9 10 11 12			University and Life	→	
		Wonder →	Worship →	Work →	Wisdom		

1. Philosophy: The love of wisdom in natural, moral, and divine reality; this contains all the subjects (e.g., chemistry, economics, psychology, biology, etc.) except theology.
2. Natural Philosophy: Natural philosophy is the locus of integration for the subjects of natural science.
3. Moral philosophy is the love of wisdom regarding man and human society; it is the locus of integration for the subjects of social science. "Fundamentally, the focus of Christian moral philosophy is comprehending man as the image of God and his actions and relations within the human society he inhabits" (page 166).
4. Liberal Arts: The tools of learning; the skills used to justify knowledge; the traditional path to train the reason consisting of the Trivium and Quadrivium.
5. Music: "It is a total education including the heart—the memory and passions and imagination—as well as the body and intelligence" (page 19).
6. Gymnastic: Physical training and discipline which creates discipline, perseverance, and patience.

Perennialists promote education that engages students with great ideas. The *foci* of this education include reading great books and pursuing truth, wisdom, and virtue. Cultivation of the intellect is a priority, but so is cultivation of the soul.

The person committed to a biblical philosophy of Christian school education can find much in Perennialism that is valuable and helpful. The caution becomes not removing Christ from their formulas of freedom, flourishing, and forever, or from the standards of what is considered perennial, or from the values of *Veritas, Sapience, Virtu*.[34] It is God and God alone that is the same yesterday, today, and forever. Any attempt at perennialism apart from *soli scriptura, soli gratia, soli fide,* and *soli Deo gloria* is neither as timeless nor as durative as its name *perennialism* might otherwise suggest.

---

34. I.e., Truth, Wisdom, Virtue, which is a representative motto among many Perennialists.

Chapter 16

Toward a Biblical Philosophy of Christian School Education

FROM AT LEAST AS early as the *Shemah* of Deuteronomy 6 about 1400 BC, the people of God had received direct mandate from God to reach and teach the next generation about him and the way life ought to be lived under him. As discussed earlier, the ten domains delineated in Deut 6:4–9 seem to entail a decalogue of *all* of life. In other words, from the moment the child wakes in the morning until the moment the child goes to sleep at night—and all of the moments in between—it is incumbent upon the parent(s) to impress upon the hearts of their children the nature of who God is and how he wants life to be lived. *All* of life ought to be seen through the lens of God and his revealed beauty, goodness, and truth. *This* all-encompassing, Godward worldview is a critical component of a biblical philosophy of Christian school education—its *sine qua non*.

This model gets articulated throughout Scripture. Many such biblical passages have already been discussed. This model also gets articulated through many good and godly folks' philosophies of education over the centuries. The remainder of this chapter provides a representative sampling of some of those.[1]

---

1. At least as much as in any of the preceding twelve chapters on schools of thought within the philosophy of education, this chapter is selective. In at least one way this chapter is arguably even *more* selective. In this chapter, for example, *only* followers of Jesus who have a high regard for the word of God and for the God of the word are included. In some of the other chapters there are people who fit that description, as well—and are included in *that* chapter rather than in this one. One illustration seems

Justin Martyr (ca. 100–ca. 165) believed that "philosophy is indeed compatible with the gospel. He came to see that his pagan quest to know and understand the *logos* of philosophy had, in fact, prepared him to meet the true *Logos*, the Word-made-Flesh, and the revelation of truth in Jesus Christ. So, Justin retained his robe and, in Rome, conducted his own school."[2]

Titus Flavious Clemens (ca. 150–ca. 215), known as Clement of Alexandria, described philosophy as a "schoolmaster to bring the Hellenic mind—as the Law, the Hebrews—to Christ."[3] He impactfully penned *Paedagogus: The Instructor*, personifying the Lord Jesus Christ as the Author and Instructor whose benevolence, knowledge, authority, and divinity deserve our utmost attention. "But our Educator is the holy God, Jesus, the Word guiding all mankind."[4] "Now the instruction which is of God is the right direction of truth to the contemplation of God, and the exhibition of holy deeds in everlasting perseverance."[5] Clement proposed a kind of early Christian humanism, articulating what could be considered a "maximalist" position of integration, that *all* truth is God's truth—regardless of its human source.

On the other hand, Tertullian (ca. 155–240) argued,

> What indeed has Athens to do with Jerusalem? What concord is there between the Academy and the Church? What between heretics and Christians? Our instruction comes from the porch of Solomon, who had himself taught that the Lord should be sought in simplicity of heart. Away with all attempts to produce a mottled Christianity of Stoic, Platonic, and dialectic composition! We want no serious disputation after possessing Christ Jesus, no inquisition after enjoying the gospel. With our faith, we desire no further belief.[6]

---

representative. Douglass Wilson is included in the chapter on Perennialism. He is a conservative, evangelical follower of Jesus; a pastor, a preacher, and a Christian author; and a founder of a Christian school, a Christian college, and the Association of Classical Christian Schools. He could have been included in *this* chapter, but with his penchant for Perennialism, he fit that previous chapter. By default, therefore, he is included there and not here.

2. Lockerbie, *Passion for Learning*, 43.
3. Lockerbie, *Passion for Learning*, 46.
4. Gamble, *Great Tradition*, 163.
5. Lockerbie, *Passion for Learning*, 47.
6. Kienel, *History of Christian School Education*, 1:5.

TOWARD A BIBLICAL PHILOSOPHY OF CHRISTIAN SCHOOL EDUCATION 225

Origen (ca. 185–ca. 254) urged his student(s) to

> extract from the philosophy of Greeks what may serve as a course of study or a preparation for Christianity, and from geometry and astronomy what will serve to explain the sacred Scriptures, in order that all that the sons of the philosophers are wont to say about geometry and music, grammar, rhetoric, and astronomy, as fellow-helpers to philosophy, we many say about philosophy itself, in relation to Christianity. . . . Do then, my son, diligently apply yourself to the reading of the sacred Scriptures.[7]

Basil the Great's (ca. 329–379) sermon "To Young Men, on How They Might Derive Profit from Pagan Literature" continues to be translated and published today and has become one of the definitive statements on Christianity's response to pagan culture in the context of education.

> So, we also must consider that a contest, the greatest of all contests, lies before us, for which we must do all things, and, in preparation for it, must strive to the best of our power, and must associate with poets and writers of prose and orators, and with all men from whom there is any prospect of benefit with reference to the care of the soul.[8]

Conversant in Greek and Latin, Eusebius Hieronymus Sophronius, not infrequently referred to as Jerome (ca. 342–420), translated the Vulgate Scriptures, opened a monastery in Bethlehem, and wrote more than one hundred letters presently extant, in which he demonstrates his integrationist approach to education.

> Is it surprising that I, too, admiring the fairness of her form and the grace of her eloquence, desire to make that secular wisdom, which is my captive and my handmaid, a matron of true Israel? I now read the books of God with a zeal even greater than I had previously given to the books of men.[9]

Trained as a lawyer after he was baptized, John Chrysostom (ca. 345–407) became a monk and subsequently a priest. He studied theology in Antioch, whose methods were more Aristotelian than Platonic. "Chrysostom's continuity with the classical tradition is obvious. Laistner writes, 'His main point, in which he is merely repeating with a Christian

---

7. Lockerbie, *Passion for Learning*, 51–52.
8. Gamble, *Great Tradition*, 181.
9. Gamble, *Great Tradition*, 206–8.

slant what the greatest pagan educators, from Plato and Isocrates to Quintilian, had stated emphatically long before, is that the moral purpose of education is more important than anything else.'"[10] In that spirit, Chrysostom wrote his "Address on Vainglory and the Right Way for Parents to Bring Up Their Children."

> What will become of boys from earliest youth if they are without teachers? I shall not cease exhorting and begging and supplicating you before all else to discipline your sons from the first. . . . Raise up an athlete for Christ and teach him though he is living in the world to be reverent from his earliest youth. . . . Let us them implant in him this wisdom and let us exercise him therein, that he may know the meaning of human desires, wealth, reputation, power, and may disdain these and strive after the highest.[11]

"While St. Patrick (ca. 385–461) was not well educated—his having been kidnapped and enslaved robbed him of formal education, he promoted learning among his primitive converts."[12] His syncretism of Irish paganism and biblical Christianity marked much of his missionary campaign to evangelize and educate the commoners of his homeland. In addition to his humble writings, his numerous baptisms, and his extensive preaching, his impact on education can also be seen through the history of the dioceses in Ireland which he helped organize and establish. These dioceses became the purveyors of Christian education throughout his native country.

Cassiodorus's (ca. 485–ca. 585) *Institutions of Divine and Secular Learning* defends the use of secular studies oriented toward the glory of God.

> For learning taken from the ancients in the midst of praising the Lord is not considered boasting. Therefore, dearest brothers, after the soldiers of Christ have filled themselves with divine study and, grown strong by regular reading, have begun to recognize passages cited as circumstances indicate, then they may profit from going through this guide. In this way indifference and negligence and vital knowledge sought by minds set aflame in the training school of Christ.[13]

10. Gamble, *Great Tradition*, 192.
11. Gamble, *Great Tradition*, 191–205.
12. Lockerbie, *Passion for Learning*, 65.
13. Gamble, *Great Tradition*, 228–30.

Among the esteemed "Doctors of the Church,"[14] Gregory the Great (ca. 540–604) composed *Pastoral Care*, which King Alfred later had translated from Greek into English and renamed *The Shepherd's Book*. "No one ventures to teach any art unless he has learned it after deep thought. With what rashness, then, would the pastoral office be undertaken by the unfit, seeing that the government of souls is the art of arts."[15]

Classically educated, Gregory the Great founded six Benedictine monasteries and authored many homilies, including a series on the book of Ezekiel, from which this educational insight is gleaned: "And indeed exceedingly lovely is the sweetness of the contemplative life which carries the soul above itself, opens the heavens, shows that earthly cares should be scorned, discloses spiritual truths to the eyes of the mind, and hides those of the body."[16]

Being convicted that Orthodox belief and biblical doctrine deserved precise and clear articulation, Charlemagne (742–814) founded a school at his palace in Aachen and hired the renowned European educator Alcuin (ca. 735–804) to be its first Master of the Palace School. In one of his letters, Alcuin writes,

> Your holy wisdom should provide masters for the boys, and the clerks. Let there be separate spheres for those who read books, who serve singing, who are assigned to the writing school. Have special masters for each of these classes, lest having leisure time they wander about the place and practice empty games or be employed in other futilities. Let your most wise prudence, my most beloved son, consider all this, so that a well of goodness and learning may be found in the principal seat of our nation, from which the thirsty traveler of the lover of church learning, may draw whatever his soul desires. Teach the boys and young men diligently the learning of books in the way of God, that they may become worthy successors in your honors and intercessors for you. . . . May the light of learning remain among you.[17]

Among his reforms, Roger Bacon (ca. 1214–ca. 1292) brought "a new emphasis on the importance of mathematics and empirical science to a theological education." Additionally, he referred to the Bible as an academic subject. "Every other faculty uses its basic text in its classroom

---

14. Ambrose, Jerome, and Augustine.
15. Lockerbie, *Passion for Learning*, 65.
16. Gamble, *Great Tradition*, 237.
17. Gamble, *Great Tradition*, 243–48.

instruction; for it is around this text that the material of the faculty is organized since this is the end for which texts are written. This applies so much more to the Bible text since it had been given to the world by the mouth of God and by the Saints."[18]

John Wycliffe's (1329–1384) educational priorities included general literacy, biblical literacy, and English as *lingua franca*. Of this morning star of the Reformation, it has been said, "To Wycliffe we owe, more than to any one person who can be mentioned, our English language, our English Bible, and our religion."[19] Each of these has been fundamentally invaluable to the development of education in the West.

John Huss (1373–1415) emphasized literacy in general and literacy of the Scriptures in particular. Despite widespread illiteracy among pagans at the time, referring to Huss's evangelical schools that predated the Reformation, "All children could read and write . . . important passages of Scripture were given as copy for writing, and [were] also learned by rote. . . . Before Luther's Reformation, the Hussites had printed the Scriptures in the vernacular, and they possessed a good system of schools and a celebrated university."[20]

Thomas à Kempis (ca. 1380–1471), a priest, monk, and author, apparently preferred the solace and deep thought of his cell more than the practical affairs of administration. He devoted most of his time to prayer, study, copying manuscripts, teaching nascents, conducting mass, and hearing confessions. He prioritized simplicity and sincerity.

Regarding the philosophy of education, in particular, he wrote,

> What good does it do, then, to debate about the Trinity, if by a lack of humility you are displeasing to the Trinity? I would much rather feel profound sorrow for my sins than to be able to define the theological term for it. . . . This is the highest wisdom: to see the world as it truly is, fallen and fleeting; to love not the world for its own sake but for God's, and to direct all your effort toward achieving the kingdom of heaven. . . . Learn to see yourself as God sees you. . . . This is the greatest lesson. . . . And, he is very learned indeed who knows God's will and makes it his own.[21]

---

18. Lockerbie, *Passion for Learning*, 103–4.
19. Kienel, *History of Christian School Education*, 1:137.
20. Kienel, *History of Christian School Education*, 1:142.
21. Kempis, *Imitation of Christ*, 3–6.

Mapheus Vegius (1405–1458) was a humanist, a poet, a philosopher, and a priest. He authored "the longest and most important educational discussion of his time."[22] This treatise consists of six volumes elucidating education and moral development; the first three volumes address parents, and the last three address children. The work is notably Christian in its content although rather humanistic in its themes. For example, it allows the reading of secular texts, but only in conjunction with the study of the Scriptures. It prioritizes sound moral development as the apex of learning.

Here is a brief excerpt:

> May the youth of happy disposition seize knowledge and dedicate himself to it, since it has in view great benefits . . . He receives the best guidance of how one may live a modest, earnest, and pious life, how one should love parent and fatherland, reverence God and avoid evil and despise sensuality. . . . Knowledge furnishes youth the greatest pleasure; knowledge of the changes of fate, of times and peoples and their history has something alluring. The doctrines that it offers are not merely of great moral influence, but conduce also to prudent judgments, to ripe reflection upon mastery over the tasks of life. Scientific studies furnish relief and refreshment in those countless difficulties of which human life is full, and they cause us to forget them. . . . Knowledge is an ornament of mankind.[23]

Martin Luther (1483–1546) supported the shift of educational authority from private to public jurisdiction, from voluntary to compulsory participation, and from associative to institutional organization.

> Luther, the Educational Reformer, is by no means just one more slice of the reformer's career. It is an issue that lies at the very heart of understanding Luther. . . . Certainly, he was a great theologian, a pastor, and a biblical scholar, but from the beginning of his career to its end, he was also an educational reformer, who not only spoke his mind but also acted on his convictions.[24]

Luther wrote:

> My idea is that boys should spend an hour to two hours a day in school, and the rest of the time work at home, learn some trade,

---

22. Eby, *Ancient and Medieval*, 884.
23. Eby, *Ancient and Medieval*, 892.
24. Kienel, *History of Christian School Education*, 1:154.

and do whatever is desired, so that study and work may go on together, while the children are young and can attend to both. In like manner, a girl has time to go to school for an hour a day, and yet attend to her work at home, for she sleeps, dances, and plays away more than that. The real difficulty is found alone in the absence of an earnest desire to educate the young, and to aid and benefit mankind with accomplished citizens. The devil much prefers blockheads and drones, that men may have more abundant trials and sorrows in the world.[25]

Arguably more humanistic than many of his Protestant Reformation predecessors or even contemporaries, Ulrich Zwingli (1484–1531) nonetheless wrote, "While the humanist holds that education may contribute to increased piety and even salvation, the reformer holds that all learning is subject to the grace of God. Therefore, all those who would be truly learned should pray that he who alone can give faith will illuminate by His Spirit those whom we instruct in his Word." He summarized his philosophy of Christian education in his *How to Educate the Young in Good Manners and Christian Discipline*.

Francois Rabelais (ca. 1485–1553) was known to be an influential educational reformer of his day, whose program is described as varied and exhausting,[26] and included prayer, Bible reading, discussion, recitation, reference books, Greek, Latin, Hebrew, Arabic, manners, card tricks, apothecary, horsemanship, swordsmanship, hunting, wrestling, painting, wood carving, metallurgy, numerical sciences, geometry, and instrumental music.

Johann Bugenhagen (1485–1558) did "even more than Luther in the cause of Protestant schools in Germany."[27] He promoted four types of schools, all of which he advocated being under local authority:

1. Vernacular schools for town boys.

2. Vernacular schools for town girls.

3. Latin schools for upper-class boys.

4. Latin schools for upper-class girls.

---

25. Kienel, *History of Christian School Education*, 1:195–96.
26. Eby, *Development of Modern Education*, 211.
27. Kienel, *History of Christian School Education*, 1:251.

He based much of his educational thought upon the following aphorism: "The protestant religion was taught together with the secular subjects."[28]

Martin Bucer (1491–1551) recommended Christian education of youth as the highest priority in his *Code of Recommendations*. His second highest was that all children would be taught to read and write. So convinced of these priorities, he persuaded many local authorities to release funds that had been collected for local religious orders. Bucer, a Protestant, utilized Catholic monies to fund his Protestant schools. His schools taught reading, writing, Christianity, music, and the liberal arts.[29]

A classmate of John Calvin's at the University of Paris, Ignatius Loyola (1491–1556) founded the Jesuits, campaigned aggressively against the French Huguenot school system, and established ninety-two Jesuit high schools. Eventually emerging from Loyola's ecclesiastical and educational movement, *Ratio atque Institutio Studiorum Societatis Iesu* (The Official Plan for Jesuit Education) was published in 1599. Often abbreviated as *Ratio Studiorum* (Plan of Studies), Loyola's educational tract codified the global system of Jesuit education. "Let our scholastics strive especially to preserve purity of mind and right intention in their studies: seeking nothing further in these than Divine glory and profit of souls."[30] The Jesuit motto, *ad majorem Dei gloriam*,[31] resonates in its mission to develop well-rounded Christians of service in the world—a world "charged with the grandeur of God."[32]

In his influential *De Tradendis Disciplinis* (The Transmission of Knowledge), Juan Luis Vives (1492–1540) envisioned education which cultivated wisdom, served the community, and honored God.

> For if you learn well, then it is God's gift, and you will displease Him, if you do not ascribe to Him all the glory which accrues to you through your learning. If a learned man intends to go into the sight and haunts of men, then should he have thought over his preparation for this purpose, as if he were training for a fight, so that he should not be taken possession of by any of those debased passions which attack and beset us on every side. ... Then he will adore, with humble mind, the Giver of all good

---

28. Kienel, *History of Christian School Education*, 1:252.
29. Kienel, *History of Christian School Education*, 1:258.
30. Gamble, *Great Tradition*, 458.
31. "For the greater glory of God."
32. "Jesuit Tradition," www.ignatius.vic.edu.au/about-us/jesuit-tradition#200.

gifts, and return thanks that He has held him worthy of gifts in richer proportion than He has imparted to others, and that He has willed him to be the instrument of any part of His counsel and His work, for all of us are instruments of His will.[33]

Like his English predecessor John Wycliffe, William Tyndale (1494–1536) promoted English as the *lingua franca*, general literacy, and biblical literacy—especially among the English-speaking laity and children.

Displaying his separatist tendencies, even within the context of his philosophy of education, Menno Simons (1496–1561) once wrote:

> For true evangelical faith is of such a nature that it cannot lie dormant, but manifests itself in all righteousness and works of love, it dies unto flesh and blood, destroys all forbidden lusts and desires, cordially seeks, serves, and fears God, clothes the naked, feeds the hungry, consoles the afflicted, shelters the miserable, aids and consoles all the oppressed, returns good for evil, serves those that injure it, prays for those that persecute it, teaches, admonishes, and reproves with the Word of the Lord, seeks that which is lost, binds up that which is wounded, heals that which is diseased and saves that which is sound.[34]

"[Simons] appears to recognize that children are not just small-framed adults, and that they should be given the freedom in their earliest years to 'nurse, drink, laugh, cry, warm themselves, play, etc. with few parental expectations and few worries about their imperfections.'"[35]

Philip Melanchthon (1497–1560) developed the *Saxony School Plan*. His plan articulated the following:

> The first group should consist of those children who are learning to read. . . . They are first to be taught the children's manual, containing the alphabet, the creed, the Lord's Prayer, and other prayers. When they have learned this, Donatus and Cato may both be given to them. The second group consists of children who have learned to read, and are now ready to go into grammar. The first hour afternoon every day all the children, large and small should be practiced in music. Then the school master must interpret the second group the fables of Aesop. After Vespers, he should explain to them the "Paedology" of Mosellanus,

---

33. Gamble, *Great Tradition*, 393–406.

34. As cited at "Menno Simons on . . . the New Life," http://www.mennosimons.net/newlife.html.

35. Bunge, *Child in Christian Thought*, 194–226.

and when this is finished, he should select from the "Colloquies" of Erasmus some that may conduce their improvement and discipline. The third group would have been well-trained in grammar. An hour after mid-day they, together with the rest are to devote to music. After this the teacher is to give an explanation of Virgil. When he has finished this, he may take up Ovid's "Metamorphoses," and in the latter part of the afternoon Cicero's "Offices" or "Letters to Friends." The boys in the second and third groups are to be required every week to write compositions, either in the form of letters or verses.[36]

"Had the reformers concerned themselves as much with training teachers as they did with preparing catechisms, universal education for religious purposes would have been attained centuries earlier."[37] Some even argue that "the triumph of humanism through the effort of Melanchthon and his disciples prevented this obvious extension of the ideals of the Reformation, and made the study of an alien culture the central interest of [schools] for more than three hundred years."[38]

Francis Xavier (1506–1552) one of the six original Jesuits under Loyola, is credited with the saying, "Give me children until they are seven years old, and anyone can take them afterwards."[39] Xavier apparently prioritized the fertile and formative years of early childhood development.

Of Johann Sturm (1507–1589), it is said that he was the most humanistic of his generation of Protestant educators. In fact, as Eby says, "Religion was not Sturm's supreme concern, but was utilized as a help to study Latin."[40] In his very successful school in Strasburg, Germany, Sturm divided the curriculum into ten graded classes, each to be taught by a different teacher and each to follow a prescribed curriculum. Learning Latin was the exclusive task of the first three years, and then Greek was added from the fourth class on. In the senior section of six years the course branched out to the seven liberal arts and the lectures were open to the public.

Although his aforementioned contemporary Martin Luther had conveyed explicit contempt for the classics such as Aristotle (whom

---

36. Kienel, *History of Christian School Education*, 1:247–50.
37. Kienel, *History of Christian School Education*, 1:206.
38. Kienel, *History of Christian School Education*, 1:246.
39. Kienel, *History of Christian School Education*, 1:285.
40. Kienel, *History of Christian School Education*, 1:255.

Luther called, "that blind heathen teacher"),[41] John Calvin (1509–1564), on the other hand, thought that leaders ought to be educated in Hebrew, Greek, and Latin in addition to the classics and the Christian Scriptures.[42] Calvin's ideals have been summarized as, "For the business of life and the purpose of eternity, to preserve the purity of religion and to fit the young for the service of Kirk and Commonwealth, to enable every man and woman to fulfill his or her 'vocation,' and by these means to promote this Godly Commonwealth."[43] Furthermore, Calvin thought teachers ought to instill traits into their students which would please God. A humanist and a biblicist, he prioritized and promoted thrift, hard work, responsibility, and an orientation of *soli Deo gloria* for all of his students in all of their subjects.[44] Calvin wrote:

> Those to whom God has given the honor of having children, let them know that they are all the more obligated to take pains that their children are duly instructed. If they wish to have good instruction, it is always necessary to begin with faith. Children could give the appearance of having all the virtue in the world, but that would be worth nothing, unless God be feared and honored by them. How frequently we see those who take great pains that their children be taught the business of the world. It is true that they provide excellent teachers for their children, but for the purpose of making a grand show, so that they might know some three words of Latin and be able to display at the dinner table that they converse easily and can put up a good front according to the world. Yet it is never a question of knowing God. That is the wrong way to proceed! It is putting the cart before the horse![45]

Nonetheless, Calvin offered the following rationale for studying pagan philosophers:

> In reading profane authors, the admirer may see full light of truth displayed in them to remind us that the human mind, however much fallen and perverted from its original integrity, is still adorned and invested with admirable gifts from the Creator. If we reflect that the Spirit of God is the only Fountain of truth,

---

41. Kienel, *History of Christian School Education*, 1:246.
42. Gutek, *Historical and Philosophical Foundations*, 116.
43. Kienel, *History of Christian School Education*, 1:294.
44. Anthony, "John Calvin," 103.
45. Kienel, *History of Christian School Education*, 1:230.

we shall be careful, as we would avoid offering and talk to Him, not to reject or condemn truth—wherever it appears.[46]

John Amos Comenius (1592–1670) is considered by many to have been the father of modern education and one of the most influential persons in the history of Christian education. "From him today knowledge and education are still considered to be the road humankind must take to reach the peaceable kingdom."[47] His views of Christian education include peace-education and *pansophism*. Comenius's *pansophism* (literally, "all knowledge") is his synthesis derived from theology, philosophy, and science.[48]

Comenius introduced pictorial textbooks composed in native languages, and he applied pedagogy based upon the gradual growth from simple to more comprehensive concepts. "Children do not train themselves spontaneously, but are shaped only by tireless labor. A young sapling, planned for a tree, must be planted, watered, hedged for protection, and propped up."[49]

Comenius's concept of Christian schooling within a Christian republic included:

1. *Schola maternal* at the mother's knee (from birth to age six)—in every home.

2. *Schola vernacular* at the vernacular school (childhood)—in every hamlet.

3. *Schola Latina* at the Latin school (boyhood)—in every city.

4. *Christian university* (for advanced students only)—in every province.

Comenius devoted a chapter in *The Great Didactic* to "Teaching Children about God and Christian Living." Therein he posited piety as the supreme purpose of education. In his mind piety was developed by means of meditation, prayer, and examination. Training in piety was to be started as soon as children began to speak.

---

46. Kienel, *History of Christian School Education*, 1:246.
47. Gutek, *Historical and Philosophical Foundations*, 130.
48. Gutek, *Historical and Philosophical Foundations*, 126.
49. Gutek, *Historical and Philosophical Foundations*, 28.

Comenius believed the Bible was God's inerrant Word. He considered it to be the most basic and the most important source of knowledge. He posited that the Scriptures were equally suitable to all—containing truth that even children could understand.[50] To him education meant bringing men to the place where they would accept Christ and by accepting him would be able to fulfill God's purposes for their lives. Comenius opposed the use of pagan classics in education.

Francis Bacon (1561–1626) appreciated both God's *word* and God's *world* as viable sources of knowledge, but "lamented the reliance on questionable traditions in both areas. He advocated greater emphasis on inductive learning, rather than blind acceptance of traditional authority."[51] His penchant and priority for theology as primary stirred disdain within him and among his followers for other epistemological and educational priorities, such as what he called: "the contentious learning of the dialecticians . . . the delicate learning of the humanists . . . and the fantastic learning of the necromancers."[52]

Johann Valentin Andrea (1586–1654) published his educational utopia entitled *Christian City (Christianopolis)* in 1619. In it he highlighted the following priorities for education: "Their first and highest exertion is to worship God with a pure and faithful soul, the second, to strive toward the best and most chaste morals, the third, to cultivate the mental powers."[53]

Among Blaise Pascal's (1623–1662) most educationally influential insights included his posit that "the heart has its reasons which reason knows nothing of." Additionally, what has become known as "Pascals' Wager" has proved helpful to many students and educators alike struggling to buttress their faith with intellectual rigor. Finally, his *Pensées*—whether read in English or French—provide Christian school students with ponderous yet poetic insights from an intelligent, authentic, and wise man of God.

August Hermann Francke (1663–1727) was a German Lutheran clergyman, philanthropist, Bible scholar, and educator who relied upon inner light. His schools ran from 7 a.m. to 3 p.m. daily. Many of them

---

50. Kienel, *History of Christian School Education*, 1:313–16.
51. Kienel, *Philosophy of Christian School Education*, 61.
52. Eby, *Development of Modern Education*, 219.
53. Eby, *Development of Modern Education*, 246.

became known as "Ragged schools,"[54] indicative of the attire of the poor children from industrialized towns attending his German schools.

> Early morning was devoted to prayer, the singing of hymns, and the reading of a passage of the Scriptures. This was followed by catechisms drills, two hours of reading instruction, an hour of writing, and an hour of arithmetic. The schoolmaster also led the pupils on daily walks, which provided physical exercise as well as an opportunity for lessons in natural history. On Sundays, the pupils accompanied the schoolmaster to worship service and Sunday school.[55]

In his *Brief and Simple Instruction How to Lead Children toward Piety and Christian Wisdom*, Francke insisted that

> in order to educate children so that they preserve true and candid piety up to their old age, teachers as well as parents, yea, all around them, must be conscious of their Christian duty. Indeed, that requires more than the intelligence of natural man. We need wisdom from above to seek always and everywhere the honor of the Almighty and the glory of His name.[56]

Cotton Mather (1663-1728) asserted that "the schoolmaster has many opportunities of doing good. God make him sensible to his obligations.... An office most laborious, yet most pleasing to God ... (and to the schoolmasters). Sirs, let it be your grand design to instill into their minds the doctrines of piety. Consider it as their chief interest, and yours also, that they may know the Holy Scriptures as to become wise."[57]

In contrast to many other eighteenth-century American revivalist preachers, Jonathan Edwards (1703-1758)

> insisted that children were capable of becoming faithful Christians. In all his sermons to children, Edwards mixed clear, logical explanation of the Bible with emotional appeals to the heart. ... At the same time as Edwards deliberately tried to frighten children, he also reassured them. No matter how much he emphasized God's anger, he always ended his [children's] sermons by imagining children in heaven.[58]

54. Kienel, *History of Christian School Education*, 1:297.
55. Kienel, *History of Christian School Education*, 1:319.
56. Kienel, *History of Christian School Education*, 1:321.
57. Kienel, *History of Christian School Education*, 1:65.
58. Bunge, *Child in Christian Thought*, 300-328.

Apparently following in the footsteps of his mother, "in order to form the minds of children, the first thing to be done is to conquer their will," from a letter from Susanna Wesley to her son, John Wesley (1703–1791),[59] the founder of Methodism preached, "Break their will, that you may save their soul."[60] To educate his people, Wesley published about five hundred works, many of which were intended for use in schools, e.g., five grammars (in English, Greek, Latin, German, and French), *Plain Account of Kingswood School*, *A Short History of Rome*, and a *Natural Philosophy*.

> His intent was to include every area of "useful learning, or practical studies." The main course of study was designed to teach reading, writing, and arithmetic, English, French, Latin, Greek, and Hebrew, history, geography, and chronology, rhetoric and logic, and geometry, algebra, physics, music, and ethics. Other topics were soon added, such as painting and astronomy. This scheme was based (largely) on the typical public-school curriculum, but added music, physics, Hebrew, religious biography, the Bible, and Christian classics."[61]

The educational reforms of Robert Raikes (1735–1811) "were occasioned by sympathy for the sorry plight of children caused by the new industrialism."[62] In 1780, for example, he opened the first Sunday school. "Under the tutelage of a paid instructor, these Lord's day sessions were charity schools providing instruction in reading, writing, arithmetic, spelling, hymns, catechism, and Scripture."[63]

A patriot, a Calvinist, a merchant, and an educational reformer, Samuel Phillips Jr. (1752–1802) advocated the spiritual development of young students. He asserted, "The object in educating youth ought to be to qualify young persons as ornaments, as blessings, and as comforts in the vineyard of the Lord."[64]

Noah Webster (1758–1843) asserted, "In my view, the Christian religion is the most important and one of the first things in which all children, under a free government ought to be instructed. No truth is more evident to my mind than that the Christian religion must be the

---

59. Bunge, *Child in Christian Thought*, 278.
60. Bunge, *Child in Christian Thought*, 279.
61. Bunge, *Child in Christian Thought*, 280–99.
62. Eby, *Development of Modern Education*, 881.
63. Eby, *Development of Modern Education*, 610.
64. Lockerbie, *Passion for Learning*, 236.

basis of any government intended to secure the rights and privileges of a free people."⁶⁵

Thomas Arnold (1795–1842) emphasized Christian piety, character formation, and intellectual development. He preached weekly sermons, encouraged team sports, and expanded his curriculum to include mathematics, French, and modern history. "It is not wisdom to make boys prodigies of information, but it is wisdom and our duty to cultivate their faculties each in its season, first the memory and imagination, and then their judgment, to furnish them with the means, and to excite the desire, of improving themselves, and to await with confidence for God's blessing on the result."⁶⁶

William Holmes McGuffey (1800–1873), a prominent college president and professor of psychology and philosophy, began publishing his readers in 1836; they began to be called *McGuffey Readers* in 1857. "There is something to be learned and something to be taught in schools, besides the mere mechanical round of book lessons."⁶⁷ He implored educators with his biblical ideals:

> Parents commit to us their richest treasures, their dearest hopes. . . . The Christian religion is the religion of our country. From it are derived our prevalent notions of the character of God, the great moral governor of the universe. From no source has the author drawn more copiously, in his selections, than from the sacred Scriptures. For this, he certainly apprehends no censure. In a Christian country, that man is to be pitied, who at this day, can honestly object to imbuing the minds of youth with the language and spirit of the Word of God. Let us then, fellow teachers, avoid, on the one hand, the inculcation of all sectarian peculiarities in religion, and on the other, let us beware of incurring the charge (which will not fail to be made) of being enemies to our country's quiet, by teaching to our pupils the crude notions, and revolutionary principles of modern infidelity.⁶⁸

Referred to as the quintessential American theologian of childhood,⁶⁹ Horace Bushnell (1802–1876) wrote *Christian Nurture* in 1847.

---

65. Kienel, *History of Christian School Education*, 1:85.
66. Gamble, *Great Tradition*, 514.
67. Conway, *American Literacy*, 70.
68. Lockerbie, *Passion for Learning*, 266–72.
69. Bunge, *Child in Christian Thought*, 350.

> Central to Bushnell's argument was his critique of revivalism. . . . Bushnell emphatically denounced such "ostrich nurture," comparing revivalism to an ostrich laying eggs, covering them up in the sand, and leaving them to hatch alone. . . . Bushnell envisioned true Christian nurture as a thoroughly natural process—the authentic sign of a godly home. . . . The process literally began at birth . . . emphasizing what he called an organic conception of family life. . . . Bushnell also emphasized the importance of specific training in the creeds, Christian doctrine, and the content of Scripture, as long as the method and timing was sensitive to the child's needs and understanding. . . . Bushnell believed that each child came into the world as the recipient of a unique spiritual legacy. . . . No summary of Bushnell's though would be complete without noting that he enjoyed children for their own sake because of—not in spite of—their inherent vulnerability.[70]

Abraham Kuyper (1837–1920), who famously said, "There is not one square inch on the whole plain of human existence over which Christ, who is Lord over all, does not proclaim, 'This is Mine!'"[71] Adhering to and applying the tenets of its namesake, Kuyper College is committed to—as they say it—*Bringing God's grace into today's culture.*

> Your education at Kuyper will be grounded in our belief that the Bible is the Word of God and guides our teaching, philosophy, and lifestyle. Affirming that all people are made in the image of God to declare His glory, we integrate faith into all aspects of your student experience—helping you to develop academically, spiritually, socially, and morally into a Christ-centered leader.[72]

Herman Bavinck (1854–1921) was a systematic theologian trained in the liberal theology of his day, but nonetheless remained in the Dutch Reformed tradition. He taught under Kuyper at the Free University. Perhaps best known for his four-volume *Reformed Dogmatics*, Bavinck wrote a lot about psychology and pedagogy later in his career.[73]

---

70. Bunge, *Child in Christian Thought*, 350–64.

71. Kuyper, *Sphere Sovereignty*, 26.

72. Kyper College, "Academics," para. 1, https://www.kuyper.edu/academics/. Nicholas Wolterstorff et al. refer to this as "The Regent Model of Learning." Wolterstorff, *Educating for Shalom*, 199–225.

73. Parsons, *Since We Are Justified*, 143.

Clarence H. Benson (1879–1954), founder and president of the Evangelical Teacher Training Association (ETTA) and arguably known most for his work at the Moody Bible Institute and in the Sunday school movement, contributed significantly to the Christian educational philosophical discussion of his day. Benson's taxonomy of the task of Christian education included the Christian teacher reaching the student's:

1. Mentality.

   - "Sensation is the great door through which knowledge of the outer world comes into the mind. For this purpose, we find the body and mind are closely connected."[74]
   - "Perception is the ability to interpret information given by senses. Sensations are the raw material of knowledge. Percepts are the first objects from this raw material."[75]
   - "The acquisition of knowledge for the intellect is similar to the acquisition of food for the body. When we sit down to partake of food, our primary objective is acquisition. Knowledge, in the same way, is acquired through the five gates provided for that purpose."[76]

2. Personality.

   - "[Each student is] a God-given individual, with the power of choice, will, and self-control."[77]
   - "Teaching is not complete unless it in some way affects or influences the pupil."[78]
     - Receptive contact.
     - Responsive contact.

3. Spirituality.

   - "Man can pass from one plane to another. His endowment of self-determination enables him to sit like a king between heaven and earth."[79]

---

74. Benson, *Christian Teacher*, 15–16.
75. Benson, *Christian Teacher*, 16.
76. Benson, *Christian Teacher*, 17.
77. Benson, *Christian Teacher*, 21.
78. Benson, *Christian Teacher*, 23.
79. Benson, *Christian Teacher*, 33.

- "Now, while men may learn *about* God through their senses, in the same way as they have been conscious of the world about them, these faculties are not sufficient for a personal or soul acquaintance *with* Him."[80]

In summary, "The teacher who teaches the mentality is preparing the individual for *knowledge*, but the teacher who reaches the personality is preparing the pupil for *life*, while the Christian teacher, in going beyond this and reaching the spirituality, is preparing the pupil for *eternity*."[81]

T. S. Eliot (1888–1965) prioritized thinking Christianly. In that regard he penned this poignant prose: "The purpose of Christian education would not be merely to make men and women pious Christians. . . . A Christian education would primarily train people to be able to think in Christian categories."[82]

Paul Herman Vieth (1895–1978), a German evangelical, promoted theocentric Christian education. Perhaps best known for his contributions in conceptualizing objectives for Christian education, Vieth emphasized the importance of Bible-centered content and experience.

> Teaching is the finest of fine arts. It is more noble than painting, for the teacher does not represent his ideal on canvas, but makes it to live in the lives of men. It is more worthy than architecture, for the arches and pillars of a noble character will stand not simply for one or twenty centuries, but will last throughout eternity, since the sculptor works with inanimate stone—the teacher exercises his art with living material.[83] Teaching exists for the sake of life, and not life for the sake of teaching. Its purpose is served when it has helped its pupils to live more abundantly.[84] Subject-matter, then, is the means which the pupil utilizes, under the guidance of the leader, to bring about an enrichment of his experience, and to bring it under his control so that he may realize his Christian objectives.[85]

---

80. Benson, *Christian Teacher*, 34.
81. Benson, *Christian Teacher*, 46.
82. Eliot, *Christianity and Culture*, 22.
83. Sayers, *Lost Tools of Learning*, 13.
84. Sayers, *Lost Tools of Learning*, 53.
85. Paul Herman Vieth, quoted in Steibel, "Paul Herman Vieth," para. 42, https://www.biola.edu/talbot/ce20/database/paul-herman-vieth#authors.

Frank Gaebelein (1899–1983) famously declared, "Education by its nature is dedicated to changing those who are taught. . . . Truth is the ultimate object of the educational quest."[86]

> We do indeed give primacy to that spiritual truth revealed in the Bible and incarnate in Christ. That does not mean, however, that those aspects of truth discoverable by man in the realm of mathematics, chemistry, or geography, are any whit less God's truth than the truth as it is in Christ. . . . Truth about Christ pertains to salvation; that about physics does not . . . But all the time there is the unity of all truth under God.[87]

Gordon H. Clark (1902–1985), analytic philosopher and Calvinist theologian, argued that all truth was propositional. He defended realism against the empiricisms of his day. He critiqued secular philosophy in general and secular approaches to epistemology and education in particular.

> Parents, however, because of the exigencies of life, cannot personally give the children the instruction they need. Schools are necessary. But to what sort of school should Christian parents send their children? Does it seem reasonable that a Christian child should be given pagan instruction? Just because a young man survives pagan instruction is no reason for subjecting him to it. . . . Children sometimes survive diphtheria or infantile paralysis, but we do not try to give it to them. . . . Now, in public schools, children receive a pagan education. . . . Any Christian, it seems to me, should have sense enough to see that subjection to pagan influences works an injustice to the child. . . . What suggestion can be made to help the parent in the present situation? There is one very concrete suggestion-whether it is practicable or not the parents must decide for themselves. Suffice is to be said that the suggestion is in actual operation in a number of places. The suggestion simply is that Christian parents band together to form Christian schools. . . . A system of Christian schools will give us a knowledge of Christianity as it embraces the whole of life, and will produce a complete Christian culture for a complete man.[88]

---

86. Gaebelein, *Christian Education in Democracy*, 30–31.
87. Lockerbie, *Passion for Learning*, 386.
88. Clark, "Relationship of Public Education," para. 17, 18, 22.

Calvin College professor Henry Zylstra (1909–1956) declared, "Christian education must be both *education* and *Christian* if it is to justify itself and meet the secular challenge.... Our schools must be *schools*—that for one. And, then again, they must be *Christian*—that for another thing. And in making these two points I shall want to insist, of course, that they must be both at once."[89]

Lois E. LeBar (1907–1998), professor of Christian education at Wheaton College from 1945 to 1975, known as a demanding teacher, she specialized in educational philosophy and curriculum design. She outlines methods that "consistently emphasize biblical content and the centrality of Christ.... Following in the tradition of Comenius, LeBar emphasizes both authoritative content and the actual experience of students."[90] LeBar is perhaps best known for her 1958 text, *Education That Is Christian*, a philosophy of Christian education that emphasizes themes in teaching, learning, and curriculum development. In that textbook, LeBar identifies three aims for any *Education That Is Christian*:

1. Transformation.

2. Formation.

3. Service.

William Frankena (1908–1985) was a professor of philosophy of education at the University of Michigan for decades. It is said of Frankena that he

> gives us one of the most helpful models for integrating our philosophical beliefs into a coherent philosophy of Christian education. His model is made up of *five boxes*, each representing an aspect of one's philosophy of education. Each of the boxes relates systematically to another box, thus ensuring a certain cohesiveness to the overall philosophy. This helps to prevent the Christian educator from uncritically borrowing presuppositions or methods from non-Christian worldviews.
>
> Box A, in Frankena's model, contains a statement about the ultimate purpose of humankind. Choices for this box usually include humankind's responsibility to glorify, serve, love, honor, obey, or worship God. The statement in Box A provides thematic unity to the other four boxes.

---

89. Zylstra, *Testament of Vision*, 138.
90. Pazmiño, *Foundational Issues*, 160–61.

Box B includes both philosophical and empirical premises about human nature, life, and the world. Included in this box are the foundational beliefs that undergird one's philosophy of education. Often included in this box are the educator's beliefs concerning the Bible, the Godhead, the church, the family, principles of human development, the role of the Holy Spirit, and other important theological and empirical foundational beliefs.

There is a direct connection between "Box A-Ultimate Purpose" and "Box B-Premises," and the next category, "Box C-Excellencies." Excellencies refers to the characteristics one's educational philosophy is designed to produce, based upon the foundational ideas mentioned in the Ultimate Purpose and the Premises. The excellencies, collectively, paint a picture of the ideal person. Christian educators often draw on Jesus' teachings from his "Sermon on the Mount" or Paul's teaching on "the fruit of the spirit" to describe their excellencies.

Box D contains explanations based on empirical and scientific theory about how to produce the stated excellencies. The learning theories explained in this box are derived primarily from social science research. Care must be taken to critically evaluate the presuppositions of the theories used before applying them within a Christian context.

Box E contains the specific educational strategy with goals and objectives related to every aspect of the educational practice. The details described in this section, related to curriculum, methods, and organizational structure, are based on the data from the first four boxes, thus ensuring a cohesive educational philosophy.

The "Frankena Model" helps the Christian educator integrate theory and practice in articulating a statement of philosophy of Christian education. This guards against one of the greatest dangers in educational ministry, that of utilizing methods that are not well thought out philosophically, theologically, and educationally.[91]

Bob Jones Jr. (1911–1997), a fundamentalist like his father, Bob Jones Sr. (1883–1968), and successor to the BJU presidency, founded and edited *Faith for the Family* (1973–1986), an issues-oriented fundamentalist periodical. His separatist views of education drove him to open a publishing house to produce uniquely Christian curricula.

Drs. Arlin and Beka Horton graduated from Bob Jones University in 1951 and moved to Pensacola, Florida, in 1952 to found a Christian

---

91. Newton, "Frankena Model," 534–35.

school. That school, Pensacola Christian School, opened in 1954 and was later renamed Pensacola Christian Academy. In 1974, the Hortons opened Pensacola Christian College to further their vision of "Education from a [fundamental] Christian Perspective." Pensacola Theological Seminary, an extension of PCC's graduate school, was founded in 1998. The Hortons' educational philosophy according to their own words "is based upon the Word of God. The primary purpose of the school is to train the student in the Christian way of life and to give the student a good general education. . . . The academic program through the traditional approach, is developed to provide students with the best possible program of studies."[92] The heart of their traditional, separatist, and conservatively Christian philosophy of education is based upon four principles:

1. Traditional education is God-centered.
2. Traditional education is authoritarian in its approach.
3. These two commitments result in sound, Scriptural discipline and also in
4. Godly character training.

> All of these combine to set the stage for an excellent education [in which] you learn . . . the Bible, that God created, the worth of your soul, the 3 R's and other subjects, to sit up straight and pay attention, that it is not right to cheat, to recite when called upon, to honor and respect your parents, respect for authority, that a man's word is his bond, that a job worth doing is worth doing well, personal initiative, develop pride in America, that the free enterprise system is still the best system, that competition is healthy.[93]

Having been tutored by C. S. Lewis at Oxford University, Harry Blamires (1916–2017), a novelist, literary critic, and Anglican theologian, argues that education should be about *cultivating* five domains—as he famously framed the philosophical focus in the title of his book—*The Christian Mind*:

1. Acute sensitivity to providence.

2. Supernatural orientation.

3. Awareness of evil.

---

92. Baker, *Successful Christian School*, 188.
93. Baker, *Successful Christian School*, 35.

4. Conception of truth.

5. Acceptance of authority.

6. Concern for the person.

7. Sacramental view of all of life.[94]

Pope John Paul II (1920–2005) famously addressed a gathering of students in Madison Square Garden in October 1979. His comments became quite paradigmatic for parochial education.

> I would like to say something about Catholic education, to tell you why the Church considers it so important and expends so much energy in order to provide you and millions of other young people with a Catholic education. The answer can be communicated in one word, in one person—Jesus Christ. The Church wants to communicate Christ to you. This is what education is all about; this is the meaning of life—to know Christ. . . . And so the purpose of Catholic education is to communicate Christ to you so that your attitude towards others will be that of Christ.[95]

Arthur F. Holmes's (1924–2011) vision for education included the following emphases:

1. All truth is [rightly acknowledged as] God's truth.

2. The comprehensiveness, coherence, and unity of truth.

3. The usefulness of liberal arts as preparation for life and service to church and society, in which "knowledge of the past is a condition of practical wisdom for the present."

    - Breadth of learning gives access to the wealth of human learning and to the diversity of human experience.
    - Transferable skills (verbal, analytic, quantitative, communication, and social skills) are applicable to any kind of work.
    - Historical and conceptual contexts interrelate the particulars of experience and enable one to uncover assumptions and underlying worldviews.

---

94. Blamires, *Christian Mind*, 63.
95. Lockerbie, *Passion for Learning*, 362–65.

- Engagement with moral values and social issues sensitizes and informs the conscience and contributes to character development.
- Aesthetic experience nurtures and refines the imagination and develops an appreciation of beauty.
- Holistic development (intellectual, cultural, moral, and spiritual) is the result.

4. The viable role of contemplative and doxological learning.
5. The care of the soul via spiritual formation.[96]

Howard G. Hendricks (1924–2013), the Yale-educated, renowned professor of Christian education at Dallas Theological Seminary, summarized highlights of education, which he referred to as *Teaching to Change Lives*:

1. Teacher: Stop growing today, and you stop teaching tomorrow.
2. Education: How people learn determines how you teach.
3. Activity: Maximum learning is always the result of maximum involvement.
4. Communication: To truly impart information requires the building of bridges.
5. Heart: Teaching that impacts is not head-to-head, but heart-to-heart.
6. Encouragement: Teaching tends to be most effective when the learner is most motivated.
7. Readiness: The teaching-learning process will be most effective when both student and teacher are adequately prepared.[97]

Ted W. Ward (1930–2016) served as a professor of education at Michigan State University and professor of Christian education and mission at Trinity Evangelical Divinity School, where he also served as dean of International Studies, Mission, and Education. Dr. Ward's interests and involvement included moral development, teacher education, nontraditional theological education in Third World countries, missions, and the family.[98]

Jerry Falwell (1933–2007) saw secular humanism as the greatest threat to all educational endeavor. An evangelical, a Southern Baptist

---

96. Holmes, *Building the Christian Academy*, 1–7.

97. Hendricks, *Teaching to Change Lives*.

98. Hoke and Cannell, "Ted Warren Ward," para. 1, https://www.biola.edu/talbot/ce20/database/ted-warren-ward.

pastor, and founder of a Christian school, college, graduate school, and seminary, Falwell "crusaded not only to get the three R's back into the classroom, but especially to get the fourth R—religion—[back] into the center of education."[99]

Paul A. Kienel (1933–2020) cites "Ten Reasons Why You Should Send Your Child to a Christian School."

1. You are accountable to God for what your children are taught in school.
2. Christian schools offer a better level of instruction.
3. The Bible does not teach that children should be exposed to all kinds of sin.
4. The Christian school is right for your child, because it has not cut itself off from the most important book in the world—the Bible.
5. The Christian school provides an opportunity for your child to witness for Christ.
6. Christian schools teach all subject matters from a Christian context.
7. Christian schools support the family as the number one institution of society.
8. Atheists have, for all practical purposes, taken over public education in this country.
9. Christian schools maintain discipline.
10. Christian schools (like Christian parents) believe that our children are gifts from the Lord, and that we are, therefore, responsible to train them according to his word not only at home *and* in the church, but in school, as well.[100]

John H. Westerhoff III (b. 1933), an Episcopal priest, scholar, teacher, seminary professor, and writer, edited *Religious Education*, a professional journal, and authored more than two dozen books, including *Will Our Children Have Faith?* In such publications he wrote about four stages of faith and eight aspects of Christian school life that can contribute to faith development, as Christian educators "consciously attempt to fashion persons who embody the Christian life of faith."[101]

1. Experienced faith: a child's observations.

---

99. Knight, *Philosophy and Education*, 121.
100. Kienel, *Reasons for Christian Schools*, 13–18.
101. Lockerbie, *Passion for Learning*, 378–83.

2. Affiliate faith: an older child seeks to identify with a community of faith.

3. Searching faith: characterized by doubt or critical opinions.

4. Owned faith: whose personal value derives from it being real—not merely cultural, familial, or traditional.[102]

The following list delineates aspects of Christian school life that Westerhoff argued can contribute to the development of *owned faith*:

1. Environment.

2. Ritual participation.

3. Ordering time.

4. Organization of life.

5. Interactions.

6. Discipline.

7. Role models.

8. Language.[103]

D. Bruce Lockerbie (b. 1935) followed closely in the footsteps of his headmaster, Frank Gaebelein, in what Lockerbie describes as the DNA of the vocation of the Christian school.

> Here, then, is the nexus between "the unity of all truth under God" and our work as school board members, heads-of-schools, administrators, and teachers. We are summoned as leaders to know the Truth that sets us free and to act upon it. We are commissioned to provide in our schools a setting in which an awareness—a conscious intentionality—asserts that "the unity of all truth" under God pervades every board policy, every head-of-school appointment, every administrative decision, and thereby every faculty member's lesson and example to his or her students.[104]

---

102. Lockerbie, *Passion for Learning*, 378–83.
103. Lockerbie, *Passion for Learning*, 388.
104. Lockerbie, *Passion for Learning*, 389.

Kenneth O. Gangel (1935–2009) wrote prolifically and practically about the integration of faith and learning. "The phrase 'integration of truth' refers to the teaching of all subjects as a part of the total truth of God, thereby enabling the student to see the unity of natural and special revelation."[105]

He distills five principles for the process of such integration.

1. The teacher who would integrate faith and learning must constantly be about the all-important task of theological sieve-building.

2. Every teacher must be at least an amateur theologian.

3. The teachers must help students "get it all together" in a Christian worldview.

4. Teachers must learn (and help students learn) to walk a carefully balanced line between open-mindedness and unchallengeable doctrine.

5. Teachers must remember that the task of integration should be approached with reverence, relevance, and relaxation.[106]

Ronald Nash (1936–2006) speaks of three kinds of illiteracy: functional, cultural, and moral. These three kinds of illiteracy are found in people who cannot read, in those who cannot engage with the historically great ideas, and in those whose "values have been replaced with the relativistic nonsense, irrational ideas, and moral bankruptcy that set [Matthew] Arnold (author or Dover Beach, footnote the entire poem) into eternal sadness." Nash goes on to assert that "the restoration of functional, cultural, and moral literacy requires that we know who the enemies are. We must find ways to loosen their destructive control over the education of future generations of young people. And we must act then in cooperation with others in our society who want to see an end to the crisis of American education."[107]

Michigan State University–educated and Asbury College professor of the philosophy of education Catherine M. Stonehouse (b. 1940) advocates a mutual respect among teacher and learner in a community of education.

---

105. Lockerbie, *Passion for Learning*, 372.
106. Gangel, "Integrating Faith and Learning," 99–108.
107. Nash, *Closing of American Heart*, 59.

Mutual respect, then, requires that adults honestly respect children. Another factor that influences the atmosphere of mutual respect is the teacher's view of his or her role. Often we tend to think of the teacher as the one who knows and the student as the one who is to learn. The teacher is the one who has the facts or truths that are to be transmitted to the learners. Many times, the methods we use indicate that we think teachers can transplant full-grown concepts into the minds of learners as they passively listen to the teacher. This view of the teacher's role destroys mutual respect and inhibits development. Mutual respect calls for teachers who see themselves as learners.[108]

Bruce Wilkinson (b. 1940) teaches the *Seven Laws of the Learner*:

1. *The Law of the Learner.* "Cause to learn." The teacher should accept the responsibility of causing the student to learn.

2. *The Law of Expectation.* "Expect the best." The teacher should influence his students' learning and behavior by adjusting expectations.

3. *The Law of Application.* "Apply for life change." The teacher should always teach for the purpose of life change.

4. *The Law of Retention.* "Master the minimum." The teacher should enable all students to enjoy maximum mastery of the Irreducible Minimum.

5. *The Law of Need.* "Build the need." The teacher should build the need before teaching the content.

6. *The Law of Equipping.* "Equip for service." The teacher should train students for a life of service and edification.

7. *The Law of Revival.* "Revive the heart." The teacher should encourage an ongoing personal revival in students' lives.[109]

Contra Kohlberg, Craig Richard Dykstra (b. 1947) argues that moral development is *not* primarily a function of age and stage, but rather primarily a function of organic aspects such as one's own community, experiences, and disciplines.

---

108. Stonehouse, *Patterns in Moral Development*, 73.
109. Wilkinson, *Almost Every Answer*.

> Exploring the range and depth of a single practice could take a lifetime. That is partly because each is so rich and various. Every practice has taken an astonishing variety of specific forms, in history and around the world today. Moreover, every practice is a place of mystery: a gracious vessel that can be broken by loveless acts. Practices call for a lifetime of exploration because we are constantly learning more about what it means to do them well—and learning it right in the middle of our doing it. . . . Education in Christian practices is always going on within the life of Christian communities. It happens as parents teach children the economics of a household or as friends surround a widow in her time of grief. Our most important education for practice happens in the course of life-in-community. It is education that takes place in the ongoing patterns of life together. . . . This kind of learning—communal but unplanned—takes place all the time.[110]

Dan Egeler asserts that "true learning, however, is not complete until the truth being taught has been *understood, fully appreciated*, and *internalized*."[111] This recent president of ACSI (Association of Christian Schools International) advocates Christian teachers take a mentoring approach to their role—especially among a generation of millennial learners.

Another contemporary theory-practitioner, Glen Schultz, summarizes the educational endeavor by what he calls four key principles:

1. Parents have been given the assignment to raise godly offspring.
2. The training process (education) must be based upon truth.
3. The end goal of this assignment is to raise children who know Jesus Christ as Savior and think and act from a biblical worldview.
4. Parents must choose able men and women who "fear God, love truth, and hate covetousness" to help them with this assignment.[112]

Curtiss Hancock (born c. 1950) simply states, "To educate is to habituate."[113] He explains that

> the word *habit* means *having*. Habits are acquired dispositions or qualities that modify natural human activity. Habits are inclinations we have, developed in our natural abilities by repeated

---

110. Bass, *Practicing our faith*, 195–204.
111. Egeler, *Mentoring Millennials*, 71.
112. Schultz, *Kingdom Education*, 83.
113. Hancock, *Recovering Catholic Philosophy*, 81.

actions. They bring new qualities to human life by enabling us to initiate specific activities in our natural abilities in controlled and purposeful ways. . . . One scholar has called habits *operational structures*. As an acquired operational tendency, a habit is curiously situated in its relationship to power and to activity. A habit is not identical with knowledge or appetite.[114] . . . *Happiness ultimately depends on ordering its life around the things of God.*[115]

Mark Eckel (born c. 1960) portrays the enterprise of education in the context of a Covenantal Christian school as a pyramid as follows, with pedigree as the capstone and with philosophy as the foundation:

1. *Philosophy*: A school's philosophy includes a *mission* that defines its identity, a *vision* that tells where it is headed, and *core virtues* that explain how it plans to get there based upon biblical truths.

2. *Posture*: The posture of a covenantal school entails commitment to certain habits of the heart. These habits include Christian intellect, interiority, and involvement in the community in ways that intersect and infuse the life of the school.

3. *Personnel*: Christian teachers *are* the school. God-gifted educators demonstrate the school's philosophy and live the school's posture.

4. *Principle*: The underlying principle of covenantal education is that all of life is unified, and it all belongs to God.

5. *Process*: The aforementioned principle is incorporated through the process of integrating biblical truth into all school subject matter and for all of life.

6. *Program*: The curriculum needs to be distinctly Christian.

7. *Pedigree*: Children are indoctrinated Christianly in order to eventually transform culture through their vocational lives.[116]

Former headmaster of Prestonwood Christian Academy, current president of ACSI, and author of *Running with the Horses: A Parenting Guide for Raising Children to be Servant-Leaders for Christ*, Dr. Larry

---

114. Hancock, *Recovering Catholic Philosophy*, 82.
115. Hancock, *Recovering Catholic Philosophy*, 32.
116. Jones, *Perspectives on Your Child's Education*, 60–79.

Taylor promotes a "unique training program designed to assist schools in adopting a strategic, intentional, and holistic plan that directly impacts the culture of their school community." He strives to have "schools learn about a proven training paradigm and educational model that prepares students to:

1. Think, write, and speak Christianly, critically, and intelligently.
2. Reason with and about other worldviews.
3. Persuade non-believers to follow Christ.[117]

Jim Wilhoit advocates a transformational approach to education, which he contrasts with other approaches:[118]

	Transformational	Developmental	Transmissive	Romantic
Aim	Transforming the learner.	Equipping the learner with useful tools.	Transmitting knowledge and skills.	Personal growth and self-fulfillment.
Focus	The individual person as a potential recipient of the transforming grace of God.	The individual within society.	Society.	The individual.
Process	Interaction between personal experiences and transforming truths.	Accumulation and interaction between experiences, perspective, and society.	Absorption of skills and knowledge.	Unfolding inborn traits and characteristics, which are assumed to be good.
Knowledge	A tool to be wielded as God intended.	A tool to be used.	Highly organized factual information.	Experiences and activities which help a person grow.

Dr. Wilhoit enumerates the content and the character of such education:

1. Critical reflection on life.

---

117. Taylor, *Running with the Horses*.
118. Wilhoit, *Search for Meaning*, 73–103.

2. An emphasis on relationships.

3. A sense of mystery and wonder.

4. A balance between support and challenge.

5. Knowledge of Scripture and its practical application.

6. Knowledge of God and appropriate worship.

7. A foundational God-centeredness.

8. A focus on the person and work of Christ.

9. Guidance as to how best to follow Jesus.

10. A realization of the centrality of the grace of God.

Educated at both Harvard University and Oxford University, educational psychologist Adam Saenz, writes about *The Power of a Teacher*. He asserts that the potency of education and educators is to restore hope and to change lives. He speaks about this holistic concept of well-being entailing the following domains:

1. Occupational

2. Emotional

3. Financial

4. Spiritual

5. Physical

Saenz writes about what he sees as the *sine qua non* of wellness, i.e., that the teacher needs to be holistically well in order to impact the student toward wellness. "The teacher intent on a lifetime journey on the road of education is wise to consistently invest meaningful qualities of oil of his or her attention on the wheel that matters most: the wheel of personal wellbeing. You [teacher] do have the power to make lives better, including your own."[119]

Donovan Graham enumerates five critical considerations:

1. The purpose of education.

---

119. Saenz, *Power of a Teacher*, 34.

2. The nature of the learner.

3. The learning process.

4. The view of the subject matter.

5. The person and offices of the teacher.[120]

He goes on to describe the teacher in such an educational context:

1. Jesus as the model.

2. The teacher as an image-bearer of God.

3. Finite, fallen, and redeemed.

4. Prophet, priest, and king.[121]

Graham enumerates considerations for Christian school curriculum.[122]

1. *Biblical truth is the framework for all inquiry.* "It enables us to explore reality and have a perspective through which we can see it truthfully."[123]

2. *Knowledge is diverse and unified.* Borrowing Whitehead's term, "seamless coat of learning," Graham posits knowledge that is both diverse and unified. That knowledge is diverse is attested to by the variety within creation. That it is unified is attested to by the aseity God and the fact that Jesus Christ is that which holds it all together. To be properly understood and utilized, both unity and diversity must be embraced.

3. *Knowing also entails a concomitant responsibility of doing.* True knowledge involves an understanding of information, the implications of that information, and a response to both.

Robert Pazmiño (b. 1948), a Columbia-educated, evangelical professor of the philosophy of education, asserts that twenty-first-century education should include more than just cognitive development. He calls for educational "invitations that encourage theological reflection,

---

120. Graham, *Biblical Yardstick for Teaching*, 1.
121. Graham, *Biblical Yardstick for Teaching*, 130–31.
122. Graham, *Biblical Yardstick for Teaching*, 111.
123. Graham, *Biblical Yardstick for Teaching*, 101.

spiritual imagination, and transformative practice in Christian education beyond current efforts."[124]

Human flourishing does not happen in a vacuum, it takes place within a context. Michael Peterson, a Christian educational philosopher, describes critical components of that context within a Christian school and its philosophy of education.

1. Has a creational outlook: God brought everything [else] into being.

2. Develops an incarnational mindset: God identifies himself intimately with humanity.

3. Maintains a sacramental orientation: An overall understanding of life as sacramental envisions many created realities as potential channels of God's grace.

4. Grows in deep regard for humans: God pronounced [human] creation very good.

5. Teaches that Truth is based upon the way things really are.

6. Recognizes evil—even while acknowledging supreme goodness and absolute power of God and while affirming the original, intrinsic goodness of the creation.

7. Increases one's sensitivity to others. Understanding the fragility of our existence is a precursor to compassion that motivates efforts to alleviate the suffering of others.[125]

Christian epistemologist W. Jay Wood calls academic and spiritual disciplines "deeply anchored habits of the mind that contribute to the success of our many intellectual endeavors and ultimately to our ability to lead excellent lives."[126] He lists wisdom, understanding, foresight, and love of truth, and observes that "there is nothing new, of course, about approaching epistemological concerns with matters of intellectual virtue and vice uppermost in mind; indeed this approach was once the staple of Judeo-Christian as well as ancient Greek ways of thinking."[127]

---

124. Pazmiño, *Foundational Issues*, 266–74.
125. Peterson, *With All Your Mind*, 208–12.
126. Wood, *Epistemology*, 7.
127. Wood, *Epistemology*, 8.

Human flourishing, Wood argues, is the soil from within which intellectual virtues grow. Whether Aristotelian *eudaemonia*, Stoic *apatheia*, or Christian beatific vision, the determination of whether an intellectual quality is virtuous arises from the calculus of whether lives ought to be headed in that direction. "Thus, what we regard as intellectually virtuous and vicious behavior will vary as we are committed to one or another account of human flourishing."[128]

According to Wood, such virtues include:

1. Acquired

2. Maintained

3. Communicated

4. Applied

and that they fall into at least one of the following four categories:

1. Motivational

2. Dialectical

3. Pedagogical

4. Practical

with what he calls fine and fuzzy lines demarcating the categories.[129]

Philip Dow, a Cambridge University PhD and a Christian head of school, cites fifteen research-based strategies for fostering intellectual virtues in a Christian school.[130]

1. Create a culture of thinking: A community of learners in which individual and collective thinking are valued and promoted as part of the regular, day-to-day experience of everyone within the school.

2. Hire and develop intellectually virtuous faculty and staff: An intellectual virtues educational model must be owned, supported, and implemented by educators who genuinely understand and are passionate about intellectual virtues.

---

128. Wood, *Epistemology*, 46.
129. Wood, *Epistemology*, 38–42.
130. Dow, *Virtuous Minds*, 187–91.

3. Direct instruction: Intellectual virtues must be taught and taught about.

4. Family support: A culture conducive to intellectual character growth requires strong family involvement to foster intellectual virtues in and among their children.

5. Advisory groups: Provide a safe environment for ongoing positive relationships, conversation, goal-setting, and encouragement.

6. Ongoing reflection: Self-awareness and self-assessment are critical for growth.

7. Modeling: Provide attractive and informative examples of various traits of intellectual virtue for sake of admiration, inspiration and even imitation.

8. Positive reinforcement: Calling attention to successful approximations of intellectual virtues encourages more intellectual virtue.

9. Reflective teaching and learning: Routinely reorient to the primary aspects of teaching and learning through the consideration of intellectual virtues.

10. Thinking routines: Incorporate simple cognitive patterns and structures to develop, practice, and cultivate intellectual virtues.

11. Making thinking visible: Incorporate this Harvard-approach by providing explicit representations and framework of intellectual virtues.

12. Metacognition: Self-regulative means by which students learn to increasingly be aware of, understand, and manage their thinking, feeling, and acting.

13. Critical thinking pedagogy: Intellectually disciplined processes of actively and skillfully conceptualizing, applying, analyzing, synthesizing, and evaluating information gathered from observation, experience, reflection, and reasoning.

14. Agenda of understanding: Pushing students into situations in which they are confronted by their own and others' ideas.

15. Incorporate intellectual virtue concepts into standards and assessments: Identify goals and modes of measurability of aspects of the development of intellectual virtues.

In their book, entitled *A Vision with a Task: Christian Schooling for Responsive Discipleship*, Stronks and Blomberg summarize their twelve chapters with twelve recommendations for Christian schools:

1. That Christian schools discuss the nature and task of learning [Christianly].

2. That Christian schools analyze the social factors affecting their school.

3. That Christian schools develop a mission statement and corresponding objectives.

4. That Christian schools schedule planning sessions for teachers to develop lessons consonant with the school mission.

5. That Christian schools develop peer associates for prayer, active listening, encouragement, and discernment.

6. That Christian schools encourage love and respect among all constituents.

7. That Christian schools intentionalize developing underdeveloped domains within schools, e.g., spiritual, ethical, aesthetic, spatial, intrapersonal, and interpersonal.

8. That Christian schools implement an integral curriculum in which knowledge entails a personal response of insight and service.

9. That Christian schools develop structures that facilitate the school's vision.

10. That Christian schools ensure that integral units cultivated creational integrity.

11. That Christian schools use their mission statement and objectives to formulate principles to student assessment and evaluation.

12. That Christian schools regularly pursue professional development.[131]

131. Stronks and Blomberg, *Vision with a Task*, 304–8.

Steven Vryhof, a University of Chicago–educated former Christian school teacher who became a professor at Calvin College, distills the Christian Schools International approach to Christian school education in particular in two of his books, *A Vision with a Task: Christian Schooling for Responsive Discipleship* and *Twelve Affirmations: Reformed Christian Schooling for the 21st Century*; the latter enumerates and elucidates the following priorities:

1. The Christian school's mission is clarified to shape all curricular goals and practices.

2. The Christian school community stresses the restorative power of God's grace in individual lives within the world community.

3. Trusting the Holy Spirit's guidance to the student's lives, the Christian school community offers opportunities and fosters responsibilities to exercise *discernment*.

4. The Christian school experience preserves in students the ability to express and share the full range of God-given emotions.

5. Christian school teachers and students take the future seriously by confronting the realities of how, where, and with whom students will spend their lives.

6. The Christian school curriculum is designed to address real problems, and its students are prepared to generate real products.

7. In the Christian school, students learn key knowledge and develop essential skills.

8. The Christian school pays attention to and affirms each student level.

9. The curriculum in the Christian School reflects the complexity of God's world.

10. The Christian school is a community in the biblical sense.

11. The Christian school allows teachers' strengths and artistry to be fully utilized.

12. The Christian school community continuously seeks a more excellent way by planning and structuring for change.

TOWARD A BIBLICAL PHILOSOPHY OF CHRISTIAN SCHOOL EDUCATION

Based upon the working definitions and the purposes of this book: *philosophy of education is both the academic discipline which studies the fundamental nature of education, its foundational constituents, and its theoretical bases; as well as the theory, attitude, and orientation that acts as a guiding principle for one's approach to education, viz. the act, the process, or the product of imparting or acquiring knowledge or understanding, or of developing skills or competencies, or of cultivating the capacities of reasoning, judgment, values, or virtues—thereby preparing oneself or others for mature and flourishing life.* From that starting, the closing section of this book summarizes the *summum bonum* of education within the context of a biblical philosophy of Christian school education.

Although the present author acknowledges a vast array of denotations, a broad scope of connotations, and an abundant aforementioned list of illustrations of the term *biblical philosophy of Christian school education*—a vast array of meanings that may in fact provide viable contributions to general understanding of Christian school education, within the context of this book, the present author offers the following aspects of a biblical philosophy of Christian school education.

Noetic

1. Regain that which was lost in the fall.

2. Teach students to think God's thoughts after him.

3. Renew minds and concomitantly transform learners by means of the liberating mechanisms of Beauty, Goodness, and Truth.

4. Demonstrate the theocentric foundations of each and of all of the academic disciplines and cocurricular domains for development.

5. Promote a sense of divine *Weltanschauung, apologia,* and *vocare* within each student as a steward of God's stuff—truth, time, talent, treasure, and *creation continuo.*

Relational

1. Reach and teach the next generation by God's grace and for God's glory.

2. Cultivate great commandment and great commission living.

3. Engage in the "one another's" of the New Testament for God's people doing God's work in God's way.[132]

4. Cultivate an individual spirit of and a collective culture of love, joy, peace, patience, kindness, goodness, faithfulness, gentleness, and self-control.

5. Speak the truth in love.

Doxological

1. Do all of this in such a way (i.e., the *quality* of arête) and to such an extent (i.e., the *quantity* of arête)—excellently and wholeheartedly as unto the Lord (i.e., the impetus, the motive, and the goal of *soli Deo gloria*).

2. Reorient and recalibrate teachers' and learners' modes, means, and motives as to being from God, through God, and to(wards) God (cf. Rom 11:33–36).

Thus, a biblical philosophy of a Christian school education is that which incorporates the aforementioned noetic, relational, and doxological aspects into education. What seems to do so succinctly, substantively, and scripturally is *Arête: Pursuing excellence for the glory of God!*

---

132. "One another" comes from the Greek term *allelon* (ἀλλήλων), which occurs one hundred times in ninety-four verses containing forty-seven admonitions to Christians on how to comfort themselves and how to interact with others. These become the standard for relationships among all the constituents of a Christian school.

As poetically and profoundly as Bernard of Cluny (ca. 1100–ca. 1150) penned it nearly a millennium ago, "*There God, our King and portion, in fullness of his grace, shall we behold forever, and worship face to face.*"[133]

May God's people live *this* day in light of *that* day. May God's people do God's work in God's way—by God's grace and for God's glory. May that work *include*—and by the very nature of that inclusion—*not* be limited *to* Christian school education. May God's people commit themselves and their educational endeavors to . . .

Arête:
Pursuing excellence for the glory of God!

---

133. McGrath, *Passionate Intellect*, 43.

Appendix 1

Ars Gratia Ars—Soli Deo Gloria: A Critical Review of Nicholas Wolterstorff's *Art in Action: Toward a Christian Aesthetic*

INTRODUCTION

NICHOLAS WOLTERSTORFF'S (NW) ART *in Action: Toward a Christian Aesthetic* (*AA*) distills the essence of NW's argument presented with more analytics and acumen in his *Works and Worlds of Art* (*WW*). Both texts seem to have served as helpful correctives to (or at least challenges to) many twentieth-century tendencies in and around art, arts, and aesthetics. The former also serves as the focus for this appendix, which shall attempt to summarize NW's view of art in *AA*, to commend several contributions of NW via *AA*, and to consider several internal considerations and several external considerations that might contribute to the argument and application of *AA*.

DEFINITION OF WOLTERSTORFF'S (NW) VIEW OF ART IN *ART IN ACTION* (*AA*)

In his preface, NW asserts that *AA* is his attempt "to relate my 'aesthetic to the central Christian dogmas.'"[1] Alluding to Dorothy Sayers's essay

---

1. *AA*, ix.

on the subject,[2] NW proceeds to explain that *AA* "represents an attempt to articulate how I as a Christian see art and the aesthetic dimension of reality." Finally, he suggests that in *AA* he is not attempting "to relate Christianity to arts or arts to Christianity."[3]

In *AA*, NW utilizes an instrumental theory of aesthetics. He describes his particular approach to instrumentalism as "a *functional* approach to art."[4] Two-thirds of the way through *AA*, NW delineates the particular *qualified* instrumentalism which he adopts:

> I have also, be it noted, adopted a qualified instrumentalist theory of artistic value. For I have said that the quality of a work of art—like that of any other artifact produced or distributed for a purpose—inheres in how effectively it serves that purpose. Therein lies the instrumentalist component. But I have added that it also inheres in how good and satisfying it proves in general to use for the purpose intended (the side-effect clause). Therein lies the qualification.[5]

DESCRIPTION OF WHAT WOLTERSTORFF'S VIEW OF ART IN ART IN ACTION CONTRIBUTES[6]

Among other contributions, *AA* seems to have contributed helpful correctives to several tendencies in and around art and aesthetics prevalent during the twentieth century.

Contra nihilism, *AA* argues that the world is knowable, that some of that knowableness is known in part through action—even in art in action. The nothingness and unknowableness of nihilism as an approach to

---

2. Sayers, "Towards a Christian Aesthetic," 69.

3. *AA*, ix. Although NW makes this claim, a reader could argue that actually NW does quite a bit of what could be called by some as relating Christianity to art and art to Christianity both in *AA* as well as in his more analytic and more philosophical *WW*.

4. *AA*, x.

5. *AA*, 158.

6. Prior to proceeding to considering contributions and critiques of *AA*, there are at least three other nontrivial aspects of NW's *AA* which ought to be mentioned, viz. his describing art as a gracious gift which enlists human responsibility, his employment of role analysis, and his teleological norm that art ought to contribute to human experience of *shalom*. (The present author finds pp. 67–121 in *AA* particularly valuable in their contribution to a Christian perspective of art and artists as stewards of the Sovereign and for *shalom*.)

art is addressed in the substantiveness and knowableness of art in action. The action of the art concretizes it, and it does so knowably.

Contra deconstructivism, *AA* argues that an artist's intent and content convey particular and substantive meaning. An observer, therefore, is not warranted in deconstructing the work of art and reconstructing as it were some observer-imposed meaning. The meaning of the work of art inheres in the artist and in the art itself.

Contra technologism, *AA* would argue that newer is not necessarily truer. Some perennial metanarratives and master narratives offer something, at least in some cases (such as art and artists moving themselves and their audiences closer to shalom)—something that is even more valuable and durative than so-called progress or technique.

Contra contemplativism (and its concomitant elitism), which divorces art (and the artist) from the rest of life, which elevates the artist above the rest of humanity, and which promotes an aestheticism without true responsibility,[7] *AA* calls for a more egalitarian approach to art and artists and expects art and artists to act responsibly in moving themselves and their audiences closer to shalom.[8]

DELINEATION OF WHAT WOLTERSTORFF'S VIEW IN ART IN ACTION SEEMS TO MISS OR AT LEAST MIGHT BENEFIT FROM MORE EXPRESSLY CONSIDERING

1. Internal Considerations

First, NW seems to lack definitional clarity or consistency. For example, at one point, NW seems to suggest that the artist's *intent* is what matters, and at another time he seems to suggest that the art accomplishes

---

7. A careful reader of *AA* and of cultural trends precipitating its writing might also notice significant ways in which NW also contributes to countering other twentieth-century tendencies in and around art, e.g., Impoverishment, Neo-Dadaism, Minimalism, Conceptualism, and Popism—just to name a few.

8. Although this call to a responsibility of art and artists to move themselves, their art, and their audiences closer to shalom, the present author cites two caveats or cautions. First NW rightly eschews idolatry in the arts, but shalom itself could become for artists, arts, and audiences just another idol. Second, NW rightly eschews abstraction and obfuscation, but it seems rather abstract if not obfuscatory as to how an artist or art moves its audience by responsibility, intention, and design closer to shalom.

something *other than* what the artist intends. A careful reader is left wondering, "Which is it?!" Is what art *does* as action intentional, incidental, both, or neither? Perhaps the best illustration of this problem is NW's recurring thought experiment of a young musician he calls Johnny. NW argues that Johnny's action of art is to delight his teacher, but in so doing Johnny incidentally bores his young sister. So, the careful reader would not be out of line to wonder whether Johnny *does* his art to delight his old teacher or to bore his young sister, or does that even matter since both actually happen. In other words, the very example NW uses seems to argue against what NW seems to be trying to argue for, i.e., concrete and particular artist intent.

A second significant example of a lack of definitional clarity or consistency is NW's Donald Duck illustration.[9] Donald Duck is considered in NW's illustrations as an entity at one time, and not as an entity at another. So, which is it? In NW's qualified instrumentalism, is Donald Duck an entity, or not? If he is *both* an entity *and* not an entity, he cannot be both an entity and not an entity at the same time and in the same way, but it is not clear that NW has explicitly addressed the way(s) in which Donald Duck ought to be considered an entity and in which way(s) he ought not to be.

A third significant example of a lack of definitional clarity or consistency is what NW seems to say about the music in the composer's mind itself being the *work of art*, but he does not seem to address the scenario of the composition staying *only* there (in the composer's mind) as to whether it would be a work of art in that case. There seem to be at least two loopholes at this point in NW's argument. First, it is unclear as to whether an unwritten, unperformed *work of art* (e.g., the music in the composer's mind) is actually a *work* at all. If it is actually a work, how does it satisfy the terms of NW's qualified instrumentalism as cited above? Per his definition of music being a work of art in the composer's

---

9. This recurring illustration occurs among other places on p. 20 of *WW*. "Donald Duck is of course represented without *there being* [NW's emphasis] some entity, Donald Duck (DD)." Actually, there is an entity Donald Duck, albeit a cartoon entity. Second, even NW describes DD as an "insouciant fowl" and a "sequence of drawings" which was "photographically copied." For something to be insouciant, it needs to *be*; for something to be a fowl, it needs to *be*; likewise, for something to be a sequence, a drawing, a photograph, and a copy, it needs to *be*—even if *be*-ing only fictionally. NW cannot have it both ways: either DD is an entity that truly exists fictionally, or NW cannot describe this nonentity in such entity-ways (*Fiction*, http://plato.stanford.edu/entries/fiction/.)

mind, a reader might be inclined to think NW's position would be that the "in the mind only" composition would in fact be a work of art, and yet, per his definition of a work of art, the "in the mind only" composition does not seem to be a *work*.

In addition to what appear to be a few lapses of definitional clarity or consistency, NW seems to commit a few fallacies, as well. First, in characterizing non-*AA* approaches, NW seems to create both a straw man[10] and a false dilemma. He postulates only his view or extreme views, which he describes as follows: "One will distort arts or find them inscrutable."[11] NW insists that neglecting the embeddedness inherent in his particular view of art in action "bounds" an observer to one of the two aforementioned horns. Certainly, his art in action cannot be the only legitimate *tertium quid*. One could inquire of NW, for example, what he means by "bound" to "distort" art. It appears in context to mean that any view other than his particular view of art in action is a distortion of what actually is the true view, i.e., *his*. Whether NW actually intended such a statement to convey such hubris that to the present author it seems to convey is not clear to the present author, but what seems clear is that NW does not graciously present his argument. Rather he seems to implicitly insist that any other argument about art being something other than (or more than just) *art as action* is distorted. This seems to create both a false dilemma between his view and any other view, as well as a straw man out of any variant view.[12]

Second, NW seems to equivocate at times: "*Work* of art" vs. "art as *work*." Fundamentally, this seems to be as much a factor of his utilizing the same English word for a "*work* of art" as he does for "art as *work*." It is unclear to the present author as to whether NW does this wittingly, or not. Either case (whether he does so wittingly, or he does so unwittingly) would be problematic. If he does so unwittingly, he seems to fail

---

10. One of multiple examples can be found in NW's countering contemplative approaches to art. "Let us say that aesthetic contemplation is undertaken for the sake of the satisfaction to be gotten in the contemplation" (*AA*, 17–18). One, however, who might be inclined to a contemplative approach to art might contest such a myopic and egoistic end as the "satisfaction to be gotten"; perhaps they would suggest that NW contemplates a work of art such as Mel Gibson's *The Passion of the Christ* not for satisfaction, but for aesthetic wonder, as well as for conviction, for contrition, or even for worship.

11. *AA*, 5.

12. In *AA*, 67, NW goes from straw man to *ad hominem*. He speaks of the "bewitchment" of the contemplation view of high art.

to appropriately distinguish the nuance of semantic domain between the two words *work* in his expressions "*work* of art" and "art as *work*."[13] On the other hand, if he does so wittingly, then he seems guilty of *petitio principii* in at least three regards: *Id est* if he does so wittingly, NW seems to beg the questions of definition, of ontology, and of universality.

In terms of NW begging the question of definition, this seems to the present author to be the most obvious and the most fundamentally egregious. If NW is knowingly using the word *work* (as in "*work* of art" and "art as *work*") in the same way with the same meaning (and there does not seem to be any particular clarity or clarification that he is *not*), then his essential argument in *AA* is really not an argument at all, it is merely rearranging the order of the words—tantamount to a tautology. In other words, if NW is knowingly using the word *work* (as in "*work* of art" and "art as *work*") in the same way with the same meaning, then all his argument basically boils down to is that *art is work*, for it cannot *not* be work and *be* a work of art because a work of art by definition is art *and* work.

Second, in terms of NW's begging the question, ontologically speaking,[14] speech acts (sometimes referred to in *AA* and *WW* as event-acts and occurrence-acts and elsewhere in NW as performance-acts)[15]

---

13. Perhaps NW and the argument he attempts to make in *AA* and *WW* could benefit from utilizing words from another language (e.g., Latin, Greek, French, or German) that might help nuance the different aspects of the English term *work* with appropriate and clarifying distinction. Latin terms worth considering might include *opus, eventus, actus, factum, artificium, fabrica, erit artis opus*, etc. Greek terms worth considering might include *poiema, techni, ergo, ergo techni, ergasia, sumban, praxe, pragmatopoiese*, etc. French terms worth considering might include *art, artifice, ouvre d'art, realisation, ouvrage, evenement, effet*, etc. German terms worth considering might include *Kunst, Kunstwerk, Arbeit, Werk, Tat, Vorgang, Geschehnis, Vorkommnis, Veranstaltung, Gestaltung, Wirkung*, etc.

14. One such *petitio principi* ontologically speaking in NW's argument occurs on p. 36 of *WW*, on which he says, "Occurrences are events." No clarification; no caveats; no conditions. Just a plain, *un*-argued assertion that (all) occurrences are events. Some occurrences, however, are not events. One counterexample shall suffice: the occurrence of a stationary stone stationed still on the stable's stoop would be an occurrence of such and so said stone, but not an event. Perhaps NW writing about such a stone, an artist painting such a stone, or the equestrian placing such a stone can be called events, but certainly not the stationary stone itself. Three pages earlier NW tries to anticipate this defeater by using the term instance (rather than event or occurrence)—which he admits is "a rather ambiguous word" (*WW*, 33); but again NW fails to define the semantic domain of *that* term, to assuage the reader's concerns about the admitted ambiguity, or to demonstrate how that answers the question he begs three pages later.

15. NW commendably concedes that defining such terms with ontologically clarity is "immensely perplexing" (*WW*, 36). He even goes as far as to say that "the

seem to be a significant source[16] for NW's concept of art as action.[17] Among other disanalogies and other potentially problematic aspects of NW drawing so heavily upon speech acts as a source for his ontological concepts in *AA*, speech acts seem to be an oversimplification of the causality of acts and of action. Thus, the present author contends that to utilize such as a source for conclusions about art as (only) action obfuscates, adumbrates, or truncates other (non-action) aspects of art. In other words, even if art *is* action and even if art *as* action is a legitimate, reasonable, and helpful way to look at art, that does not make it the only legitimate, reasonable, and helpful way to look at art, nor does it preclude art from *being* anything *but* action—both of which NW seems to argue that it is.[18]

---

perceptible artifacts of art are not all alike in their ontological status" (*WW*, 37). He proceeds to elucidate some of what he sees as distinguishing between, for example, the existence of a fictional character in some senses, but the non-existence of the same character in another; he explores the concept of compositions existing in a composer's head; he even gives a nod to improvisation as something other than an art-work (*WW*, 41), but he seems to fall short of drawing clearly delineating and defining lines for the key terms in his argument, e.g., what *is* art, what is *not* art, what is *action*, what is something *other than* action—if anything at all, what is art *as* action, and what might be art as something *other than just* action—if anything at all.

16. Zuidervaart, review of *AA*, 88.

17. NW admits to his being "ontologically profligate" (*WW*, 4) in regards to failing to define *acts* or *action*, and even in assuming that examples of each exist ontologically—presupposing (or even presuming) a justification for his use of such terms as *acts* and *action* as foundational to his argument.

18. Although no small part of such an ontological discussion arguably lies outside of the scope of this present book, at least one further point seems pertinent at present. Using event-act almost synonymously with speech-act (*WW*, 193–97), NW defines *event* as consisting "of (i.e., *is*) [parenthetical note and italics original] an entity's actually having a certain property, or one or more entities actually standing in a certain relation." Again, this seems fraught with several difficulties, including: (1) Even such an *action* term as *event* poses a challenge for NW to define using *action*-terms and not *being*-terms; perhaps contra Lucas and NW—and contra more than just the front flap of *AA*—substance, not action is the most important and fundamental category of thought, i.e., that by which other terms are even defined. (2) Additionally, NW fails to distinguish how something that is obviously *not* an event, e.g., a stationary stone stationed still on the stable's stoop does not have certain properties and does not stand in relationship to other entities, etc.; in other words, his definition for *event* (which he uses synonymously with *action*) is too broad and imprecise—not unlikely (among other things) betraying his action-bias. (3) Even granting NW his definition and even giving him the benefit of the doubt in terms of *art* as event/action in some regard, it still seems an unwarranted *non sequitur* for NW to claim that is *all* art is; could not art be action *and* something other than action? (There will be more on this in the final

Finally, in terms of universality, "The universality of art corresponds only to a diversity and flux of purposes, not to some pervasive and unique purposes. . . . For one thing, one cannot escape the impression that there is in man a deep desire for concreteness."[19] Furthermore, to put it another way, NW in *WW* suggests that not only does there exist animals walking, but the walking of the animals doing the walking does itself exist. However, as NW admits, the animals which do the walking exist, too, so does that not by analogy mean that art universally exists even "prior" to it walking, so to speak?[20]

2. External Considerations

To critique NW's *AA* an astute reader need look no further than NW's preface in *AA* to stumble upon a clue as to how to proceed. As stated above, NW asserts in his preface that *AA* is his attempt "to relate my 'aesthetic to the central Christian dogmas.'"[21] Admittedly alluding to Dorothy Sayers's essay on the subject,[22] NW proceeds to explain that *AA* "represents an attempt to articulate how I as a Christian see art and the aesthetic dimension of reality." The present author contends that if in fact NW did intend to relate his aesthetic to central Christian dogmas, he would have done well to follow Dorothy Sayers's model in "Towards a Christian Aesthetic." Therein the latter seems to relate her aesthetic to one of the most aesthetically pertinent and historically foundational Christian dogmas—from the opening chapter of Scripture, i.e., Creation.

First the present author will attempt to argue for the pertinence of this dogma, second to distill the essence of Sayers's use of this dogma in her model, third to demonstrate the way she actually accomplished what NW said that he set out to accomplish even better than what NW actually accomplished.

Although admittedly Christians and Christianity have not held singularly to a single interpretation of the Creation narrative itself, nonetheless *Creation* has perennially been an historic Christian dogma.

---

section of this book under the heading of Another Consideration.)

19. The irony being that NW utilizes abstraction to make his case for concretization.
20. *WW*, 1.
21. *AA*, ix.
22. Sayers, "Towards a Christian Aesthetic," 69.

i. Although Christianity (and its dogma) is more than just its historic creeds, it is not less than them.

ii. The historic creeds of Christianity include the Apostles' Creed, the first Nicene Creed, and the amended Nicene (Niceno-Constantinopolitan) Creed.

iii. These three historic Christian creeds have historically and conventionally been viewed as a distillation of Christian dogma.

iv. These three creeds all explicitly affirm Creation as a Christian dogma.

   a. The Apostles' Creed states: "I believe in God, the Father almighty, Creator of heaven and earth."
   b. The Nicene Creed states: "We believe in one God, the Father Almighty, Maker of all things visible and invisible."
   c. The Niceno-Constantinopolitan Creed states: "We believe in one God, the Father Almighty, Maker of heaven and earth, and of all things visible and invisible."

v. Not only do these creeds *state* Creation as a Christian dogma, they each cite Creation in their first statement.

   a. Citing Creation in their first statement seems to acknowledge the logical priorness of Creation to the other Christian dogmas stated in the statements.
   b. Citing Creation in their first statement seems also to illustrate the conceptual priorness of Creation to the other Christian dogmas.

      i. The universe might have come about another way, but it did not.

      ii. If it had come about in a different way, *that* means or method would have presumably been stated in Scripture, codified in creeds, and cited as conceptually prior to other Christian doctrines.

      iii. The universe might have come about another way, but it did not.

      iv. Whatever way that was in fact, it was in fact through Creation—whatever the particulars, persons, time frames, and mechanisms therein—as alluded to in Scripture no matter how literal or allegorical a particular Christian's interpretation, this is conventionally and Christianly known as *Creation*.

v. Creation—however it actually came about—is a *sin qua non* of Christian dogma.
  1. If Creation had not transpired, then man would not have existed.
  2. If man would not have existed, man would not have sinned.
  3. If man would not have sinned, Christ would not have died for their sins according to the Scriptures.
  4. If Christ had not died for man's sins according to the Scriptures, then he would not have risen from the dead.
  5. If Christ had not risen from the dead, then Christians would be among men most miserable.
      a. Their faith would be in vain.
      b. Their dogma would be vacuous.
  vi. But Christians' faith is not in vain, their dogma is not vacuous, their Christ did rise from the dead having died for their sins, which they committed subsequent to having been created as part of Creation.

vi. Furthermore, as Sayers mentions and as NW fails to substantively address, man was not just created as an *arbitrary* part of Creation, man was created as a *particular* part of creation.

vii. The particular part: Man was created in the image of God (*imago Dei*).

viii. Of no other creature was it said that it was created in the *imago Dei*.

ix. *Imago Dei*, therefore, is a distinct feature of man as a creature.

x. Not only is *imago Dei* a distinct feature of man as creature, it is a pertinent feature of man in the context of a discussion on art, arts, and aesthetics:

  a. A discussion that NW asserted he was engaging in *in AA*.
  b. Thus, it ought to be a pertinent feature of NW's aesthetic in *AA*.
  c. It does not seem to be.
  d. It was, however, in Sayers's work on the subject.
      xi. Admittedly the concept of *imago Dei* has precipitated copious consideration over the millennia.

xii. Arguably whatever *imago Dei* does in fact entail, a reasonable place to begin seems to be in the text itself in which this concept of Creation commences, Genesis 1.
   a. In Genesis 1 a careful reader observes that man is made in the image of God (*imago Dei*).
   b. In Genesis 1 a careful reader observes that God creates.
   c. From Genesis 1 a careful reader would reasonably infer that at least part of what being made in the image of God (*imago Dei*) entails would be that man—like the God in whose image man is made—is a creator.
   d. As a creator, man is to create.
   e. To create is to put the *imago Dei* on display to the rest of the universe—and to God!

xiii. Now, whatever art may be (and the ontics and other ontological particulars of all that art *is* and is *not* goes beyond the scope of this present book), it is not less than something related to creating.[23]

xiv. If art has something to do with creating, it seems reasonable that one whose self-stated thesis were to relate his aesthetic to the central Christian dogmas, would at least build upon the historical Christian dogmas on the matter at hand.

xv. Thus, it would seem reasonable to include the *imago Dei* of the Creation account.

xvi. Sayers seems to construct her model on this foundation; NW does not.

xvii. NW begins his work with an allusion to Sayers, opening his preface interacting with her words, "We have no Christian aesthetic."

xviii. The present author—even after having read NW's *AA*—echoes Sayers: "We [still] have no Christian aesthetic."

xix. Arguably what NW did in *AA* is related to aesthetics, but it seems to the present author that one cannot compellingly argue that NW's aesthetic in *AA* is Christian—at least not in any substantive and scriptural way, since NW failed to build upon such foundational

---

23. In all fairness to NW, the present author commends the former for his more lucid treatment of some pertinent principles, predicates, properties, and phenomenologies of the ontics and ontology of art, arts, and aesthetics in his article "Toward an Ontology of Art Works," than what he seemed to overlook or understate in the popular *AA*, or even than what he seemed to obfuscate in the more convoluted *WW*.

aspects of Christianity in general and of a Christian aesthetic in particular as Creation, *imago Dei*, God as Creator, and man as creator.

    a. NW failed to do so.
    b. Sayers did not.

xx. Sayers's view included her assertion that every work of art is an image made *by* an image that is also an image-*maker*, and each image as such is a projected image of the artist analogical in some way or another to the triune God.[24]

xxi. Sayers's argument included three phases:

    a. The nature of man.
        i. Man is *imago Dei*.
        ii. God is Creator.
        iii. Therefore, man is a creator.
    b. The nature of art.
        i. Art is an image—not a copy, nor is it a copy of a copy (cf. mimesis).
        ii. As such art is an image created *by* an image and image-*maker* created (among other things) to create—even as the Creator in whose image man was created was and is a Creator.
    c. The nature of man as artist.
        i. Sayers famously declared, "Man is most himself—man is most manlike—when engaged in creative activity."
        ii. Sayers is in good company with such a declaration.
            1. Stanford Reid's, *A Reformed Approach to Christian Aesthetics*:
                a. "Man's highest responsibility being the work of interpreting and enjoying nature to glory of God.
                b. "As he increases in understanding, more and more he recognizes the ultimate unity of all things in the creative and providential activity of God, and also acknowledges that there is a divinely ordained pattern in the universe, external to man, which man must endeavor to discover for this is man's duty given to him from the beginning of time.

---

24. Even NW makes a passing allusion to the artist being compared to God. He attributes this analogy (not to Augustine, etc.) but to Christoforo Landino as cited in Tigerstedt, "Poet as Creator."

c. "God is the ultimate Artist from whom and to whom must go and come all true aesthetic reactions."[25]
  2. Flannery O'Connor.
     a. Whereas NW might say art *represents*.
     b. FOC would say art *re*-presents.
  3. Herman Bavinck's theological aesthetic:[26]
     a. Reclaim beauty as part of a revelation of God, who is not only True and Good, but Beautiful, as well.
        i. That which is True in revelation, whether general or special, harkens the careful observer back to God the Father.
        ii. That which is Good in revelation, whether general or special, harkens the careful observer back to God the Son.
        iii. That which is Beautiful in revelation, whether general or special, harkens the careful observer back to God the Spirit.
     b. Seek to understand and appreciate God's glorious handiwork.
     c. Strive for independence from mere artistic convention.
     d. Enjoy art and God, the Ultimate Artist.

xxii. This *imago Dei* approach to a Christian aesthetic points the careful and caring Christian aesthetician in two additional directions in terms of integrating Christian dogma with art and aesthetics:

  a. *Sub specie aeternitatis*:
     i. To see all of life (including art, arts, and aesthetics) from the perspective of the eternal.
     ii. All of the beauty, goodness, and truth of life has its source, meaning, and destiny in God, the One who is Eternal.
  b. *Coram Deo*:
     i. To *see* all of life (including art, arts, and aesthetics) from the perspective of the eternal, is to see all of life and all of how we engage all of life as *seen* by the Eternal.

---

25. Reid, "Reformed Approach," 211–19.
26. Covolo, "Herman Bavinck's Theological Aesthetics, 43–58.

> ii. All the beauty, goodness, and truth of life is rightly displayed before the all-seeing eyes of God—by his grace and for his glory.

xxiii. This *imago Dei* approach to a Christian aesthetic points the careful and caring Christian aesthetician in one ultimate direction in terms of integrating Christian dogma with art and aesthetics, i.e., to God alone be the glory (*soli Deo gloria*).

xxiv. *Soli Deo gloria* seems to be what NW was looking for when reading Sayers and when penning his preface.[27]

> a. In *soli Deo gloria* a Christian finds an integrating origin, purpose, and destiny not only of Truth and Goodness, but of Beauty, as well.
> b. In *soli Deo gloria* a Christian finds a means by which to "relate his aesthetic to the central Christian dogmas."
> c. In *soli Deo gloria* a Christian finds a lens thru which to "see art and the aesthetic dimension of reality."
> d. In *soli Deo gloria* a Christian finds meaning to art in action.

Prior to drawing this appendix to a close, it seems pertinent to prompt further external consideration in one other potentially profitable direction—one that does not yet seem to have been taken in the literature swirling around NW's vortex stirred up by *AA*. In *AA*, NW seems to react against notions like *ars gratia ars* (AGA),[28] and rightly so—at least in some regard(s). In this appendix, the present author contends that NW (although getting a bigger picture than *ars gratia ars* seems to get) does not get a big *enough* picture—one that is portrayed quite pertinently via *imago Dei, sub specie aeternitatis, coram Deo,* and *soli Deo gloria* (SDG).[29] What the present author would like to propose for further consideration in another book[30] is the possibility of these three different approaches (i.e., *AA*, AGA, and SDG), which may seem on the surface to be quite contradictory to each other, at another level could be seen not as contradictory, but as potentially complementary as follows.

---

27. Rom 11:33–36; Col 3:1–23; 1 Cor 10:31; Eccl 12:13.

28. Both for sake of ease as well as for correspondence to NW's approach being referred to as *AA*.

29. As famously penned by J. S. Bach at the foot of many of his compositions.

30. And that perhaps by another author.

AGA acknowledges art in a visceral way. Herein molecular aspects of the art itself can be talked about at this level.[31] For the sake of discussion, this could be called *micro*-analysis.

AA seems to approach art in a conceptual way. Herein philosophical (and even sociological) aspects of the art in context of its work and world are talked about. For the sake of discussion, this could be called *mezzo*-analysis.[32]

SDG seems to approach art in a teleological way. Herein doxological aspects of the art are talked about. For the sake of discussion, this could be called *macro*-analysis.

What the present author is proposing for further consideration in some future book(s) is analogous to lenses in science. In science, scientists have benefitted from using different levels of lenses for different types of observation and investigation. At times, in certain contexts, and with particular application, micro-, mezzo-, and macro-analyses are appropriately and astutely applied—each complementing the other. Perhaps by analogy, a similar application of all three lenses is potentially beneficial in art and aesthetics, as well—i.e., the apt utilization of micro- (AGA), mezzo- (AA), and macro- (SDG) analyses not in contradistinction and contradiction to one another, but in complement. Perhaps this could even contribute to answering the perennially elusive question of what is art, and perhaps it would contribute to NW and others like him who desire to attempt to relate their Christian dogma to aesthetics. Perhaps this complementary approach would provide careful and caring observers of art a visceral, conceptual, and teleological levels to be equipped with a more comprehensive (and thereby more comprehending) lens through which to observe art molecularly, philosophically, and doxologically.

As early as the front flap of *AA*, a careful reader can begin to observe where NW is coming from and where he is going: "Action, not substance, will be our most important category of thought."[33] Whereas many aesthetic and artistic missteps of the twentieth century may be countered via this

---

31. In music, for example, this level of consideration would examine form and analyses such as melody, harmony, rhythm, texture, timbre, instrumentation, orchestration, etc.

32. Even NW cracks the door open for this kind of conceptual complementarianism in his own description of his own approach in *AA* as a "wider scene" than AGA on p. 90. Furthermore he invokes a similar complementarianism in literary analysis and uses the metaphor of Chinese boxes to illustrate the different levels from which fiction can be viewed, "box within a box" (*WW*, 171).

33. *AA* attributes this quote from its front flap to Lucas, *Freedom and Grace*, 111.

Art as Action approach, the present author concludes that NW's polemic oversteps an overarching principle of a Christian approach to aesthetics and art, i.e., the implications of *imago dei* in Creation and in creating. That notwithstanding, a complementary conglomeration of *ars gratia ars* (AGA), art in action (*AA*), and *soli Deo gloria* (SDG) might provide future Christian aestheticians with a more full-orbed set of lenses through which to see art and arts for what they truly are, whether from a visceral, philosophical, or teleological perspective. To overlook or to underutilize the other two (i.e., AGA and SDG), NW seems to have done a disservice to art, to arts, to aesthetics, and to Christians. The action to which NW refers in *AA* cannot exist without substance, and it would otherwise exist for no reason were it to exist without *teleos*. Seeing art through the lens of Creation like Sayers affords the aesthetician a model that upholds the micro, mezzo, and macro elements of art, arts, and aesthetics.

Appendix 2

Toward a Summative Capstone Project for Students in a K–12 Christian School

BASED UPON A BIBLICAL PHILOSOPHY OF CHRISTIAN SCHOOL EDUCATION

I. Chapter 1: *Weltanschauung*. What is Truth; what do I believe; what is my worldview?
   a. The student is to delineate, detail, and defend his/her views of orthodox Christianity per the ten loci of a biblical theology.
   b. The student's treatment of each of the ten loci listed below should include two pertinent Scripture references as well as some demonstration of some understanding of the different positions on these issues among the body of Christ.
   c. Chapter 1 should cover approximately five to ten pages.
      i. Prolegomena and Bibliology.
      ii. Theology.
      iii. Christology.
      iv. Pneumatology.
      v. Anthropology.
      vi. Hamartiology.
      vii. Soteriology.
      viii. Ecclesiology.

          ix. Angelology.
          x. Eschatology.
II. Chapter 2: *Apologia*. What is a reasonable defense of Christianity that engages a particular cultural contraindication?
   a. The student is to articulate an apologetic for one of the following theological themes concomitant to his/her biblical, Christian *Weltanschauung* and *vocare*.
   b. The treatment of this section must include at least five Scripture references.
   c. Chapter 2 should cover approximately three to five pages.
          i. Abortion or euthanasia.
          ii. Stem cell research or genetic engineering.
          iii. The problem of evil.
          iv. The existence of God.
          v. The origin of the universe.
          vi. The right role of government.
          vii. The validity of absolute truth.
          viii. The historicity of the resurrection of Jesus.
          ix. The authenticity, accuracy, and authority of Scripture.
          x. A doxological teleology of relationship, stewardship, and worship.
          xi. Toward a biblical philosophy of Christian school education in light of secular trends in schooling and contemporary trends in educational philosophy.
III. Chapter 3: *Vocare*. What might God want me to be and do in light of the Truth?
   a. The student is to integrate a proposed professional path from the aforementioned worldview and apologetic.
   b. Chapter 3 should incorporate information received from the required interview of a professional in ones intended career field, as well as additional research.
   c. Chapter 3 should be approximately three to five pages.

Appendix 3

Sample School Profile Based upon a Biblical Philosophy of a Christian School Education

BLESSED CHRISTIAN SCHOOL

VISION:

Educational excellence for the glory of God.

MISSION:

Equipping students to impact the world for Christ.

VALUES:

A family of families.
Speaking the truth in love.
Serving God and one another.
By God's grace and for God's glory.

PURPOSE:

A ministry whose business is education, Blessed Christian School exists to provide a Christian, classical, college preparatory education which integrates biblical faith and learning from a conservative, evangelical, interdenominational perspective.

PHILOSOPHY:

A Christ-centered school that is based upon biblical principles, Blessed Christian School grows students by means of a classical education designed to develop spiritual, academic, physical, and relational excellence by God's grace and for God's glory.

PILLARS:

With its foundation being the word of God, Blessed Christian School builds upon its three pillars, i.e., *Veritas* (Truth), *Sapientia* (Wisdom), *Virtu* (Virtue).

GOALS & OBJECTIVES:

1. Partnering with parents.
   - BCS will identify and welcome parents who desire to raise a Christ-honoring family.
   - BCS will provide a Christian educational experience for students whose parents desire to develop next generation Christian servant-leaders.
2. Educating students.
   - BCS will develop the whole child—spiritual, academic, physical, and relational.
   - BCS will cultivate a passion for Jesus Christ, a joy for learning, and a lifelong quest for Truth, Wisdom, and Virtue.
3. Producing graduates.
   - BCS will develop graduates who are committed to spiritual, academic, physical, and relational development per its *Ideal Graduate Profile*.

- BCS will develop graduates who are pursuing excellence for the glory of God.

4. Developing faculty.
   - BCS will identify, hire, and develop credentialed, capable, competent, and caring Christian faculty that will enable the school to fulfill its mission.
   - BCS will recruit, reward, and retain faculty that align with its *Ideal Faculty Profile*.

5. Sustaining operations.
   - BCS will govern itself, its budget, and its policies and procedures according to a sound integration of biblical principles and best practices.
   - BCS will recruit and retain board members, administrators, faculty, and staff who know Jesus personally as their Savior and Lord, who actively participate in a local evangelical church, and whose actions and attitudes model Christ.

6. Cultivating stewardship.
   - BCS will recognize each of its resources as a gift from God, and will therefore steward those resources faithfully and well.
   - BCS will acquire, develop, and maintain land and facilities in a way that will honor the Lord and meet the students' needs.

7. Pursuing excellence.
   - BCS will integrate biblical Truth, Wisdom, and Virtue into every aspect of the school.
   - BCS will endeavor to do everything it does at the highest quality, to the best of its abilities, and for the glory of God.

IDEAL GRADUATE PROFILE:

Spiritual

The graduate would love the Lord God with all his/her heart, soul, mind, and strength.
- The graduate would embrace his/her identity and purpose in Christ.

Academic

The graduate would have mastered a college-preparatory curriculum, developing a biblical worldview and honing skills to think and to communicate both clearly and effectively.
- The graduate would cultivate intellectual curiosity

Physical

- The graduate would recognize his/her body as the temple of the Holy Spirit and would steward it accordingly.
- The graduate would have experienced a breadth of athletic opportunities to encourage a lifestyle of wellness.

Relational

- The graduate would have developed good patterns of interacting with God, self, and others.
- The graduate would demonstrate servant-leadership and a desire to impact the world for Christ through God's call on his/her life.

IDEAL FACULTY PROFILE:

Love God and others

- People who recognize their own sinfulness and neediness of a Savior.
- People who see others as sheep needing a Shepherd.

Follow Jesus authentically and energetically

- People who have experienced the unconditional love of God and are not cynical or sarcastic.
- People who have experienced such forgiveness that they readily forgive others.

Relate to others God-honoringly

- People whose cups are full enough to handle challenges that may occur.
- People who are honest in admitting their own need for growth.

Genuinely like kids and their parents

- People who assume the care of every student every time.
- People who remember that we are partnered with parents and the local church.

Are team players

- People who desire to serve the whole school, not just their own class.
- People who do not complain.

Are responsible

- People who perform routine tasks routinely, correctly, and well.
- People who clean up their own messes.

Are good instructors and who like to teach

- People who know and love their subject matter and their students.
- People who remember what it was like "not to get it" and who are eager to help.

Are committed to Truth, Wisdom, and Virtue

- People who value, read, and submit to the Bible as God's inspired and infallible Word.
- People who desire to know God and to make him known by word and deed.

DOCTRINAL STATEMENT:

This BCS Doctrinal Statement summarizes the essential beliefs and teaching position to which Blessed Christian School adheres.

8. We believe the Bible to be the only inspired, inerrant, infallible, and authoritative word of God.

9. We believe in one God eternally existent in three persons: Father, Son, and Holy Spirit.

10. We believe in the deity of Christ, in his virgin birth, in his sinless life, in his substitutionary and atoning death, in his resurrection from the dead, in his ascension to the right hand of the Father, and in his eventual, personal return to power and glory.

11. We believe in the necessity of regeneration by the Holy Spirit for salvation due to the exceeding sinfulness of humanity, and that individuals are justified by grace through faith solely by the accomplished work of Christ.

12. We believe in the resurrection of those so saved to glorification in heaven and of all others to damnation in hell.

13. We believe in the spiritual unity of all true believers in Christ.

INTERDENOMINATIONAL STATEMENT:

Blessed Christian School desires that the interdenominational position of our school be understood and sustained. Within that context, different viewpoints may be presented for classroom discussion with the final teaching being left to the family and to the local church. Some examples of such topics may include, but are not limited to:
- Baptism
- Communion
- Eschatology
- Church government
- Baptism and gifts of the Holy Spirit (e.g., tongues, healing, prophecy, etc.)

APPENDIX 4

Sample Alphabetized Quotes Pertinent to a Biblical Philosophy of a Christian School Education

SINCE A BIBLICAL, EDUCATIONAL philosophy in the context of a Christian school is not just analytical, abstract, or esoteric, but rather feet-to-the-ground, vis-à-vis real people engaging real people in real ways, the following statements are intended to inform and inspire educators and learners in ways consistent with the definitional qualities of this book.

1. A battle for the mind and for the heart is being waged in the classroom.

2. "A Christian education would primarily train people to be able to think in Christian categories" (T. S. Eliot).

3. "A Christian school is Christian if and only if Christian content is central to the whole understanding. Every subject of study is to be seen from the perspective of Christianity" (Frank Spina).

4. "A journey of a thousand miles begins with a single step" (Lao-tzu).

5. "A part of Being is the being, man, who verbalizes" (cf. Martin Heidegger).

6. "All that you say, I will do" (Ruth 3:5).

7. "All truth is God's truth" (Arthur Holmes).

8. "Alone we can do so little, together we can do so much" (Helen Keller).

9. "Any autonomy is wrong" (Francis Schaeffer).

10. A.B.C ... *Academics. Behavior. Christ-follower.*

11. A.B.C ... *Accept. Believe. Confess.*

12. A.R.E ... *Ask. Receive. Explore.*

13. A.S.K ... *Ask. Seek. Knock.*

14. Αρητη (excellence).

15. "*Ars recte loquendi recteque scribendi initium fundamentum omnium disicplinarium*" ("The arts of correct speaking and writing is the beginning and basis of all knowledge," Nicholas Perotti).

16. "Ασκεσις" ("Training," Socrates).

17. "Attempt great things for God. Expect great things from God" (William Carey).

18. Being God's people doing God's work in God's way.

19. Being content does not mean having it all, but being thankful to the Lord for all you have.

20. Biblical principles. Best practices. Board policies.

21. "Breakfast is the most important meal of the day" (Jillian Michaels).

22. By God's grace and for God's glory.

23. "Childhood—we get only one pass at it, and yet it dictates the quality of the rest of our lives" (Wes Stafford).

24. "Children learn what they live" (a poem by Dorothy Law Nolte).

25. "Christian education is neither" (James Pluddemann).

26. "Christians should stop laughing and take such men seriously. Then we shall have the right to speak again to our generation" (Francis Schaeffer).

27. "Classics: Hooks to catch the souls" (Gilbert Highet).

28. Clear head. Clean hands. Close heart.

29. Committed. Competent. Communicative. Creative. (Howard Hendricks).

30. "Competition is for horses, not artists" (Bela Bartok).

31. *Correct* (challenge/convince . . . Tell them what they need to know . . . HEAD).
    Rebuke (warn/reprove . . . Tell them when they are wrong . . . HEART).
    Encourage (urge/exhort . . . Cheer them on with words of hope . . . HANDS)
    "Preach the Word. Be prepared in season and out of season. Correct. Rebuke. Encourage. With patience and careful instruction" (cf. railroad tracks of shepherding for life from 2 Tim 4:2).

32. Decisions determine direction.

33. "Diligent risks" (Mike Rose).

34. Do more than belong, Participate.
    Do more than care, Help.
    Do more than believe, Practice.
    Do more than react, Respond.
    Do more than be fair, Be kind.
    Do more than forgive, Forget.
    Do more than dream, Work.
    Do more than think, Love.

35. Don't give a man a fish, teach him to fish—and give him access to the pond.

36. "Education is the most powerful weapon that you can use to change the world" (Nelson Mendela).

37. Efficiency. Effectiveness. Eternal significance.

38. Either you will control your thoughts, or they will control you.

39. Enter their world, like Jesus entered ours.

40. "*Every* relationship should be characterized by mutual respect and by recognition on the part of each that the other is an image-bearer of the Creator" (Robert Littlejohn).

41. Everything is either a tool to be used or an idol to be worshipped.

42. "Fear God and keep his commandments, for this is the whole duty of man" (Qoheleth).

43. "Free at last! Free at last! Thank God almighty, we are free at last!" (Martin Luther King Jr.)

44. "From the cowardice that dares not face new truth, from the laziness that is contented with half-truth, from the arrogance that thinks it knows all truth, Good Lord, deliver me. Amen!" (Kenyan prayer).

45. God chose to reveal himself to us through his *Word*:
    a. Creation
    b. Christ
    c. Counselor
    d. Canon
    e. Conscience
    f. Conviction
    g. Condemnation
    h. Consummation

46. "God is central; both students and subjects are essential to the process, but neither one is central" (Norman De Jong).

47. God's people doing God's work in God's way.

48. Good. Better. Best. Never let it rest. Until your good is better, and your better is best.

49. "Grace does not eliminate intelligent effort, though it does eliminate earning" (Dallas Willard).

50. "Grace plus anything is anything but grace" (Andy Stanley).

51. "Happy is the man who can recognize in the work of today a connected portion of the work of life, and an embodiment of the work of Eternity" (Clerk Maxwell).

52. "He must learn another language—that of thought-forms of the people to whom he speaks" (Francis Schaeffer).

53. Head. Heart. Hands.

54. Hear and Heed (Gen 2:16–17; Exod 20:5–6; Eccl 12:1–13; Deut 6:4; Job 38–42; Ps 1; Prov 8; John 14:15; Rev 22:18–19).

55. "He is to be educated because he is a man, not because he is to make shoes, nails, or pins" (William Ellery).

56. "How you see your future is much more important than what happened in your past" (Zig Ziglar).

57. "I believe in Christianity as I believe that the *sun* has risen, not only because I *see* it, but because by it I *see everything else*" (C. S. Lewis).

58. "I have never let my schooling interfere with my education" (Mark Twain).

59. "I know of no safe repository of the ultimate powers of the society but the people themselves, and if we think them not enlightened enough to exercise control with a wholesome discretion, the remedy is not to take it from them, but to inform their discretion by education" (Thomas Jefferson).

60. "I play the notes as they are written, but it is God who makes the music" (J. S. Bach).

61. "If you win, say nothing. If you lose, say less" (Paul Brown).

62. "In the world it is called Tolerance, but in hell it is called Despair" (Dorothy Sayers).

63. "Intelligence plus character—that is the goal of true education" (Martin Luther King Jr.).

64. ". . . intelligent, culturally sensitive, and passionate fidelity to the gospel of Jesus Christ" (D. A. Carson).

65. "It's not the dreams you dream, it's the choices you make" (Joseph Stowell).

66. "It is part of education to learn to interest ourselves in subjects for which we have no aptitude" (T. S. Eliot).

67. "It seems astonishing, archaic, and anachronistic any more to combine one's religious convictions with one's vocational ambitions" (Robert Littlejohn).

68. "It would be a pity if we overlooked the possibilities of education as a means of acquiring wisdom" (T. S. Eliot).

69. Jesus is the . . .
    a. *Way*: the ultimate metaphysical reality.
    b. *Truth*: the ultimate epistemological purity.
    c. *Life*: the ultimate axiological model and substitute.

70. Jesus is the *True Tao*.

71. Knowing who God is. Knowing who we are in relationship to God. Responding appropriately.

72. "Knowledge has a unique and irreplaceable function in human life" (Dallas Willard).

73. "Lead me to imitate you, and enjoy your well-deserved rest" (Jean Jacques Rousseau).

74. "Learning is therefore a spiritual calling, properly done, it attaches us to God" (Cornelius Plantinga Jr.)

75. "Let knowledge grow from more to more, But more of reverence is us dwell" (Alfred Lord Tennyson).

76. "Let us notice that the system of the Bible is excitingly different from any other because it is the only system in religion or philosophy that tells us why a person may do what every man must do, that is, begin with himself" (Francis Schaeffer).

77. "Literature is our guide to the true meaning of the past, to a right estimate of the present, and to a sound forecast of the future" (Pope Pius II).

78. Living curriculum: Ones who incarnate truth, beauty, and goodness—like Jesus did!

79. "Love—and the unity it attests to—is the mark Christ gave Christians to wear before the world. Only with this mark may the world know that Christians are indeed Christians and that Jesus was sent by the Father" (Francis Schaeffer).

80. "May God grant his richest blessing on this partnership of the Christian school, the local church, and the Christian family by his grace and for his glory!" (present author).

81. M.B.E . . . *Ministry whose Business is Education.*

82. M.B.W.A . . . *Management By Walking About.*

83. Memorable. Meaningful. Ministerial.

84. Mimesis. . . . Re: that part of my teaching technique that I would not infrequently use for CES chapels, the ancients used to call it "mimesis." It's a Greek term from which we get the term "mimic." It's one of many strategies of what's referred to as "mnemonic" devices. Mnemonic is also from Greek and meant something related to or aiding in memory. Mnemonics come in *lots* of different shapes and sizes—including a cow stuck in the mud. . . . Generally mnemonics come in 3 categories: Visual (seeing, picturing, imagining), Auditory (hearing self or another), and Kinesthetic (touching, doing, moving, etc.). Generally speaking, each of us use all of them; some of us learners learn better with one than with another, etc. But, also, generally speaking, the more the merrier. . . . In other words if someone can see, hear, and do something with the stuff they're learning, it creates more synaptic pathways in the brain, thereby engaging more of your brain to retain and to recall that which was learned. (Some folks have memorized the entire New Testament using primarily visual mnemonics to "picture" in their mind what the text says.). . . . In terms of breaking the verse down, I generally am intuitive. I just kind of do what feels like makes the most sense—generally *small* syntactical chunks (especially the younger the learners).

85. Model for ministry. Paradigm for pedagogy. Template for teaching.

86. "Much education today is monumentally ineffective. All too often we are giving young people cut flowers when we should be teaching them to grow their own plants" (John Gardner).

87. "Music expresses that which cannot be said and on which it is impossible to be silent" (Victor Hugo).

88. "Never, never, never, never give up!" (Sir Winston Churchill).

89. No meaning. No purpose. No significance. (Human life without God and absolutes.)

90. "Nothing you ever do for children is ever wasted. They seem not to notice us, hovering, averting our eyes, and they seldom offer thanks, but what we do for them is never wasted" (Garrison Keillor).

91. "Once you stop learning, you start dying" (Albert Einstein).

92. Our patterns in life determine our paths in life.

93. "Our progress as a nation can be no swifter than our progress in education. The human mind is our fundamental resource" (John F. Kennedy).

94. Our response is our responsibility, their response is their responsibility.

95. *Our* responsibility is to respond to *God's* ability.

96. *Paideia* (Education, enculturation, and more!).

97. Past mistakes don't have to determine future direction.

98. Plan your work, work your plan.

99. Pray. Prepare. Present. Probe. Provide.

100. Partner with parents: Proactive. Positive. Personable. Pedagogical. Practical. Prayerful.

101. Post-everything (i.e., post-modern, post-history, post-sociology, post-Christian, etc.).

102. Purpose. People. Principles. Programs.

103. "Rational unity between the particulars and the universals. . . . [An] insistence on a unified field of knowledge" (Francis Schaeffer).

APPENDIX 4

104. "Relativistic pluralism is *the* battlefield of our time" (Timothy Tennent).

105. Root. Chute. Fruit.

106. Say what you mean. Mean what you say. Do what you say you're going to do.

107. *Sehnsucht* (seeking, searching).

108. Serious. Separate. Sold-out.

109. "So then let us pursue what makes for peace and for mutual upbuilding" (Rom 14:19).

110. *Sola scriptura. Sola gratia. Sola fide. Solus Christus. Soli Deo gloria.*

111. "Some men see things as they are and ask why, I dream of things that never were and ask why not" (George Bernard Shaw).

112. Strengths (what are you doing well). Struggles (what you could be doing better). Strategies (how you will go about doing better).

113. Students are designed . . .
    a. To be (Rom 8:29).
    b. To know (John 8:32).
    c. To do (Rom 12:2; Eph 2:10).

114. "Superficiality is the curse of our age" (Richard Foster).

115. "Supposedly we know, and we do not purposely suppress the truth, our education is neither inefficient nor irresponsible, and there is no rampant ignorance and irreligion, consequently, whoever is intelligent, educated and presumably honest should in all fairness be allowed to publish his arguments against current doctrine" (John Milton).

116. T.E.A.C.H.E.R.—Teacher, Education, Activity, Communication, Heart, Encouragement, Readiness (Howard Hendricks).

117. "The aim and final end of all music should be none other than the glory of God and the refreshment of the soul" (J. S. Bach).

118. "The area of creativity, therefore, is no minor footnote to the Christian life, but it is essential" (Franky Schaeffer).

119. "The best educated human being is the one who understands the most about the life in which he is placed" (Helen Keller).

120. "The biblical presentation is . . . true truth. In this way we know true truth about God, true truth about man, and something truly about nature. Thus on the basis of the Scriptures, while we do not have exhaustive knowledge, we have true and unified knowledge" (Francis Schaeffer).

121. "The body is the servant of the mind" (James Allen).

122. "The central job of schools is to maximize the capacity of each student" (Carol Ann Tomlinson).

123. "[The church's] responsibility is not only to hold to the basic, scriptural principles of the Christian faith, but to communicate these unchanging truths 'into' the generation in which it is living" (Francis Schaeffer).

124. "The end, then, of learning is to repair the ruins of our first parents by regaining to know God aright, and out of that knowledge to love Him, to imitate Him, and to be like Him" (John Milton).

125. "The fallenness of man does not lead to machine-ness, but to fallen man-ness" (Francis Schaeffer).

126. "The greatest evidence of how we have been transformed is not how little we have sinned, but how well we have loved" (Bill Tell).

127. "The history of educational theory is marked by opposition between the idea that education is development from within and that it is formation from without" (John Dewey).

128. "The human being is the only creature that needs to be educated" (Immanuel Kant).

129. "The mathematician does not study pure mathematics because it is useful, he studies it because he delights in it, and he delights in it because it is beautiful" (J. H. Poincare).

130. "The mediocre teacher tells. The good teacher explains. The superior teacher demonstrates. The great teacher inspires" (William Arthur Ward).

131. "The noblest work in education is to make a reasoning man, and we expect to train a young child by making him reason! This is beginning at the end, this is making an instrument of a result. If children understood how to reason, they would not need to be educated" (Jean Jacques Rousseau).

132. "The only purpose of education is to teach a student how to live his life by developing his mind and equipping him to deal with reality. The training he needs is theoretical, i.e., conceptual. He has to be taught to think, to understand, to integrate, to prove. He has to be taught the essentials of the knowledge discovered in the past, and he has to be equipped to acquire further knowledge by his own effort" (Ayn Rand).

133. "The present moment is the only moment available to us. And it is the door to all moments" (Thich Nhat Hanh).

134. "The purpose of learning is growth, and our minds, unlike our bodies, can continue growing as we continue to live" (Mortimer Adler).

135. "The supreme end of education is expert discernment in all things—the power to tell the good from the bad, the genuine from the counterfeit, and to prefer the good and the genuine to the bad and the counterfeit" (Samuel Johnson).

136. "The test and the use of a man's education is that he finds pleasure in the exercise of the mind" (Jacques Barzun).

137. "The true function of the teacher is to create the most favorable conditions for self-learning" (John Milton Gregory).

138. "The universe is before our eyes like a beautiful book in which all creatures, great and small, are as letters to make us ponder the invisible things of God" (The Belgic Confession, Article 2).

139. "The vision that you glorify in your mind, the Ideal that you enthrone in your heart—this you will build your life by, this you will become" (James Allen).

140. The whole Word for the whole world.

141. "There is not a square inch on the whole plain of human existence over which Christ, who is Lord over all, does not proclaim: 'This is Mine!'" (Abraham Kuyper).

142. Time is short, and eternity is sure.

143. "To educate a person in mind and not in morals is to educate a menace to society" (Theodore Roosevelt).

144. "To study without thinking is futile. To think without studying is dangerous" (Confucius).

145. "To teach is to learn twice" (Joseph Joubert).

146. "Today we have a weakness in our educational process in failing to understand the natural associations between the disciplines" (Francis Schaeffer).

147. Truth for students:
   a. The family for incubation.
   b. The church for indoctrination.
   c. The school for integration.

148. U.F.O.—God's truth is U*nchanging*, F*orever*, O*bjective*.

149. *Veritas* (Harvard University).

150. ". . . vision for a more faithful, robust, engaged Christianity" (Timothy Tennent).

151. "We all teach and learn, all our lives" (Gilbert Highet).

152. "We are far too easily pleased" (C. S. Lewis).

153. "We are what we repeatedly do, excellence, therefore, is not an act, but a habit" (Aristotle).

154. "We are witnessing the rise of the global brain, when a buzzing hive of knowledge, connectivity, technology, and access unites the human and the machine, the physical and the digital, in previously unimaginable ways" (Beth Comstock).

155. "We cannot deal with people like human beings, we cannot deal with them on the high level of their humanity, unless we really know their origin—who they are. God tells us that he created man in his image. So man is something wonderful" (Francis Schaeffer).

156. "We cannot despair humanity, because we ourselves are human" (Albert Einstein).

157. "We have failed to stand for truth, failed to articulate, defend, and advance an intelligent and coherent Christian worldview" (Charles Colson).

158. "We have the right to believe whatever we want, but everything we believe is not right" (Ravi Zacharias).

159. "We must teach music in our schools, a schoolmaster ought to have skill in music, or I would not regard him, neither should we ordain men as preachers unless they have been well exercised in music" (Martin Luther).

160. "We should love good art. But art as art does not have the right to speak ex cathedra regardless of content" (Francis Schaeffer).

161. "When I look at the world I'm pessimistic, but when I look at people I am optimistic" (Carl Rogers).

162. "While we might not like the word *system*, because it sounds rather cold, this does not mean that the biblical teaching is not a system. Everything goes back to the beginning and thus the system has unique beauty and perfection because everything is under the apex of the system" (Francis Schaeffer).

163. "Worship is to quicken the conscience by the holiness of God, to feed the mind with the truth of God, to purge the imagination by the beauty of God, to open the heart to the love of God, to devote the will to the purpose of God" (William Temple).

164. "You are a work of God created to work with God" (Greg Holder).

165. You are more than welcome here, you are not welcome to behave that way here.

166. You get what you expect—and what you inspect.

167. "... you'll be a man, my son" (Rudyard Kipling).

Appendix 5

Sample Taxonomy Table of a Multifaceted, Holistic, Eclectic Pedagogy Based upon a Biblical Philosophy of a Christian School Education

This taxonomy table portends to be used by teachers at a Christian school committed to implementing programs and pedagogy consistent with a biblical philosophy of a Christian school education. Its design and delivery offer a paradigm and particulars pertinent to a pedagogue's priority and practice of preparing plans and executing lessons. This table offers a lesson-cycle grid through which a teacher can filter various subjects, topics, units, lessons, etc., to stimulate consideration of a comprehensive, coherent, Christian lesson cycle. A lesson cycle may include something not necessarily inclusive or exclusive to a particular column, but a lesson should have something from/in each column.

Propositional	Personal	Practical
Head	Heart	Hands
To know	To be	To do
Thoughts	Feelings	Actions
Cognition	Affect	Behavior
Reason	Faith	Habit
Content	Commitment	Conduct
Content	Commitment	Carry-thru
Content	Concept	Construct

APPENDIX 5

Authorial intent	Inferred content	Applied extent
Apprehend	Attest	Apply
Intellectual	Volitional	Behavioral
Knowing	Believing	Doing
Acknowledging	Accepting	Becoming
Assimilating	Accommodating	Acting and Actualizing
Absolute	Analogy	Applied
Book	Look	Took
What	So what	Now what
Observe	Interpret	Apply
Observe content	Infer intent	Determine extent
What it meant	What it means	What difference it makes
Then & There	Here & Now	I & Thou . . . What & How
Substance	Self	Salience
Logos	Pathos	Ethos
Doctrine	Duties	Doings
Love God with Mind	Love God with Heart	Love God with Soul/ Might
Know the Truth	Truth will set you free	You will be free indeed
Justly	Mercifully	Humbly
Word	Wonder	Worship and Work
From God	Through God	To God
God's Truth, Goodness, Beauty	God's grace	God's glory
God	God's gift	God's glory
Truth	Goodness	Beauty
Truth	True	Truly
His Being	Our being	Our becoming
Being	Believing	Becoming
Ontos	Episteme	Ethics/Aesthetics
Ontology	Epistemology	Axiology
Metaphysics	Epistemics	Ethics/Aesthetics
What is	What we know	What we do
Deity	Decision	Direction
The ocean	The boat	The rowing
Vortex	View	Value

APPENDIX 5

Paradigm	Perspective	Pertinence
The Ground of Being	The grasp of being	The gasp of being
Origin	Purpose	Destiny
God	Human	Creation
Creation	Fall	Redemption/Consummation
Imago Dei	Non posse non pecarre	Poiema
Creator	Redeemer	Sustainer
Weltanschauung	Apologia	Vocare
Veritas	Sapientia	Virtu

Book	Look	Hook	Took
Hermeneutics		Homiletics	
What		So what	Now what
Inform		Transform	
What the text says.	What the text meant.	What the text means.	How the text applies.
There and then		Here and now	
Investigation		Interpretation	
Then	Always	Now	
Precept	Principle	Practice	
Knowing who God is	Knowing who I am in relation to God	Responding appropriately	
Original audience	Propositional revelation	Contemporary audience	

Appendix 6

A Covenant for Excellence

IN THE SPRING AND summer of 1993, believing that Christian schooling lacked a common statement calling for excellence in our schools, PAIDEIA, Inc. produced *A Covenant for Excellence*, first signed by delegates to our annual conference at Eastern University, St. Davids, Pennsylvania, on June 30, 1993.

As colleagues in Christian schooling, we hereby solemnly declare and affirm ***A Covenant for Excellence*** in our calling as Christian educators:

Whereas, we acknowledge that we are sinners redeemed by the grace of God through faith in Jesus Christ, and
Whereas, we have submitted ourselves to the Lordship of Jesus Christ and to the authority of Holy Scripture as God's Word, and
Whereas, God's Word declares that the fear of the Lord is the beginning of godly wisdom, knowledge, and understanding, and
Whereas, God's Word commands us to make disciples of all persons everywhere, especially our own children, by the training and instruction of the Lord,
Therefore, we affirm that
—godly *wisdom* comes only by special revelation through the Person of Christ, Holy Scripture, and the whole counsel of God given by the Holy Spirit through the Church,

—godly *knowledge* comes by general revelation through formal and informal study and contemplation of nature and human nature, in pursuit of an academic curriculum, and in work and play,

—godly *understanding* comes only when the whole of life's experience passes through the lens of a biblical worldview, meaning that all truth is framed by biblical reality and everything that is ultimately of God is true.

We further affirm that

—God who is perfect and holy commands of us service that aspires to be both perfect and holy, therefore excellent,

—lacking in ourselves the capacity to fulfill
this command, we are nonetheless summoned to know and strive after the highest attainment of our gifts, while humbly ascribing only to God all glory for our lowly efforts,

—to keep back anything that would honor God is sin, to endeavor to achieve less than our best is sin, to commend ourselves for doing what is only our duty is sin, to judge others whose achievement is either more or less than our own is sin,

—for these our sins of omission and commission, we most earnestly repent.

We further affirm that

—the goal of achieving excellence in any sphere of human service to God is essential to the good stewardship of our gifts and calling,

—both the example of Holy Scripture and the work of God in history commend the founding and sustaining of schools honoring
to the Lord Jesus Christ by the excellence of their stewardship,

—both objective and subjective standards of excellence exist for measuring the quality of our schools and our work in them,

—these standards of excellence reflect both biblical virtues and cultural values compatible with Scripture,

—among the biblical virtues are the objective spiritual qualities of Christian living enumerated by St. Paul as exemplary of the life transformed and the mind renewed (Rom 12:1—15:13): humility, sobriety, proportion, love, honor for one another, zeal, joy, hope, patience, faithfulness in prayer, generosity, hospitality, forgiveness, sympathy, harmony, peaceable behavior, absence of vengefulness, submission to authority, justice, good citizenship, fiscal responsibility, non-judgmental spirit, absence of legalism and license, mutual acceptance—all evidences of the powerful work of the Holy Spirit,

—among those cultural values acknowledged by our society and compatible with Scripture are these subjective temporal qualities, exemplary of academic, artistic, athletic, and social attainment, such as personal or communal recognition for scholastic honors, artistic originality, athletic skill and sportsmanship, social maturity and responsibility, and altruistic deeds,

—among other cultural values acknowledged by our society and compatible with Scripture are excellence of professional skills in teaching and administering, business practice and financial management, maintenance of resources, and valid recognition by one's peers of work worthy of commendation.

Therefore, be it resolved by all those undersigned that the schools we found or sustain be institutions where

—governing boards, administrators, teachers, staff, and supporters recognize the holistic and interdependent nature of our work together, as set forth in St. Paul's analogy for the Body of Christ,

—governing boards, administrators, teachers, staff, and supporters all recognize and act upon their distinct and separate roles and responsibilities in our schools,

—as those called to hone the intellect and shape the will of our students to imitate "the mind of Christ," our calling may be recognized and respected for its own unique contribution to the Body of Christ.

Be it further resolved by all those undersigned that our students

—be stimulated, challenged, and encouraged to make the best possible use of the intellectual, aesthetic, physical, social, and spiritual gifts given to them,

—be offered every opportunity to excel in academic studies, athletic competition, artistic performance, and social growth, while keeping before them their need for spiritual maturity in proportion to their age and experience in faith,

—be provided with examples of excellence worthy of emulation, not only by their teachers and by their own participation in learning, testing, exhibition, competition at the highest appropriate levels, but also by the finest quality of human endeavor by guests invited to our schools or by visits to lectures, concerts, exhibits at museums or galleries, theatrical productions, and sporting events,

—become inculcated by biblical virtues leading to excellence, taught by example and precept in the living and teaching of those who govern, administer, teach, serve, and support,

—be taught only those cultural values leading to excellence that are compatible with Scripture, such as intellectual integrity or athletic courage, and fostered as corollaries to biblical virtues,

—be urged to recognize the grace of God apparent throughout the whole human race and in every nation and culture,

—be pointed toward every possible adult field of service worthy of God's call and their gifts, fully assured that God is no respecter of the hierarchy, favor, nationality or gender of persons.

Finally, let it be our covenant together to examine our work daily against the highest standard of our Lord's excellent example of teaching; let us also follow the injunction of St. Paul, who urges, "Whatever is true, noble, right, pure, lovely, admirable—if anything is excellent or praiseworthy—think about such things" (Phil 4:8).

SIGNED TO AFFIRM MY COVENANT:

PAIDEIA, Inc., PO Box 26, Stony Brook, NY 11790
(used by permission)

Bibliography

Abbott, Edwin A. *Flatland.* New York: Dover, 1952.
Adams, A. K. M., et al. *Reading Scripture with the Church: Toward a Hermeneutic for Theological Interpretation.* Grand Rapids: Baker Academic, 2006.
Adams, Jay E. *Back to the Blackboard: Design for a Biblical Christian School.* Stanley, NC: Timeless Texts, 1998.
Adkins, A. W. H. "Theoria versus Praxis in the Nicomachean Ethics and the Republic." *Classical Philology* 73 (October 1978) 297–313.
Adler, Mortimer J. *Art, the Arts, and the Great Ideas.* New York: Macmillan, 1994.
———. *How to Think about God: A Guide for the 20th Century Pagan.* New York: Macmillan, 1980.
———. *The Paideia Proposal: An Educational Manifesto.* New York: Macmillan, 1982.
———. *A Synopticon: An Index to the Great Ideas.* Chicago: University of Chicago Press, 1952.
———. *Ten Philosophical Mistakes: Basic Errors in Modern Thought; How They Came About, Their Consequences, and How to Avoid Them.* New York: Macmillan, 1985.
Alcott, William. *The Young Man's Guide: Classic Wisdom for Improving Mind, Manners, and Morals.* Avon, MA: Adams, 2013.
Allard-Nelson, Susan K. "Virtue in Aristotle's Rhetoric: A Metaphysical and Ethical Capacity." *Philosophy and Rhetoric* 34 (2001) 245–59.
Allen, Diogenes. *Philosophy for Understanding Theology.* Atlanta: John Knox, 1985.
Allen, Diogenes, and Eric O. Springsted, eds. *Primary Readings in Philosophy for Understanding Theology.* Louisville: John Knox, 1992.
Allen, James. *As a Man Thinketh.* N.p.: Watchmaker, 2010.
Allport, Gordon W. *Becoming: Basic Considerations for a Psychology of Personality.* New Haven: Yale University Press, 1955.
Anderson, Charles. *Prescribing the Life of the Mind: An Essay on the Purpose of the University, the Aims of Liberal Education, the Competence of Citizens, and the Cultivation of Practical Reason.* Madison: University of Wisconsin Press, 1993.
Anderson, Clifford. "A Pragmatic Reading of Karl Barth's Theological Epistemology." *American Journal of Theology & Philosophy* 22 (September 2001) 241–69.
Anderson, David A. *Gracism: The Art of Inclusion.* Downers Grove: InterVarsity, 2007.

Angeles, Peter A., and Eugene Ehrlich. *The HarperCollins Dictionary of Philosophy: In-Depth Explanations and Examples Covering over 3,000 Entries.* 2nd ed. New York: Harper Perennial, 1992.
Anthony, Michael J., ed. *Evangelical Dictionary of Christian Education.* Grand Rapids: Baker Academic, 2001.
Aristotle. *Metaphysics.* Translated by Richard Hope. Ann Arbor: University of Michigan Press, 1960.
———. *The Rhetoric and the Poetics of Aristotle.* Introduction by Edward P. J. Corbett. *Rhetoric* translated by W. Rhys Roberts; *Poetics* translated by Ingram Bywater. New York: Modern Library, 1984.
Armstrong, Thomas. *The Multiple Intelligences of Reading and Writing: Making the Words Come Alive.* Alexandria, VA: ASCD, 2003.
Augustine. *Confessions.* Translated by Rex Warner. New York: New American Library, 1963.
Bahnsen, Greg L. *An Answer to Frame's Critique of Van Til: Profound Differences between the Traditional and Presuppositional Methods.* Glenside, PA: Westminster Seminary Bookstore, 2003.
———. *The Apologetic Implications of Self-Deception.* Nacogdoches, TX: Covenant, 2011.
Baker, A. A. *The Successful Christian School: Foundational Principles for Starting and Operating a Successful Christian School.* Pensacola, FL: Beka, 1979.
Baldwin, Louis. *Triumph over the Odds: Inspiration Success Stories.* New York: Carol, 1994.
Barna, George. *Transforming Children into Spiritual Champions: Why Children Should Be Your Church's #1 Priority.* Ventura, CA: Regal, 2003.
Barnes, Jonathan. *Aristotle.* New York: Oxford University Press, 1982.
———, ed. *The Complete Works of Aristotle.* Rev. Oxford trans. Vol. 2. Princeton: Princeton University Press, 1984.
Barrett, Justin L. *Cognitive Science, Religion, and Theology: From Human Minds to Divine Minds.* Conshohocken, PA: Templeton, 2011.
Barth, Karl. *Church Dogmatics.* Edinburgh: T. & T. Clark, 1961.
Barzun, Jacques, and Henry F. Graff. *The Modern Researcher.* 6th ed. Belmont, CA: Wadsworth, 2004.
Bayne, Tim. *Thought: A Very Short Introduction.* New York: Oxford University Press, 2013.
Beausay, William. *The Leadership Genius of Jesus: Ancient Wisdom for Modern Business.* Nashville: Nelson, 1997.
Beers, Stephen T., ed. *The Soul of a Christian University: A Field Guide for Educators.* Abilene, TX: Abilene Christian University Press, 2008.
Graham, George. "Behaviorism." *Stanford Encyclopedia of Philosophy*, edited by Edward N. Zalta. 2019. https://plato.stanford.edu/entries/behaviorism/.
Bellah, Robert N., et al. *Habits of the Heart: Individualism and Commitment in American Life.* Berkeley: University of California Press, 1985.
Benner, David G., and Peter C. Hill. *Baker Encyclopedia of Psychology & Counseling.* 2nd ed. Grand Rapids: Baker, 1999.
Benson, Clarence H. *The Christian Teacher.* Chicago: Moody, 1950.
Berkhof, Louis. *Introduction to Systematic Theology.* Grand Rapids: Baker, 1979.

Berkhof, Louis, and Cornelius Van Til. *Foundations of Christian Education: Addresses to Christian Teachers*. Phillipsburg, NJ: Presbyterian and Reformed, 1990.
Bernard, Harold W. *Psychology of Learning and Teaching*. 2nd ed. New York: McGraw-Hill, 1965.
Berryman, Sylvia. "Democritus." *Stanford Encyclopedia of Philosophy*, edited by Edward N. Zalta. Fall 2010 ed. http://plato.stanford.edu/archives/fall2010/entries/democritus/.
Best, Harold. "Creative Diversity, Authenticity and Excellence." *Arts Education Policy Review* 1 (May/June 1994) 2–8.
Best, John W. *Research in Education*. 3rd ed. Englewood Cliffs, NJ: Prentice Hall, 1977.
Beversluis, Nicholas Henry. *Christian Philosophy of Education*. Study Guide ed. Grand Rapids: National Union of Christian Schools, 1971.
Blake, Nigel, et al., eds. *The Blackwell Guide to the Philosophy of Education*. Malden, MA: Blackwell, 2003.
Blamires, Harry. *The Christian Mind: How Should a Christian Think?* Ann Arbor, MI: Servant, 1978.
Bloom, Allan. *The Closing of the American Mind*. New York: Simon & Schuster, 1987.
Bono, Edward de. *Six Thinking Hats*. Boston: Little, Brown, 1985.
Boyd, William. *The History of Western Education*. London: Black, 1950.
Boyer, Steven D., and Christopher A. Hall. *The Mystery of God: Theology for Knowing the Unknowable*. Grand Rapids: Baker, 2012.
Boys, Mary. *Biblical Interpretation in Religious Education: A Study of the Kerygmatic Era*. Birmingham, AL: Religious Education, 1980.
Braaten, Carl E., and Robert W. Jenson. *The Two Cities of God: The Church's Responsibility for the Earthly City*. Grand Rapids: Eerdmans, 1997.
Braley, James, et al., eds. *Foundations of Christian School Education: Perspectives on Christian Teaching*. Colorado Springs: Purposeful Design, 2003.
Brand, Holly. *Christ and Culture*. N.p.: DrHollyBrand.com, 2015.
Brauch, Manfred T. *Abusing Scripture: The Consequences of Misreading the Bible*. Downers Grove: IVP Academic, 2009.
Brennen, Annick M. "Philosophy of Education." *Sounds of Encouragement* (Annick Brennen and Barrington Brennen's website). 2001. http://www.soencouragement.org/Essays%20on%20Education%20and%20Educational%20PhilosophyHTML2.htm.
Brighouse, Harry. *On Education: Thinking in Action*. New York: Routledge, 2006.
Bromiley, Geoffrey W. *Theological Dictionary of the New Testament*. Edited by Gerhard Kittel and Gerhard Friedrich. Grand Rapids: Eerdmans, 1985.
Broudy, Harry S. "How Philosophical Can Philosophy of Education Be?" *Journal of Philosophy* 52 (December 1955) 612–22.
———. *The Uses of Schooling*. New York: Routledge, 1988.
Brown, Colin. *Philosophy and the Christian Faith*. Downers Grove: InterVarsity, 1968.
Brown, John Seely, and Paul Duguid. *The Social Life of Information*. Boston: Harvard Business School Press, 2000.
Brown, Montague. *Restoration of Reason: The Eclipse and Recovery of Truth, Goodness, and Beauty*. Grand Rapids: Baker Academic, 2006.
Brunner, Emil. *Revelation and Reason: The Christian Doctrine of Faith and Knowledge*. Translated by Olive Wyon. Philadelphia: Westminster, 1946.
Buber, Martin. *Between Man and Man*. Boston: Beacon, 1955.

———. *The Way of Man: According to the Teaching of Hasidism*. New York: Kensington, 1994.

Buckalew, M. Walker. *Twenty Principles for Teaching Excellence: The Teacher's Workbook*. Wilmington, DE: Independent School Management, 1992.

Budd, John M. *Higher Education's Purpose: Intellectual and Social Progress*. Lanham, MD: University Press of America, 2009.

Budziszewski, J., et al. *Evangelicals in the Public Square: Four Formative Voices on Political Thought and Action*. Grand Rapids: Baker Academic, 2006.

Bunge, Marcia J., ed. *The Child in Christian Thought*. Cambridge, UK: Eerdmans, 2001.

Burleson, Blake, and John Beebe. *Pathways to Integrity: Ethics and Psychological Type*. Gainsville, FL: Center for Applications of Psychological Type, 2001.

Butts, Freeman. *Cultural History of Western Education*. New York: McGraw-Hill, 1955.

———. *The Education of the West*. New York: McGraw-Hill, 1947.

Byrne, H. W. *Achieving: Academic Integration in a Christian School Setting*. Longwood, FL: Xulon, 2003.

———. *A Christian Approach to Education: Educational Theory and Application*. Milford, MI: Mott, 1977.

Cahn, Steven M. *Classic and Contemporary Readings in the Philosophy of Education*. 2nd ed. New York: Oxford Press University, 2012.

Caldecott, Stratford. *Beauty for Truth's Sake: On the Re-enchantment of Education*. Grand Rapids: Brazos, 2009.

Calhoun, Robert L. *What Is Man*. 4th ed. New York: Association, 1939.

Campbell, Ernest T. *Christian Manifesto*. New York: Harper & Row, 1970.

Canter, Lee, and Marlene Canter. *Assertive Discipline: Positive Behavior Management for Today's Classroom*. Santa Monica, CA: Canter, 1992.

Carlson, Greg, Tim Ellis, et al. *Perspectives on Children's Spiritual Formation: Four Views*. Edited by Michael J. Anthony. Nashville: B&H, 2006.

Carr, Judy F., and Douglas E. Harris. *Succeeding with Standards: Linking Curriculum, Assessment, and Action Planning*. Alexandria, VA: ASCD, 2001.

Carr, Wilfred, ed. *The Routledge Falmer Reader in Philosophy of Education*. New York: Routledge, 2005.

Carroll, Lewis. *Symbolic Logic and the Game of Logic: Mathematical Recreations of Lewis Carroll*. New York: Dover, 1958.

Carson, Ben. *Think Big: Unleashing Your Potential for Excellence*. Grand Rapids: Zondervan, 1992.

Carson, D. A. *The Gagging of God: Christianity Confronts Pluralism*. 15th anniv. ed. Grand Rapids: Zondervan, 2011.

Carter, Craig A. *Rethinking Christ and Culture: A Post-Christendom Perspective*. Grand Rapids: Brazos, 2006.

Carter, J. Adam, and Ben Kotzee. "Epistemology of Education." *Oxford Bibliographies Online* (2016) 1–21.

Carver, John, and Miriam Mayhew Carver. *Basic Principles of Policy Governance*. San Francisco: Jossey-Bass, 1996.

———. *The CEO Role under Policy Governance*. San Francisco: Jossey-Bass, 1997.

Center for Education and Employment Law. *Keeping Your School Safe and Secure: A Practical Guide*. Malvern, PA: Center for Education and Employment Law, 2014.

Chadwick, Daniel R. *Tables for Students of Philosophy: A Supplement to Philosophical Discussion*. Lanham, MD: University Press of America, 2002.
Challies, Tim, and Josh Byers. *Visual Theology: Seeing and Understanding the Truth about God*. Grand Rapids: Zondervan, 2016.
Chesterton, G. K. *The Everlasting Man*. San Bernardino, CA: Rough Draft Printing, 2013.
Christiaens, Wim. "Basic Ontology and the Ontology of the Phenomenological Life World: A Proposal." *Foundations of Science* 11 (2006) 249–74. http://citeseerx.ist.psu.edu/viewdoc/download?doi=10.1.1.88.8408&rep=rep1&type=pdf.
Clark, Gordon H. *The Biblical Doctrine of Man*. Jefferson, MD: Trinity Foundation, 1984.
———. *A Christian Philosophy of Education*. 2nd ed. Jefferson, MD: Trinity Foundation, 1988.
———. *A Christian View of Men and Things: An Introduction to Philosophy*. 2nd ed. Jefferson, MD: Trinity Foundation, 1991.
———. *Dewey*. Phillipsburg, NJ: Presbyterian and Reformed, 1960.
———. *Essays on Ethics and Politics*. Jefferson, MD: Trinity Foundation, 1992.
———. *Historiography: Secular and Religious*. 2nd ed. Jefferson, MD: Trinity Foundation, 1994.
———. *In Defense of Theology*. Milford, MI: Mott, 1984.
———. *An Introduction to Christian Philosophy*. Jefferson, MD: Trinity Foundation, 1989.
———. *The Johannine Logos*. 2nd ed. Jefferson, MD: Trinity Foundation, 1989.
———. *Logic*. Jefferson, MD: Trinity Foundation, 1988.
———. *The Philosophy of Science and Belief in God*. 2nd ed. Jefferson, MD: Trinity Foundation, 1987.
———. "The Relationship of Public Education to Christianity." Speech, 42nd Annual Convention of the Ruling Elders' Association of Chester Presbytery, Kennett Square, Pennsylvania, October 31, 1935. http://www.trinityfoundation.org/journal.php?id=40.
———. *Religion, Reason and Revelation*. Jefferson, MD: Trinity Foundation, 1986.
———. *Thales to Dewey*. 2nd ed. Jefferson, MD: Trinity Foundation, 1989.
———. *Three Types of Religious Philosophy*. Jefferson, MD: Trinity Foundation, 1989.
Clark, Kelly James, et al. *101 Key Terms in Philosophy and Their Importance for Theology*. Louisville: Westminster John Knox, 2004.
Clark, Kevin, et al. *The Liberal Arts Tradition: A Philosophy of Christian Classical Education*. Camp Hill, PA: Classical Academic, 2013.
Clayton, Philip. *God and Contemporary Science*. Grand Rapids: Eerdmans, 1997.
Clayton, Thomas E. *Teaching and Learning: A Psychological Perspective*. Englewood Cliffs, NJ: Prentice Hall, 1965.
Coley, Kenneth S. *Ten Practices of Effective Boards: A Unique Tale about Board Governance*. Fairfield, PA: Helmsman, 2014.
Conway, J. North. *American Literacy: Fifty Books That Define Our Culture and Ourselves*. New York: Morrow, 1993.
Cooper, David E. *Authenticity and Learning: Nietzsche's Educational Philosophy*. New York: Routledge, 1983.

Copan, Paul, and Paul K. Moser, eds. *The Rationality of Theism*. New York: Routledge Taylor & Francis, 2003.
Copan, Paul, et al., eds. *Philosophy*. Vol. 1, *Christian Perspectives of the New Millennium*. Addison, TX: CLM & RZIM, 2003.
Corley, Bruce, et al. *Biblical Hermeneutics: A Comprehensive Introduction to Interpreting Scripture*. 2nd ed. Nashville: Broadman & Holman, 2002.
Correia, Fabrice, and Benjamin Schnieder, eds. *Metaphysical Grounding: Understanding the Structure of Reality*. Cambridge: Cambridge University Press, 2014.
Covolo, Robert S. "Herman Bavinck's Theological Aesthetics: A Synchronic and Diachronic Analysis." *Bavinck Review* 2 (2011) 43–58.
Cowan, Steven B., and James S. Spiegel. *The Love of Wisdom: A Christian Introduction to Philosophy*. Nashville: B&H, 2009.
Cowan, Steven B., et al., eds. *Five Views on Apologetics*. Grand Rapids: Zondervan, 2000.
Cowell, Barbara. "The Role of Christians in Religious and Moral Education." *Journal of Moral Education* 12 (1983) 161–65.
Craig, William Lane. "Hugh Ross's Extra-Dimensional Deity: A Review Article." *Journal of the Evangelical Theological Society* 42 (June 1999) 293–304.
———. *Reasonable Faith*. Rev. ed. *Christian Truth and Apologetics*. Wheaton, IL: Crossway, 1994.
Craig, William Lane, and Paul M. Gould, eds. *The Two Tasks of the Christian Scholar: Redeeming the Soul, Redeeming the Mind*. Wheaton, IL: Crossway, 2007.
Crider, Scott F. *The Office of Assertion: An Art of Rhetoric for the Academic Essay*. Wilmington, DE: ISI, 2005.
Crisp, Thomas M., et al., eds. *Knowledge and Reality: Essays in Honor of Alvin Plantinga*. Dordrecht: Springer, 2006.
Cubukcu, Feryal. "Gadamer's Philosophical Hermeneutics on Education." *Journal of Education and Instructional Studies in the World* 2 (May 2012) 110–16.
Cunningham, James D., and Anthony C. Fortosis. *Education in Christian Schools: A Perspective and Training Model*. Whittier, CA: Association of Christian Schools International, 1987.
Curren, Randall, ed. *A Companion to the Philosophy of Education*. Malden, MA: Blackwell, 2003.
Curtler, Hugh Mercer. *Ethical Argument: Critical Thinking in Ethics*. 2nd ed. New York: Oxford University Press, 2004.
Cutpers, Stefaan E., and Christopher Martin, eds. *Reading R. S. Peters Today: Analysis, Ethics, and the Aims of Education*. West Sussex, UK: Wiley, 2011.
Danielson, Charlotte. *Enhancing Student Achievement: A Framework for School Improvement*. Alexandria, VA: ASCD, 2002.
Davidheiser, Bolton. *Science and the Bible*. Grand Rapids: Baker, 1971.
Davidson, Harriet. *T. S. Eliot and Hermeneutics: Absence and Interpretation in the Waste Land*. Baton Rouge: Louisiana State University Press, 1985.
Davies, Stephen. *The Philosophy of Art*. Malden, MA: Blackwell, 2006.
Davis, Stephen T. *Logic and the Nature of God*. Grand Rapids: Eerdmans, 1983.
De Beer, John, and Cornelius Jaarsma. *Toward a Philosophy of Christian Education*. Grand Rapids: National Union of Christian Schools, 1958.
DeJong, Norman. *Teaching for a Change: A Transformational Approach to Education*. Phillipsburg, NJ: Presbyterian and Reformed, 2001.

Dembski, William A., and James M. Kushiner, eds. *Signs of Intelligence: Understanding Intelligent Design*. Grand Rapids: Brazos, 2001.
Dennett, Daniel, ed. *The Philosophical Lexicon*. Newark, DE: American Philosophical Association, 1987.
DeWeese, Garrett J. *Doing Philosophy as a Christian*. Downers Grove: InterVarsity, 2011.
Dewey, John. *Experience and Education*. New York: Collier, 1967.
Dickson, John. *Humilitas: A Lost Key to Life, Love, and Leadership*. Grand Rapids: Zondervan, 2011.
Diehl, David E. "Educational Philosophies Definitions and Comparison Chart." In "A Study of Faculty-Related Variables and Competence in Integrating Instructional Technologies into Pedagogical Practices." PhD diss., Texas Southern University, 2005.
Dobson, James. *Bringing Up Boys: Practical Advice and Encouragement for Those Shaping the Next Generation of Men*. Wheaton, IL: Tyndale, 2001.
———. *Bringing Up Girls: Practical Advice and Encouragement for Those Shaping the Next Generation of Women*. Carol Stream, IL: Tyndale, 2010.
Dockery, David S., and Gregory Alan Thornbury, eds. *Shaping a Christian Worldview: The Foundations of Christian Higher Education*. Nashville: Broadman & Holman, 2002.
Dombrowski, Eileen, et al. *Theory of Knowledge: Course Companion*. New York: Oxford University Press, 2007.
Dow, Philip E. *Virtuous Minds: Intellectual Character Development for Students, Educators, and Parents*. Downers Grove: IVP Academic, 2013.
Downs, Perry G. *Teaching for Spiritual Growth: An Introduction to Christian Education*. Grand Rapids: Zondervan, 1994.
Drago-Severson, Eleanor. *Leading Adult Learning: Supporting Adult Development in Our Schools*. Thousand Oaks, CA: Corwin, 2009.
Drexler, James L. *Nurturing the School Community: Teacher Induction and Professional Learning Communities*. Colorado Springs: Purposeful Design, 2011.
Dueck, Alvin C. *Between Jerusalem & Athens: Ethical Perspectives on Culture, Religion, and Psychotherapy*. Grand Rapids: Baker, 1995.
Dunn, James D. G. "The Colossian Philosophy: A Confident Jewish Apologia." *Biblica* 76 (1995) 153–81.
Dupre, Ben. *Fifty Philosophy Ideas You Really Need to Know*. New York: Barnes and Noble, 2013.
Duska, Ronald, and Mariellen Whelan. *Moral Development: A Guide to Piaget and Kohlberg*. New York: Paulist, 1975.
Eagleton, Terry. *The Ideology of the Aesthetic*. Oxford: Blackwell, 1990.
Eby, Frederick, and Charles Flinn Arrowood. *The Development of Modern Education: In Theory, Organization, and Practice*. New York: Prentice Hall, 1934.
———. *The History and Philosophy of Education: Ancient and Medieval*. Englewood Cliffs, NJ: Prentice Hall, 1940.
Eckel, Mark. *The Whole Truth: Classroom Strategies for Biblical Integration*. Maitland, FL: Xulon, 2003.
Eckel, Mark, et al. *Perspectives on Your Child's Education: Four Views*. Edited by Paul Jones. Nashville: B&H, 2009.

Eckel, Peter D. *The Shifting Frontiers of Academic Decision Making: Responding to New Priorities, Following New Pathways*. American Council on Education / Praeger Series on Higher Education. Westport, CT: Praeger, 2006.

Edgar, William. *Lifting the Veil: The Face of Truth*. Phillipsburg, NJ: P&R, 2001.

Edge, Findley B. *Teaching for Results*. Rev. ed. Nashville: Broadman and Holman, 1995.

Edlin, Richard. *The Cause of Christian Education*. 3rd ed. Colorado Springs: National Institute for Christian Schools, 1999.

Edwards, Anne Michaels. *Writing to Learn: An Introduction to Writing Philosophical Essays*. Boston: McGraw Hill, 2000.

Egeler, Daniel. *Mentoring Millennials: Shaping the Next Generation*. Colorado Springs: NavPress, 2003.

Einstein, Albert. *Cosmic Religion and Other Opinions and Aphorisms*. New York: Covici-Friede, 1931.

Eliot, T. S. *Christianity and Culture: The Idea of a Christian Society*. New York: Harcourt, Brace, 1940.

Elkind, David. *The Hurried Child: Growing Up Too Fast Too Soon*. Reading, MA: Addison-Wesley, 1981.

———. *A Sympathetic Understanding of the Child: Birth to Sixteen*. Boston: Allyn and Bacon, 1971.

English, Fenwick W. *The Art of Education Leadership: Balancing Performance and Accountability*. Los Angeles: Sage, 2008.

Erickson, Erik H. *Childhood and Society*. 2nd ed. New York: Norton, 1963.

———. "Erikson's Stages of Development." Learning-Theories.com. https://www.learning-theories.com/eriksons-stages-of-development.html.

Erickson, Millard J. *Christian Theology*. 2nd ed. Grand Rapids: Baker, 1998.

Erickson, Millard J., et al., eds. *Reclaiming the Center: Confronting Evangelical Accommodation in Postmodern Times*. Wheaton, IL: Crossway, 2004.

Erwin, Jonathan C. *Inspiring the Best in Students*. Alexandria, VA: ASCD, 2010.

Evans, C. Stephen. *Philosophy of Religion: Thinking about Faith*. Downers Grove: InterVarsity, 1985.

———. *Preserving the Person: A Look at the Human Sciences*. Downers Grove: InterVarsity, 1977.

Evans, Malcolm D. *Whitehead and Philosophy of Education: The Seamless Coat of Learning*. Value Inquiry Book Series 74. Atlanta: Rodopi, 1998.

Fackre, Gabriel. "The Theological Commonplaces of Christian Education." *Christian Education Journal* 15 (Spring 1995) 27–36.

Fakkema, Mark. *Christian Philosophy: Its Educational Implications*. Chicago: National Union of Christian Schools, 1952.

Feinberg, John S. *No One Like Him: The Doctrine of God*. Wheaton, IL: Crossway, 2006.

Ferguson, David. *The Great Commandment Principle*. Wheaton, IL: Tyndale, 1998.

Ferguson, David, et al. *Relational Foundations: Experiencing Relevance in Life and Ministry*. Austin, TX: Relationship, 2004.

Fitzgibbons, R. E. "Peters's Analysis of Education: The Pathology of an Argument." *British Journal of Educational Studies* 23 (February 1975) 77–78.

Fleshman, Arthur Cary. *The Metaphysics of Education*. Boston: Mayhew, 1914.

Foster, David. *The Philosophical Scientists*. London: Hurst, 1985.

Foucalt, Michael. *Politics, Philosophy, Culture*. New York: Routledge, Chapman, and Hall, 1988.

Fowler, James W. *Stages of Faith: The Psychology of Human Development and the Quest for Meaning.* New York: HarperCollins, 1981.
Frame, John M. *The Doctrine of the Knowledge of God.* Phillipsburg, NJ: P&R, 1987.
———. *A History of Western Philosophy and Theology.* Phillipsburg, NJ: P&R, 2015.
Franke, John R. *The Character of Theology: An Introduction to Its Nature, Task, and Purpose.* Grand Rapids: Baker Academic, 2005.
Frankena, William K. *Philosophy of Education.* New York: Macmillan, 1965.
———. *Three Historical Philosophies of Education: Aristotle, Kant, Dewey.* Glenview, IL: Foresman, 1965.
Frankl, Viktor E. *The Doctor and the Soul: From Psychotherapy to Logotherapy; A New Approach to the Neurotic Personality Which Emphasizes Man's Spiritual Values and the Quest for Meaning in Life.* 2nd ed. New York: Vintage, 1973.
———. *Man's Search for Meaning: An Introduction to Logotherapy.* Rev. ed. New York: Pocket, 1963.
———. *The Will to Meaning: Foundations and Applications of Logotherapy.* Expanded ed. New York: Penguin, 2014.
Freud, Sigmund. *The Future of Illusion.* Translated by W. D. Robson-Scott. Revised and edited by James Strachey. Garden City: Doubleday, 1964.
Friedman Foundation for Educational Choice. *ABCs of School Choice: Rising Tide.* Indianapolis: Friedman Foundation for Educational Choice, 2012.
Friesen, J. Glenn. *Neo-Calvinism and Christian Theosophy: Franz Von Baader, Abraham Kuyper, Herman Dooyeweerd.* Calgary: Aevum, 2015.
Frost, Gene. *Learning from the Best: Growing Greatness in the Christian School.* Grand Rapids: Christian Schools International, 2010.
Fry, L. W. "Research in Spirituality from Concept to Application." Meeting of the National Academy of Management, Denver, Colorado, October 19, 2016.
———. "Spiritual Leadership as Intrinsic Motivation through Vision, Hope, Faith, and Altruistic Love." Meeting of the National Academy of Management, Seattle, August 5, 2003.
———. "Toward a Theory of Spiritual Leadership." *Leadership Quarterly* 14 (2003) 693–727.
Fry, L. W., and P. Malone. "Transforming Schools through Spiritual Leadership." Association for Supervision and Curriculum and Development National Conference, San Antonio, Texas, September 2002.
Fry, L. W., and R. A. Giacalone. "Exploring Critical Issues to Aid Recognition of Management, Spirituality, and Religion as a Legitimate Domain for Social Science Inquiry." Meeting of the National Academy of Management, Seattle, August 4, 2003.
Fuller, Edmund, ed. *The Christian Idea of Education.* New Haven: Yale University Press, 1960.
Fuller, Steve. *Social Epistemology.* Bloomington: Indiana University Press, 1991.
Furtak, Rick Anthony. "Henry David Thoreau." *Stanford Encyclopedia of Philosophy*, edited by Edward N. Zalta. Fall 2014 ed. http://plato.stanford.edu/archives/fall2014/entries/thoreau/.
Gaebelein, Frank. *Christian Education in a Democracy.* Colorado Springs: Association of Christian Schools International, 1995.
———. *Inside the Christian School.* Whittier, CA: Association of Christian Schools International, 1980.

———. *The Pattern of God's Truth: A Basic Contribution to Christian Educational Philosophy.* Chicago: Moody, 1968.

———. *The Pattern of God's Truth: The Integration of Faith and Learning.* Colorado Springs: Association of Christian Schools International, 1968.

Gamble, Richard M., ed. *The Great Tradition: Classic Readings on What It Means to Be an Educated Human Being.* Wilmington, DE: ISI, 2008.

Gangel, Kenneth O. "Integrating Faith and Learning: Principles and Process." *Bibliotheca Sacra* 135 (April–June 1978) 99–108.

Gangel, Kenneth O., and Warren S. Benson. *Christian Education: Its History and Philosophy.* Chicago: Moody, 1983.

Garcia, Shirley, and David Cottrell. *Listen Up, Teacher! You Are Making a Difference!* Dallas: Corner Stone Leadership Institute, 2002.

Gardner, Howard. *Changing Minds: The Art and Science of Changing Our Own and Other People's Minds.* Boston: Harvard Business School Press, 2004.

———. *The Disciplined Mind: Beyond Facts and Standardized Tests; The K–12 Education That Every Child Deserves.* New York: Penguin, 2000.

———. *Five Minds for the Future.* Boston: Harvard Business School Press, 2006.

Gates, Henry Louis, Jr., and Terri Hume Oliver, eds. *W. E. B. Du Bois: The Souls of Black Folk; Authoritative Text, Contexts, Criticism.* New York: Norton, 1999.

Gatto, John Taylor. *Dumbing Us Down: The Hidden Curriculum of Compulsory Schooling.* Gabriola Island, BC: New Society, 2002.

Gedge, Peter S. "Christian Contributions to Moral Education." *Journal of Moral Education* 11 (October 1982) 266–73.

Geisler, Norman. *Introduction to Philosophy: A Christian Perspective.* Grand Rapids: Baker, 1987.

———. *Systematic Theology.* Vol. 1, *Introduction Bible.* Minneapolis: Bethany House, 2002.

———. *Systematic Theology.* Vol. 2, *God Creation.* Minneapolis: Bethany House, 2003.

———. *Systematic Theology.* Vol. 3, *Sin Salvation.* Minneapolis: Bethany House, 2004.

———. *Systematic Theology.* Vol. 4, *Church Last Things.* Minneapolis: Bethany House, 2005.

Ggita, Allan. *The Education Philosophy of Jacques Maritain: Towards a Liberal and Integral Human Development.* Herstellung, Germany: Lambert Academic, 2012.

Gleason, Robert W., ed. *The Essential Pascal.* New York: New American Library, 1966.

Gibbs, Ollie E., and Jerry L. Haddock. *Classroom Discipline: A Management Guide for Christian School Teachers.* Colorado Springs: Association of Christian Schools International, 1995.

Gilson, Etienne. *God and Philosophy.* 2nd ed. New Haven: Yale University Press, 2002.

Golman, Daniel. *Social Intelligence: The New Science of Human Relationships.* New York: Bantam, 2006.

Goodman, Russell. "Transcendentalism." *Stanford Encyclopedia of Philosophy,* edited by Edward N. Zalta. Fall 2015 ed. http://plato.stanford.edu/archives/fall2015/entries/transcendentalism/.

Goodrich, Rachel M. "Neo-Thomism and Education." *British Journal of Education Studies* 7 (November 1958) 27–35.

Graham, Donovan L. *A Biblical Yardstick for Teaching.* Lookout Mountain, GA: Covenant College, 1991.

———. *Teaching Redemptively: Bringing Grace and Truth into Your Classroom.* 2nd ed. Colorado Springs: Purposeful Design, 2009.
Greene, Albert E. *Reclaiming the Future of Christian Education: A Transforming Vision.* Colorado Springs: Association of Christian Schools International, 1998.
Greenleaf, Robert K., et al., eds. *On Becoming a Servant-Leader.* San Francisco: Jossey-Bass, 1996.
Grenz, Stanley J. *The Social and Relational Self: A Trinitarian Theology of the Imago Dei.* Louisville: Westminster John Knox, 2001.
Groothuis, Douglas. *Philosophy in Seven Sentences: A Small Introduction to a Vast Topic.* Downers Grove: InterVarsity, 2016.
Gruden, Wayne. *Systematic Theology: An Introduction to Biblical Doctrine.* Leicester: InterVarsity, 1994.
Gundersen, Dennis. *Your Child's Profession of Faith.* Amityville, NY: Calvary, 1994.
Gutek, Gerald L. *Historical and Philosophical Foundations of Education: A Biographical Introduction.* 4th ed. Upper Saddle River, NJ: Pearson, 2005.
———. *New Perspectives on Philosophy and Education.* Columbus: Pearson, 2009.
———. "A Secular Contract, A Sacred Calling: Jacques Maritain and John Dewey on Education; A Reconsideration." *Educational Horizons* 83 (Summer 2005) 247–63.
Gutting, Gary. *What Philosophers Know: Case Studies in Recent Analytic Philosophy.* New York: Cambridge University Press, 2009.
Guyer, Paul, and Rolf-Peter Horstmann. "Idealism." *Stanford Encyclopedia of Philosophy*, edited by Edward N. Zalta. Fall 2015 ed. https://plato.stanford.edu/archives/fall2015/entries/idealism/.
Haack, R. J. "Philosophies of Education." *Royal Institute of Philosophy* 51 (1976) 3–4.
Habermas, Gary R. "The Recent Evangelical Debate on the Bodily Resurrection of Jesus: A Review Article." *Journal of the Evangelical Theological Society* 33 (1990) 375–78.
Habermas, Ronald, and Klaus Issler. *Teaching for Reconciliation: Foundations and Practice of Christian Educational Ministry.* Grand Rapids: Baker, 1992.
Halpin, David. "The Nature of Hope and Its Significance for Education." *British Journal of Education Studies* 49 (December 2001) 392–410.
Hancock, Curtis L. *Recovering a Catholic Philosophy of Elementary Education.* Mount Pocono, PA: Newman House, 2005.
Hare, William. "Russell's Contribution to Philosophy of Education." *Russell* 7 (1987) 25–41.
Harman, Gilbert. "Moral Philosophy Meets Social Philosophy: Virtue Ethics and the Fundamental Attribution Error." *Proceedings of the Aristotelian Society*, n.s., 99 (1999) 315–31.
Harris, Maria, and Gabriel Moran. *Reshaping Religious Education: Conversations on Contemporary Practice.* Louisville: Westminster John Knox, 1998.
Harris, Robert. *Integration of Faith and Learning: A Worldview Approach.* Eugene, OR: Cascade, 2004.
Harvey, Thomas, et al. *Leading for Excellence: A Twelve Step Program to Student Achievement.* Lanham, MD: Rowman and Littlefield Education, 2014.
Hasker, William. "Humanness as the Mirror of God." *Philosophia Christi*, 2nd ser., 1 (1999) 105–10.

———. *Metaphysics: Constructing a World View*. Contours of Christian Philosophy. Downers Grove: InterVarsity, 1983.
Healy, Mary, and Robin Parry, eds. *The Bible and Biblical Soundings on the Knowledge of God: Epistemology*. Colorado Springs: Paternoster, 2007.
Hearne, Donna H. *Everything You Need to Know to Win the Long War against Common Core*. St. Louis: Freedom Basics, 2015.
Heddendorf, Russell, and Matthew Vos. *Hidden Threads: A Christian Critique of Sociological Theory*. Lanham, MD: University Press of America, 2010.
Heidenry, Margaret. "My Parents Were Home-Schooling Anarchists." *New York Times*, November 8, 2011. https://www.nytimes.com/2011/11/13/magazine/my-parents-were-home-schooling-anarchists.html?_r=0.
Helm, Paul, ed. *Faith and Reason*. New York: Oxford University Press, 1999.
Hendricks, Howard G. *Color Outside the Lines: A Revolutionary Approach to Creative Leadership*. Nashville: Word, 1998.
———. *Heaven Help the Home: The Art and Joy of Successful Family Living*. Wheaton, IL: Victor, 1982.
———. *Teaching to Change Lives: Seven Proven Ways to Make Your Teaching Come Alive*. Sisters, OR: Multnomah, 1987.
Henninger, Mark G. "The Adolescent's Making of Meaning: The Pedagogy of Augustine's Confessions." *Journal of Moral Education* 18 (1989) 32–44.
Henry, Carl F. H. *God, Revelation, and Authority*. Vol. 1. Waco, TX: Word, 1976.
———. *Twilight of a Great Civilization: The Drift toward Neo-Paganism*. Westchester, IL: Crossway, 1988.
Henry, Nelson B., ed. *Modern Philosophies and Education*. Fifty-Fourth Yearbook of the National Society for the Study of Education, pt. 1. Chicago: University of Chicago Press, 1955.
Hick, John. *Philosophy of Religion*. Foundations of Philosophy series. Englewood Cliff, NJ: Prentice Hall, 1963.
Hicks, David V. *Norms and Nobility: A Treatise on Education*. New York: University Press of America, 1999.
Highet, Gilbert. *The Art of Teaching*. New York: Vintage, 1977.
Hirsch, E. D., Jr. *Cultural Literacy: What Every American Needs to Know*. New York: Houghton Mifflin, 1988.
Hirst, P. H., and R. S. Peters. *The Logic of Education*. Students Library of Education series. New York: Routledge, 1970.
Hoch, David. "Explaining Education-Based Athletics to Parents." *High School Today* (October 2014) 34–35.
Hodgson, Peter C. *God's Wisdom: Toward a Theology of Education*. Louisville: Westminster John Knox, 1999.
Hoekema, A. *Created in God's Image*, Grand Rapids: Eerdmans, 1994.
Hogan, Padraig. "Gadamer and the Philosophy of Education." In *Encyclopedia of Educational Philosophy and Theory*, edited by Michael Peters. Singapore: Springer, 2015. https://doi.org/10.1007/978-981-287-532-7_171-1.
Holland, John H. *Complexity: A Very Short Introduction*. New York: Oxford University Press, 2014.
Holmes, Arthur F. *All Truth Is God's Truth*. Downers Grove: InterVarsity, 1977.
———. *Building the Christian Academy*. Grand Rapids: Eerdmans, 2001.

———. *Contours of a World View. Studies in a Christian World View.* Grand Rapids: Eerdmans, 1983.
———. *Philosophy: A Christian Perspective; An Introductory Essay.* Rev. ed. Downers Grove: InterVarsity, 1978.
Hooks, Bell. *Teaching to Transgress: Education as the Practice of Freedom.* New York: Routledge, 1994.
Horton, Michael. *Core Christianity: Finding Yourself in God's Story.* Grand Rapids: Zondervan, 2016.
Horton, Ronald A., ed. *Christian Education: Its Mandate and Mission.* Greenville, SC: Journey Forth, 1992.
Hudson, Frederic M. *The Adult Years: Mastering the Art of Self-Renewal.* Rev. ed. San Francisco: Jossey-Bass, 1999.
Hummel, Charles E. *The Galileo Connection: Resolving Conflicts between Science & the Bible.* Downers Grove: InterVarsity, 1986.
Hunter, James C. *The Servant: A Simple Story about the True Essence of Leadership.* Roseville, CA: Prima, 1998.
"Idealism and Education," Pearson. 2011. Accessed on December 17, 2016. http://catalogue.pearsoned.co.uk/assets/hip/gb/hip_gb_pearsonhighered/samplechapter/0132540746.pdf.
Idleman, Kyle. *AHA: The God Moment That Changes Everything.* Colorado Springs: Cook, 2014.
Illich, Ivan. *Deschooling Society.* New York: Harper and Row, 1971.
———. *Tools for Conviviality.* New York: Boyars, 1973.
Imel, Susan, et al., eds. *Addressing the Spiritual Dimensions of Adult Learning: What Educators Can Do.* San Francisco: Jossey-Bass, 2000.
Irmscher, H. Dietrich. "Johann Gottfried von Herder: German Philosopher." *Britannica.com.* December 14, 2020. https://www.britannica.com/biography/Johann-Gottfried-von-Herder.
Jaarsma, Cornelius R. *Fundamentals in Christian Education: Theory and Practice.* Grand Rapids: Eerdmans, 1953.
Jaeger, Werner. *Early Christianity and Greek Paideia.* Cambridge: Harvard University Press, 1961.
Jensen, Eric. *Teaching with the Brain in Mind.* Alexandria, VA: ASCD, 1998.
Job, Rueben P. *Three Simple Rules: A Wesleyan Way of Living.* Nashville: Abingdon, 2007.
Johnson, Tony W., and Ronald F. Reed. *Philosophical Documents in Education.* 4th ed. Boston: Pearson, 2012.
Kane, Robert. *The Significance of Free Will.* New York: Oxford University Press, 1998.
Kantzer, Kenneth S., and Carl F. Henry, eds. *Evangelical Affirmations.* Grand Rapids: Academic, 1990.
Keck, Leander E. "Paul as Thinker." *Interpretation* 47 (1993) 27–38.
Keefe, Carolyn, ed. *C. S. Lewis Speaker and Teacher.* Grand Rapids: Zondervan, 1971.
Keith, Chris. "In My Own Hand: Grapho-Literacy and the Apostle Paul." *Biblica* 89 (2008) 39–58.
Keller, Joseph. "The Logic of Religious Discovery." *American Journal of Theology and Philosophy* 10 (September 1989) 143–52.
Kelly, John Norman Davidson. *Early Christian Doctrines.* Rev. ed. New York: HarperCollins, 1978.

Keyes, Ralph. *The Post-Truth Era: Dishonesty and Deception in Contemporary Life*. New York: St. Martin's, 2004.
Kienel, Paul A. *A History of Christian School Education*. Vol. 1. Colorado Springs: Association of Christian Schools International, 1998.
———. *A History of Christian School Education*. Vol. 2. Colorado Springs: Purposeful Design, 2005.
———. *Philosophy of Christian School Education*. Rev. ed. Whittier, CA: Association of Christian Schools International, 1983.
———. *Reasons for Christian Schools*. Milford, MI: Mott, 1981.
Knight, George R. *Philosophy and Education: An Introduction in Christian Perspective*. 4th ed. Berrien Springs, MI: Andrews University Press, 2006.
Knowles, Malcolm S., et al. *The Adult Learner: The Definitive Classic in Adult Education and Human Resource Development (Managing Cultural Differences)*. Houston: Gulf, 1998.
Kohl, Herbert. *The Open Classroom: A Practical Guide to a New Way of Teaching*. New York: Vintage, 1969.
Kohli, Wendy, ed. *Critical Conversations in Philosophy of Education*. New York: Routledge, 1995.
Koji, Tachibana. "How Aristotle's Theory of Education Has Been Studied in Our Century." *Studia Classica* 3 (2012) 21–67.
Kostenberger, Andreas J. *Excellence: The Character of God and the Pursuit of Scholarly Virtue*. Wheaton, IL: Crossway, 2011.
———, ed. *Whatever Happened to Truth?* Wheaton, IL: Crossway, 2005.
Kroon, Fred, and Alberto Voltolini. "Fiction." *Stanford Encyclopedia of Philosophy*, edited by Edward N. Zalta. Fall 2011 ed. http://plato.stanford.edu/archives/fall2011/entries/fiction/.
Kuhn, Thomas. *The Copernican Revolution: Planetary Astronomy in the Development of Western Thought*. New York: Vintage, 1959.
Kuyper, Abraham. *Sphere Sovereignty: A Public Address Delivered at the Inauguration of the Free University, October 20, 1880*. Translated by George Kamps. Paper. http://www.reformationalpublishingproject.com/pdf_books/Scanned_Books_PDF/SphereSovereignty_English.pdf.
Kvanvig, Jonathan L., ed. *Oxford Studies in Philosophy of Religion*. Vol. 1. Oxford: Oxford University Press, 2008.
———. *Rationality and Reflection: How to Think about What to Think*. Oxford: Oxford University Press, 2014.
———. *The Value of Knowledge and the Pursuit of Understanding*. Cambridge: Cambridge University Press, 2003.
———, ed. *Warrant in Contemporary Epistemology: Essays in Honor of Plantinga's Theory of Knowledge*. Lanham, MD: Rowman and Littlefield, 1996.
Lammi, Walter. "The Conflict of Paideias in Gadamer's Thought." *Paideias Philosophy of Education*. https://www.bu.edu/wcp/Papers/Educ/EducLamm.htm.
Leach, Javier. *Mathematics and Religion: Our Languages of Sign and Symbol*. Conshohocken, PA: Templeton, 2010.
Lebar, Lois E. *Education That Is Christian*. Colorado Springs: Chariot Victor, 1995.
Ledbetter, Brett. *What Drives Winning: Building Character Gets Results*. O'Fallon, MO: Green Dot, 2015.
Lewis, C. S. *The Abolition of Man*. New York: HarperCollins, 1974.

———. *An Experiment in Criticism*. New York: Cambridge University Press, 1961.

———. *Mere Christianity*. Rev. ed. New York: HarperSanFrancisco, 2001.

Littlejohn, Robert, and Charles T. Evans. *Wisdom and Eloquence: A Christian Paradigm for Classical Learning*. Wheaton, IL: Crossway, 2006.

Lockerbie, D. Bruce. *A Christian Paideia: The Habitual Vision of Greatness*. Colorado Springs: Purposeful Design, 2005.

———. *A Passion for Learning: A History of Christian Thought on Education*. 2nd ed. Colorado Springs: Purposeful Design, 2007.

Lotz, Philip Henry, ed. *Orientation in Religious Education*. New York: Abingdon-Cokesbury, 1950.

Lowrie, Roy W. *Inside the Christian School: From the Headmaster's Diary*. Whittier, CA: Association of Christian Schools International, 1980.

———. *Insights for Christian School Board Members*. Whittier, CA: Association of Christian Schools International, 1985.

Lucas, Christopher J. *What Is Philosophy of Education?* New York: MacMillan, 1969.

Lyotard, Jean-François. *The Postmodern Condition*. Minneapolis: University of Minnesota, 1984.

Mabbott, J. D. "Is Plato's Republic Utilitarian?" *Mind* 46 (1937) 468–74. https://doi.org/10.1093/mind/XLVI.184.468.

MacCullough, Martha E. *By Design: Developing a Philosophy of Education Informed by a Christian Worldview*. Langhorne, PA: Cairn University, 2013.

MacDonald, Neil B. *Metaphysics and the God of Israel: Systematic Theology of the Old and the New Testaments*. Grand Rapids: Baker Academic, 2006.

Machen, J. Gresham. *Education, Christianity, and the State*. Unicoi, TN: Trinity Foundation, 2004.

Machen, J. Gresham, and John W. Robbins, eds. *Education, Christianity, and the State: Essays*. Jefferson, MD: Trinity Foundation, 1987.

Malone, P., and L. W. Fry. "Transforming Schools through Spiritual Leadership: A Field Experiment." Meeting of the National Academy of Management, Seattle, August 6, 2003.

Mandelbaum, Eric. "Associationist Theories of Thought." *Stanford Encyclopedia of Philosophy*, edited by Edward N. Zalta. Summer 2016 ed. http://plato.stanford.edu/archives/sum2016/entries/associationist-thought/.

Maritain, Jacques. *Education at the Crossroads*. New Haven: Yale University Press, 1971.

Martin, Troy W. "Scythian Perspective or Elusive Chiasm: A Reply to Douglas A. Campbell." *Couplet Barbarian/Scythian in Colossians* 3 (1999) 256–64.

Marzano, Robert J. *What Works in Schools: Translating Research into Action*. Alexandria, VA: ASCD, 2003.

Maslow, Abraham H. *The Farther Reaches of Human Nature*. New York: Viking, 1971.

Mason, Charlotte, and Karen Glass. *Mind to Mind: An Essay Towards a Philosophy of Education*. San Bernardino, CA: Karen Glass, 2015.

Mason, Mark, ed. *Complexity Theory and the Philosophy of Education*. Hoboken, NJ: Wiley-Blackwell, 2008.

Matheny, Mike, et al. *The Matheny Manifesto: A Young Manager's Old-School Views on Success in Sports and Life*. New York: Crown Archetype, 2015.

Mayers, Marvin K., et al. *Reshaping Evangelical Higher Education*. Grand Rapids: Zondervan, 1972.

McCall, Thomas H. *An Invitation to Analytic Christian Theology.* Downers Grove: InterVarsity, 2015.
McCauley, H. C. "On the Philosophy of Education." *Maynooth Review* (November 1979) 80–94.
McGrath, Alister. *The Passionate Intellect: Christian Faith and the Discipleship of the Mind.* Downers Grove: InterVarsity, 2010.
McInerny, Daniel, ed. *The Common Things: Essays on Thomism and Education.* Washington, DC: Catholic University of America Press, 1999.
McLeod, Saul. *Carl Rogers.* Simply Psychology. 2014. www.simplypsychology.org/carl-rogers.html.
McMurrin, Sterling M. "What about the Philosophy of Education." *Journal of Philosophy* 59 (October 25, 1962) 629–37.
McQuilken, J. R. "The Behavioral Sciences under the Authority of Scripture." *Journal of the Evangelical Theological Society* 20 (1977) 31–43.
Meadors, Gary T., ed. *Four Views on Moving Beyond the Bible to Theology.* Grand Rapids: Zondervan, 2009.
Mercer, Neil. *Words and Minds: How We Use Language to Think Together.* London: Routledge, 2000.
Merriam, Sharan B., and Rosemary S. Caffarella. *Learning in Adulthood: A Comprehensive Guide.* 2nd ed. San Francisco: Jossey-Bass, 1999.
Merry, Michael S. "Should the State Fund Religious Schools?" *Journal of Applied Philosophy* 24 (2007) 255–70.
Mikulecky, Donald C. "Complexity Science as an Aspect of the Complexity of Science." *Worldviews, Science and Us* (2007) 30–52. https://www.researchgate.net/publication/241614882_Complexity_Science_as_an_Aspect_of_the_Complexity_of_Science.
Miller, George David. *Negotiating Toward Truth: The Extinction of Teachers and Students.* Value Inquiry Book series 62. Atlanta: Rodopi, 1998.
———. *Peace, Value, and Wisdom: The Educational Philosophy of Daisaku Ikeda.* New York: Rodopi, 2002.
Miller, Mark, and Patrick Lencioni. *The Heart of Leadership: Becoming a Leader People Want to Follow.* San Francisco: Berett-Koehler, 2013.
Miller, Matt. *The Two Percent Solution: Fixing America's Problems in Ways Liberals and Conservatives Can Love.* New York: Public Affairs, 2003.
Miller, Randolph Crump. "Rethinking Empiricism in Theology." *American Journal of Theology and Philosophy* 10 (September 1989) 159–70.
Miller, Stephen G. *Arete.* 3rd ed. Berkeley: University of California Press, 2012.
Mills, Jon, ed. *A Pedagogy of Becoming.* Value Inquiry Book series 116. New York: Rodopi, 2002.
Moltmann, Jurgen. *Man: Christian Anthropology in the Conflicts of the Present.* Translated by John Sturdy. Philadelphia: Fortress, 1973.
Montgomery, George R. *Leibniz.* 2nd ed. *Discourse on Metaphysics: Correspondence with Arnauld and Monadology.* Chicago: Open Court, 1918.
Moreland, J. P. *Christianity and the Nature of Science: A Philosophical Investigation.* Grand Rapids: Baker, 1989.
———. *Kingdom Triangle: Recover the Christian Mind; Renovate the Soul; Restore the Spirit's Power.* Grand Rapids: Zondervan, 2007.
———. "A Reluctant Traveler's Guide for Slouching Towards Theism: A Philosophical

Note on Nagel's *Mind and Cosmos*." *Philosophia Christi* 14 (2012) 429–38.
———. *Scaling the Secular City: A Defense of Christianity*. Grand Rapids: Baker, 1987.
———. "What Are the Three Laws of Logic?" Apologetics Resource Center. January 6, 2015. https://arcapologetics.org/three-laws-logic/.
Moreland, J. P., and William Lane Craig. *Philosophical Foundations for a Christian Worldview*. Downers Grove: InterVarsity, 2003.
Mouw, Richard J. *The Challenges of Cultural Discipleship: Essays in the Line of Abraham Kuyper*. Grand Rapids: Eerdmans, 2012.
———. *Distorted Truth: What Every Christian Needs to Know about the Battle for the Mind*. San Francisco: Harper and Row, 1989.
———. *He Shines in All That's Fair: Culture and Common Grace*. Grand Rapids: Eerdmans, 2001.
———. *Uncommon Decency: Christian Civility in an Uncivil World*. Downers Grove: InterVarsity, 1992.
Mulvey, J. H., ed. *The Nature of Matter*. New York: Oxford University Press, 1981.
Muratore, Giulio. "Review." *Science and Society* 9 (Summer 1945) 284–88.
Murch, James DeForest. *Christian Education and the Local Church: History, Principles, Practice*. Cincinnati: Standard, 1943.
Murphy, F. "The Paradox of Freedom in R. S. Peters' Analysis of Education as Initiation." *British Journal of Educational Studies* 21 (1973) 5–33.
Myers, David G. *Psychology*. New York: Worth, 2004.
Myers, Jeff, et al. *Cultivate: Forming the Emerging Generation through Life-on-Life Mentoring*. Manitou Springs, CO: Summit Ministries, 2016.
Nadler, Steven. "Baruch Spinoza." *Stanford Encyclopedia of Philosophy*, edited by Edward N. Zalta. Fall 2016 ed. http://plato.stanford.edu/archives/fall2016/entries/spinoza/.
Nagel, Greta. *The Tao of Teaching: The Ageless Wisdom of Taoism and the Art of Teaching*. New York: Plume, 1998.
Nagel, Thomas. *Mind and Cosmos: Why the Materialist Neo-Darwinian Conception of Nature Is Almost Certainly False*. New York: Oxford University Press, 2012.
———. "Public Education and Intelligent Design." *Philosophy & Public Affairs* 36 (2008) 187–205.
Nash, Ronald H. *The Closing of the American Heart: What's Really Wrong with America's Schools*. Plano, TX: Probe Ministries International, 1991.
———. *The Word of God and the Mind of Man: The Crisis of Revealed Truth in Contemporary Theology*. Phillipsburg, NJ: P&R, 1992.
National Association of Independent Schools. *Marketing Independent Schools in the 21st Century*. Washington, DC: National Association of Independent Schools, 2001.
Naugle, David K. *Worldview: The History of a Concept*. Grand Rapids: Eerdmans, 2002.
Newberg, Andrew B. *Principles of Neurotheology*. Burlington, VT: Ashgate, 2010.
Newberg, Andrew B., and Mark Robert Waldman. *How God Changes Your Brain: Breakthrough Findings from a Leading Neuroscientist*. New York: Ballantine, 2010.
Newbigin, Lesslie. *Proper Confidence: Faith, Doubt, and Certainty in Christian Discipleship*. Grand Rapids: Eerdmans, 1995.
Niebuhr, H. Richard. *Christ and Culture*. New York: Harper and Row, 1951.

———. *Resurrection and Historical Reason: A Study of Theological Method.* New York: Scribner, 1957.
Nissen, Johannes. *New Testament and Mission: Historical and Hermeneutical Perspectives.* New York: Lang, 1996.
Noddings, Nel. *Philosophy of Education.* 3rd ed. Boulder, CO: Westview, 2012.
Noll, Mark A. *The Scandal of the Evangelical Mind.* Grand Rapids: Eerdmans, 1994.
Nouwen, Henri J. M. *In the Name of Jesus: Reflections on Christian Leadership.* New York: Crossroad, 2002.
Nussbaum, Martha C. *Cultivating Humanity: A Classical Defense of Reform in Liberal Education.* Cambridge: Harvard University Press, 1997.
———. "Virtue Ethics: A Misleading Category?" *Journal of Ethics* 3 (1999) 163–201.
Okasha, Samir. *Philosophy of Science: A Very Short Introduction.* New York: Oxford University Press, 2002.
Oliphint, K. Scott. *The Battle Belongs to the Lord: The Power of Scripture for Defending Our Faith.* Phillipsburg, NJ: P&R, 2003.
———. *The Consistency of Van Til's Methodology.* Scarsdale, NY: Westminster Discount Book Service, n.d.
———. *Cornelius Van Til and the Reformation of Christian Apologetics.* Scarsdale, NY: Westminster Discount Book Service, n.d.
Ornstein, Allan C. "Philosophy as a Basis for Curriculum Decisions." *High School Journal* 74 (January 1991) 102–9.
Ortwein, Mark. "Virtue Epistemology and Education." In *Encyclopedia of Educational Philosophy and Theory,* edited by Michael Peters. Singapore: Springer, 2015. https://doi.org/10.1007/978-981-287-532-7_371-1.
Osborne, Grant R. *The Hermeneutical Spiral: A Comprehensive Introduction to Biblical Interpretation.* Downers Grove: InterVarsity, 1991.
Ozmon, Howard. "Idealism and Education." Chapter 1 in *Philosophical Foundations of Education.* Boston: Pearson, 2012.
Packer, J. I. *Knowing God.* Downers Grove: InterVarsity, 1985.
Parsons, Michael, ed. *Since We Are Justified by Faith: Justification in the Theologies of the Protestant Reformation.* Crownhill, UK: Paternoster, 2012.
Patzia, Michael. "Anaxagoras (c. 500–428 B.C.E.)." *Internet Encyclopedia of Philosophy.* https://iep.utm.edu/anaxagor/.
Paul, Richard, and Linda Elder. *A Miniature Guide for Students on How to Study and Learn: A Discipline Using Critical Thinking Concepts and Tools.* Dillon Beach, CA: Critical Thinking Consortium, 2001.
Pazmiño, Robert W. *By What Authority Do We Teach? Sources for Empowering Christian Educators.* Grand Rapids: Baker, 1994.
———. *Foundational Issues in Christian Education: An Introduction in Evangelical Perspective.* 3rd ed. Grand Rapids: Baker Academic, 2008.
———. *God Our Teacher: Theological Basics in Christian Education.* Grand Rapids: Baker Academic, 2001.
Pearcey, Nancy. *Total Truth: Liberating Christianity from its Cultural Captivity.* Wheaton, IL: Crossway, 2008.
Pennings, Ray. *Cardus Education Survey: Do the Motivations for Private Religious Catholic and Protestant Schooling in North America Align with Graduate Outcomes?* Pasadena, CA: Cardus, 2011.

Perrin, Christopher A. *An Introduction to Classical Education: A Guide for Parents.* Camp Hill, PA: Classical Academic, 2004.
Peters, R. S. *Ethics & Education.* London: Allen & Unwin, 1966.
———, ed. *The Philosophy of Education: Oxford Readings in Philosophy.* Oxford: Oxford University Press, 1973.
Peterson, Michael L. *Philosophy of Education: Issues and Options.* Edited by C. Stephen Evans. Downers Grove: InterVarsity, 1986.
———. *With All Your Mind: A Christian Philosophy of Education.* Notre Dame: University of Notre Dame Press, 2001.
Phaman, Dylan. "Alexis De Tocqueville and the Character of American Education." Acton Institute PowerBlog. November 21, 2012. https://blog.acton.org/archives/45852-alexis-de-tocqueville-and-the-character-of-american-education.html.
Phillips, D. C., and Siegel, Harvey. "Philosophy of Education." *Stanford Encyclopedia of Philosophy*, edited by Edward N. Zalta. Winter 2015 ed. http://plato.stanford.edu/archives/win2015/entries/education-philosophy/.
Phillips, Timothy R., and Dennis L. Okholm. *Christian Apologetics in the Postmodern World.* Downers Grove: InterVarsity, 1995.
Piaget, Jean, and Barbel Inhelder. *The Psychology of the Child.* New York: Basic Books, 1969.
Piattelli-Palmarini, Massimo, and Keith Botsford. *Inevitable Illusions: How Mistakes of Reason Rule Our Minds.* New York: Wiley, 1994.
Pierce, John R. *An Introduction to Information Theory: Symbols, Signals, and Noise.* 2nd ed. New York: Dover, 1980.
Pinnock, Clark H., and Barry L. Callen. *The Scripture Principle: Reclaiming the Full Authority of the Bible.* 2nd ed. Grand Rapids: Baker Academic, 2006.
Piper, John. *The Pleasures of God: Meditations on God's Delight in Being God.* Rev. ed. Sisters, OR: Multnomah, 2000.
Piper, John, and Justin Taylor, eds. *The Supremacy of Christ in a Postmodern World.* Wheaton, IL: Crossway, 2007.
Piper, Mary. *How Schools and Families Can Save the World.* Grosse Pointe Farms, MI: Grosse Pointe Academy, 2001.
Plantinga, Alvin. "Advice to Christian Philosophers." *Faith and Philosophy* 1 (1984) 253–71.
———. *Warrant: The Current Debate.* New York: Oxford University Press, 1993.
———. *Warrant and Proper Function.* New York: Oxford University Press, 1993.
———. *Warranted Christian Belief.* New York: Oxford University Press, 2000.
———. *Where the Conflict Really Lies: Science, Religion, and Naturalism.* New York: Oxford University Press, 2011.
Plantinga, Alvin, and Nicholas Wolterstorff, eds. *Reason and Belief in God.* Notre Dame: University of Notre Dame Press, 1983.
Plantinga, Cornelius. *Engaging God's World: A Christian Vision of Faith, Learning, and Living.* Grand Rapids: Eerdmans, 2002.
Plato. *Phaedrus.* New York: Andesite, 2015.
Poggeler, Otto, and John Bailiff. *The Paths of Heidegger's Life and Thought.* Amherst, MA: Humanity, 1998.
Pojman, Louis P., and Lewis Vaughn. *Classics of Philosophy.* 3rd ed. New York: Oxford University Press, 2011.

Polanyi, Michael. *Personal Knowledge: Towards a Post-Critical Philosophy.* London: Routledge & Kegan Paul, 1958.
———. *The Study of Man.* Mansfield Centre, CT: Martino, 2014.
Polkinghorne, John. *Faith, Science, and Understanding.* New Haven: Yale University Press, 2000.
———. *Quantum Theory: A Very Short Introduction.* New York: Oxford University Press, 2002.
———. *Science and Theology: An Introduction.* Minneapolis: Fortress, 1998.
Pollack, William S. *Toward a New Model of Boys and Schools: How Elementary Schools Can Give a Good Start toward Manhood.* Grosse Pointe Farms, MI: Grosse Pointe Academy, 2000.
Pollard, William G., et al. *The Christian Idea of Education.* Edited by Edmund Fuller. New Haven: Yale University Press, 1960.
Polzin, Robert M. *Biblical Structuralism: Method and Subjectivity in the Study of Ancient Texts.* Philadelphia: Fortress, 1977.
Poplin, Mary. *Is Reality Secular: Testing the Assumptions of Four Global Worldviews.* Downers Grove: InterVarsity, 2014.
Porrovecchio, Mark Joseph. "F. C. S. Schiller and the Style of Pragmatic Humanism." PhD diss., University of Pittsburgh, 2006.
Porter, Stanley E., and Beth Stovell, eds. *Biblical Hermeneutics: Five Views.* Downers Grove: InterVarsity, 2012.
Porter, Stanley E., and Kent D. Clarke. "Canonical-Critical Perspective and the Relationship of Colossians and Ephesians." *Biblica* 78 (1997) 57–86.
Potts, Michael. *Aerobics for the Mind: Practical Exercises in Philosophy That Anybody Can Do.* Tullahoma, TN: Word Crafts, 2014.
Powell, Jim. *Postmodernism for Beginners.* Danbury, CT: For Beginners, 1998.
Powers, Bruce P. *Christian Education Handbook: A Revised and Completely Updated Edition.* Phillipsburg, NJ: Presbyterian and Reformed, 1996.
Poythress, Vern S. *God Centered: Biblical Interpretation.* Phillipsburg, NJ: P&R, 1999.
———. *Redeeming Philosophy: A God-Centered Approach to the Big Questions.* Wheaton, IL: Crossway, 2014.
———. *Symphonic Theology: The Validity of Multiple Perspectives in Theology.* Phillipsburg, NJ: P&R, 2001.
Quinn, Robert E. *Deep Change: Discovering the Leader Within.* San Francisco: Jossey-Bass, 1996.
Ramm, Bernard L., et al. *Hermeneutics.* Grand Rapids: Baker, 1987.
Rana, Fazale. *The Cell's Design: How Chemistry Reveals the Creator's Artistry.* Grand Rapids: Baker, 2008.
Rayner, Leslie, and Christopher Perrin. *The Classical Reader: A Comprehensive Reading Guide for K-12 Students.* Camp Hill, PA: Classical Academic, 2015.
Redpath, Peter A. *A Not-So-Elementary Christian Metaphysics: Written in the Hope of Ending the Centuries-Old Separation between Philosophy and Science and Science and Wisdom.* Vol. 1. St. Louis: En Route, 2015.
Reid, W. Stanford. "The Beginning of Wisdom." *Evangelical Quarterly* 43 (July–September 1976) 144–53.
———. "The Covenant Interpretation of Culture." *Evangelical Quarterly* 26 (1954) 33–42.

———. "A Reformed Approach to Christian Aesthetics." *Evangelical Quarterly* 37 (May–June 1965) 68–81.
Rice, J. Valentine. "Jacques Maritain and the Problem of Christian Philosophy." *Hermathena* 134 (Summer 1983) 7–34.
Richard, Mark. *When Truth Gives Out*. New York: Oxford University Press, 2008.
Richards, Lawrence O. *A Theology of Christian Education*. Grand Rapids: Ministry Resources Library, 1975.
Riesen, Richard A. *The Academic Imperative: A Reassessment of Christian Education's Priorities*. Colorado Springs: Purposeful Design, 2010.
Rigsby, Rick. *Lessons from a Third Grade Dropout: How Timeless Wisdom of One Man Can Impact an Entire Generation*. Nashville: Nelson, 2006.
Ripley, Amanda. *The Smartest Kids in the World and How They Got That Way*. New York: Simon and Schuster, 2013.
Robb, Felix C. "Aristotle and Education." *Peabody Journal of Education* 20 (1943) 202–13.
Roberts, Robert C., and W. Jay Wood. *Intellectual Virtues: An Essay in Regulative Epistemology*. New York: Clarendon, 2007.
———. *A Psychology of Christian Virtues*. Grand Rapids: Eerdmans, 2007.
Robins, Henry Ephraim. *The Christian Idea of Education as Distinguished from the Secular Idea of Education*. Classic Reprint series. London: Forgotten, 2015.
Rocha, Samuel D. *A Primer for Philosophy and Education*. Eugene, OR: Cascade, 2014.
Rogers, Carl R. *Client-Centered Therapy: Its Current Practice, Implications and Theory*. London: Constable, 1951.
———. *Freedom to Learn*. Edited by William R. Coulson. Studies of the Person series. Columbus, OH: Merrill, 1969.
———. *On Becoming a Person: A Therapist's View of Psychotherapy*. Sentry ed. Boston: Houghton Mifflin, 1961.
———. "A Theory of Therapy, Personality and Interpersonal Relationships as Developed in the Client-Centered Framework." In *Psychology: A Study of a Science*, vol. 3, *Formulations of the Person and the Social Context*, edited by S. Koch. New York: McGraw Hill, 1959.
Rogers, Carl, et al. *Person to Person: The Problem of Being Human; A New Trend in Psychology*. Lafayette, CA: Real People, 1967.
Rookmaaker, Hans R. *Art Needs No Justification*. Vancouver, BC: Regent College, 1978.
Rorty, Richard. *Philosophy and the Mirror of Nature*. Princeton: Princeton University Press, 1979.
Rose, Colin, and Malcolm J. Nicholl. *Accelerated Learning for the 21st Century: The Six-Step Plan to Unlock Your Master-Mind*. New York: Delacorte, 1997.
Rose, Mike. *Why School: Reclaiming Education for All*. New York: New Press, 2014.
Royalty, Robert M. "Dwelling on Visions: On the Nature of the So-Called 'Colossians Heresy.'" *Biblica* 83 (2002) 329–57.
Ruitenberg, Claudia. *What Do Philosophers of Education Do? (And How Do They Do It?)*. Hoboken, NJ: Wiley-Blackwell, 2010.
Rushdoony, Rousas J. *The Messianic Character of American Education: Studies in the History of the Philosophy of Education*. Vallecito, CA: Ross House, 1995.
Ryan, Thomas G. "Philosophical Orientation in Pre-Service." *Journal of Educational Thought* 2 (2008) 247–60.

Saenz, Adam L. *The Power of a Teacher: Restoring Hope and Well-Being to Change Lives.* Peoria, AZ: Intermedia, 2012.

Sayers, Dorothy. *The Lost Tools of Learning.* Reprint. New York: Trinity Forum, 2004.

———. *The Whimsical Christian: 18 Essays: Reflections on God and Man by the Creator of Lord Peter Wimsey.* New York: Collier, 1987.

Schachter-Shalomi, Zalman, and Ronald S. Miller. *From Age-ing to Sage-ing: A Profound New Vision of Growing Older.* New York: Warner, 1995.

Schaeffer, Francis A. *Art and the Bible.* Downers Grove: InterVarsity, 2006.

———. *The Complete Works of Francis A. Schaeffer.* Vol. 1, *A Christian View of Philosophy and Culture.* Westchester, IL: Crossway, 1982.

———. *Escape from Reason.* Downers Grove: InterVarsity, 2006.

———. *The Mark of the Christian.* Downers Grove: InterVarsity, 1970.

Schaeffer, Franky. *Addicted to Mediocrity: 20th Century Christians and the Arts.* Westchester, IL: Crossway, 1981.

Schafer, R. Murray. *The Rhinoceros in the Classroom.* London: Halston, 1975.

Schaffer, Jonathan. "Grounding, Transitivity, and Contrastivity." In *Metaphysical Grounding: Understanding the Structure of Reality,* edited by Fabrice Correia and Benjamin Schnieder, 122–38. Cambridge: Cambridge University Press, 2012.

Schimmels, Cliff. *I Was a High School Drop-In.* Old Tappan, NJ: Revell, 1986.

Schlissel, Steven M. *The Standard Bearer: A Festschrift for Greg L. Bahnsen.* Nacogdoches, TX: Covenant, 2002.

Schultz, Glen. *Kingdom Education: God's Plan for Educating Future Generations.* 2nd ed. Nashville: Lifeway, 1998.

Schweitzer, Albert. *The Light within Us.* New York: Polyglot, 1959.

Scott, Charles E., and John Sallis. *Interrogating the Tradition: Hermeneutics and the History of Philosophy.* New York: State University of New York Press, 2000.

Scott, Ian W. *Paul's Way of Knowing: Story, Experience, and the Spirit.* Grand Rapids: Baker Academic, 2009.

Scruton, Roger. *Beauty: A Very Short Introduction.* New York: Oxford University Press, 2011.

Sealey, John. *Religious Education: Philosophical Perspectives.* Crow's Nest, Australia: Unwin Hyman, 1985.

Sennett, James F., ed. *The Analytic Theist: An Alvin Plantinga Reader.* Grand Rapids: Eerdmans, 1998.

Seymour, Jack L., and Donald E. Miller, eds. *Theological Approaches to Christian Education.* Nashville: Abingdon, 1990.

Shand, John. *Philosophy and Philosophers: An Introduction to Western Philosophy.* Montreal: McGill-Queen's University Press, 2002.

Shapiro, Stewart. "Classical Logic." *Stanford Encyclopedia of Philosophy,* edited by Edward N. Zalta. Winter 2013 ed. http://plato.stanford.edu/archives/win2013/entries/logic-classical/.

Siegel, Harvey, ed. *The Oxford Handbook of Philosophy of Education.* New York: Oxford University Press, 2009.

Simmons, Tracy Lee. *Climbing Parnassus: A New Apologia for Greek and Latin.* Wilmington, DE: ISI, 2002.

Simpson, Douglas J. *Christian Education: An Introduction to Its Scope.* Nashville: Randall House, 1979.

Simpson, Peter. "Contemporary Virtue Ethics and Aristotle." *Review of Metaphysics* 45 (March 1992) 503–24.
Smith, Christian, and Melinda Lundquist Denton. *Soul Searching: The Religious and Spiritual Lives of American Teenagers*. New York: Oxford University Press, 2005.
Smith, James K. A. *How (Not) to Be Secular: Reading Charles Taylor*. Grand Rapids: Eerdmans, 2014.
Smith, M. Cecil. *Adult Learning and Development: Perspectives from Educational Psychology*. Mahwah, NJ: Erlbaum, 1998.
Smith, Robin. "Aristotle's Logic." *Stanford Encyclopedia of Philosophy*, edited by Edward N. Zalta. Winter 2016 ed. http://plato.stanford.edu/archives/win2016/entries/aristotle-logic/.
Solzhenitsyn, Aleksander. *A World Split Apart*. McLean, VA: Trinity Forum, 2002.
Spear, Paul D., and Steven R. Loomis. *Education for Human Flourishing: A Christian Perspective*. Downers Grove: IVP Academic, 2009.
Sproul, R. C. *Not a Chance: The Myth of Chance in Modern Science and Cosmology*. Grand Rapids: Baker, 1997.
Stafford, Wess. *Too Small to Ignore: Why Children Are the Next Big Thing*. Colorado Springs: WaterBrook, 2005.
Stetzer, Ed. "Calvin Miller Has Died: In Memoriam and His 'Letter to the Church.'" Pastors.com. August 26, 2012. https://pastors.com/calvin-miller-has-died-in-memoriam-and-his-letter-to-the-church/.
Stewart, Vivien. *A World-Class Education: Learning from International Models of Excellence and Innovation*. Alexandria, VA: ASCD, 2012.
Stonehouse, C. *Patterns in Moral Development*. Waco, TX: Word, 1980.
Stott, John. *Your Mind Matters: The Place of the Mind in the Christian Life*. Downers Grove: InterVarsity, 2006.
Straughan, Roger, and John Wilson, eds. *Philosophers on Education*. Totowa, NJ: Barnes and Noble, 1987.
Strauss, D. F. M. *Philosophy: Discipline of the Disciplines*. Grand Rapids: Paideia, 2009.
Strauss, Gerald. *Luther's House of Learning*. Baltimore: Johns Hopkins University Press, 1952.
Stronks, Gloria Goris, and Doug Blomberg, eds. *A Vision with a Task: Christian Schooling for Responsive Discipleship*. Grand Rapids: Baker, 1993.
Sweet, William. "Jacques Maritain." *Stanford Encyclopedia of Philosophy*, edited by Edward N. Zalta. Summer 2019 ed. https://plato.stanford.edu/archives/sum2019/entries/maritain/.
Swenson, Richard A. *Hurtling toward Oblivion: A Logical Argument for the End of the Age*. Colorado Springs: NavPress, 1999.
Taggart, Andrew J. "Nagel on Aristotle on Identifying with the 'Highest Part of Ourselves.'" AndrewTaggart.com. April 16, 2013. https://andrewjtaggart.com/2013/04/16/nagel-on-aristotle-on-identifying-with-the-highest-part-of-ourselves/.
Tanabe, Jennifer. "Benjamin Bloom." *New World Encyclopedia*. January 2013. https://www.newworldencyclopedia.org/p/index.php?title=Benjamin_Bloom&oldid=966656.
Taylor, Charles. *The Ethics of Authenticity*. Cambridge: Harvard University Press, 1992.
———. *A Secular Age*. Cambridge: Harvard University Press, 2007.

Taylor, Daniel. *The Myth of Certainty: The Reflective Christian and the Risk of Commitment*. Downers Grove: InterVarsity, 1992.

Taylor, Larry. *Running with the Horses: A Parenting Guide for Raising Children to Be Servant-Leaders for Christ*. Bloomington, IN: Westbow, 2013.

Taylor, Richard Shelley. *The Disciplined Life*. Kansas City, MO: Beacon Hill, 1962.

Tayo, Ademola S. "B. F. Skinner's Theory and Education: A Christian Critique." Paper prepared for the 28th International Faith and Learning Seminar, Babcock University, Nigeria, June 17–28, 2001. Institute for Christian Teaching. https://christintheclassroom.org/vol_28/28cc_441-460.htm.

Thiessen, Gesa Elsbeth, ed. *Theological Aesthetics: A Reader*. Grand Rapids: Eerdmans, 2004.

Thomas à Kempis. *The Imitation of Christ*. Translated by William C. Creasy. Macon, GA: Mercer University, 1989.

Thomas, Gary. *Education: A Very Short Introduction*. New York: Oxford University Press, 2013.

Thomasson, Amie L. "The Ontology of Art." In *The Blackwell Guide to Aesthetics*, edited by Peter Kivy, 78–92. Malden, MA: Blackwell, 2004.

Thompson, Norma H. *Religious Education and Theology*. Birmingham, AL: Religious Education, 1982.

Thomson, Iain. "Heidegger on Ontological Education; or, How We Become What We Are." *Inquiry* 44 (2001) 243–68.

Tigerstedt, E. N. "The Poet as Creator: Origins of a Metaphor." *Comparative Literature Studies* 5 (1968) 455–88.

Tillich, Paul. *The Courage to Be*. New Haven: Yale University Press, 1952.

———. *The New Being*. New York: Scribner, 1955.

Torrance, Thomas F. *Reality and Evangelical Theology*. Philadelphia: Westminster, 1982.

———. *Theological Science*. Edinburgh, Scotland: T. & T. Clark, 1996.

Tournier, Paul. *The Healing of Persons*. Westchester, IL: Good News, 1967.

———. *To Resist or to Surrender?* Richmond, VA: John Knox, 1969.

Towns, Elmer L. *A History of Religious Educators*. Grand Rapids: Baker, 1985.

Trianosky, Gregory. "What Is Virtue Ethics All About?" *American Philosophical Quarterly* 27 (October 1990) 335–44.

Tripp, Paul David. *Age of Opportunity: A Biblical Guide to Parenting Teens*. Phillipsburg, NJ: P&R, 1997.

———. *Your Christian School: A Culture of Grace?* DVD-ROM. Philadelphia: Tripp, 2009.

Troost, Andree. *What Is Reformational Philosophy? An Introduction to the Cosmonomic Philosophy of Herman Dooyeweerd*. Grand Rapids: Paideia, 2012.

Turley, Stephen R. *Awakening Wonder: A Classical Truth, Goodness, and Beauty*. Camp Hill, PA: Classical Academic, 2014.

Uebersax, John. "Areté—Definition and Meaning." John-Uebersax.com (personal website). https://www.john-uebersax.com/plato/words/arete.htm.

Vandrunen, David. *God's Glory Alone: The Majestic Heart of Christian Faith and Life; What the Reformers Taught . . . and Why It Still Matters*. Grand Rapids: Zondervan, 2015.

Van Inwagen, Peter. "Materialism and the Psychological-Continuity Account of Personal Identity." *Philosophical Perspectives* 11 (1997) 305–19.

Van Patten, James J. "Model for Philosophy of Education." *Journal of Thought* (1973) 286–95.
Van Til, Cornelius. *The Defense of the Faith.* 3rd ed. Philadelphia: Presbyterian and Reformed, 1967.
Vedral, Vlatko. *Decoding Reality: The Universe as Quantum Information.* New York: Oxford University Press, 2010.
Veith, Gene Edward, Jr. *Postmodern Times: A Christian Guide to Contemporary Thought and Culture.* Wheaton, IL: Crossway, 1994.
———. *Reading between the Lines: A Christian Guide to Literature.* Wheaton, IL: Crossway, 1990.
Veith, Gene Edward, Jr., and Andrew Kern. *Classical Education: The Movement Sweeping America.* Washington, DC: Capital Research Center, 2001.
Vryhof, Steven, et al. *12 Affirmations: Reformed Christian Schooling for the 21st Century.* Grand Rapids: Baker, 1989.
Vygotsky, Lev. *Mind in Society: The Development of Higher Psychological Processes.* Cambridge: Harvard University Press, 1978.
Wallach, Lisa, and Michael A. Wallach. *Seven Views of Mind.* New York: Psychology, 2013.
Ward, Leo R. "Maritain's Philosophy of Education for Freedom." *Review of Politics* 40.4, fortieth anniversary issue (October 1978) 499–513.
Washington, Booker T. *Up from Slavery: An Autobiography by Booker T. Washington.* New York: Doubleday and Page, 1901.
Watson, J. B. "Animal Education: An Experimental Study on the Psychical Development of the White Rat, Correlated with the Growth of Its Nervous System." PhD diss., University of Chicago, 1903.
———. *Behaviorism.* Chicago: University of Chicago Press, 1930.
———. "Psychology as the Behaviorist Views It." *Psychological Review* 20 (1913) 158–77.
Westphal, Merold, ed. *Postmodern Philosophy and Christian Thought.* Bloomington: Indiana University Press, 1999.
Whitehead, Alfred North. *Adventures of Ideas.* New York: Free Press, 1967.
———. *The Aims of Education and Other Essays.* Paperback ed. New York: Free Press, 1968.
———. *Process and Reality.* Edited by David Ray Griffin et al. Corrected ed. New York: Free Press, 1978.
Wiens, Timothy P., and Kathryn L. Wiens, eds. *Building a Better School: Essays on Exemplary Christian School Leadership.* Stony Brook: Paideia, 2012.
Wilhoit, Jim. *Christian Education and the Search for Meaning.* 2nd ed. Grand Rapids: Baker, 2000.
Wilhoit, James C., and John M. Dettoni, eds. *Nurture That Is Christian: Developmental Perspectives on Christian Education.* Ada, MI: Baker 1995.
Wilkins, John S., and David Hull. "Replication and Reproduction." *Stanford Encyclopedia of Philosophy*, edited by Edward N. Zalta. Spring 2014 ed. http://plato.stanford.edu/archives/spr2014/entries/replication/.
Wilkinson, Bruce, ed. *Almost Every Answer for Practically Any Teacher: The Seven Laws of the Learner Series.* Colorado Springs: Multnomah, 1992.
———. *The Seven Laws of the Learner: How to Teach Almost Anything to Practically Anyone!* Colorado Springs: Multnomah, 1992.

Willard, Dallas. *A Place for Truth: Leading Thinkers Explore Life's Hardest Questions*. Downers Grove: InterVarsity, 2010.
Willis, Wayne. "Liberating the Liberal Arts." *Journal of General Education* 39 (1988) 193–205.
Wilson, Clifford. *Jesus the Teacher*. Victoria, Australia: Word of Truth, 1974.
Wilson, Douglas. *The Case for Classical Christian Education*. Wheaton, IL: Crossway, 2003.
———. *The Paideia of God and Other Essays on Education*. Moscow, ID: Canon, 1999.
———. *Recovering the Lost Tools of Learning: An Approach to Distinctively Christian Education*. Wheaton, IL: Crossway, 1991.
Wilson, Edward. *Consilience: The Unity of Knowledge*. New York: Knopf, 1998.
Wilson, John, and Barbara Cowell. "Applying Philosophy." *Journal of Applied Philosophy* 2 (1985) 127–31.
Winch, Christopher. "The Honey Trap: The Social and Cognitive Adequacy of Language in Educational Contexts." *Journal of Applied Philosophy* 5 (1988) 211–24.
Winch, Christopher, and John Gingell. *Key Concepts in the Philosophy of Education*. New York: Routledge, 2005.
Witham, Larry. *By Design: Science and the Search for God*. San Francisco: Encounter, 2003.
Witherall, Arthur. "The Value of Truth and the Care of the Soul." *Journal of Applied Philosophy* 13 (1996) 189–97.
Wittgenstein, Ludwig. *Philosophical Investigations*. New York: Oxford University Press, 1968.
Wolfe, David L. *Epistemology: The Justification of Belief*. Downers Grove: InterVarsity, 1982.
Wolterstorff, Nicholas. *Art in Action: Toward a Christian Aesthetic*. Grand Rapids: Eerdmans, 1980.
———. *Educating for Responsible Action*. Reprint. Grand Rapids: CSI, 1981.
———. *Educating for Shalom: Essays on Christian Higher Education*. Grand Rapids: Eerdmans, 2004.
———. "To Theologians from One Who Cares about Theology, but Is Not One of You." *Theological Education* 40 (2005) 79–102.
———. "Toward an Ontology of Art Works." *Nous* 9 (May 1975) 115–42.
———. *Works and Worlds of Art*. London: Oxford University Press, 1980.
Wolterstorff, Nicholas, et al., eds. *Educating for Life: Reflections on Christian Teaching and Learning*. Grand Rapids: Baker Academic, 2002.
Wood, W. Jay. *Epistemology: Becoming Intellectually Virtuous*. Contours of Christian Philosophy. Downers Grove: InterVarsity, 1998.
Woodfin, Yandall. *With All Your Mind: A Christian Philosophy*. Nashville: Abingdon, 1980.
Woodward, John B. *Man as Spirit, Soul, and Body: A Study of Biblical Psychology*. Pigeon Forge, TN: Grace Fell International, 2007.
Woodward, William Harrison. *Vittorino da Feltre and Other Humanist Educators*. Toronto: University of Toronto Press, 1996.
Wright, Jason S. "Morality and Hebraic Christian Religion." *Journal of Moral Education* 11 (1981) 32–40.
Yoder, John H. *The Politics of Jesus: Vicit Agnus Noster*. Grand Rapids: Eerdmans, 1940.

Ziefle, Helmut W. *Modern Theological German: A Reader and Dictionary.* Grand Rapids: Baker, 1997.
Zimmerman, Larry L. *Truth and the Transcendent: The Origin, Nature, and Purpose of Mathematics.* Hebron, KY: Answers in Genesis, 2000.
Zuck, Roy. *Teaching How Jesus Taught.* Grand Rapids: Baker, 1995.
Zuidervaart, Lambert. Review of *Art in Action: Toward a Christian Aesthetic,* by NicholasWolterstorff. *Philosophia Reformata* 48 (1983) 87-90.
Zylstra, Henry. *Testament of Vision.* Grand Rapids: Eerdmans, 1958.